11-23-04
29.95
Cms

DAMAGED

Torn Cover

Basil Chicken over Angel Hair, page 198

Classy Chicken, page 181

BLT Wraps, page 242

Three Bean Salad I, page 282

Amaretto Divine, page 308

all recipes

30 minutes to cook

Oxmoor House

ISBN: 0-8487-2819-X
Library of Congress Control Number: 2004112821
Printed in the United States of America
First Printing 2004

To order additional publications, call 1-800-765-6400.

For more books to enrich your life, visit
oxmoorhouse.com

Cover: Fruit Pizza with White Chocolate (page 319)

Allrecipes.com, Inc.
President: Bill Moore
Senior VP Development: Tim Hunt
Vice President Marketing: Esmée Williams
Production Manager: Maya Smith
Senior Recipe Editor: Sydny Carter
Senior Food Editor: Jennifer Anderson
Recipe Editors: Emily Brune, Richard Kozel,
    Lesley Peterson, Britt Swearingen
Creative Direction: Yann Oehl, Jeff Cummings

Allrecipes.com, Inc.
400 Mercer Street, Suite 302
Seattle, WA 98109
(206) 292-3990
www.Allrecipes.com

Oxmoor House, Inc.
Editor in Chief: Nancy Fitzpatrick Wyatt
Executive Editor: Susan Carlisle Payne
Art Director: Cynthia Rose Cooper
Copy Chief: Allison Long Lowery

Allrecipes 30 Minutes to Cook
Editor: McCharen Pratt
Copy Editor: Diane Rose
Editorial Assistant: Shannon Friedmann
Senior Photographer: Jim Bathie
Photographer: Brit Huckabay
Senior Photo Stylist: Kay E. Clarke
Photo Stylist: Amy Wilson
Director, Test Kitchens: Elizabeth Tyler Luckett
Assistant Director, Test Kitchens: Julie Christopher
Test Kitchens Staff: Kristi Carter, Nicole Lee Faber,
    Kathleen Royal Phillips, Elise Weis, Kelley Wilton
Publishing Systems Administrator: Rick Tucker
Color Specialist: Jim Sheetz
Director of Production: Phillip Lee
Production Manager: Theresa L. Beste
Production Assistant: Faye Porter Bonner

Contributors:
Designer: Carol Damsky
Indexer: Mary Ann Laurens
Photographer: Ralph Anderson
Photo Stylist: Mindy Shapiro
Editorial Interns: Amber Ballew, Sheila Egts,
    Jessica Lynn Dorsey

Table of Contents

Welcome from the Staff of Allrecipes!

Dear Friends:

We live in a busy world, and with all the demands for our time, it's not surprising that cooking meals tends to fall to the bottom of the to-do list. Finding the time to give your family a delicious home-cooked meal can be challenging. The millions of home cooks at **Allrecipes.com** have been helping each other solve that problem every day for over 7 years, and we've gathered the best of their time-saving recipes here for you. For this all-new cookbook, we've selected over 400 top-rated recipes—rated and reviewed by the online community of **Allrecipes.com**—and organized them into an easy-to-follow book that will get you in and out of the kitchen faster than your family can say, "We're hungry!" Take a look at some of our favorite features:

- **10** *Quick & Easy Menus* **promise entire meals that can go from kitchen to table in less time than it takes to have a pizza delivered. Accompanying each menu is a game plan to help you organize your time and take all the guesswork out of meal planning.**
- **3 bonus chapters: With the best** *30-Minute Brand-Name Recipes,* **you can use brand-name products you love in recipes tested and approved by home cooks like you.** *Fast & Healthy* **provides recipes to help you feed your family the well-rounded meals they deserve. And you can turn to** *No-Cook Creations* **when cooking is not an option.**
- **An** *Allrecipes.com* **reader review for each recipe provides valuable tips, serving suggestions, or substitution ideas from someone who tested the recipe in his or her own home.**
- **48 pages of all-new color photography prove that "quick" doesn't have to mean "bland." Yes, you** *can* **have gorgeous food on the table in just minutes!**
- **All-new ways to help you find the fastest, easiest recipes: Look for recipes marked 30 Minutes or Less, 20 Minutes or Less, and 10 Minutes or Less, as well as those sporting our 3 new recipe banners: 5 Ingredients or Less, Freezer Fresh, and From the Pantry.**

And don't forget that every single recipe in these pages cooks in 30 minutes or less. In fact, if you add up the prep time and cook time for any recipe here, you won't be busy for more than 45 minutes. We also state chill times, marinate times—any hands-off time that you can spend out of the kitchen and with your family. After you've flipped through these pages, be sure to take your own family recipes and kitchen secrets to **Allrecipes.com** and share them with us. You may find yourself in next year's volume of home-tested favorites!

Happy Cooking,

The Staff of Allrecipes

What is Allrecipes.com?

It's an interactive recipe swap that's helping over 6 million people get dinner on the table with confidence.

Seven years ago, we created a place for home cooks to share their favorite recipes via the Internet. As word spread, others joined in, and in no time, **Allrecipes.com** grew into the world's largest community of home cooks—over 6 million strong—and became the number-one source for online recipes. On the website, recipes are posted for everyday home cooks to put them to the test and then rate and review them online.

About the recipes

Every recipe in this book includes a brief **comment from the contributor.** This may be a serving suggestion, details on where the recipe came from, or other valuable information about the dish. We always preserve the character of the contributed recipe, but we make slight changes where necessary to ensure consistency, accuracy, and completeness in the published version.

On **Allrecipes.com,** visitors post **recipe reviews,** and for this book, we've included the most helpful reviews alongside the recipes. Look for **"What other cooks have done"** in the box beside every recipe for these reviews that give serving suggestions and cooking tips.

Veterans of the website know to look not only to the **highest-rated, but also the most-rated recipes** when they're looking for winners. This means that lots of people have tried these recipes at home and rated them online. We've included the

rating for each recipe. For this book, only 4- or 5-star recipes (out of a possible **5 stars**) were included. Once you've made a few of these recipes, go online and share your thoughts. Look on the next two pages for a list of the most rated and reviewed recipes from this book.

You may wonder why some of the recipe titles have **Roman numerals** attached to them, like Chicken Piccata III on page 197 or Pig Picking Cake II on page 307. Contributors submit multiple recipes with these titles, so we assign them a number to help keep up with all the variations. In this book, you'll find only one of the variations—the highest-rated, most-reviewed version—but you can find all the different takes on classic recipes online.

Prep and cook times are included as a basic guide with each recipe to help you plan meals. Remember that these times are approximate. How fast you chop, the accuracy of your oven's temperature, humidity, and other variations can affect your prep and cook time.

Need more information?

You'll find helpful tip boxes and charts throughout the book to help you with basic cooking and baking questions, and you can visit us online if you need more information. Check out the "Cooking Advice" section at **Allrecipes.com** where you can browse through articles and step-by-step cooking tutorials.

Recipe Hall of Fame

Check out the all-star recipes with the most ratings and reviews from the website—the best of the best from this year's cookbook, Allrecipes 30 Minutes to Cook. The following recipes received hundreds of ratings from the online community and come with the testimonials of home cooks everywhere who acclaim these as their all-time favorites. Listen to what people are saying about these great-tasting recipes.

▶ **Chocolate Éclair Dessert** (page 27)
"This was absolutely fantastic. It's even better because it can be put together so easily! It was really neat-looking, too, with all the layers. I took it to a church luncheon, and it was all gobbled up."

▶ **Broiled Pork Chops** (page 86)
"I made these for dinner tonight, and they came out fabulous! My older brother, who is a notoriously picky eater and rarely will try anything I make, ate two pork chops! I consider that a definite sign of success. Plus, this was simple and easy to prepare."

▶ **Taco Bake I** (page 170)
"What a great recipe! It's so easy to make, which is the best part. Never fails!"

▶ **Salisbury Steak** (page 171)
"It was salisbury-licious. This was very good. My whole family devoured it. So easy to make and very satisfying to have the kids eat all their dinner for a change. Thanks for the recipe—it's a keeper!"

▶ **Skillet Chops with Mushroom Gravy** (page 175)
"This is a great recipe when you need a good meal in a hurry, but you want it to taste like it took all afternoon! I served it with noodles and it was a big hit. The meat comes out very tender, and the gravy picks up the flavor of the chops. Wonderful!"

▶ **Sausage Gravy I** (page 179)
"This is the best recipe I have come across in years. Ever since my grandmother passed away, I have missed her sausage biscuits and gravy. Now I have found the joy of Sunday breakfast again—and the great memory of my grandmother. This recipe tastes just like hers used to."

▶ **Aussie Chicken** (page 182)
"This was fabulous! It was a huge hit with my family. My husband, who has a reputation for being strictly a beef and potato man, enjoyed this and was telling other family members about the dish and how good it was. The recipe is very simple. Most of the ingredients are ones that everyone usually has on hand. The leftovers were even better the next day. A really terrific dish. I will definitely fix it again."

▶ Lemon-Mushroom-Herb Chicken
(page 182)

"My family and I loved this! I've never had a caper, so I tasted one when I got home. Yuck! But I savored the taste when mixed with the other ingredients in this recipe. Truly a great blend! I'll make this over and over and over! I am glad I have found another recipe for my family to enjoy."

▶ Acapulco Chicken (page 193)

"I'm not usually fond of Mexican food, but I wanted to try something different. I'm always looking for some spicy food, and I came upon this recipe. It was the best! This meal will be served in my home at least four times a month."

▶ Arrabbiata Sauce (page 214)

"My family loved this sauce, and we will definitely have this again. We are always eating pasta, and this sauce has a kick to it that makes it yummy and different."

▶ Champagne Shrimp and Pasta
(page 215)

"This recipe is amazing! It's so easy to make, doesn't take long to cook at all, and when it's finished, it looks and tastes amazing. I recommend this to anyone who is looking for a simple dish with 5-star restaurant quality!"

▶ Tuscan Soup (page 254)

"Wow, this is fantastic! This smelled so wonderful while cooking that I just couldn't stop taste-testing it. I can't wait to make it again, and I'll double it for leftovers or for a crowd."

▶ Cheesy Ranch New Red Potatoes
(page 272)

"It's hard to go wrong with these little potatoes; they were great. Everyone loved them so much that I had to make a second batch just to get through dinner."

▶ Oven-Roasted Potatoes
(page 272)

"I love this recipe! I was glad to find it because I was getting sick of mashed and baked potatoes. The flavor was great, and it made the kitchen smell amazing. Even my picky daughter cleaned her plate. Definitely a keeper."

▶ Ramen Coleslaw (page 281)

"This a very simple, nice twist on regular coleslaw, which my family usually does not like much. When I saw this recipe, I thought it might work. Everyone enjoyed it! Perfect to make and take to an outdoor summer gathering."

▶ Basic Crêpes (page 294)

"This recipe is definitely a winner! After visiting Europe and eating their wonderful crêpes, I wanted to learn how to make my own. This was my first try, and they came out just perfect. My mom tried them and said I should become a professional chef."

▶ Aunt Anne's Coffee Cake (page 312)

"Loved this recipe. Very simple to make, and it's not too heavy at all. I've had the recipe requested many times. When my three-year-old nephew comes to visit, he asks for it as soon as he walks in the door! I could eat half the cake fresh out of the oven."

▶ Classic Tiramisu (page 313)

"This recipe was excellent. I got rave reviews from people who said they had never eaten such a good dessert, and it was better than any tiramisu at a restaurant! Not a drop left on the plate."

▶ Apple Enchilada Dessert (page 321)

"I am always looking for recipes that my teenagers can make. This was a super dessert for budding cooks, and it will definitely become a dessert to serve to company."

▶ Aunt Cora's World's Greatest Cookies (page 334)

"Aunt Cora was a genius. This is the best cookie I have ever tasted, and I have tried a whole lot of cookies. The batter is smooth and creamy, and the texture of the cookie is light and just about melts in your mouth. Everyone who likes peanut butter and chocolate chips should make this recipe."

▶ Chewiest Brownies (page 339)

"These are exactly what my definition of brownies should be: rich, chocolaty, slightly chewy, and heavy. These are the best I've tried and are a hit with my family, too. Very easy to make. They go great with ice cream or on their own."

Recipe Highlights

Every single recipe in Allrecipes 30 Minutes to Cook *has a banner to help you identify favorite features. Here's a guide to all the banners scattered throughout the book. Look for them in the index for more help in finding the perfect recipe for your needs.*

Around-the-World Cuisine ▼

Open your mind and your palate with these recipes that feature exotic flavors from around the globe.

Blue Ribbon Winner ▼

Contributors share some of their special prizewinning fare from around the world.

Classic Comfort Food ▼

Chicken and Dumplings, Meatloaf, Macaroni and Cheese, Bread Pudding . . . need we say more?

Company is Coming ▼

When you need a meal to impress your guests, look for this banner to fill your entertaining needs.

Covered-Dish Favorite ▼

Whether it's a church potluck or a family reunion, you'll have the right dish to carry along.

Crowd-Pleaser ▼

These recipes yield enough for a large party and are fit for all kinds of celebrations.

Family Favorite ▼

When it's reliable, family-pleasing recipes you're looking for, try these foolproof picks.

5 Ingredients or Less ▼

Speed up your prep time with recipes that feature five ingredients or less, excluding salt, pepper, and water.

Freezer Fresh ▼

Fill your freezer with delicious dishes that hold up well to freezing and reheating for easy, ready meals.

From the Grill ▼

Add a little spice to backyard barbecuing with these new approaches to grilling your favorite meals.

From the Pantry ▼

You probably have everything you need to make these recipes that call for common pantry and fridge items.

Holiday Fare ▼

We've made it easy to find the best recipes to celebrate the holidays with your family and friends.

Holiday Gift Giving ▼

Give a gift of the heart with these recipes for wonderful homemade gifts from your kitchen.

Hot & Spicy ▼

Hot and spicy fans can find their next indulgence here. Remember that you can adjust the seasonings to taste.

Kid-Friendly ▼

Pull out these recipes for surefire hits with little ones and adults alike. Everyone will clean their plates.

Make-Ahead ▼

For parties or weeknight meals, plan ahead and make life easier with recipes that can be made ahead.

Meatless Main Dish ▼

Looking for a break from meat and potatoes? These vegetarian delights will please even die-hard meat-eaters.

One-Dish Meal ▼

Dinner can't get much easier than a whole meal in one dish. You'll enjoy all the flavor without all the fuss.

Out-of-the-Ordinary ▼

Shake up things at the dinner table with recipes that turn everyday meals into extraordinary feasts.

Party Food ▼

Put on your party hat and get cooking. You'll set the mood for your next gathering with style.

Restaurant Fare ▼

Make standout dishes from your favorite restaurant at home with these classic recipes.

Quick & Easy Menus

Meal Planning Made Easy

Casual Company Dinner

Easy and fun, a lobsterfest on the grill is a flavorful way to entertain friends. Add grill-friendly vegetables, such as corn on the cob or mushrooms on skewers, to round out these fast recipes.

MENU PREP PLAN

1. Prepare Lemon Syllabub and refrigerate until ready to serve.

2. Preheat grill. While grill heats, prepare lobster marinade and brush lobster tails with marinade.

3. Grill corn with lobster tails. (To grill husked corn on the cob, season ears with salt and pepper to taste and wrap tightly with aluminum foil. Grill 15 minutes, turning often.)

MENU

Grilled Rock Lobster Tails

grilled corn on the cob

Lemon Syllabub

Serves 6

---

30 minutes or less

Grilled Rock Lobster Tails *(pictured on page 40)*

Submitted by: **Joe Nekrasz**
"Marinated Grilled Rock Lobster Tails take very little cooking time and are so good!"

½	cup olive oil	⅛	teaspoon white pepper
1	tablespoon lemon juice	⅛	teaspoon garlic powder
1	teaspoon salt	6	(10 ounce) rock lobster tails
1	teaspoon paprika		Lemon slices (optional)

1. Lightly oil cold grill rack and preheat grill for high heat.
2. In a small bowl, combine olive oil and lemon juice. Stir in salt, paprika, white pepper, and garlic powder. Split lobster tails lengthwise with a large knife. Brush meat side of tail with marinade.
3. Place tails, meat side down, on the prepared grill and cook for 6 minutes. Turn lobster tails and cook, brushing often with remaining marinade, 6 to 8 more minutes or until lobster is opaque and firm to the touch. Serve with lemon slices, if desired. **Yield:** 6 servings.

Per serving: 416 calories, 53g protein, 2g carbohydrate, 21g fat, 0g fiber, 269mg cholesterol, 1233mg sodium

FROM THE GRILL ▶

Prep Time: 15 minutes

Cook Time: 14 minutes

Average Rating: ★★★★★

What other cooks have done:

"Really, really good! I used fresh garlic instead of garlic powder, and cayenne pepper instead of paprika. Delicious!"

Lemon Syllabub *(pictured on page 41)*

Submitted by: **Sarah-neko**

"This is a deliciously light, creamy, sophisticated little dessert from days gone by. I first tasted it at a supper given by a lecturer in seventeenth-century literature when I was at college, and it took our taste buds right back to the Restoration. It can be prepared as either a parfait or a punch. Please note that both versions contain alcohol, so don't serve either to younger family members."

1	cup heavy whipping cream, chilled	2	tablespoons fresh lemon juice
½	cup white sugar	¼	teaspoon ground nutmeg
¼	cup white wine		Fresh mint leaves
1	teaspoon grated lemon zest		Lemon slices

1. Whip cream and sugar in a chilled bowl until cream begins to thicken. Gradually whip in white wine, lemon zest, and lemon juice. Continue to whip until light and fluffy but not grainy. Cover the mixture and chill at least 15 minutes.

2. Serve in chilled parfait glasses. Garnish with nutmeg, mint, and lemon slices. **Yield:** 6 servings.

For Syllabub Punch:
Add additional white wine to the whipped mixture until the mixture reaches a drinking consistency.

Per serving: 212 calories, 1g protein, 19g carbohydrate, 15g fat, 0g fiber, 54mg cholesterol, 16mg sodium

◀ OUT-OF-THE-ORDINARY

Prep Time: 15 minutes

Chill Time: 15 minutes

Average Rating: ★★★★☆

What other cooks have done:

"Light and delicious, as well as being quick and easy to prepare. Makes a great alternative to a zabaglione for a dinner party, since it's made in advance."

Love Your Lobster

Decided to indulge in some lobster, but not sure where to begin? No need to hesitate any longer—we'll turn you into a fearless lobster aficionado in no time.

You'll likely find either spiny (rock) lobsters or Maine lobsters at your local supermarket. Rock lobsters are easily distinguished from Maine lobsters by the fact that Maine lobsters have a pair of large, heavy claws, while rock lobsters have no claws. The meat of rock lobsters, which is mostly in the tail, is firmer and less sweet than that of Maine lobsters. Outside California and Florida, most of the rock lobster meat sold in this country is in the form of frozen tails, usually labeled "rock lobster tails."

If you serve whole lobster, help your dinner guests get a head start by doing a little shell cracking first. Turn the lobsters upside down and cut lengthwise through the tail shell using kitchen shears or a big sharp knife. Try not to cut through the meat; just split the shell. If your lobster has claws, take a hammer or meat tenderizer and rap the claws sharply until there are some substantial cracks in them. You don't want to pulverize them, but you want them to be cracked enough so everyone can split them by hand.

Besides the delicate white meat, you'll probably encounter some green and red stuff inside your lobster. The green matter inside the body cavity is the liver (tomalley) which is highly prized by lobster connoisseurs. The red clumps you may find in the tail are eggs (coral), and they are good eating, too.

The classic way to serve fresh lobster is simply with small dishes of melted butter, lemon wedges, and bibs. For more information, visit **Allrecipes.com**

Fall Family Gathering

When family gathers for dinner, you don't want to be chained to the stove. Use the microwave to speed up prep and cook times, and transform a bakery pound cake with homemade frosting to get to the table quicker.

MENU PREP PLAN

1. Toast almonds for salad. Meanwhile, prepare Whipped Cream Frosting and frost pound cake. Chill cake until ready to serve.

2. Halve and seed squash. Microwave squash halves and prepare stuffing.

3. Stuff squash halves and return to microwave. Meanwhile, assemble salad. Dress half of salad for menu, reserving remaining salad and dressing for another meal.

MENU

Green Salad with Cranberry Vinaigrette

Stuffed Acorn Squash Supreme

bakery pound cake with Whipped Cream Frosting

Serves 4

20 *minutes or less*

Green Salad with Cranberry Vinaigrette

Submitted by: **Nancy**
"This green salad is especially pretty to serve during the Christmas holidays."

1	cup sliced almonds	½	teaspoon ground black pepper
3	tablespoons red wine vinegar	2	tablespoons water
⅓	cup olive oil	½	red onion, thinly sliced
¼	cup fresh cranberries	4	ounces crumbled blue cheese
1	tablespoon prepared Dijon-style mustard	1	(11 ounce) bag mixed salad greens
½	teaspoon minced garlic		
½	teaspoon salt		

1. Preheat oven to 375°F (190°C).
2. Arrange almonds in a single layer on a baking sheet. Toast in the preheated oven for 5 minutes or until nuts begin to brown.
3. In a blender or food processor, combine vinegar, oil, cranberries, mustard, garlic, salt, pepper, and water. Process until smooth.
4. In a large bowl, toss the almonds, onion, blue cheese, and greens with the dressing until evenly coated. **Yield:** 8 servings.

Per serving: 219 calories, 7g protein, 6g carbohydrate, 19g fat, 3g fiber, 11mg cholesterol, 405mg sodium

HOLIDAY FARE ▶

Prep Time: 15 minutes

Cook Time: 5 minutes

Average Rating: ★★★★★

What other cooks have done:

"I had a New Year's Eve dinner party and served this salad as my second course. I added a teaspoon of white sugar to the dressing and substituted feta cheese for the blue cheese. It tasted like a salad from an expensive restaurant. All of my guests just loved it—especially the crunchy almonds."

Stuffed Acorn Squash
Supreme *(pictured on page 39)*

Submitted by: **Patrice Gerard**
"Acorn squash is partially cooked in the microwave and then filled with turkey sausage, broccoli-cheese rice, and apples."

1	(6 ounce) package broccoli and cheese-flavored rice mix	½	cup chopped apple
2	medium acorn squash, halved and seeded	2	teaspoons crushed coriander seed
1	pound turkey breakfast sausage	½	cup shredded Monterey Jack cheese

1. Prepare rice mix according to package directions; cover and set aside.
2. Meanwhile, place 2 squash halves, cut side down, on a microwave-safe plate. Microwave on high for 5 minutes or until tender but firm. Repeat with remaining squash.
3. In a medium skillet over medium heat, cook sausage until evenly browned; drain and set aside.
4. In a large bowl, mix together the prepared rice, sausage, apple, and coriander. Stuff each squash half with the mixture.
5. Cover stuffed squash halves with heavy-duty plastic wrap and microwave on high for 5 minutes or until cooked through and soft. Remove plastic and top stuffed squash with cheese. Continue to microwave until cheese is melted, about 1 minute. **Yield:** 4 servings.

Per serving: 586 calories, 28g protein, 59g carbohydrate, 28g fat, 5g fiber, 107mg cholesterol, 1381mg sodium

◄ **COMPANY IS COMING**

Prep Time: 10 minutes

Cook Time: 20 minutes

Average Rating: ★★★★☆

What other cooks have done:

"I doctored this recipe a little by using maple sausage and adding a quarter of a can of pumpkin and a half can of evaporated milk to it. It was hearty and wonderful. The acorn squash was so sweet. A great combination."

Whipped Cream Frosting

Submitted by: **Tom Parker**
"A heavenly coating for any cake. Whipped cream is gently folded into sweetened cream cheese."

1	(8 ounce) package cream cheese, softened	⅛	teaspoon salt
1	cup white sugar	1	teaspoon vanilla extract
		1½	cups heavy cream

1. In a large bowl, beat cream cheese, sugar, salt, and vanilla until smooth. In a small bowl, whip the heavy cream until stiff peaks form. Fold into the cream cheese mixture or beat with an electric mixer on low. **Yield:** 12 servings.

Per serving: 233 calories, 2g protein, 18g carbohydrate, 18g fat, 0g fiber, 61mg cholesterol, 91mg sodium

◄ **RESTAURANT FARE**

Prep Time: 5 minutes

Average Rating: ★★★★★

What other cooks have done:

"I wasn't very successful folding the whipped cream into the cream cheese mixture. I used my mixer on low instead, and it worked great."

Fish 'n' Chips

Kid-friendly to the max, this menu matches the classic pairing of fried fish and french fries with the easiest ice cream topping to ever hit your spoon. A pint or two of coleslaw from your supermarket's deli makes a perfect side dish.

MENU PREP PLAN

1. Prepare Supreme Strawberry Topping a day ahead, if desired, and store in refrigerator.

2. While oil for frying heats, prepare batter for fish. Fry fish in batches, draining cooked fish on paper towels. While fish fries, bake frozen french fries according to package instructions.

3. Serve fish and french fries alongside coleslaw purchased from your supermarket's deli section. Remove strawberry topping from fridge. Stir and pour over scoops of vanilla ice cream.

MENU

Beer Batter for Fish

french fries

deli coleslaw

Supreme Strawberry Topping
with vanilla ice cream

Serves 6

FAMILY FAVORITE ▶

Prep Time: 10 minutes

Cook Time: 5 minutes per batch

Average Rating: ★★★★★

What other cooks have done:

"This made a very good batter. I added additional beer since it was thick at first. I also added 1 tablespoon of Old Bay® seasoning. The fish turned out with a perfect golden brown coating. Just what I was looking for!"

Beer Batter for Fish *(pictured on page 43)*

Submitted by: **Wilma Scott**
"This basic beer batter is good for almost any white-fleshed fish."

2	quarts vegetable oil	¼	teaspoon ground black pepper
4	cups pastry flour or all-purpose flour	⅛	teaspoon garlic powder
1	tablespoon baking powder	3	eggs
½	teaspoon baking soda	1½	cups milk
2	tablespoons cornstarch	¾	cup beer
½	teaspoon salt	1½	pounds cod fillets
			Lemon wedges

1. Heat oil to 375°F (190°C) in a deep fryer or a large, heavy saucepan.
2. Meanwhile, in a medium bowl, stir together flour, baking powder, baking soda, cornstarch, salt, pepper, and garlic powder.
3. In a large bowl, beat together eggs and milk. Mix in beer. Stir flour mixture into egg mixture.
4. Coat fish in batter and submerge fish, in batches, in hot oil. Fry until golden brown, about 4 to 5 minutes. Serve hot with lemon wedges. **Yield:** 6 servings.

Per serving: 773 calories, 29g protein, 75g carbohydrate, 42g fat, 11g fiber, 155mg cholesterol, 494mg sodium

Supreme Strawberry Topping (pictured on page 42)

Submitted by: **Brad Reynolds**

"Awesome restaurant-style strawberry topping. Serve cold over cheesecake or ice cream."

1	pint strawberries, cleaned and stemmed	⅓	cup white sugar
		1	teaspoon vanilla extract

1. Cut strawberries in half. In a saucepan over medium–high heat, combine strawberries, sugar, and vanilla. Cook, stirring occasionally, until sauce thickens, about 5 minutes. Remove from heat. In a blender, puree about a third of sauce and mix back into remainder. Store in refrigerator. **Yield:** 6 servings.

Per serving: 60 calories, 0g protein, 15g carbohydrate, 0g fat, 1g fiber, 0mg cholesterol, 1mg sodium

◄ **5 INGREDIENTS OR LESS**

Prep Time: 8 minutes

Cook Time: 5 minutes

Average Rating: ★★★★★

What other cooks have done:

"Be careful with how many strawberries you puree. The first time I made it, I pureed a few too many of the berries, and it was a bit soupy. (I like a few big strawberry pieces rather than just a sauce.) The next time, I didn't puree as much, and it was perfect!"

Deep-Frying Dos and Don'ts

Deep-frying can be a lot of fun and is a great way to cook many treats like the delicious battered fish recipe at left. However, deep-frying can be a dangerous process because of the extreme temperature the oil must be for frying. We cannot stress enough the fact that you should be very careful when deep-frying.

• When deep-frying, it is best to use neutrally-flavored oil like safflower or peanut oil. Oils like extra virgin olive oil have a low smoking point, which means that they will burn at a much lower temperature, making whatever you are frying taste scorched and bitter.
• Use enough oil to cover whatever items you intend to fry.
• Use a candy thermometer to keep track of the oil's temperature. Temperatures between 350° and 375°F (175° and 190°C) are ideal. Oils will begin to burn between 400° and 450°F (200° and 230°C) and will catch fire at around 500°F (260°C).
• Once the oil has reached the desired temperature, reduce the heat to low. If the temperature on the thermometer begins to drop, turn the stove up a small amount until the temperature has risen to the desired level.

• To avoid splashing hot oil when dropping your battered fish (or other ingredients) into the oil, use a long spoon and place the ingredients into the oil gently.
• Don't drop items to be fried into the oil from a distance; the splash would be dangerous. The closer to the surface of the oil you can get before dropping the items into the oil without burning yourself, the safer deep-frying will be.
• Once the first fish fillet dropped into the oil has a golden brown exterior, test to see if it has cooked all the way through. If it is golden brown on the outside but undercooked on the inside, reduce the oil's heat and try again.
• Be careful not to crowd the oil with too many items. Crowding will cause the oil's temperature to drop dramatically, which will result in a greasy product. Crowding will also increase the likelihood that the fried bits and pieces will stick to each other.
• Remove the cooked items with a slotted metal spoon and let them drain on paper towels or cooling racks. Season, if desired, and enjoy!

For more information, visit **Allrecipes.com**

Buona Sera, Amici!

A hearty Italian-style meal is just the thing to tempt family and friends to your table. Scoop several flavors of sorbet into pretty glasses and garnish with biscotti to create an alluring dessert. Your supermarket should have plenty of sorbet flavors (and colors) to choose from.

MENU PREP PLAN

1. Prepare spread for garlic bread and store in refrigerator.

2. Put water for pasta on to boil and prepare Sirloin Marinara.

3. Cook pasta while sirloin cooks; drain and set aside. During sirloin's final simmer, spread baguette with garlic mixture, sprinkle with cheese, and broil.

> ### MENU
>
> **Sirloin Marinara**
>
> **spaghetti noodles**
>
> **Garlic Bread Fantastique**
>
> **store-bought sorbet and biscotti**
>
> *Serves 6*

Sirloin Marinara *(pictured on page 44)*

Submitted by: **Lanelle**
"My family loved this. Try serving over pasta or garlic mashed potatoes."

2 tablespoons olive oil	2 cups chunky pasta sauce
1 onion, thinly sliced	2 cloves garlic, minced
2 pounds top sirloin steak, sliced	½ cup dry red wine

1. Heat the oil in a large skillet over medium-high heat. Add the onion and sauté 5 minutes or until tender. Add the steak strips and cook 10 minutes, turning so all sides get browned.
2. Add pasta sauce, garlic, and red wine. Reduce heat to low and simmer for 10 minutes or until the steak is cooked through. **Yield:** 6 servings.

Per serving: 328 calories, 23g protein, 7g carbohydrate, 22g fat, 1g fiber, 76mg cholesterol, 319mg sodium

AROUND-THE-WORLD CUISINE ▶

Prep Time: 13 minutes

Cook Time: 25 minutes

Average Rating: ★★★★☆

What other cooks have done:

"An absolutely wonderful recipe! I made this for my boyfriend, and he loved it. We ate it with garlic mashed potatoes. My boyfriend suggested spicing it up with some red pepper or jalapeños if you want some heat."

Garlic Bread Fantastique *(pictured on page 44)*

Submitted by: **Sharon Whan**

"A zippy change from the usual garlic bread. It will surely be your favorite ever!"

½	cup butter, softened	1	teaspoon ground black pepper
2	tablespoons mayonnaise		
¼	teaspoon dried sage	1	French baguette, halved lengthwise
3	cloves garlic, chopped		
2	teaspoons dried oregano	¼	cup shredded Parmesan cheese
1	teaspoon salt		

1. Preheat broiler.

2. In a medium bowl, combine butter, mayonnaise, sage, garlic, oregano, salt, and pepper. Place baguette halves on a baking sheet. Spread mixture evenly on bread and sprinkle with Parmesan cheese.

3. Broil in the preheated oven for 5 minutes or until lightly toasted.

Yield: 6 servings.

Per serving: 388 calories, 8g protein, 41g carbohydrate, 22g fat, 3g fiber, 45mg cholesterol, 1062mg sodium

◄ **KID-FRIENDLY**

Prep Time: 10 minutes

Cook Time: 5 minutes

Average Rating: ★★★★☆

What other cooks have done:

"Only some guess the sage, and no one realizes there's mayo. Just delicious— surely the best garlic bread you'll ever make. The butter mixture keeps well in the fridge, too."

Perfect Pair: Pasta and Sauce

What comes in a box and is ready to eat in about 10 minutes? Pasta, of course! In the time it takes pasta to cook to perfection, you can whip up a simple but divine sauce—or the fabulous sirloin recipe at left—providing you with one of the world's quickest homemade meals.

And pasta's nutritional profile isn't too shabby either: One cup of cooked pasta is low in fat and provides complex carbohydrates, B vitamins, and some protein. When choosing pasta, select the whole wheat version more often if you can, as this variety has more protein and fiber than pasta made just from wheat flour.

What makes pasta a fattening meal is not the pasta itself but the rich, abundant sauces that many of us use to drown our noodles. Fresh, simple sauces are the best choice. In Italy, the sauces complement, not overpower, the pasta, so a little sauce can go a long way. The 2 cups of sauce called for in the recipe at left can come from any source you like, including the aisles of the grocery store, the container of Mom's famous homemade spaghetti sauce in your refrigerator, or the tomatoes in your garden. Here's an idea: Go to your supermarket salad bar and load up on fresh precut vegetables. Sauté them in a little olive oil and add to the sirloin recipe or toss with cooked pasta.

So add a little pasta to your menu: It's easy, fast, and always tastes great!

For more information, visit **Allrecipes.com**

Easy Summer Afternoon

When sunshine and warm weather are calling you outside, take dinner with you! A store-bought lemon icebox pie ends this easy meal on a tangy, sweet note.

MENU PREP PLAN

1. Prepare and marinate tuna. Start green beans on stovetop while tuna marinates in refrigerator. Prepare rice pilaf according to package directions.

2. Grill tuna.

3. Once beans reach desired degree of doneness, remove from stovetop and serve with tuna and pilaf.

MENU

Grilled Teriyaki Tuna

rice pilaf

Fasoliyyeh Bi Z-Zayt
(Syrian Green Beans with Olive Oil)

lemon icebox pie

Serves 4

Grilled Teriyaki Tuna

Submitted by: **Steve Dreibelbis**

"Yellowfin tuna is always delicious when grilled. This is great at a tailgate party or at your Saturday afternoon summer barbecue. You can add a little cayenne pepper or minced fresh ginger to the marinade to give it a little extra kick."

FROM THE GRILL ▶

Prep Time: 5 minutes

Marinate Time: 15 minutes

Cook Time: 16 minutes

Average Rating: ★★★★★

What other cooks have done:

"I made extra marinade for chicken breasts. Instead of grilling the tuna, I cooked it on the stovetop. I served it with rice pilaf and asparagus. My husband and I also drank pineapple wine from Maui with our meal. It reminded us of our trips to Maui."

1	cup teriyaki sauce	1	teaspoon ground black
¾	cup olive oil		pepper
2	tablespoons minced	4	(4 ounce) yellowfin tuna
	garlic		fillets

1. In a large heavy-duty, zip-top plastic bag, combine teriyaki sauce, oil, garlic, and pepper. Place tuna in bag, turning to coat. Seal bag with as little air in it as possible. Marinate for 15 minutes in the refrigerator.
2. Lightly oil cold grill rack and preheat grill for high heat.
3. Remove tuna from marinade. Cook on the prepared grill for 5 to 8 minutes per side or to desired degree of doneness. **Yield:** 4 servings.

Note: Cooking times will vary depending on the thickness of the fillets and the heat of the grill. Check the doneness of the fish by making an incision with a knife and checking the color in the middle.

Per serving: 548 calories, 31g protein, 13g carbohydrate, 42g fat, 0g fiber, 51mg cholesterol, 2802mg sodium

Fasoliyyeh Bi Z-Zayt
(Syrian Green Beans with Olive Oil)

Submitted by: **tasneem**

"I learned how to make this while visiting my husband's family in Syria. It can be a healthy, fast vegetarian entrée that is surprisingly filling when eaten with pita bread, or it can be a flavorful side dish. Syrians like it cooked until the green beans start turning brownish in color. The idea is not to sauté them, but to let them steam in the moisture released by the ice crystals."

1 (16 ounce) package frozen cut green beans	Salt to taste
¼ cup extra virgin olive oil	¼ cup chopped fresh cilantro
	1 clove garlic, minced

1. Place the green beans in a large pot and drizzle with olive oil. Season with salt to taste and cover.

2. Cook over medium-high heat, stirring occasionally, until beans are cooked to desired degree of doneness.

3. Add cilantro and garlic to beans and continue to cook just until cilantro has started to wilt. Eat as a main course by scooping up the beans with warm pita bread or serve as a side dish. **Yield:** 4 servings.

Per serving: 164 calories, 2g protein, 8g carbohydrate, 14g fat, 3g fiber, 0mg cholesterol, 74mg sodium

◄ AROUND-THE-WORLD CUISINE

Prep Time: 5 minutes

Cook Time: 15 minutes

Average Rating: ★★★★

What other cooks have done:

"Loved these! I cut back a little on the olive oil and added extra garlic and a splash of red wine vinegar. My husband wanted thirds and asked why I had not made enough. (I made four servings and it was just two of us!) I plan to make these for Thanksgiving and will add diced cooked bacon."

Weeknight Vegetarian

Take a break from fare that weighs heavy on your palate and enjoy this deceivingly delicious vegetarian menu. No one will guess the pudding's secret ingredient!

MENU PREP PLAN

1. Prepare chocolate pudding up to a day ahead and chill until ready to serve.

2. Prepare eggplant and put in the oven. Prepare salad dressing and store in refrigerator until ready to serve.

3. Turn eggplant and continue to bake. Dress store-bought salad greens. Store leftover dressing in the refrigerator. Serve eggplant with store-bought marinara sauce and salad on the side.

> ### MENU
>
> **Creamy Cucumber Dressing with salad greens**
>
> **Baked Fried Eggplant**
>
> **Tofu Chocolate Pudding**
>
> *Serves 4*

20 minutes or less

Creamy Cucumber Dressing

Submitted by: **Michele O'Sullivan**
"Use this delicious dressing on a fresh green salad."

1	(8 ounce) container plain yogurt	1	clove garlic, minced
½	cucumber, peeled, seeded, and coarsely chopped	½	teaspoon salt
1	teaspoon fresh lemon juice	½	teaspoon ground white pepper

1. In a blender, combine all ingredients. Blend until smooth and refrigerate until chilled. **Yield:** 8 servings.

Per serving: 21 calories, 1g protein, 2g carbohydrate, 1g fat, 0g fiber, 4mg cholesterol, 160mg sodium

MAKE-AHEAD ▶

Prep Time: 15 minutes

Average Rating: ★★★★☆

What other cooks have done:

"A little anchovy paste would make it Caesaresque. Fresh savory would be good, too. Be careful not to overblend—stop at the somewhat chunky gazpacho stage and resist the temptation to hit the liquefy button."

Baked Fried Eggplant

Submitted by: **Kris**

"I love fried eggplant but absolutely hate the mushy texture. I've found a great way to get the fried eggplant taste without the mush. And the sour cream added to the batter gives it a wonderful flavor."

1 eggplant
1 egg, lightly beaten
1 (8 ounce) container sour cream
3 tablespoons all-purpose flour
2 cups Italian-style breadcrumbs
1 jar marinara sauce (optional)

1. Preheat oven to 375°F (190°C). Lightly grease a baking sheet.
2. Wash eggplant and slice into ¼ inch slices. In a medium bowl, stir together egg and sour cream until well blended. Toss the eggplant slices in flour to coat. Dip 1 eggplant slice at a time into the egg batter and coat with breadcrumbs. Place coated eggplant on the prepared baking sheet and spray the tops with vegetable cooking spray.
3. Bake in the preheated oven for 15 minutes. Turn the slices over and cook 15 more minutes or until both sides are brown and crisp. Serve with marinara sauce, if desired. **Yield:** 4 servings.

Per serving: 417 calories, 13g protein, 55g carbohydrate, 17g fat, 6g fiber, 78mg cholesterol, 910mg sodium

◄ FAMILY FAVORITE
Prep Time: 15 minutes
Cook Time: 30 minutes
Average Rating: ★★★★☆
What other cooks have done:
"Excellent recipe! Tastes just like it does in the restaurants. I added thinly sliced fresh mozzarella from the deli and four-cheese spaghetti sauce. It was awesome and tasted just like fried eggplant."

Tofu Chocolate Pudding

Submitted by: **Jenni**

"A dreamy, creamy chocolate pudding that uses tofu."

1 cup semisweet chocolate chips
1 (16 ounce) package firm tofu, drained
¼ cup soy or skim milk
1 tablespoon vanilla extract

1. Microwave the chocolate on high for 30 seconds or until melted. Stir during melting, if necessary.
2. In a blender or food processor, combine tofu with the melted chocolate, milk, and vanilla. Process until mixture is smooth. Cover and chill at least 1 hour and serve. **Yield:** 6 servings.

Per serving: 201 calories, 8g protein, 20g carbohydrate, 12g fat, 2g fiber, 0mg cholesterol, 11mg sodium

◄ KID-FRIENDLY
Prep Time: 10 minutes
Chill Time: 1 hour
Average Rating: ★★★★☆
What other cooks have done:
"This pudding is wonderful. I added some sweetener for a little extra sweetness and 1 teaspoon of apple cider vinegar. Serve this with fat-free whipped topping for a very healthy, delicious dessert."

Low-Key Holiday

The holiday season is busy enough; don't let dinnertime add to your to-do list. This impressive menu is easy on the cook and heaven for the taste buds.

MENU PREP PLAN

1. Prepare Chocolate Éclair Dessert up to a day ahead and chill until ready to serve.

2. Prepare seasoning for chicken, and rub onto breasts. Set seasoned chicken aside and start Orange-Maple Glaze.

3. Put orzo on to boil and sauté chicken. While chicken cooks, cook carrots.

4. Add Orange-Maple Glaze to chicken. Drain cooked orzo. Serve chicken over orzo with carrots on the side.

MENU

Rosemary Chicken with Orange-Maple Glaze

orzo

Balsamic-Glazed Carrots

Chocolate Éclair Dessert

Serves 4

Rosemary Chicken with Orange-Maple Glaze

Submitted by: **Linda W.**
"The wonderfully rich glaze makes this an elegant dinner to serve to guests."

2	teaspoons chopped fresh rosemary	1	cup orange juice
½	teaspoon salt	½	cup dry white wine
½	teaspoon freshly ground black pepper	½	cup maple-flavored syrup
4	skinless, boneless chicken breast halves	2	tablespoons butter
		2	tablespoons olive oil

1. In a small bowl, mix together the rosemary, salt, and pepper. Rub mixture on both sides of chicken breasts and set aside.
2. Bring orange juice and wine to a boil in a small saucepan. Reduce heat slightly, continuing a low boil for 5 minutes, stirring occasionally. Stir in maple syrup and continue boiling for 5 more minutes, stirring frequently, until glossy and just slightly thickened. Set aside.
3. Melt butter with olive oil in a large skillet over medium-high heat. Add chicken breasts. Cover skillet and sauté for 5 minutes on each side or until lightly browned. Pour orange-maple mixture over chicken. (Mixture will boil and bubble.) Reduce heat and simmer, uncovered, 10 minutes, basting occasionally, until chicken is cooked through and sauce has turned into a rich, thick glaze. **Yield:** 4 servings.

Per serving: 395 calories, 28g protein, 34g carbohydrate, 14g fat, 0g fiber, 84mg cholesterol, 452mg sodium

COMPANY IS COMING ▶

Prep Time: 10 minutes

Cook Time: 30 minutes

Average Rating: ★★★★☆

What other cooks have done:

"I forgot the wine and made the sauce with just orange juice and maple syrup. Wonderful, wonderful. Even the kids liked it!"

 *minutes or less*

Balsamic-Glazed Carrots

Submitted by: **Harry Wetzel**
"Carrots sautéed in olive oil are tossed with balsamic vinegar and brown sugar in this deceptively simple side dish."

1 tablespoon olive oil	1 tablespoon brown sugar
3 cups baby carrots	
1½ tablespoons balsamic vinegar	

1. Heat oil in a skillet over medium-high heat. Sauté carrots in oil for about 10 minutes or until tender. Add balsamic vinegar and brown sugar; stir to coat and serve. **Yield:** 4 servings.

Per serving: 85 calories, 1g protein, 12g carbohydrate, 4g fat, 2g fiber, 0mg cholesterol, 38mg sodium

20 minutes or less

Chocolate Éclair Dessert

Submitted by: **Kristie Behrens**
"Everyone loves this no-bake pudding dessert that's so quick and easy to make. I always keep the ingredients on hand in case I need a speedy dessert."

½ (14.4 ounce) box graham crackers, divided	3 cups milk
2 (3.4 ounce) packages instant vanilla pudding mix	1 (8 ounce) container frozen whipped topping, thawed
	1 (16 ounce) container chocolate frosting

1. Line the bottom of a 9x13 inch pan with one-third of graham crackers. In a large bowl, combine pudding mix and milk. Stir well. Stir in whipped topping. Spread half of mixture over graham cracker layer. Top with another third of graham crackers and the remaining pudding. Top all with the final third of graham crackers. Frost with chocolate frosting. Refrigerate until serving. **Yield:** 12 servings.

Per serving: 401 calories, 4g protein, 66g carbohydrate, 14g fat, 1g fiber, 5mg cholesterol, 487mg sodium

◄ **5 INGREDIENTS OR LESS**

Prep Time: 5 minutes

Cook Time: 10 minutes

Average Rating: ★★★★☆

What other cooks have done:

"Instead of baby carrots, I peeled regular carrots and sliced them into about ¼ inch round slices. Also, I used a little bit more brown sugar than what the recipe called for. They taste great the next day, too!"

◄ **KID-FRIENDLY**

Prep Time: 15 minutes

Average Rating: ★★★★★

What other cooks have done:

"Excellent! I microwaved the frosting for 45 seconds. (Be sure to remove the foil under the plastic lid and put the lid back on.) This gave me an easy-to-spread frosting that left a smooth top. I also grated a little chocolate to sprinkle over the dessert."

Hearty Homestyle

A simple casserole is just the thing to satisfy the whole family. With a bountiful salad and buttery breadsticks from your supermarket's bakery section, there may not be room left for dessert, but just in case, we've included some fantastic fudge.

MENU PREP PLAN

1. Prepare fudge up to a day ahead, if desired. Prepare salad dressing and store in refrigerator.

2. Cook pasta. Prepare cheese mixture for casserole while pasta cooks.

3. Start fudge if not prepared the day ahead. While cheese and butter melt, sauté chicken. Stir together remaining fudge ingredients and press into pan.

4. Assemble salad using precooked bacon. Dress part of salad for menu, reserving remaining salad and dressing for another meal. Assemble casserole. Cut fudge into squares.

MENU

Farmer's Salad

Chicken Rotini Stovetop Casserole

bakery breadsticks

No-Cook Never-Fail Fudge

Serves 6

---

10 *minutes or less*

Farmer's Salad

Submitted by: **Marsha Gray**
"This is a great-tasting salad that is easy to prepare. The main ingredients— lettuce, broccoli, and bacon—are normally on hand."

FAMILY FAVORITE ▶

Prep Time: 10 minutes

Average Rating: ★★★★★

What other cooks have done:

"This salad is a favorite with everyone. I've added cheese and sunflower seeds to it, and there's never enough left at the bottom of the bowl for lunch the next day! Absolutely wonderful and simple."

1	(16 ounce) bag lettuce	1	tablespoon distilled white vinegar
1	(12 ounce) bag broccoli florets	1	cup crumbled precooked bacon
¾	cup mayonnaise		
3	tablespoons white sugar		

1. In a large bowl, combine the lettuce and broccoli.
2. Whisk together the mayonnaise, sugar, and vinegar.
3. Pour dressing over lettuce mixture and toss evenly to coat. Sprinkle with bacon and refrigerate until ready to serve. Serve cold. **Yield:** 8 servings.

Per serving: 500 calories, 7g protein, 9g carbohydrate, 50g fat, 2g fiber, 50mg cholesterol, 548mg sodium

Chicken Rotini Stovetop Casserole

Submitted by: **Terry**

"Rotini pasta tossed with chicken, bell peppers, and a creamy herb sauce—all prepared on the stovetop! Very quick and easy recipe. You can improvise to accommodate certain tastes. Serve it for any occasion."

1	(12 ounce) package rotini pasta	½	teaspoon chopped fresh parsley
2	cups half-and-half	4	skinless, boneless chicken breast halves, cubed
½	cup butter or margarine	2	tablespoons vegetable oil
⅔	cup freshly grated Parmesan cheese	½	green bell pepper, chopped
½	teaspoon dried basil	½	red bell pepper, chopped
½	teaspoon dried oregano		
½	teaspoon chopped fresh chives		

1. Bring a large pot of lightly salted water to a boil. Add pasta and cook for 8 to 10 minutes or until al dente; drain.

2. Meanwhile, combine half-and-half and butter in a saucepan over medium heat. Boil gently, stirring occasionally, until mixture has reduced to 1½ to 1⅔ cups. Remove pan from heat; whisk in cheese, basil, oregano, chives, and parsley. Cover and set aside.

3. Sauté chicken in oil in a large skillet 5 minutes on each side or until lightly browned. Stir in green and red bell pepper, and cook until vegetables are tender and chicken is no longer pink and juices run clear.

4. In a casserole dish, combine the hot cooked pasta, chicken mixture, and sauce. Mix well and serve immediately. **Yield:** 6 servings.

Per serving: 480 calories, 28g protein, 23g carbohydrate, 31g fat, 1g fiber, 128mg cholesterol, 444mg sodium

◄ COVERED-DISH FAVORITE

Prep Time: 15 minutes

Cook Time: 25 minutes

Average Rating: ★★★★★

What other cooks have done:

"I added a good dose of garlic to the sauce and some garlic, onion, and mushrooms to the chicken and peppers. I added ½ teaspoon of cornstarch to get the sauce to thicken. I will be using this recipe again and again."

No-Cook Never-Fail Fudge

Submitted by: **Mary**

"This recipe came from a dear friend of mine. It is an unbelievably delicious fudge! This fudge has been a hit with all who have tried it. Don't let them know the ingredients until they have tasted it; no one will ever believe it has cheese in it. Pecans can be substituted for walnuts. This fudge can be frozen."

FREEZER FRESH ▶

Prep Time: 10 minutes

Cook Time: 10 minutes

Cool Time: 20 minutes

Average Rating: ★★★★★

What other cooks have done:

"This is an excellent recipe. It makes a very smooth, creamy, and chewy fudge. It reminds me of fudge I've gotten from bakeries. It's easy to make but requires a lot of stirring. It gets stiff very quickly, so I wound up kneading it with my hands. I took it to a party, and everyone raved over it."

½	pound processed cheese, cubed	½	cup unsweetened cocoa powder
½	pound butter	1½	cups chopped walnuts
2	pounds confectioners' sugar	½	tablespoon vanilla extract

1. Lightly grease a 9x13 inch pan.

2. Melt cheese and butter together in a nonstick saucepan; stir until smooth. Keep mixture over low heat. In a mixing bowl, sift confectioners' sugar and cocoa together until thoroughly mixed and no lumps remain.

3. Combine the sugar mixture with the melted butter and cheese. Stir until very smooth. Stir in nuts and vanilla.

4. Press mixture into prepared pan; let cool until firm. Cut into small squares. Store in refrigerator. **Yield:** 20 servings.

Per square: 360 calories, 4g protein, 49g carbohydrate, 18g fat, 1g fiber, 32mg cholesterol, 205mg sodium

Grill Thrill

Flex your grilling muscles with this menu that's rich in colors and flavors. Banana pudding helps cool the heat of spicy Tandoori Chicken.

MENU

Tandoori Chicken II

Marinated Veggies

Uncooked Banana Pudding

Serves 4

MENU PREP PLAN

1. Preslice veggies a day ahead, if desired, and store, refrigerated, in a zip-top plastic bag.

2. Prepare vegetable marinade. Slice vegetables if not done ahead. Marinate veggies.

3. Prepare chicken rub. Rub chicken and refrigerate. Prepare banana pudding and chill until ready to serve.

4. Grill chicken and vegetables.

Tandoori Chicken II

Submitted by: **Bonnie**

"A paste made from a combination of spices and dried peppers is the secret to this grilled chicken recipe. Since no long marinating time is required, the chicken can be prepared in the time it takes to preheat the grill."

½ teaspoon curry powder	¼ teaspoon ground cinnamon
½ teaspoon crushed red pepper flakes	¼ teaspoon ground turmeric
½ teaspoon coarse kosher salt	2 tablespoons water
¼ teaspoon ground ginger	4 skinless, boneless chicken breast halves
¼ teaspoon paprika	

1. In a medium bowl, combine curry powder, red pepper flakes, salt, ginger, paprika, cinnamon, turmeric, and water to form a smooth paste.
2. Rub paste onto chicken. Cover chicken and refrigerate for 15 minutes.
3. Lightly oil cold grill rack and preheat grill for medium-high heat.
4. Cook on the prepared grill for 6 minutes per side or until chicken is no longer pink and until juices run clear. **Yield:** 4 servings.

Per serving: 265 calories, 49g protein, 1g carbohydrate, 6g fat, 0g fiber, 134mg cholesterol, 353mg sodium

◄ HOT & SPICY

Prep Time: 15 minutes

Marinate Time: 15 minutes

Cook Time: 10 minutes

Average Rating: ★★★★☆

What other cooks have done:

"Excellent! I love the fact that this recipe makes chicken loaded with flavor with no added calories. It's perfect for anyone trying to follow a reduced-calorie diet. I cooked mine under the broiler, and it turned out just fine."

Marinated Veggies

Submitted by: **Mathilda Sprey**

"A tasty way to grill veggies! Makes a great sandwich, too!"

Prep Time: 10 minutes

Marinate Time: 15 minutes

Cook Time: 15 minutes

Average Rating: ★★★★☆

What other cooks have done:

"I improvised on proportions, using slightly more soy sauce than oil and lemon juice. I also added 1 to 2 tablespoons honey. It was really fabulous!"

½	cup olive oil	¼	cup sliced yellow squash
½	cup soy sauce	¼	cup sliced red onion
½	cup lemon juice	8	large fresh button
½	clove garlic, crushed		mushrooms
¼	cup thickly sliced zucchini	8	cherry tomatoes
¼	cup sliced red bell pepper		
¼	cup sliced yellow bell pepper		

1. In a large bowl, combine olive oil, soy sauce, lemon juice, and garlic; mix together.

2. Add the zucchini, red bell pepper, yellow bell pepper, squash, red onion, mushrooms, and tomatoes to olive oil mixture; stir to combine.

3. Cover bowl and marinate in refrigerator for 15 minutes.

4. Lightly oil cold grill rack and preheat grill for medium–high heat.

5. Place vegetables in a grill basket, discarding marinade. Cook on the prepared grill for 10 to 12 minutes or until tender. **Yield:** 4 servings.

Per serving: 160 calories, 3g protein, 8g carbohydrate, 14g fat, 2g fiber, 0mg cholesterol, 917mg sodium

Get Grilling!

Everything tastes better off the grill. And nothing could be simpler, right? Well, there is more to barbeque than tossing a steak on the grill. Experience is a great teacher, but before you spend years perfecting that secret recipe, you might want to go over the basics.

Preheating the Grill

The right temperature is always important. Reliable grill thermometers are widely available, but will only give an accurate reading when the grill is covered. That being said, the standard is still the caveman method. This consists of holding your hand approximately 6 inches above the coals or heat source (about the spot where the food will be cooking) and counting how many seconds you can keep your hand in this position. Count "one-barbeque, two-barbeque…."

- High Heat: 3 seconds or 500°F (260°C)
- Medium-High Heat: 5 seconds or 400°F (200°C)
- Medium Heat: 7 seconds or 350°F (175°C)
- Medium-Low Heat: 10 seconds or 325°F (165°C)
- Low Heat: 12 seconds or 300°F (150°C)

Direct Heat vs. Indirect Heat

There are primarily two methods of using a grill. Cooking directly over the heat source is known as grilling over direct heat. The food is cooked for mere minutes on a hot grill, and the lid is rarely, if ever, closed. Thin cuts of meat, fillets, kabobs, and vegetables are good candidates for this method. Indirect heat is used for larger pieces of meat, such as thick steaks, roasts, and whole fish. In this method, the food is cooked just off the heat; the lid is closed, and the cooking times are somewhat longer. On a gas grill, fire up the two outside burners, and cook the meat over the middle, unlit burner. When using charcoal, push the coals to the sides, leaving a place in the middle to cook.

Timing is Everything

Avoid turning your juicy chop into tough, dry shoe leather by checking for doneness at the approximate time given in the recipe. An instant-read thermometer is a good tool for this. Insert it into the thickest part of the meat to measure the internal temperature of the food.

For more information, visit **Allrecipes.com**

Uncooked Banana Pudding

Submitted by: **LeAnne**
"Dessert in 10 minutes with vanilla pudding mix, bananas, sour cream, and whipped topping."

1	(8 ounce) container sour cream	2	cups whole milk
1	(8 ounce) container frozen whipped topping, thawed	1	(12 ounce) package vanilla wafers
1	(5.1 ounce) package instant vanilla pudding mix	4	bananas, peeled and sliced

1. In large bowl, combine sour cream, whipped topping, pudding mix, and milk. Stir well.
2. In the bottom of a trifle bowl or other glass serving dish, place a layer of vanilla wafers, then a layer of pudding mixture, and then a layer of bananas. Repeat until all ingredients are used. Refrigerate until serving. **Yield:** 10 servings.

Per serving: 447 calories, 5g protein, 64g carbohydrate, 19g fat, 2g fiber, 17mg cholesterol, 375mg sodium

◄ **CLASSIC COMFORT FOOD**

Prep Time: 10 minutes

Average Rating: ★★★★★

What other cooks have done:

"I used this pudding as a topping on a 9x13 inch cake and wow—it was gone in no time! When using it as a topping, just mix in the bananas and crumble vanilla wafers on top."

Busy Night Soup & Sandwich

When everyone's running in a different direction, a bowlful of hearty soup and a mile-high club sandwich that's a snap to assemble will make dinnertime a calm in the storm.

MENU PREP PLAN

1. Prepare and bake cookies.

2. While cookies bake, cook vegetables for soup.

3. Combine remaining soup ingredients. Cook bacon for sandwiches while soup heats. Remove cookies from oven to cool.

4. Assemble sandwiches and serve with bowls of soup.

MENU

Lorraine's Club Sandwich

Potato, Broccoli, and Cheese Soup

Cowboy Oatmeal Cookies

Serves 4

KID-FRIENDLY ▶

Prep Time: 5 minutes

Cook Time: 5 minutes

Average Rating: ★★★★★

What other cooks have done:

"We tried a sandwich with three pieces of toast but prefer to cram all the meat and veggies between two pieces. I also added some red onion and a squirt of Dijon mustard."

10 minutes or less

Lorraine's Club Sandwich *(pictured on page 38)*

Submitted by: **Lorraine Winkel**
"An easy, quick, and delicious sandwich to eat anytime."

8	slices bacon	8	leaves lettuce
12	slices bread, toasted	8	slices tomato
⅓	cup mayonnaise		
8	(1 ounce) slices cooked deli turkey breast		

1. Place bacon in a large, deep skillet. Cook over medium–high heat until evenly brown. Drain on paper towels.
2. Spread each slice of toast with mayonnaise. On 1 slice of toast, layer 2 slices turkey and 2 leaves lettuce. Cover with a slice of toast. Add 2 slices bacon and 2 slices tomato. Top with a slice of toast. Repeat procedure for remaining sandwiches. **Yield:** 4 servings.

Per serving: 874 calories, 21g protein, 43g carbohydrate, 69g fat, 3g fiber, 85mg cholesterol, 1711mg sodium

Potato, Broccoli, and Cheese Soup

(pictured on page 38)

Submitted by: **Ruth A. Burbage**

"A cheesy potato-broccoli soup that tastes great."

2	cups chopped onion	4	chicken bouillon cubes
2	tablespoons butter or margarine	3	cups frozen broccoli florets
2½	pounds potatoes, peeled and cubed		Salt and ground black pepper to taste
5	cups boiling water	3	cups shredded Cheddar cheese

1. In a large pot, sauté onion in butter. Add potatoes, water, and bouillon cubes. Cover and bring to boil. Reduce heat to medium and cook until potatoes are tender, about 15 minutes.

2. Meanwhile, cook broccoli according to package directions. Drain and add to soup.

3. In a blender or food processor, puree half of the soup and return to pot. Season with salt and pepper to taste.

4. Add cheese and heat soup through until cheese is melted. Serve warm. **Yield:** 6 servings.

Per serving: 448 calories, 20g protein, 43g carbohydrate, 23g fat, 7g fiber, 60mg cholesterol, 1193mg sodium

◄ CLASSIC COMFORT FOOD

Prep Time: 15 minutes

Cook Time: 30 minutes

Average Rating: ★★★★★

What other cooks have done:

"I have been looking for a great recipe for broccoli-cheese soup, and this is definitely it! It is not time-consuming, and it tastes wonderful. I have added some fresh garlic to the recipe to add even more flavor."

A Little Dab Will Do You

When serving soup, don't overlook the wonderful world of garnishes. Not only will they make your soup look beautiful, but the right garnish will add a whole new dimension of taste to each mouthful. By introducing a contrasting flavor or texture, or by accenting one of the minor ingredients and bringing it to the forefront, a little garnish does wonders for any kind of soup.

• Try a sprinkling of freshly minced herbs (whichever kind you used in cooking the soup).

• To cool down a spicy soup or add just a touch of creaminess, stir either lime juice, a little grated ginger, some finely chopped orange zest, or perhaps a dash of curry powder into some fat-free sour cream or fat-free plain yogurt. Dollop this mixture on top of each bowl of soup right before serving. You can, of course, change the flavorings according to the kind of soup you've made.

• Toasted bread, unbuttered croutons, crackers, or baked tortilla chips add a satisfying crunch without piling on the pounds.

• A spoonful of salsa, chopped tomatoes, bell peppers, scallions, or cucumbers adds a cool, fresh taste to your soup.

• A dusting of finely grated hard cheese, such as Parmesan, Romano, or Emmentaler, adds lots of flavor but not much fat.

For more information, visit **Allrecipes.com**

Cowboy Oatmeal Cookies *(pictured on facing page)*

Submitted by: **Ellie Davies**

"This great cookie is one of my kids' favorites. This doesn't call for nuts, but I sometimes add about ½ cup of them, chopped."

KID-FRIENDLY ▶

Prep Time: 15 minutes

Cook Time: 12 minutes per batch

Cool Time: 5 minutes per batch

Average Rating: ★★★★★

What other cooks have done:

"My family thought these cookies were terrific. I substituted chocolate chips, nuts, and candy-coated chocolate pieces for the cup of butterscotch chips. The recipe was very forgiving—I'm sure we added almost 2 cups of goodies, and it still turned out great."

2	cups all-purpose flour	1	cup packed brown sugar
½	teaspoon baking powder	1	cup white sugar
1	teaspoon baking soda	2	eggs
½	teaspoon salt	2	cups quick cooking oats
½	cup butter or margarine, softened	1	cup butterscotch chips
½	cup vegetable oil		

1. Preheat oven to 350°F (175°C).

2. In a large bowl, sift together flour, baking powder, baking soda, and salt; set aside.

3. In a separate large bowl, cream butter, oil, brown sugar, and white sugar until smooth. Beat in eggs, 1 at a time. Gradually stir in the sifted ingredients until well blended. Mix in oats and butterscotch chips. Drop by teaspoonfuls onto ungreased baking sheets.

4. Bake in the preheated oven for 10 to 12 minutes or until edges are golden. Cool on baking sheets for 5 minutes before transferring to wire racks to cool completely. **Yield:** 3 dozen.

Per cookie: 167 calories, 2g protein, 23g carbohydrate, 8g fat, 1g fiber, 12mg cholesterol, 115mg sodium

Cowboy Oatmeal Cookies

Lorraine's Club Sandwich, page 34,
and Potato, Broccoli, and Cheese Soup, page 35

Stuffed Acorn Squash Supreme,
page 17

Grilled Rock Lobster Tails, page 14

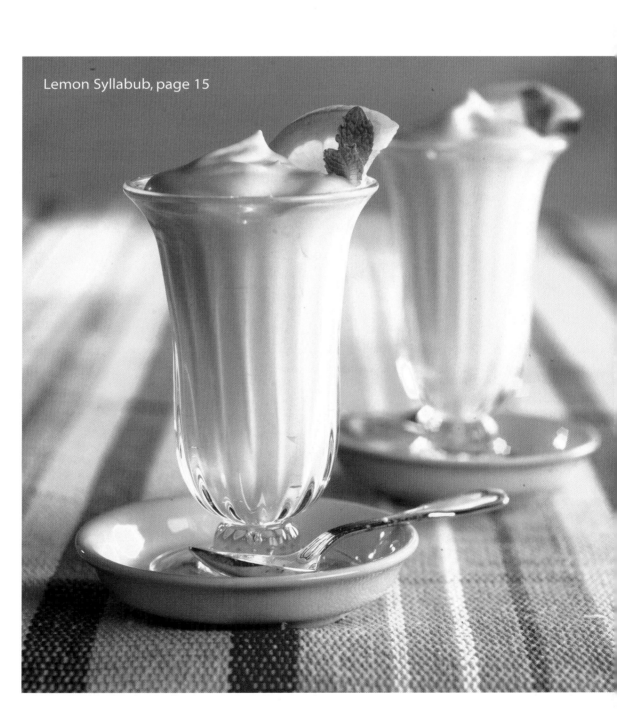

Lemon Syllabub, page 15

Supreme Strawberry Topping,
page 19

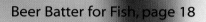
Beer Batter for Fish, page 18

Sirloin Marinara, page 20,
and Garlic Bread Fantastique, page 21

30-Minute Brand-Name Recipes

7-Layer Dip

Submitted by: **Bush's Best® Beans**

"This creamy, irresistible Mexican-style dip is perfect for parties!"

PARTY FOOD ▶

Prep Time: 20 minutes

Chill Time: 30 minutes

Cook Time: 10 minutes

Average Rating: ★★★★★

What other cooks have done:

"I use a deep-dish pie plate or quiche dish instead of an 11x13 pan. There are never any leftovers."

1 (16 ounce) container sour cream

1 (1.25 ounce) package taco seasoning

1½ (16 ounce) cans BUSH'S BEST® Pinto Beans★, mashed

1 (16 ounce) jar chunky salsa

2 cups shredded Cheddar cheese

1 (4 ounce) can sliced black olives

2 cups shredded lettuce

1 large tomato, chopped

2 avocados, diced

½ cup chopped green onions Tortilla chips

1. Mix sour cream and taco seasoning. Chill for 30 minutes.
2. In a saucepan, combine BUSH'S BEST® Pinto Beans and salsa. Heat on medium and stir until evenly blended. Let cool.
3. Take cooled BUSH'S BEST® Pinto Beans and salsa and spread in an 11x13 inch pan. Spread sour cream/taco seasoning mixture over beans.
4. Layer the cheese, olives, lettuce, tomatoes, avocados, and green onions in that order evenly in pan. Serve with tortilla chips. **Yield:** 8 servings.

Per serving: 474 calories, 17g protein, 32g carbohydrate, 33g fat, 9g fiber, 55mg cholesterol, 1232mg sodium

★Substitute 1½ cans BUSH'S BEST® Refried Beans, if desired.

Creamy Crab and Artichoke Dip

Submitted by: **Keebler® Kitchens**

"Serve this delicious warm dip with Town House® Crackers."

HOLIDAY FARE ▶

Prep Time: 16 minutes

Cook Time: 15 minutes

Average Rating: ★★★★☆

What other cooks have done:

"This was great and easy. My family loved it on Christmas Eve."

1 (8 ounce) package cream cheese, softened

1 cup mayonnaise

1 (6 ounce) package imitation crab

⅓ cup chopped onion

1 (13.75 ounce) can artichoke hearts, drained and chopped

¾ cup shredded Parmesan cheese KEEBLER® TOWN HOUSE® Crackers

1. Preheat oven to 375°F (190°C).
2. In a medium bowl, blend together cream cheese and mayonnaise until smooth. Stir in next 4 ingredients; spoon mixture into a pie plate.
3. Bake, uncovered, in the preheated oven for 15 minutes or until lightly browned. Serve with TOWN HOUSE® Crackers. **Yield:** 8 servings.

Per serving: 388 calories, 11g protein, 10g carbohydrate, 35g fat, 2g fiber, 59mg cholesterol, 889mg sodium

Herbed White Bean Spread on Garlic-Toasted Bruschetta

Submitted by: **Hormel Foods Corporation**

"A rich spread made with cannellini beans, fresh sage, and Parmesan cheese is spread onto baguette slices and broiled until bursting with Italian flavor."

2	tablespoons CARAPELLI® olive oil, divided	1	cup water
3	green onions, chopped	1	teaspoon HERB-OX® Chicken Flavored Bouillon Granules
2	cloves garlic, minced		
1	tablespoon chopped fresh sage	¼	cup grated Parmesan cheese
1	(16 ounce) can cannellini beans, rinsed and drained	12	(1 inch thick) French baguette slices
		1	clove garlic, halved

1. Heat 1 tablespoon oil in a skillet. Add the green onions, garlic, and sage and cook for about 2 minutes. Add beans, water, and bouillon granules and continue to cook until liquid is absorbed, about 5 minutes; add the cheese. Cool to room temperature. Place bean mixture in a food processor and process until smooth.
2. Preheat broiler.
3. Rub the bread on both sides with the cut side of garlic and brush lightly with remaining 1 tablespoon oil. Place on a baking sheet.
4. Broil in the preheated oven for about 1 minute or until golden on 1 side. Turn and cook 1 more minute. Place about 2 tablespoons of spread on each slice. **Yield:** 12 servings.

Per serving: 102 calories, 4g protein, 14g carbohydrate, 4g fat, 2g fiber, 2mg cholesterol, 212mg sodium

◀ PARTY FOOD

Prep Time: 15 minutes

Cook Time: 10 minutes

Average Rating: ★★★★★

What other cooks have done:

"I made this with vegetable bouillon and omitted the cheese for my vegan sister. I also added a minced shallot to the onion mixture. It was a hit with my family."

Cold Smoked Salmon Spread

Submitted by: **Keebler® Kitchens**
"This simple, savory spread combines the classic flavors of salmon, cream cheese, and dill. The ideal accompaniment for buttery Town House® crackers."

MAKE-AHEAD ▶

Prep Time: 12 minutes

Chill Time: 1 hour

Average Rating: ★★★★☆

What other cooks have done:

"This also tastes great stuffed in celery sticks or spread on cauliflower or broccoli. It's a great way to use up leftover salmon."

1	(8 ounce) package cream cheese, softened	1	tablespoon chopped fresh dill
4	ounces smoked salmon, chopped	1	tablespoon lemon juice
3	tablespoons finely chopped chives		Fresh dill (optional)
2	tablespoons capers		Lemon peel (optional)
			KEEBLER® TOWN HOUSE® Crackers

1. Combine cream cheese and smoked salmon in a medium bowl. Add next 4 ingredients. Spoon into a serving bowl or onto a plate. Garnish with fresh dill and lemon peel, if desired. Chill at least 1 hour; serve with TOWN HOUSE® Crackers. **Yield:** 24 servings.

Per serving: 39 calories, 2g protein, 0g carbohydrate, 4g fat, 0g fiber, 11mg cholesterol, 86mg sodium

10 minutes or less

Roasted Sweet Red Pepper Spread

Submitted by: **Keebler® Kitchens**
"Piquant roasted red bell peppers mingle with tangy tomato paste, garlic, and ground red pepper in this flavorful spread."

HOLIDAY GIFT GIVING ▶

Prep Time: 10 minutes

Average Rating: ★★★★★

What other cooks have done:

"This has great roasted red pepper flavor, while the ground red pepper adds some bite. The recipe as stated yields a lot. Next time, I plan on cutting the recipe in half."

2	(12 ounce) jars roasted red peppers, drained	2	teaspoons white sugar
1	(16 ounce) can tomato paste	1	teaspoon garlic salt
1	tablespoon chopped fresh thyme	1	teaspoon ground red pepper
1	tablespoon olive oil	1	teaspoon salt
			KEEBLER® TOWN HOUSE® Crackers

1. Place roasted peppers in a blender or food processor. Cover; blend or process until finely chopped. Add tomato paste, thyme, olive oil, sugar, garlic salt, ground red pepper, and salt. Cover; blend or process until nearly smooth. Serve at once or cover and chill up to 1 week. Serve with TOWN HOUSE® Crackers. **Yield:** 12 servings.

Per serving: 98 calories, 3g protein, 15g carbohydrate, 4g fat, 2g fiber, 0mg cholesterol, 914mg sodium

Fiesta Cracker Spread

Submitted by: **Keebler® Kitchens**

"Sharp Cheddar and jalapeños add a pleasing bite to this festive spread that's delicious on a crisp Town House® Cracker."

1 (8 ounce) package cream cheese
1 tablespoon seltzer water
½ cup shredded sharp Cheddar cheese
1 teaspoon dry Mexican or taco seasoning
1 tablespoon salsa
2 tablespoons finely chopped red bell pepper

¼ cup chopped green onions
¼ cup corn (optional)
1 tablespoon diced jalapeño pepper (optional)
KEEBLER® TOWN HOUSE® Crackers
Cilantro leaves, red bell pepper, or jalapeño slices (optional)

◄ **PARTY FOOD**

Prep Time: 15 minutes

Average Rating: ★★★★★

What other cooks have done:

"This is fast and so easy! I used a canned mix of corn and peppers, so I skipped chopping the red peppers. I added extra jalapeños for more zip. This definitely should be made one day ahead so the flavors can combine."

1. Mix cream cheese, seltzer water, Cheddar cheese, and seasoning at medium speed with an electric mixer until smooth. Fold in next 5 ingredients. Refrigerate until serving. Serve with TOWN HOUSE® Crackers. Garnish with cilantro leaves, red bell pepper, or jalapeño slices, if desired. **Yield:** 16 servings.

Per serving: 67 calories, 2g protein, 1g carbohydrate, 6g fat, 0g fiber, 19mg cholesterol, 91mg sodium

Baked Cranberry Almond Brie

Submitted by: **Land O'Lakes, Inc.**

"Cranberry sauce, toasted almonds, and a soft cream cheese pastry are the perfect way to dress up warm Brie. Serve with apple slices, pear slices, or crackers."

PARTY FOOD ▶

Prep Time: 15 minutes

Chill Time: 1 hour

Cook Time: 20 minutes

Stand Time: 30 minutes

Average Rating: ★★★★★

What other cooks have done:

"Instead of the cranberry-almond mixture, I used a cranberry chutney with pecans, pears, apples, orange, and dried fruit."

Pastry
¾ cup all-purpose flour
¼ cup LAND O LAKES® Ultra Creamy™ Butter, softened
1 (3 ounce) package cream cheese, softened

Filling
1 (8 ounce) wheel Brie cheese

3 tablespoons cranberry-orange sauce
3 tablespoons chopped toasted almonds

Topping
1 egg
1 teaspoon water

1. Combine flour, butter, and cream cheese in a large bowl. Beat at low speed with an electric mixer, scraping bowl often, until mixture leaves sides of bowl and forms a dough, about 2 to 3 minutes. Divide dough in half; wrap in plastic wrap. Refrigerate until firm, about 1 hour.

2. Preheat oven to 400°F (200°C).

3. Roll each half of dough on a lightly floured surface to ⅛ inch thickness. Cut an 8 inch circle from each dough half (saving dough scraps for decoration, if desired). Place 1 circle on an ungreased baking sheet. Place Brie cheese on center of pastry circle. Spread cranberry sauce over top of cheese; sprinkle with toasted almonds. Top with remaining pastry circle. Pinch edges of pastry to seal. Flute edges, if desired. Decorate top with small pastry cutouts, if desired.

4. Beat egg with water in a small bowl; brush top and sides of pastry.

5. Bake in the preheated oven for 15 to 20 minutes or until golden brown. Remove from baking sheet immediately. Let stand for 30 minutes to allow cheese to set. To serve, cut into small wedges.

Yield: 8 servings.

Per serving: 257 calories, 9g protein, 12g carbohydrate, 19g fat, 1g fiber, 82mg cholesterol, 278mg sodium

Nut-Glazed Brie Served with Crackers

Submitted by: **Keebler® Kitchens**
"Entice your guests with a round of Brie topped with a sweet nut glaze."

⅓ cup packed brown sugar
¼ cup broken walnut or pecan pieces or chopped almonds
2 teaspoons water

1 (14 ounce) round Brie cheese
Assorted KEEBLER® TOASTEDS® Crackers

◀ 5 INGREDIENTS OR LESS
Prep Time: 10 minutes
Cook Time: 8 minutes
Average Rating: ★★★★★

1. Preheat oven to 500°F (260°F).
2. In small mixing bowl, stir together brown sugar, nuts, and water.
3. Place Brie on an ovenproof platter or in a 9-inch pie plate.
4. Bake in the preheated oven for 5 minutes or until cheese is slightly softened.
5. Spoon nut mixture over top; bake for 3 more minutes or until sugar is melted and cheese is heated through but not melted. Serve with assorted TOASTEDS® Crackers. **Yield:** 18 servings.

Per serving: 163 calories, 6g protein, 12g carbohydrate, 10g fat, 0g fiber, 22mg cholesterol, 259mg sodium

What other cooks have done:
"I fixed this as an appetizer for a Christmas dinner, and it disappeared in five minutes! I used a nut mix of pecans and walnuts and substituted butter for the water. It was delicious!"

Olive and Goat Cheese Crostini

Submitted by: **Lindsay® Olives**
"Scrimp on time without sacrificing flavor with these super simple, tasty crostini. Goat cheese spread on toasted baguette slices and topped with black olives and paprika makes for a perfect last-minute appetizer or anytime snack."

1 (1 pound) French baguette, sliced diagonally into 20 pieces
5½ ounces goat cheese
1 (6 ounce) can LINDSAY® Black Ripe Pitted Olives, chopped

1 teaspoon fresh oregano, chopped
Paprika to taste

◀ 5 INGREDIENTS OR LESS
Prep Time: 10 minutes
Cook Time: 10 minutes
Average Rating: ★★★★★

1. Preheat oven to 375°F (190°C).
2. Spread baguette slices on a large baking sheet and bake in the preheated oven for 5 to 10 minutes until lightly toasted. Set aside.
3. Combine goat cheese, olives, and oregano in a small bowl. Spread mixture on top of each crostini. Garnish with a light dusting of paprika just before serving. **Yield:** 10 servings.

Per serving: 262 calories, 9g protein, 31g carbohydrate, 11g fat, 2g fiber, 15mg cholesterol, 609mg sodium

What other cooks have done:
"I liked this recipe because it was extremely simple to make as well as easy—and it tasted good. Next time, I think I will brush the bread with olive oil before baking and maybe add a little garlic."

Spinach-Cheese Bites

Submitted by: **Keebler® Kitchens**

"A savory Italian cheese and spinach mixture is baked onto crackers and garnished with red and yellow bell pepper pieces. This is a fun and easy appetizer that won't keep you long in the kitchen."

COMPANY IS COMING ▶

Prep Time: 15 minutes

Cook Time: 10 minutes

Average Rating: ★★★★☆

What other cooks have done:

"I wrapped small teaspoonfuls in some puff pastry (rolled out, not too thin) and baked them at 375°F for 15 to 25 minutes."

2 teaspoons olive oil
½ teaspoon finely chopped or pressed garlic
1 (6 ounce) package fresh baby spinach, coarsely chopped
1¼ teaspoons dried Italian seasoning
¼ teaspoon salt
1¼ cups Asiago, Parmesan, or pepper Jack cheese
16 KEEBLER® TOWN HOUSE® Crackers
Diced red and yellow bell pepper

1. Preheat oven to 375°F (190°C).
2. Heat olive oil in a medium skillet over medium heat. Add garlic; stir a few seconds until fragrant. Add spinach, Italian seasoning, and salt; stir and cook for 3 to 4 minutes or until spinach wilts. Remove skillet from heat.
3. Drain spinach in small sieve or colander, pressing out liquid with the back of the spoon. Place spinach between paper towels and pat dry. Place in small bowl and stir in cheese. Place crackers on a baking sheet. Spoon about 1½ teaspoons spinach mixture onto each cracker. Bake in the preheated oven for 5 minutes or until hot. Garnish each with diced bell pepper. Serve warm. **Yield:** 16 servings.

Per serving: 75 calories, 3g protein, 5g carbohydrate, 5g fat, 1g fiber, 8mg cholesterol, 215mg sodium

Spicy Marinated Olives

Submitted by: **Lindsay® Olives**

"Marinated Lindsay® Olives are the perfect treat to have on hand for a quick appetizer or salad accompaniment. This recipe makes for a delicious trick to have up your sleeve for those unexpected entertaining moments."

1 teaspoon whole coriander seeds	½ teaspoon crushed red pepper flakes
1 teaspoon whole cumin seeds	1 bay leaf (optional)
¼ cup extra virgin olive oil	2 cloves garlic, minced
2 tablespoons sherry vinegar or champagne vinegar	2 cups LINDSAY® Black Ripe Pitted Olives, or LINDSAY® Green Ripe Select, or a combination
½ teaspoon salt	
½ teaspoon paprika	

1. Toast coriander and cumin seeds in a small skillet over medium heat, shaking skillet occasionally, until seeds are fragrant, 2 to 3 minutes.
2. In a jar with a tight-fitting lid, combine seeds and next 7 ingredients. Cover; shake well. Add olives; cover and shake well to coat olives with marinade. Refrigerate at least 2 hours or up to 1 month before serving. Serve at room temperature with wooden picks as an appetizer or add to a tossed green salad. **Yield:** 1 dozen appetizer servings (about 2 cups olives).

Per serving: 78 calories, 0g protein, 2g carbohydrate, 8g fat, 0g fiber, 0mg cholesterol, 252mg sodium

◄MAKE-AHEAD

Prep Time: 10 minutes

Cook Time: 3 minutes

Chill Time: 2 hours

Average Rating: ★★★★☆

What other cooks have done:

"These are so delicious that I tripled the recipe the second time I prepared it and gave away jars of these olives as party favors. I will be making these again for the holidays for sure."

---

10 minutes or less

Ranch Medley Mix

Submitted by: **Keebler® Kitchens**

"Combine savory Cheez-It® Crackers, crunchy cereal bits, and pretzels with the delightful tang of Ranch flavor, and you've got an unbeatable party pleaser."

5 cups CHEEZ-IT® Original Baked Snack Crackers	2 cups mini pretzel twists
	3 tablespoons vegetable oil
5 cups KELLOGG'S® Crispix Cereal	1 (1 ounce) package dry Ranch salad dressing mix

1. In a large zip-top plastic bag, combine CHEEZ-IT® Crackers, KELLOGG'S® Crispix Cereal, and pretzels. Drizzle vegetable oil over mixture. Seal bag and shake well. Add Ranch dressing mix to bag. Seal bag and shake well. Serve immediately. **Yield:** 18 servings.

Per serving: 72 calories, 1g protein, 11g carbohydrate, 3g fat, 0g fiber, 0mg cholesterol, 252mg sodium

◄5 INGREDIENTS OR LESS

Prep Time: 10 minutes

Average Rating: ★★★★★

What other cooks have done:

"My 18-month-old son loves this! I can't get him to stop eating it, and he loves to shake the bag to help mix it."

Sweet & Sour Hot Dog Bites

Submitted by: **The J.M. Smucker Company**

"Smucker's® Grape Jelly is the secret ingredient in these tantalizing sweet and sour snacks."

5 INGREDIENTS OR LESS ▶

Prep Time: 5 minutes

Cook Time: 10 minutes

Average Rating: ★★★★★

What other cooks have done:

"My great-grandsons loved it with strawberry jam, also."

¼	cup prepared mustard	1	tablespoon sweet pickle relish
½	cup SMUCKER'S® Grape Jelly	½	pound frankfurters, cooked

1. In a medium saucepan over low heat, combine mustard, SMUCKER'S® jelly, and relish. Heat, stirring constantly, until mixture is hot and well blended.

2. Slice frankfurters diagonally into bite-size pieces. Add to sauce and heat thoroughly. **Yield:** 20 snack servings.

Per serving: 59 calories, 1g protein, 6g carbohydrate, 3g fat, 0g fiber, 6mg cholesterol, 168mg sodium

Festive Tortilla Squares

Submitted by: **Land O'Lakes, Inc.**

"This appetizer features a fiesta of flavors."

PARTY FOOD ▶

Prep Time: 15 minutes

Chill Time: 1 hour

Average Rating: ★★★★★

What other cooks have done:

"This is an excellent appetizer for a bridal or baby shower. Quick, easy, and no fuss!"

1	(8 ounce) package cream cheese, softened	¼	cup sliced green onions
2	tablespoons milk	¼	cup chopped ripe olives
4	ounces Deli LAND O LAKES® Jalapeño Cheese Food, shredded	6	(8 inch) flour tortillas Toppings: cream cheese, ripe olive slices, cherry tomato slices, green olive slices

1. Place cream cheese and milk in small bowl. Beat at medium speed with an electric mixer, scraping bowl often, until smooth, 1 to 2 minutes. Stir in jalapeño cheese, green onions, and ¼ cup olives by hand.

2. Spread ⅓ cup cream cheese mixture over 1 tortilla. Top with another tortilla; spread with ⅓ cup cream cheese mixture. Repeat layering with remaining tortillas and cream cheese mixture, ending with tortilla. Wrap tightly in plastic wrap; refrigerate at least 1 hour.

3. Cut into 1 inch squares. Top each square with a cream cheese dollop and a choice of toppings: ripe olive slices, cherry tomato slices, or green olive slices. **Yield:** 48 servings.

Per square: 53 calories, 1g protein, 4g carbohydrate, 4g fat, 0g fiber, 8mg cholesterol, 117mg sodium

Grilled Steak with Olive-Blue Cheese Glaze

Submitted by: **Lindsay® Olives**

"Lindsay® Black Olives and blue cheese, swirled into a port wine and beef broth reduction, are a decadent finish for the perfect steak and an unforgettable meal."

1	tablespoon butter or olive oil	½	teaspoon salt	
½	cup thinly sliced shallots or chopped onion	½	teaspoon freshly ground black pepper	
1	cup beef broth	½	cup drained LINDSAY® Black Ripe Pitted Olives, thickly sliced	
½	cup port wine or additional beef broth	¼	cup crumbled blue or Gorgonzola cheese	
4	(6 ounce) beef tenderloin steaks★, cut 1 to 1¼ inches thick	1	tablespoon chopped fresh thyme or basil	

1. Preheat grill for medium-high heat.
2. Heat butter in a medium, heavy saucepan over medium heat. Add shallots; cook 2 minutes, stirring frequently. Add broth and wine; bring to a boil. Reduce heat; simmer uncovered, until sauce has reduced to ½ cup, about 20 minutes.
3. Meanwhile, season steaks with salt and pepper. Grill over medium-high heat or in a ridged grill pan over medium heat until cooked as desired, 4 to 5 minutes per side for medium-rare, depending on thickness of steaks.
4. Remove reduced sauce from heat; stir in olives, cheese, and thyme. Arrange steaks on warm serving plates; top with glaze.
Yield: 4 servings.

★One well-trimmed top sirloin steak, cut 1 to 1¼ inches thick may be substituted for the 4 beef tenderloin steaks. Grill for 4 to 5 minutes per side for medium-rare steak. Carve steak into thin slices; transfer to serving plates and top with glaze.

Per serving: 414 calories, 29g protein, 5g carbohydrate, 28g fat, 0g fiber, 101mg cholesterol, 815mg sodium

◀ FROM THE GRILL

Prep Time: 10 minutes

Cook Time: 25 minutes

Average Rating: ★★★★★

What other cooks have done:

"I served these awesome steaks and glaze over mashed potatoes with a sprig of fresh thyme. It's perfect for any special occasion!"

Sesame Beef Stir-Fry

Submitted by: **The J.M. Smucker Company**

"Vegetable lovers and beef lovers alike will go crazy for this flavorful Asian-style dish that's cooked in a wok."

AROUND-THE-WORLD CUISINE ▶

Prep Time: 20 minutes

Marinate Time: 15 minutes

Cook Time: 12 minutes

Average Rating: ★★★★★

What other cooks have done:

"Definitely a keeper. I tripled the marinade and used it in the stir-fry. I substituted sesame oil for canola oil and served the dish over lo mein noodles."

5 tablespoons dark soy sauce
8 tablespoons CRISCO® Canola Oil or All-Vegetable Oil, divided
2 teaspoons honey
2 teaspoons prepared Dijon-style mustard
½ teaspoon crushed red pepper flakes
1 pound flank steak, cut into thin strips
2 cloves garlic, minced
2 teaspoons minced fresh ginger

1 medium onion, thinly sliced
1 red bell pepper, thinly sliced
1 green bell pepper, thinly sliced
1 bunch broccoli, cut into florets
1 (8 ounce) can sliced water chestnuts, drained
3 tablespoons sesame seeds, toasted
   Hot cooked rice

1. Whisk together soy sauce, ¼ cup CRISCO® Oil, honey, mustard, and red pepper flakes in a medium bowl. Add steak and toss. Marinate, covered, at room temperature for 15 minutes.

2. Heat 2 tablespoons CRISCO® Oil in a wok or heavy skillet over medium-high heat until hot but not smoking. Sauté garlic, ginger, onion, red and green bell peppers, and broccoli, stirring, 5 to 7 minutes. Transfer mixture to another bowl.

3. Heat 2 tablespoons CRISCO® Oil in wok over high heat until hot, but not smoking. Sauté steak, stirring, about 2 minutes. Discard marinade.

4. Stir in sautéed vegetables, water chestnuts, and sesame seeds until heated through.

5. Serve over steamed rice. **Yield:** 4 servings.

Per serving: 514 calories, 20g protein, 25g carbohydrate, 40g fat, 6g fiber, 36mg cholesterol, 1296mg sodium

Pork Chops with Dijon-Dill Sauce

Submitted by: **Hormel Foods Corporation**

"These delicately seasoned pan-fried pork chops take hardly any time at all to cook. Served with a mustard-dill sauce, this dish will make your loved ones think they are eating at a restaurant."

1 pound ALWAYS TENDER® boneless thin pork loin chops	¼ teaspoon garlic salt
	⅛ teaspoon ground black pepper
1 teaspoon CARAPELLI® olive oil	¼ cup plain low-fat yogurt
	2 teaspoons prepared Dijon-style mustard
2 teaspoons HERB-OX® Chicken Flavored Bouillon Granules	¼ teaspoon dried dill weed
	¼ teaspoon white sugar

1. In a skillet over medium heat, cook pork chops in oil for 6 to 8 minutes or until cooked through and pork reaches an internal temperature of 155°F (68°C). Remove pork to a platter; season with bouillon, garlic salt, and pepper. In small bowl, combine yogurt, mustard, dill weed, and sugar. Serve sauce with pork chops. **Yield:** 4 servings.

Per serving: 133 calories, 15g protein, 2g carbohydrate, 7g fat, 0g fiber, 36mg cholesterol, 228mg sodium

◄ FAMILY FAVORITE

Prep Time: 5 minutes

Cook Time: 8 minutes

Average Rating: ★★★★★

What other cooks have done:

"I grilled the pork instead of frying it. I also added a teaspoon of commercial dill sauce to the Dijon-Dill Sauce. It was unbelievably good."

Glazed Pork Chops

Submitted by: **The J.M. Smucker Company**

"Ketchup, steak sauce, garlic, mustard, and Smucker's® Blackberry Jam magically blend into a sweet, tangy glaze for broiled pork chops."

6 (¾ inch thick) pork loin or rib chops	¾ cup ketchup
	¼ cup steak sauce
1 cup SMUCKER'S® Blackberry Jam	1 teaspoon dry mustard
	1 clove garlic, minced

1. Preheat broiler.
2. Broil pork chops in the preheated oven 3 to 5 inches from heat for 5 minutes. Turn; broil for 5 more minutes.
3. Meanwhile, in small saucepan, combine remaining ingredients. Heat to boiling; reduce heat and simmer for 10 minutes.
4. Brush pork with sauce. Continue broiling, turning and brushing with sauce, 5 to 8 more minutes or until pork is no longer pink in center. Bring remaining sauce to a boil; serve with pork chops. **Yield:** 6 servings.

Per serving: 275 calories, 16g protein, 45g carbohydrate, 4g fat, 1g fiber, 40mg cholesterol, 539mg sodium

◄ FAMILY FAVORITE

Prep Time: 10 minutes

Cook Time: 20 minutes

Average Rating: ★★★★☆

What other cooks have done:

"This is a very tasty dish. It is quick, flavorful, and the chops remain moist."

Pizza-Style Skillet

Submitted by: **Rice A Roni®**

"This simple supper tastes just like pizza. Pepperoni and mushrooms top a Parmesan pasta sprinkled with mozzarella cheese."

KID-FRIENDLY ▶

Prep Time: 10 minutes

Cook Time: 10 minutes

Stand Time: 5 minutes

Average Rating: ★★★★★

What other cooks have done:

"This was great! I added an extra ½ cup of both sauce and cheese, and it turned out great. Even my picky fiancé liked it."

2 cups water	¾ cup spaghetti sauce
1 (5.1 ounce) package PASTA RONI® Angel Hair Pasta with Parmesan Cheese	1 (4.5 ounce) jar sliced mushrooms, drained
½ cup chopped green bell pepper	2 ounces pepperoni slices, cut into quarters
	½ cup shredded mozzarella cheese

1. In a large skillet, bring water to a boil. Stir in pasta, Seasoning Packet, and bell pepper. Return to a boil. Reduce heat to medium.
2. Gently boil, uncovered, 4 to 5 minutes or until pasta is tender, stirring occasionally. (Sauce will be thin.)
3. Stir in spaghetti sauce, mushrooms, and pepperoni. Remove skillet from heat. Let stand for 3 to 5 minutes for sauce to thicken. Sprinkle with mozzarella cheese. **Yield:** 4 servings.

Per serving: 281 calories, 12g protein, 31g carbohydrate, 12g fat, 3g fiber, 19mg cholesterol, 1167mg sodium

30 *minutes or less*

Santa Fe Chicken Pilaf

Submitted by: **Near East®**

"Spiced-up rice pilaf with corn, fresh tomato, and pieces of chicken is an exciting and delicious meal. It's also conveniently quick."

FAMILY FAVORITE ▶

Prep Time: 10 minutes

Cook Time: 20 minutes

Average Rating: ★★★★★

What other cooks have done:

"I like to add some spices to the chicken—such as cumin, salt, and pepper—before cooking. I often use this mixture to make a burrito. Just get some tortillas and spread some sour cream or guacamole on them. Add some Santa Fe Chicken Pilaf and some cheese, and you have a burrito. Easy dinner."

1 (6.09 ounce) package NEAR EAST® Rice Pilaf Mix	2 cups chicken strips, cooked, cut into 1 inch chunks, heated
1 (14 ounce) can fat-free, reduced-sodium chicken broth	½ cup chopped fresh tomato
1 teaspoon ground cumin	1 (8.75 ounce) can whole kernel corn, drained
1 cup seasoned diced tomatoes	1 cup canned black beans, rinsed and drained
	Cheddar cheese (optional)

1. Prepare NEAR EAST® rice according to package directions, using chicken broth instead of water; add cumin with contents of Spice Sack.
2. Stir in next 5 ingredients into rice mixture. Top with Cheddar cheese, if desired. **Yield:** 6 servings.

Per serving: 287 calories, 20g protein, 38g carbohydrate, 4g fat, 4g fiber, 35mg cholesterol, 844mg sodium

Grilled Chicken Breasts with Zesty Peanut Sauce

Submitted by: **The J.M. Smucker Company**

"Chicken is marinated in a spicy peanut marinade and then grilled and served with a hot, creamy peanut sauce. Garnish with cilantro for an elegant presentation."

Chicken:
- 8 large skinless, boneless chicken breasts

Marinade:
- 1 tablespoon packed dark brown sugar
- 2 tablespoons JIF® Creamy (or extra crunchy) Peanut Butter
- ¼ cup CRISCO® All-Vegetable Oil
- ½ cup soy sauce
- ⅓ cup fresh lime juice
- 2 large cloves garlic, minced
- ½ teaspoon cayenne pepper
- ½ teaspoon salt

Peanut Sauce:
- 1 cup JIF® Creamy (or extra crunchy) Peanut Butter
- 1 cup unsweetened coconut milk
- ¼ cup fresh lime juice
- 3 tablespoons soy sauce
- 2 tablespoons packed dark brown sugar
- 2 teaspoons finely minced fresh ginger root
- 2 cloves garlic, minced
- ¼ teaspoon cayenne pepper (or to taste)
- ½ cup chicken stock
- ½ cup heavy cream
- Chopped fresh cilantro (optional)

◀ HOT & SPICY

Prep Time: 17 minutes

Marinate Time: overnight

Cook Time: 28 minutes

Average Rating: ★★★★★

What other cooks have done:

"This marinade was phenomenal. The chicken came out very tender and juicy and with a great flavor. I added more garlic and a little more cayenne, and I let the chicken marinate for about six hours. Yum!"

1. Wash, trim, and pound the chicken to ¼ inch thickness.

2. Combine chicken and next 8 ingredients in a heavy duty, zip-top plastic bag. Marinate 1 hour at room temperature or as long as overnight in the refrigerator.

3. Preheat grill.

4. Combine 1 cup JIF®, coconut milk, ¼ cup lime juice, 3 tablespoons soy sauce, 2 tablespoons brown sugar, ginger, 2 cloves garlic, and ¼ teaspoon cayenne pepper in a saucepan over medium heat. Stirring constantly, cook for about 15 minutes or until thickened. Whisk in the stock and cream. Cook for 1 more minute, whisking constantly; set aside.

5. Remove chicken from marinade and cook on the prepared grill until browned, about 4 to 6 minutes on each side (or until center is no longer pink and juices run clear, turning only once).

6. Serve hot chicken topped with the peanut sauce. Sprinkle with the cilantro, if desired. **Yield:** 8 servings.

Per serving: 683 calories, 66g protein, 19g carbohydrate, 40g fat, 3g fiber, 157mg cholesterol, 1799mg sodium

Chicken with Tomato, Orange, and Rosemary Couscous

Submitted by: **Near East®**

"Chicken is served over tasty couscous with zucchini and tomato for a quick and satisfying supper."

COMPANY IS COMING ▶

Prep Time: 10 minutes

Cook Time: 15 minutes

Stand Time: 5 minutes

Average Rating: ★★★★★

What other cooks have done:

"I added my own roasted garlic oil (made from roasting freshly minced garlic in olive oil) to give it a better aroma. Next time, I will use pineapple (instead of orange), which will certainly complement the couscous. A half cup of chicken or fish stock will also enhance the flavor."

4 skinless, boneless chicken breast halves	1 (14.5 ounce) can chopped tomatoes, drained
Salt and ground black pepper to taste	1 teaspoon fresh or dried rosemary
2 tablespoons olive oil	1 (5.8 ounce) package NEAR EAST® Roasted Garlic Olive Oil Couscous Mix
¼ cup dry white wine, such as Sauvignon Blanc, or water	
1 cup water	¾ cup peeled, seeded, and chopped orange
1 cup zucchini, cut into ½ inch slices	

1. Season chicken to taste with salt and pepper. In a large skillet, heat olive oil over medium heat. Add chicken; cook 5 to 6 minutes on each side or until chicken is no longer pink and juices run clear.

2. Meanwhile, in large saucepan, combine wine, 1 cup water, zucchini, tomatoes, and rosemary. Bring to a boil over high heat. Stir in couscous and contents of Spice Sack. Remove from heat. Cover; let stand 5 minutes.

3. Fluff couscous lightly with a fork. Stir in chopped orange and serve with chicken. **Yield:** 4 servings.

Per serving: 303 calories, 28g protein, 19g carbohydrate, 10g fat, 3g fiber, 67mg cholesterol, 369mg sodium

Chicken and Peppers

Submitted by: **Land O'Lakes, Inc.**

"This easy Southwestern meal that's made in minutes is a great way to get your family to eat their vegetables."

2	tablespoons LAND O LAKES® Butter
1	pound skinless, boneless chicken breasts, cut into 3½ inch strips
2½	teaspoons fajita seasoning
¼	teaspoon salt
½	(16 ounce) package frozen pepper stir-fry vegetable combination

1	cup frozen whole kernel corn
1	tablespoon chopped fresh cilantro
	Tortillas (optional)
	LAND O LAKES® Sour Cream (optional)

◄ FAMILY FAVORITE

Prep Time: 10 minutes

Cook Time: 13 minutes

Average Rating: ★★★★☆

What other cooks have done:
"This tastes like fajitas without the wraps. It's great over yellow rice."

1. Melt butter in 12 inch skillet until sizzling; add chicken, fajita seasoning, and salt. Cook over medium heat, stirring occasionally, until chicken is no longer pink, about 6 minutes.

2. Stir in frozen peppers and corn. Continue cooking, stirring occasionally, until chicken is fork tender and peppers are tender-crisp, about 5 to 6 minutes.

3. Stir in cilantro. Serve with warm tortillas and sour cream, if desired.

Yield: 4 servings.

Per serving: 253 calories, 29g protein, 17g carbohydrate, 8g fat, 3g fiber, 81mg cholesterol, 389mg sodium

Thai-Style Chicken Skillet

Submitted by: **Rice A Roni**®

"Try a new twist on cooking with this Thai-inspired dish. Chicken and rice are steamed with pea pods and red bell peppers in an exotic peanut sauce. This is an impressive dish."

AROUND-THE-WORLD CUISINE ▶

Prep Time: 10 minutes

Cook Time: 30 minutes

Stand Time: 3 minutes

Average Rating: ★★★★★

What other cooks have done:

"I used snap pea stir-fry veggies instead of the pea pods for a little more color."

¾ pound skinless boneless chicken breast halves, cut into thin slices
2 tablespoons soy sauce
1 (4.9 ounce) package RICE A RONI® Chicken & Broccoli Flavor
1¾ cups water
2 tablespoons creamy peanut butter
1 garlic clove, pressed
1½ cups frozen pea pods
½ cup red bell pepper strips, cut into 2-inch pieces
Peanuts (optional)

1. Toss chicken with soy sauce; set aside.

2. In a large skillet over medium heat, sauté RICE A RONI® rice-vermicelli mix according to package directions.

3. Slowly stir in water, Seasoning Packet, peanut butter, and garlic. Stir in chicken; bring to a boil. Cover; reduce heat to low. Simmer 12 minutes.

4. Stir in pea pods and bell pepper; return to a simmer. Cover and simmer for 3 to 5 minutes or until vegetables are tender-crisp. Stir; let stand 3 minutes. Top with peanuts, if desired. **Yield:** 4 servings.

Per serving: 299 calories, 25g protein, 34g carbohydrate, 8g fat, 4g fiber, 44mg cholesterol, 1138mg sodium

Mandarin Shrimp and Vegetable Stir-Fry

Submitted by: **The J.M. Smucker Company**

"Shrimp is quickly stir-fried with garlic, broccoli, and peppers and then covered in a spicy orange sauce made with Smucker's® Sweet Orange Marmalade. This tastes great sprinkled with green onions and served over steamed rice."

1	cup SMUCKER'S® Sweet Orange Marmalade	24	large fresh shrimp, peeled and deveined
3	tablespoons soy sauce	1	red bell pepper, chopped
2	tablespoons white vinegar	1	yellow or green bell pepper, chopped
2	tablespoons hot pepper sauce	3	cups broccoli florets
1½	tablespoons cornstarch	½	cup water
2	tablespoons CRISCO® All-Vegetable Oil		Salt and freshly ground black pepper to taste (optional)
1	tablespoon chopped fresh ginger	1	cup chopped green onions
1	tablespoon chopped fresh garlic		Hot cooked rice (optional)

1. Combine SMUCKER'S® Sweet Orange Marmalade, soy sauce, vinegar, hot pepper sauce, and cornstarch; stir to dissolve cornstarch. Set aside.

2. Place a large skillet or wok over high heat for 1 minute and add oil. Heat oil for 30 seconds and add ginger, garlic, and shrimp. Stir-fry for 2 to 3 minutes or until shrimp turn rosy pink. Remove shrimp from pan; set aside.

3. Add bell peppers and broccoli to pan; cook over high heat for 1 minute. Add water; cover and reduce heat to medium. Cook for 4 to 5 minutes or until vegetables are tender.

4. Uncover pan and return heat to high. Add shrimp and marmalade mixture. Cook for 2 more minutes or until sauce is thickened and shrimp are completely cooked. Season with salt and freshly ground black pepper to taste, if desired. Stir in green onions. Serve with hot cooked rice, if desired. **Yield:** 4 to 6 servings.

Per serving: 400 calories, 10g protein, 79g carbohydrate, 6g fat, 3g fiber, 43mg cholesterol, 646mg sodium

◄ COMPANY IS COMING

Prep Time: 20 minutes

Cook Time: 14 minutes

Average Rating: ★★★★★

What other cooks have done:

"My whole family enjoyed this recipe. I reduced the amount of marmalade and increased the soy sauce for a little less sweetness."

Pasta Shrimp Toss

Submitted by: **Land O'Lakes, Inc.**
"This quick gourmet dish tastes equally good with chicken or scallops."

COMPANY IS COMING ▶

Prep Time: 20 minutes

Cook Time: 10 minutes

Average Rating: ★★★★★

What other cooks have done:

"I changed the recipe a bit by adding sun-dried tomatoes instead of roma. It made an incredible difference and made this already great recipe even better!"

1	(8 ounce) package uncooked dried linguine or spaghetti	½	teaspoon salt
6	tablespoons LAND O LAKES® Butter	¼	teaspoon coarsely ground black pepper
½	cup chopped onion	¼	cup whipping cream
12	ounces fresh medium raw shrimp, peeled	1	tablespoon all-purpose flour
1	medium green bell pepper, coarsely chopped	5	roma (plum) tomatoes, cubed
1	teaspoon chopped fresh garlic	1	tablespoon chopped fresh basil leaves
		½	cup freshly shredded Parmesan cheese

1. Cook linguine according to package directions. Drain. Set aside; keep warm.

2. Meanwhile, melt butter in 10 inch skillet until sizzling; add onion, shrimp, bell pepper, garlic, salt, and black pepper. Cook over medium heat, stirring occasionally, until shrimp turn pink, 6 to 7 minutes.

3. Stir whipping cream and flour together in a small bowl until smooth; stir into shrimp mixture. Continue cooking until mixture just comes to a boil, about 1 minute. Stir in tomato and basil.

4. Place hot cooked pasta in a large pasta bowl or on a serving platter; top with shrimp mixture. Sprinkle with Parmesan cheese. **Yield:** 6 servings.

Per serving: 382 calories, 19g protein, 35g carbohydrate, 19g fat, 2g fiber, 137mg cholesterol, 777mg sodium

Golden Onion, Walnut, and Blue Cheese Pizza *(pictured on page 78)*

Submitted by: **Hormel Foods Corporation**

"Onions have a natural sweetness, but special varieties, such as Maui, Vidalia, and Texas Sweet, are super sweet and super delicious."

2	tablespoons butter	1	cup shredded mozzarella cheese
2	teaspoons HERB-OX® Chicken Flavored Bouillon Granules	1	(4 ounce) package crumbled blue cheese
2	medium sweet onions, sliced	½	cup toasted chopped walnuts
1	(12 inch) prebaked pizza shell		

1. Preheat the oven to 425°F (220°C).

2. Melt butter in a large skillet over low heat. Add bouillon granules and onion and cook slowly over low heat, stirring occasionally, until soft and golden, about 10 minutes. Cover pizza crust with shredded mozzarella cheese and top with the onion mixture. Sprinkle crumbled blue cheese and walnuts evenly over onion mixture.

3. Bake in the preheated oven for 10 minutes. **Yield:** 4 servings.

Per serving: 613 calories, 28g protein, 53g carbohydrate, 32g fat, 3g fiber, 53mg cholesterol, 1467mg sodium

◄OUT-OF-THE-ORDINARY

Prep Time: 20 minutes

Cook Time: 20 minutes

Average Rating: ★★★★☆

What other cooks have done:

"I made this for dinner last night and loved it. Instead of two medium onions, I sliced up one large Vidalia onion. I also increased the mozzarella cheese to help 'glue' everything onto the crust."

Herbed Green Bean Casserole

Submitted by: **The J.M. Smucker's Company**
"Herbs and Parmesan cheese blend perfectly in this great green bean side dish. You'll have your family begging for seconds!"

FAMILY FAVORITE ▶

Prep Time: 15 minutes

Cook Time: 30 minutes

Average Rating: ★★★★★

What other cooks have done:

"I used frozen green beans, and it took a little longer to cook, so I will use canned green beans next time."

¾ cup dry breadcrumbs, divided
2 teaspoons dried basil
½ teaspoon salt (or to taste)
½ teaspoon ground black pepper (or to taste)
½ teaspoon dried thyme
1 teaspoon dried oregano
2 teaspoons chopped parsley
1 teaspoon garlic powder
1 cup freshly grated Parmesan cheese
½ cup CRISCO® Oil
2 (14 ounce) cans cut green beans, drained

1. Preheat oven to 350°F (175°C).
2. Mix together breadcrumbs, basil, salt, pepper, thyme, oregano, parsley, garlic powder, and Parmesan cheese. Set aside 2 tablespoons of crumb mixture.
3. Mix together the remaining crumb mixture, CRISCO® Oil, and green beans. Place in an ovenproof dish and sprinkle with the reserved 2 tablespoons of crumb mixture.
4. Bake in the preheated oven for about 30 minutes or until the top is golden and crispy. **Yield:** 8 servings.

Note: You can replace the canned beans with frozen or blanched and cooled fresh beans. The dried breadcrumbs and herbs can be replaced with Italian-style breadcrumbs; add the garlic and Parmesan cheese to the breadcrumbs.

Per serving: 237 calories, 7g protein, 12g carbohydrate, 18g fat, 2g fiber, 10mg cholesterol, 816mg sodium

California Spinach Salad

Submitted by: **The California Avocado Commission**
"This fresh spinach salad that's perfect for the holiday table includes avocados, olives, red onions, and oranges."

CROWD-PLEASER ▶

Prep Time: 15 minutes

Cook Time: 5 minutes

Stand Time: 25 minutes

Average Rating: ★★★★☆

What other cooks have done:

"I use olive oil and balsamic vinegar as a dressing when short on time."

½ cup red wine vinegar
1 teaspoon dried tarragon
1 teaspoon prepared Dijon-style mustard
2 cups vegetable oil
    Salt and ground black pepper to taste
3 pounds spinach, rinsed
2 tablespoons lemon juice
5 California avocados, peeled, pitted, and cubed
1 cup black olives, thinly sliced
1 red onion, thinly sliced
1 (15 ounce) can mandarin oranges, drained and quartered

1. In a small saucepan over medium heat, bring vinegar and tarragon to a boil; set aside to cool completely, about 25 minutes.
2. Whisk together the vinegar mixture and mustard; gradually add oil, beating until well blended. Season with salt and pepper to taste.
3. Place spinach in a large mixing bowl. In a medium bowl, generously drizzle lemon juice over avocado cubes to prevent browning and enhance flavor. Gently toss avocados, olives, onion, and oranges with spinach.
4. Pour in salad dressing and toss evenly to coat. **Yield:** 12 servings.

Per serving: 519 calories, 5g protein, 16g carbohydrate, 51g fat, 8g fiber, 0mg cholesterol, 215mg sodium

Fruited Rice Salad on the Half

Submitted by: **The California Avocado Commission**
"A unique and invigorating salad of fresh avocados stuffed with rice, dried fruit, and pecans."

¼	cup vegetable oil	2	cups boiling water
1	tablespoon lemon juice	¼	cup raisins
1	tablespoon red wine vinegar	½	cup dried apricots
1	teaspoon honey	4	cups cooked brown or wild rice
¼	teaspoon ground coriander	½	cup chopped pecans
¼	teaspoon prepared Dijon-style mustard	2	California avocados
	Salt and ground black pepper to taste		

◀ HOLIDAY FARE
Prep Time: 15 minutes
Stand Time: 10 minutes
Chill Time: 30 minutes
Average Rating: ★★★★★
What other cooks have done:
"This is a delicious salad. I diced the avocado and added it to the rice mixture."

1. Prepare the vinaigrette by combining the oil, lemon juice, vinegar, honey, coriander, mustard, and salt and pepper to taste in a container with a tight-fitting lid. Shake well and set aside.
2. In a medium bowl, combine the boiling water, raisins, and apricots. Let stand for 10 minutes; drain and cool.
3. In a large bowl, combine the vinaigrette, raisins, apricots, rice, and pecans. Refrigerate until chilled.
4. Before serving, slice avocados in half, remove the seed, and peel avocado. Fill each half with rice salad and serve. **Yield:** 4 servings.

Per serving: 671 calories, 9g protein, 74g carbohydrate, 41g fat, 11g fiber, 0mg cholesterol, 27mg sodium

Tuna and White Bean Salad

Submitted by: **Chef Giuliano Hazan on behalf of Bush's Best® Beans**
"A traditional Italian salad packed with protein."

AROUND-THE-WORLD CUISINE ▶

Prep Time: 15 minutes

Average Rating: ★★★★★

What other cooks have done:

"I used 2 (4 ounce) cans of albacore tuna, white onion instead of red, and added an extra tablespoon of red wine vinegar."

1	(7 ounce) can premium canned tuna, drained	Salt and freshly ground black pepper to taste
¾	cup red onion, thinly sliced crosswise	5 tablespoons extra virgin olive oil
1	(16 ounce) can BUSH'S BEST® Great Northern Beans★, drained and rinsed	1 tablespoon red wine vinegar

1. Pour tuna into a bowl and break up with a fork. Stir in onion and BUSH'S BEST® Great Northern Beans. Season with salt and pepper to taste. Toss thoroughly with olive oil and vinegar. Serve at room temperature. **Yield:** 4 servings.

Per serving: 426 calories, 24g protein, 34g carbohydrate, 20g fat, 11g fiber, 21mg cholesterol, 1003mg sodium

★Substitute 1 can of BUSH'S BEST® Cannellini Beans, if desired.

Stuffed French Toast

Submitted by: **The J.M. Smucker Company**
"French bread slices are stuffed with a cream filling before being lightly battered and fried. A sweet glaze is drizzled over each slice for the finishing touch."

HOLIDAY FARE ▶

Prep Time: 15 minutes

Cook Time: 25 minutes

Average Rating: ★★★★★

What other cooks have done:

"I used macadamia nuts instead of walnuts or pecans, two slices of white bread for each slice of French bread, and Smucker's® Strawberry Jam instead of apricot preserves and orange juice. I had no trouble keeping the slices of bread together because the cream cheese mixture was sticky. This turned out really delicious and really filling."

1	(8 ounce) package cream cheese, softened	1 cup whipping cream or half-and-half
2	tablespoons white sugar	½ teaspoon ground nutmeg
1½	teaspoons vanilla, divided	1 (12 ounce) jar SMUCKER'S® Apricot Preserves
¼	teaspoon ground cinnamon	
½	cup chopped walnuts or pecans	½ cup orange juice
1	(1 pound) loaf French bread	½ teaspoon almond extract
4	egg whites	Fresh fruit

1. Beat together cream cheese, sugar, 1 teaspoon vanilla, and cinnamon until fluffy. Stir in nuts; set aside.
2. Cut bread into 10 to 12 (1½ to 2 inch) slices; cut pocket in top of each slice. Fill each pocket with about 1½ tablespoons of cream cheese mixture.
3. Lightly grease and heat a griddle.
4. Beat together egg whites, whipping cream, remaining ½ teaspoon vanilla, and nutmeg. Using tongs, dip bread slices in egg mixture, being careful not to squeeze out filling. Cook on hot, lightly greased

griddle until both sides are golden brown. (To keep cooked slices hot for serving, place on a baking sheet in warm oven.)

5. Meanwhile, combine SMUCKER'S® preserves and orange juice in a small saucepan over medium–low heat. Stir in almond extract and heat through. To serve, drizzle apricot mixture over French toast slices. Serve with fresh fruit. **Yield:** 10 to 12 servings.

Per serving: 394 calories, 7g protein, 52g carbohydrate, 18g fat, 2g fiber, 48mg cholesterol, 309mg sodium

10 minutes or less

5-Minute Double-Layer Chocolate Pie

Submitted by: **Keebler® Kitchens**

"This pie can be whipped up in minutes with things you may already have on hand. Perfect for unexpected company or a quick after-dinner treat. There is always room for this light dessert made of chocolate and whipped topping."

1¼   cups cold milk
2   (3.9 ounce) packages instant chocolate pudding mix
1   (8 ounce) container frozen whipped topping, thawed and divided
1   (6 ounce) READY CRUST® Graham Cracker Pie Crust

1. Beat milk, pudding, and half of the whipped topping in a medium bowl with a wire whisk for 1 minute. (Mixture will be thick.) Spread in crust.

2. Spread remaining whipped topping over pudding layer in crust.

3. Enjoy immediately or refrigerate until ready to serve. **Yield:** 8 servings.

Per serving: 311 calories, 3g protein, 46g carbohydrate, 14g fat, 1g fiber, 3mg cholesterol, 548mg sodium

◄ FROM THE PANTRY

Prep Time: 5 minutes

Average Rating: ★★★★★

What other cooks have done:

"This is such a wonderful recipe. I made it at the last minute to bring to an impromptu Memorial Day get-together, and everyone kept complimenting me on it. I used one package of chocolate pudding and one package of chocolate fudge pudding. To increase the chocolate even more, I used a chocolate crust. I added chocolate sprinkles to the top, and it looked like chocolate silk pie from a restaurant."

Harvest Pumpkin Tarts

Submitted by: **Eagle Brand®**

"One of the first recipes to come out of the Eagle Brand® kitchen, magazine ads in 1927 promised 'glorious pumpkin pie . . . the kind about which poets have sung.'"

HOLIDAY FARE ▶

Prep Time: 10 minutes

Cook Time: 26 minutes

Average Rating: ★★★★★

What other cooks have done:

"These were great and easy to make. I made crusts from scratch, and the recipe worked just the same. Great for parties or just to have around the house for snacks!"

1	(14 ounce) can EAGLE BRAND® Sweetened Condensed Milk (NOT evaporated milk)	1	egg
1¼	cups canned pumpkin puree	¼	teaspoon ground cinnamon
		¼	teaspoon ground nutmeg
2	tablespoons brown sugar	2	(10 ounce) packages unbaked tart shells

1. Preheat oven to 375°F (190°C).

2. Whisk together EAGLE BRAND® Sweetened Condensed Milk, pumpkin, brown sugar, egg, cinnamon, and nutmeg. Pour evenly into tart shells.

3. Bake in the preheated oven for 26 minutes or until center is just set and pastry is golden. **Yield:** 16 tarts.

Per tart: 202 calories, 3g protein, 30g carbohydrate, 8g fat, 1g fiber, 15mg cholesterol, 115mg sodium

Fresh Fruit Tart with Gingersnap Crust

Submitted by: **The J.M. Smucker Company**

"This entrancing fruit-topped tart has a homemade gingersnap crust and a creamy filling underneath a glorious pile of fresh fruit."

COMPANY IS COMING ▶

Prep Time: 20 minutes

Cook Time: 8 minutes

Chill Time: 2 hours

Average Rating: ★★★★★

What other cooks have done:

"Instead of crushing the cookies to make a crust, I used whole cookies. I warmed them in a low-temperature oven for five to ten minutes and then pressed the cookies into small, round patty-cake tins. This made heaps of individual tarts that were gone in a flash at our get-together."

Crust:

2	cups ground gingersnap cookies	½	cup whipping cream
2	tablespoons white sugar	2	cups sliced fresh strawberries
⅓	cup Butter Flavor CRISCO® All-Vegetable Shortening	½	cup seedless grapes
		¼	cup blueberries

Filling:

		1	kiwi, peeled and sliced
1	(8 ounce) package cream cheese, softened	1	orange, peeled and segmented
¼	cup white sugar	¼	cup SMUCKER'S® Apricot Preserves
2	teaspoons lemon juice	1	tablespoon water
			Mint leaves

1. Preheat oven to 350°F (175°C).

2. In a medium bowl, combine ground cookies and 2 tablespoons sugar. With a pastry blender or 2 knives, cut in Butter Flavor CRISCO® Shortening and mix until moist clumps form. Press mixture into bottom and up sides of a 10 inch tart pan with a removable bottom.

3. Bake in the preheated oven for 8 minutes or until golden. (Watch carefully as crust can easily burn at the end of cooking time.) Let cool.

4. Meanwhile, combine cream cheese, ¼ cup sugar, and lemon juice with an electric mixer until well blended. Add whipping cream and beat at high speed until light and fluffy. Spread in tart shell and chill at least 2 hours.

5. Arrange fruit on top of chilled filling. Combine SMUCKER'S® Apricot Preserves with water and brush over top. Garnish with mint leaves and serve. **Yield:** 8 servings.

Per serving: 465 calories, 4g protein, 50g carbohydrate, 29g fat, 2g fiber, 50mg cholesterol, 218mg sodium

Keebler® Banana Pudding

Submitted by: **Keebler® Kitchens**
"This luxurious layered banana pudding is so delicious that your loved ones may fight over every bite. Fortunately, it can also be made in individual dessert glasses."

48 KEEBLER® Golden Vanilla Wafer Cookies	1 tablespoon butter or margarine
1 (3 ounce) package non-instant vanilla pudding mix	2 medium bananas, sliced Whipped topping Banana slices
2½ cups milk	

1. Line bottom and sides of a 1½ quart or an 8x8 inch baking dish with a layer of vanilla wafers using half of the wafers.

2. Combine pudding mix, milk, and butter in a saucepan. Cook and stir over medium heat until mixture comes to a full boil. Remove from heat. Layer half of banana slices over vanilla wafers; add a layer of half of pudding. Repeat layers of vanilla wafers, bananas, and pudding.

3. Chill until firm, about 3 hours. Serve with whipped topping and garnish with banana slices. **Yield:** 6 servings.

Note: To prepare in the microwave, combine pudding mix, milk, and butter in a 1½ quart glass bowl and blend well. Microwave on high for 3 minutes. Stir. Heat about 3 more minutes, stirring after each minute, or until mixture boils. Remove from microwave and proceed as directed.

Per serving: 345 calories, 6g protein, 51g carbohydrate, 14g fat, 2g fiber, 8mg cholesterol, 301mg sodium

◄ **CLASSIC COMFORT FOOD**

Prep Time: 15 minutes

Cook Time: 5 minutes

Chill Time: 3 hours

Average Rating: ★★★★★

What other cooks have done:

"This recipe reminds me of my mother's banana pudding!"

Peanut Butter Fruit Dip

Submitted by: **The J.M. Smucker Company**

"This fluffy dip made with JIF® Reduced Fat Peanut Butter and vanilla pudding doesn't skimp on flavor and is perfect for apple slices and bananas."

KID-FRIENDLY ▶

Prep Time: 15 minutes

Average Rating: ★★★★★

What other cooks have done:

"This recipe is wonderful. I made it for a potluck at work and have gotten many requests to make it again. It's wonderful with apples, bananas, or any other fruit."

2   cups fat-free milk
½   cup light sour cream
1   (3.4 ounce) package instant vanilla pudding mix
1   cup JIF® Reduced Fat Peanut Butter
⅓   cup white sugar
Apple and banana slices (or any fruit of your choice)

1. Combine milk, sour cream, and pudding mix in a medium bowl. Whisk until smooth. Stir peanut butter and sugar into pudding mixture; mix until well blended. Serve with apple and banana slices. Store leftovers in refrigerator. If dip becomes too thick, stir in additional milk. **Yield:** 6 servings (3 cups).

Per serving: 413 calories, 15g protein, 56g carbohydrate, 16g fat, 3g fiber, 2mg cholesterol, 626mg sodium

minutes or less

Apple Pie Spread

Submitted by: **Keebler® Kitchens**

"Cinnamon and pecans enhance this fall favorite. Spread it on light, buttery Town House® crackers to create a snack any crowd will devour!"

HOLIDAY FARE ▶

Prep Time: 10 minutes

Average Rating: ★★★★☆

What other cooks have done:

"Made this for an office 'snack day,' and the response was excellent. Has a light, fresh taste of apples and cinnamon, but it's not too sweet. Serve with buttery crackers and graham crackers."

1   (8 ounce) package ⅓-less-fat cream cheese (Neufchâtel)
1   tablespoon seltzer water
2   tablespoons light brown sugar
½   teaspoon ground cinnamon
¼   cup chopped pecans
1   medium crisp red apple, chopped
KEEBLER® TOWN HOUSE® Crackers
Cinnamon, chopped pecans, or red apple slices (optional)

1. Mix cream cheese and seltzer water at medium speed with an electric mixer until smooth. Add the brown sugar and cinnamon. Fold in the pecans and apple. Refrigerate until serving. Serve with TOWN HOUSE® Crackers. Garnish with cinnamon, chopped pecans, or red apple slices, if desired. **Yield:** 16 servings.

Per serving: 61 calories, 2g protein, 4g carbohydrate, 5g fat, 1g fiber, 11mg cholesterol, 57mg sodium

Classic Sugar Cookies

Submitted by: **The J.M. Smucker Company**

"Frosted sugar cookies make excellent gifts for the holidays. Have the kids help cut out cookies in their favorite shapes."

1 cup Butter Flavor CRISCO® All-Vegetable Shortening	1½ teaspoons cream of tartar
1½ cups white sugar	1 teaspoon salt
½ cup packed brown sugar	**Buttery Cream Frosting:**
2 tablespoons milk	4 cups confectioners' sugar
3 eggs	⅓ cup Butter Flavor CRISCO® All-Vegetable Shortening
1 teaspoon vanilla extract	1½ teaspoons vanilla extract
4½ cups all-purpose flour	6½ tablespoons milk
1½ teaspoons baking soda	

1. Cream together 1 cup Butter Flavor CRISCO® All-Vegetable Shortening, white sugar, and brown sugar. Add milk. Beat in eggs, 1 at a time; add 1 teaspoon vanilla. Combine flour, baking soda, cream of tartar, and salt. Mix into creamed mixture until well blended. Chill for 1 hour.

2. Preheat oven to 350°F (175°C).

3. Divide dough into thirds. Roll out each third to about ¼ inch thickness on a floured surface. Cut out with cookie cutters. Place cookies 2 inches apart on ungreased baking sheets.

4. Bake in the preheated oven for 5 to 6 minutes or until edges are slightly golden. Remove immediately to wire racks.

5. In a medium mixing bowl, combine confectioners' sugar, ⅓ cup Butter Flavor CRISCO® All-Vegetable Shortening, and 1½ teaspoons vanilla. Slowly blend in milk to reach desired consistency. Beat at high speed for 5 minutes or until smooth and creamy. Frost cooled cookies. **Yield:** 5 dozen.

Per cookie: 138 calories, 1g protein, 23g carbohydrate, 5g fat, 0g fiber, 11mg cholesterol, 76mg sodium

◀ CROWD-PLEASER

Prep Time: 15 minutes

Chill Time: 1 hour

Cook Time: 6 minutes per batch

Average Rating: ★★★★☆

What other cooks have done:

"These turned out really soft and had a nice texture. I added a touch of lemon extract to the icing."

Caramel-Pecan Turtle Cookies

Submitted by: **The J.M. Smucker Company**
"These cute, delicious treats are easy to make, filled with sweet goodness, and topped with chocolate. Sounds like a winner!"

HOLIDAY GIFT GIVING ▶

Prep Time: 20 minutes

Chill Time: 1 hour

Cook Time: 6 minutes per batch

Average Rating: ★★★★★

What other cooks have done:

"These turned out great! A very pretty cookie."

Cookie:

1 cup Butter Flavor CRISCO® All-Vegetable Shortening
1½ cups white sugar
½ cup packed brown sugar
2 tablespoons milk
3 eggs
1 teaspoon vanilla extract
4½ cups all-purpose flour
1½ teaspoons baking soda
1½ teaspoons cream of tartar
1 teaspoon salt

Caramel and Chocolate Topping:

28 caramels, unwrapped
2 tablespoons milk
3 cups pecan halves
1 (6 ounce) package semisweet chocolate chips

1. Cream together shortening, white sugar, and brown sugar. Add milk. Beat in eggs, 1 at a time; add vanilla. In a separate bowl, combine flour, baking soda, cream of tartar, and salt. Mix into creamed mixture. Chill for 1 hour.

2. Preheat oven to 350°F (175°C).

3. Divide dough into thirds. Roll out each third to about ¼ inch thickness on a floured surface. Cut out with 2¼ inch cookie cutters. Place cookies 2 inches apart on ungreased baking sheets.

4. Bake in the preheated oven for 5 to 6 minutes or until edges are slightly golden. Remove immediately to wire racks.

5. Meanwhile, combine caramels and milk in microwave-safe bowl. Cover with wax paper. Microwave on medium (50%) for 1 minute. Stir. Repeat until smooth.

6. Drop rounded teaspoonfuls of caramel mixture over each cookie and place 3 pecan halves around edge of caramel to resemble turtle.

7. Place chocolate chips in microwave-safe cup. Microwave on medium (50%) for 1 minute. Stir. Repeat until smooth. Spread rounded teaspoonfuls of chocolate over caramel. Do not cover the pecans. Cool completely. **Yield:** 5 dozen.

Note: Caramels and chocolate can also be melted in a small saucepan over very low heat.

Per cookie: 129 calories, 2g protein, 20g carbohydrate, 5g fat, 1g fiber, 11mg cholesterol, 87mg sodium

Peanut Butter-Marshmallow Bars

Submitted by: **The J.M. Smucker Company**

"An already-yummy peanut butter brownie is topped with more JIF® Peanut Butter. Toasted marshmallows and chocolate syrup really take it over the top."

¼ cup firmly packed light brown sugar

½ cup Butter Flavor CRISCO® All-Vegetable Shortening, plus extra for greasing

½ cup JIF® Extra Crunchy Peanut Butter

¼ cup white sugar

1 egg

1¼ cups all-purpose flour

1 teaspoon baking powder

¼ teaspoon salt

½ cup JIF® Creamy Peanut Butter

4 cups miniature marshmallows

½ cup chocolate-flavored syrup

◄ FAMILY FAVORITE

Prep Time: 18 minutes

Chill Time: 15 minutes

Cook Time: 26 minutes

Average Rating: ★★★★

What other cooks have done:

"These bars are really yummy. Be careful cutting them into squares—they're gooey because of the marshmallows, but that's nothing to complain about!"

1. Preheat oven to 350°F (175°C). Grease a 9x13 inch glass baking dish.

2. Combine brown sugar, CRISCO® shortening, JIF® Extra Crunchy Peanut Butter, white sugar, and egg in a large bowl. Beat at medium speed with an electric mixer until well blended.

3. In a separate bowl, combine flour, baking powder, and salt. Add gradually to creamed mixture at low speed. Beat until well blended. Cover dough and refrigerate for 15 minutes. Press chilled cookie dough into prepared dish.

4. Bake in the preheated oven for 20 minutes or until light brown. (Do not overbake.) Cool for 2 to 3 minutes.

5. For topping, place JIF® Creamy Peanut Butter in a microwave-safe measuring cup. Microwave on high for 1 minute. Pour over baked cookie layer. Spread to cover. Cover with marshmallows. Drizzle chocolate syrup over marshmallows. Return to oven.

6. Bake in the preheated oven for 5 more minutes or until marshmallows are light brown. (Do not overbake.) Loosen from sides of dish with a knife. Remove dish to a wire rack. Cool completely. Cut into bars with a sharp greased knife. **Yield:** 2 dozen.

Per bar: 194 calories, 4g protein, 24g carbohydrate, 10g fat, 1g fiber, 9mg cholesterol, 103mg sodium

Chocolate Mint Cheesecake Bars

(pictured on facing page)

Submitted by: **Eagle Brand®**
"These festive, minty cheesecake bars with a chocolate crumb crust are sure to be popular among your holiday guests. A drizzle of chocolate and a sprinkling of mint candy pieces decorate them nicely."

PARTY FOOD ▶

Prep Time: 17 minutes

Cook Time: 28 minutes

Average Rating: ★★★★★

What other cooks have done:

"For a more festive look, add a little bit of red food coloring to the cheese mixture and make sure the mint candies are green. Sprinkle a light layer of either confectioners' sugar or shredded coconut for a 'snow' appearance!"

½ cup (1 stick) butter, melted
1 (10 ounce) package chocolate graham cookies, crushed into fine crumbs
1 (8 ounce) package cream cheese, softened
1 (14 ounce) can EAGLE BRAND® Sweetened Condensed Milk (NOT evaporated milk)

2 eggs
1 tablespoon peppermint flavoring
1 cup (6 ounces) semisweet chocolate chips
1 (4.67 ounce) package chocolate mint candies, chopped

1. Preheat oven to 325°F (165°C). Grease a 9x13 inch baking pan.
2. In a medium bowl, combine melted butter and chocolate cookie crumbs; blend well. Press firmly onto the bottom of prepared pan.
3. Bake in the preheated oven for 6 minutes and let cool.
4. In small bowl, beat cream cheese until fluffy. Gradually beat in EAGLE BRAND®, eggs, and peppermint flavoring until smooth. Pour over cooled cookie base and bake for 19 minutes. Cool completely.
5. In a heavy saucepan, melt chocolate chips and drizzle over the top of the bars. Sprinkle chopped chocolate mint candies over the top.
6. Cut into bars or desired shape. Store leftovers, covered, in refrigerator. **Yield:** 2 dozen.

Per bar: 224 calories, 4g protein, 25g carbohydrate, 13g fat, 1g fiber, 44mg cholesterol, 155mg sodium

Chocolate Mint Cheesecake Bars

Golden Onion, Walnut, and Blue
Cheese Pizza, page 65

Asian Beef with Snow Peas, page 85

Simple Lemon-Herb Chicken, page 87

Flank Steak à la Willyboy, page 84

Fast & Healthy

Pita Chips

Submitted by: **Dawn**

"These baked pita chips make a lovely accompaniment to any dip or spread. Watch carefully, as they tend to burn easily!"

KID-FRIENDLY ▶

Prep Time: 10 minutes

Cook Time: 7 minutes

Average Rating: ★★★★★

What other cooks have done:

"These are extremely easy and so tasty! The first time I made these, I served them with hummus at a party for the employees of my husband's upscale restaurant. Everyone raved about them!"

12	pita rounds	1	teaspoon garlic salt
½	cup olive oil	½	teaspoon dried basil
½	teaspoon ground black pepper	1	teaspoon dried chervil

1. Preheat oven to 400°F (200°C). Line a baking sheet with parchment paper.
2. Cut each pita round into 8 triangles. Place triangles on prepared baking sheet.
3. In a small bowl, combine the oil, pepper, garlic salt, basil, and chervil. Brush each pita triangle with oil mixture.
4. Bake in the preheated oven for 7 minutes or until lightly browned and crispy. **Yield:** 24 servings.

Per serving (4 chips): 125 calories, 3g protein, 18g carbohydrate, 5g fat, 2g fiber, 0mg cholesterol, 246mg sodium

Eggplant—Easy, Good, and Tasty

Submitted by: **Bill Wade**

"This easy-to-prepare eggplant appetizer tastes great and can be made a little bit ahead of time. It goes especially well with roasted pork tenderloin or pasta."

FAMILY FAVORITE ▶

Prep Time: 15 minutes

Cook Time: 20 minutes

Average Rating: ★★★★★

What other cooks have done:

"I lined a baking sheet with aluminum foil and sprayed it with vegetable cooking spray. I baked the eggplant slices about 7 minutes before topping them with the tomatoes."

1	tablespoon olive oil	1	tomato, chopped
⅓	large eggplant, peeled	¼	cup grated Parmesan cheese
1	egg, lightly beaten	¼	cup Italian-style salad dressing
1	tablespoon water		
1	cup dry breadcrumbs		

1. Preheat oven to 375°F (190°C). Grease a baking sheet with olive oil.
2. Slice the eggplant into 8 (½ inch thick) round slices. In a small bowl, mix together the egg and water. Place the breadcrumbs in a separate small bowl.
3. Dip the eggplant slices, 1 at a time, into the egg mixture and into the breadcrumbs. Place the coated slices in a single layer on prepared baking sheet. Top the slices evenly with tomato, Parmesan cheese, and salad dressing.
4. Bake in the preheated oven about 15 minutes. Change oven setting to broil and continue cooking 3 to 5 more minutes, checking often to avoid burning. **Yield:** 8 servings.

Per serving: 134 calories, 4g protein, 13g carbohydrate, 8g fat, 1g fiber, 29mg cholesterol, 242mg sodium

Spinach Dip in Pumpernickel

Submitted by: **Julie**

"Very good! Not your ordinary spinach dip. Serve this hot with toasted bread cubes."

2   (8 ounce) round loaves pumpernickel
1   cup low-fat cottage cheese, creamed
1   cup freshly grated Parmesan cheese
¾   cup fat-free mayonnaise
½   cup nonfat sour cream
1   tablespoon grated onion
1   teaspoon fresh lemon juice
¼   teaspoon garlic powder
1   (10 ounce) package frozen chopped spinach, thawed and drained
1   (8 ounce) can water chestnuts, drained and chopped
1   (2 ounce) jar diced pimento, drained
1   (0.4 ounce) packet dry vegetable soup mix
3   tablespoons freshly grated Parmesan cheese

◀ PARTY FOOD

Prep Time: 10 minutes

Cook Time: 30 minutes

Average Rating: ★★★★★

What other cooks have done:

"This is such a different dip from the usual cold spinach dips. I added a package of dry Italian-style dressing mix to give it a little extra zest."

1. Preheat oven to 350°F (175°C).
2. Remove the top and interior of one pumpernickel loaf, forming a bowl. Cube the second loaf and leftover bread from the first loaf.
3. Place the bread bowl on a medium baking sheet and bake in the preheated oven for 10 to 15 minutes or until dry and firm.
4. In a large bowl, mix the cottage cheese, 1 cup Parmesan cheese, mayonnaise, sour cream, onion, lemon juice, garlic powder, spinach, water chestnuts, pimento, and dry vegetable soup mix. Spoon mixture into bread bowl. Top with 3 tablespoons Parmesan cheese.
5. Bake in the preheated oven for 15 minutes or until bubbly and lightly browned. Heat cubed bread until lightly toasted and serve with dip. **Yield:** 20 servings.

Per serving: 58 calories, 5g protein, 6g carbohydrate, 2g fat, 1g fiber, 6mg cholesterol, 215mg sodium

Flank Steak à la Willyboy *(pictured on page 80)*

Submitted by: **Willyboyz in the kitchen again**

"You have to let this steak sit overnight—the payoff is worth it. This staple in our household is a favorite of all who try it. You can grill this in the summer or broil it in the winter for a filling meal. I like corn on the cob and rice to complement this mouth-watering steak."

FROM THE GRILL ▶

Prep Time: 5 minutes

Stand Time: 25 minutes

Marinate Time: overnight

Cook Time: 14 minutes

Average Rating: ★★★★★

What other cooks have done:

"I added extra garlic because I love garlic. This tasted like the steak at my favorite restaurant, but even better! This steak is more sweet than salty, so if you do not like your meat a little sweet, then you may not like it. Give it a try anyway because it's so good!"

¼   cup honey
¼   cup soy sauce
½   cup red wine
1   clove garlic, crushed
1   pinch dried rosemary,
      crushed

Pinch hot chili powder
   (optional)
Pinch ground black pepper
1   pound flank steak

1. In a medium bowl, mix together the honey, soy sauce, and red wine. Season with garlic, rosemary, chili powder, and pepper. Let stand for 15 minutes to blend the flavors.

2. Place the marinade and the steak into a heavy-duty, zip-top plastic bag. Seal and lay flat in the refrigerator. Refrigerate overnight, turning once.

3. Lightly oil cold grill rack and preheat grill for high heat.

4. Grill the flank steak 7 minutes on each side for medium-rare or to desired doneness. Let stand for 10 minutes before thinly slicing against the grain. **Yield:** 4 servings.

Per serving: 228 calories, 15g protein, 20g carbohydrate, 8g fat, 0g fiber, 36mg cholesterol, 951mg sodium

Asian Beef with Snow Peas *(pictured on page 79)*

Submitted by: **Holly**

"Stir-fried beef in a light ginger sauce. Serve over steamed rice or hot egg noodles for a delicious, easy meal."

3	tablespoons soy sauce	
2	tablespoons rice wine	
1	tablespoon brown sugar	
½	teaspoon cornstarch	
1	tablespoon vegetable oil	
1	tablespoon minced fresh ginger root	

1	tablespoon minced garlic
1	pound beef round steak or sirloin tip steak, cut into thin strips
8	ounces snow peas
½	cup red bell pepper strips

◄ AROUND-THE-WORLD CUISINE

Prep Time: 10 minutes

Cook Time: 10 minutes

Average Rating: ★★★★☆

What other cooks have done:

"This was wonderful! I added thinly sliced onion and water chestnuts. I used rice vinegar instead of rice wine, and my dish turned out fabulous."

1. In a small bowl, combine the soy sauce, rice wine, brown sugar, and cornstarch. Set aside.

2. Heat oil in a wok or skillet over medium–high heat. Stir-fry ginger and garlic for 30 seconds. Add the steak and stir-fry for 2 minutes or until evenly browned. Add the snow peas and bell pepper strips and stir-fry for an additional 3 minutes. Add the soy sauce mixture; bring to a boil, stirring constantly. Lower heat and simmer until the sauce is thick and smooth. Serve immediately. **Yield:** 4 servings.

Per serving: 303 calories, 28g protein, 10g carbohydrate, 15g fat, 2g fiber, 69mg cholesterol, 757mg sodium

The Basics of Healthy Eating

The US Department of Health and Human Services' food guide pyramid is one of the simplest to use and easiest to understand of all the nutritional tools available. Keep in mind that you will need to alter the general plan that the food pyramid provides for individual use according to your height, weight, physical condition, activity level, and age.

Make Friends with the Food Guide Pyramid

It is recommended that you work food from each food group into each meal to maintain a well-balanced diet.

Foods that belong to the bread, cereal, rice, and pasta group should be the centerpiece of a meal. The food guide pyramid recommends 6 to 11 servings daily. A serving from this group can be a slice of bread or ½ cup cooked rice or pasta.

Second only to grains, vegetables are the food you should be eating the most, preferably 3 to 5 servings a day. Steaming and boiling are two excellent no-fat options for cooking veggies. You can get one serving of vegetables by eating ½ cup cooked or chopped raw veggies or 1 cup raw leafy vegetables.

You can easily eat your 2 to 4 servings of fruit by taking them along to school or work to eat as a snack. One medium apple, banana, or orange equals one serving.

Take note of how much cheese and other dairy products you use when cooking. You only need 2 to 3 servings of milk, yogurt, or cheese per day—easily accomplished when 1 cup of milk or yogurt equals one serving.

The meat group can be the hardest area of the food guide pyramid to follow; a serving of meat is a lot smaller than many people believe. One serving of cooked meat is equivalent to the size of a deck of playing cards, or you can enjoy 4 tablespoons of peanut butter, an egg, or ½ cup cooked dried beans.

- Tammy Weisberger

For more information, visit **Allrecipes.com**

Broiled Pork Chops

Submitted by: **Jan Taylor**

"These are fabulous pork chops. Pork is very lean, and this broiling method keeps the meat juicy and succulent. Serve with steamed veggies and mashed potatoes for a complete meal."

¾ cup ketchup
¾ cup water
2 tablespoons distilled white vinegar
1 tablespoon Worcestershire sauce
2 teaspoons brown sugar
1 teaspoon salt
½ teaspoon paprika
½ teaspoon chili powder
⅛ teaspoon ground black pepper
6 (¾ inch) thick pork chops

1. In a medium saucepan, combine the ketchup, water, vinegar, Worcestershire sauce, brown sugar, salt, paprika, chili powder, and pepper. Bring to a boil. Reduce heat to low and simmer, stirring occasionally, for 5 minutes. Set aside half of the sauce to serve with chops.
2. Preheat broiler.
3. Brush both sides of the chops with remaining half of sauce. Place chops on broiler pan rack; broil in the preheated oven about 4 inches from heat for 4 minutes on each side. Brush with more sauce. Continue broiling, turning and basting every 3 to 4 minutes, until pork is done and juices run clear. Discard remaining basting sauce. Serve with reserved sauce. **Yield:** 6 servings.

Per serving: 198 calories, 24g protein, 10g carbohydrate, 7g fat, 1g fiber, 58mg cholesterol, 823mg sodium

30 minutes or less

Bahama-Mama Pork Chops

Submitted by: **Christine Johnson**

"Pineapple, raisins, and spices perk pork chops up nicely. Serve over cooked rice."

1 (8 ounce) can pineapple chunks, juice reserved
1 tablespoon cornstarch
⅔ cup chile sauce
⅓ cup raisins
1 tablespoon brown sugar
⅛ teaspoon ground cinnamon
1 tablespoon vegetable oil
4 pork chops

1. In medium bowl, blend pineapple juice and cornstarch; stir in pineapple, chili sauce, raisins, sugar, and cinnamon; set aside.
2. Heat oil in large skillet over medium heat; add chops and brown lightly. Pour pineapple mixture over chops. Cover and simmer for 15 minutes or until pork is done and juices run clear. **Yield:** 4 servings.

Per serving: 236 calories, 15g protein, 23g carbohydrate, 10g fat, 1g fiber, 37mg cholesterol, 24mg sodium

Simple Lemon-Herb Chicken *(pictured on page 79)*

Submitted by: **Carolyn Stilwell**

"This is a simple, quick, and delicious dish. All you need are a few spices and, of course, the chicken! The amount of spices are completely up to you. Enjoy!"

1	lemon		Ground black pepper to taste
2	skinless, boneless chicken breast halves	¼	teaspoon dried oregano
		2	sprigs fresh parsley
	Salt to taste		Lemon slices
1	tablespoon vegetable oil		

1. Cut lemon in half and squeeze juice from half of lemon over chicken. Season with salt to taste. Heat oil in a small skillet over medium heat.

2. When oil is hot, add chicken to skillet. Add juice from other half of lemon, pepper to taste, and oregano. Cook for 6 minutes each side or until chicken is no longer pink and juices run clear. Garnish with parsley and lemon slices before serving. **Yield:** 2 servings.

Per serving: 250 calories, 39g protein, 0g carbohydrate, 9g fat, 0g fiber, 99mg cholesterol, 111mg sodium

◄ 5 INGREDIENTS OR LESS

Prep Time: 10 minutes

Cook Time: 15 minutes

Average Rating: ★★★★★

What other cooks have done:

"This was very tasty! I marinated the chicken for 30 minutes in ¼ cup lemon juice, rosemary, garlic, and basil. Then my husband grilled it. Yummy with a nice salad."

Lime Chicken Picante

Submitted by: **Donna Townsend**

"Quick, easy, spicy chicken."

½	cup chunky salsa	2	tablespoons butter
¼	cup prepared Dijon-style mustard	6	tablespoons plain yogurt
		6	lime wedges
2	tablespoons fresh lime juice		
6	skinless, boneless chicken breasts		

1. In a shallow dish or bowl, combine the salsa, mustard, and lime juice. Mix well. Add chicken; cover and refrigerate. Marinate for at least 30 minutes.

2. Melt butter in a large skillet over medium heat. Remove chicken from marinade and add to skillet, reserving marinade. Sauté, turning frequently, until browned on all sides. Meanwhile, boil reserved marinade in a saucepan for 4 to 5 minutes.

3. Add boiled marinade to chicken and sauté 3 to 5 more minutes or until chicken is no longer pink and juices run clear. Remove chicken to a serving platter; increase heat to high and boil marinade 1 minute. Spoon marinade over chicken and top evenly with yogurt and lime wedges. **Yield:** 6 servings.

Per serving: 196 calories, 29g protein, 5g carbohydrate, 7g fat, 1g fiber, 81mg cholesterol, 469mg sodium

◄ COMPANY IS COMING

Prep Time: 10 minutes

Marinate Time: 30 minutes

Cook Time: 22 minutes

Average Rating: ★★★★★

What other cooks have done:

"This has great flavor. I doubled the sauce the second time I made it and only used three chicken breasts. It allowed us to have plenty of sauce to serve over rice."

California Sherry Chicken

Submitted by: **Nikki**

"Chicken with a hint of lemon, sherry, and garlic served with zucchini and carrots. Like, totally California Sherry Chicken. Serve with roasted potatoes or fettuccine Alfredo, if desired."

4	skinless, boneless chicken breast halves	½	cup cooking sherry
¼	cup all-purpose flour	½	cup chicken broth
1	teaspoon salt	1	clove garlic, minced
1	teaspoon ground black pepper	½	lemon, juiced
1	tablespoon olive oil	4	carrots, julienned
		4	zucchini squash, julienned

1. Place chicken in a zip-top plastic bag with flour, salt, and pepper. Seal bag and shake to coat. Remove chicken from bag, shaking off excess flour.

2. Heat oil in a large skillet over medium-high heat. Brown chicken for 5 minutes on each side or until golden. Remove from skillet and set aside.

3. Combine sherry, broth, garlic, and lemon juice. Add to skillet and bring to a boil. Return chicken to skillet; reduce heat to low and simmer for 15 minutes or until chicken is no longer pink and juices run clear.

4. Meanwhile, sauté carrots and zucchini in a separate skillet until tender. Add to simmering chicken and sauce and heat through before serving. **Yield:** 4 servings.

Per serving: 284 calories, 32g protein, 26g carbohydrate, 6g fat, 6g fiber, 68mg cholesterol, 994mg sodium

Quick Chicken and Wine

Submitted by: **Mayra Martinez**

"This is a very simple chicken breast recipe that's excellent for any occasion. Goes well with white rice or pasta. Serve with a smile—that's an order!"

4	skinless, boneless chicken breast halves, cut into strips	1	cup grated Parmesan cheese
	Pinch salt	2	eggs, beaten
	Pinch ground black pepper	5	tablespoons butter
		½	cup white wine

1. Season chicken with salt and pepper to taste. In a shallow plate, spread Parmesan cheese. Dip seasoned chicken in egg, and coat well with Parmesan cheese. Repeat until all of the chicken pieces are well coated.

2. Melt butter in a medium skillet over medium heat. Divide chicken into 2 batches. Cook first batch of chicken in skillet 3 minutes on each side or until chicken is no longer pink and juices run clear. Remove cooked chicken from skillet. Repeat with second batch of chicken. Return all cooked chicken to skillet.

3. Reduce heat to low and add wine. Cover and simmer over low heat for 10 minutes. **Yield:** 6 servings.

Per serving: 292 calories, 34g protein, 1g carbohydrate, 16g fat, 0g fiber, 173mg cholesterol, 419mg sodium

◄ **COMPANY IS COMING**

Prep Time: 15 minutes

Cook Time: 22 minutes

Average Rating: ★★★★★

What other cooks have done:

"Here is the secret to making any crust stick to chicken: After thoroughly drying chicken, dip it in a little bit of flour before dipping in the egg. This will make any crust stick, unless you're boiling the chicken. I used cutlets instead of cutting strips, and I eliminated the salt."

Ranch Crispy Chicken

Submitted by: **Christine Johnson**

"This recipe is both delicious and insanely easy!"

2	(1 ounce) packages dry Ranch-style dressing mix	8	skinless, boneless chicken breast halves
¼	cup dry breadcrumbs		

1. Preheat oven to 375°F (190°C).

2. Combine dressing mix and breadcrumbs in a zip-top plastic bag. Add chicken and shake to coat. Place chicken pieces on an ungreased baking sheet.

3. Bake in the preheated oven for 25 to 30 minutes or until chicken is no longer pink and juices run clear. **Yield:** 8 servings.

Per serving: 161 calories, 28g protein, 6g carbohydrate, 2g fat, 0g fiber, 68mg cholesterol, 666mg sodium

◄ **5 INGREDIENTS OR LESS**

Prep Time: 10 minutes

Cook Time: 30 minutes

Average Rating: ★★★★★

What other cooks have done:

"This was outstanding! I doubled the breadcrumbs and left the seasoning as is. I served it with mashed potatoes and fresh corn for a quick, delicious dinner."

Skillet Herbed Chicken with Mustard

Submitted by: **Angela B.**

"This is one version of a classic French recipe that I have adapted for quick and easy preparation. Adjust the tarragon to taste."

AROUND-THE-WORLD CUISINE ▶

Prep Time: 20 minutes

Cook Time: 25 minutes

Average Rating: ★★★★☆

What other cooks have done:

"Really quick, really easy, and delicious. I fixed a nice salad while it simmered. I used fresh herbs and added a few sprigs of rosemary."

3 tablespoons prepared Dijon-style mustard
2 tablespoons honey
2 tablespoons dried tarragon
2 teaspoons dried basil
2 teaspoons dried thyme
⅛ teaspoon salt
⅛ teaspoon ground black pepper
2 tablespoons vegetable oil
4 skinless, boneless chicken breast halves
1 cup white wine, divided

1. In a small bowl, blend mustard and honey. Mix in the tarragon, basil, thyme, salt, and pepper.
2. Heat oil in a large skillet over medium heat. Brush chicken on both sides with mustard mixture and add to the skillet. Pour ¼ cup wine around the chicken. Reduce heat, cover, and simmer about 10 minutes or until liquid is reduced.
3. Add another ¼ cup wine to skillet and continue to cook 5 more minutes or until chicken is no longer pink and juices run clear. Remove chicken, reserving liquid in skillet.
4. Mix remaining wine into the skillet, stirring to loosen any browned bits. Increase heat to medium and cook, stirring occasionally, until liquid is reduced by about one-third. Serve as a sauce over the chicken.
Yield: 4 servings.

Per serving: 291 calories, 29g protein, 13g carbohydrate, 10g fat, 1g fiber, 68mg cholesterol, 439mg sodium

Caryn's Chicken

Submitted by: **Caryn**
"This is a scrumptious low-fat recipe that is requested again and again. If desired, serve with a crisp green salad."

6 oranges, juiced	4 skinless, boneless chicken
3 tablespoons thinly sliced green onions	breast halves, pounded thin
Ground black pepper to taste	

1. Combine orange juice, green onions, and pepper in a large skillet over medium heat.
2. Add the chicken to skillet and simmer about 10 minutes or until chicken is no longer pink and juices run clear. To serve, place the chicken on a serving plate and pour some of the juice mixture over top. **Yield:** 4 servings.

Per serving: 250 calories, 30g protein, 30g carbohydrate, 2g fat, 6g fiber, 68mg cholesterol, 77mg sodium

◄ 5 INGREDIENTS OR LESS
Prep Time: 10 minutes
Cook Time: 10 minutes
Average Rating: ★★★★☆
What other cooks have done:
"I used fresh chives from my garden and squeezed fresh oranges. In 10 minutes, I had the most wonderful meal. I served it with some leftover white rice that I added right into the juice after removing the cooked chicken."

Chicken Perkelt

Submitted by: **Silvia**
"This Eastern European favorite is light and tender. My husband asks for this at least once a week. Serve over hot rice or pasta."

3 tablespoons vegetable oil	Salt and ground black pepper to taste
6 skinless, boneless chicken breast halves, cubed	1 (4.5 ounce) can mushrooms, undrained
½ large onion, chopped	3 tablespoons sour cream
2 chicken bouillon cubes	
1 teaspoon paprika	

1. Heat oil in a large skillet over medium heat and add chicken and onion. Season with bouillon cubes, paprika, and salt and pepper to taste. Sauté chicken until almost cooked through. Stir in mushrooms and liquid. Cover the skillet and cook for 5 more minutes or until the mushrooms are tender and the chicken is no longer pink and juices run clear.
2. Stir in the sour cream and remove skillet from heat. **Yield:** 6 servings.

Per serving: 221 calories, 28g protein, 3g carbohydrate, 10g fat, 1g fiber, 72mg cholesterol, 554mg sodium

◄ FAMILY FAVORITE
Prep Time: 15 minutes
Cook Time: 25 minutes
Average Rating: ★★★★☆
What other cooks have done:
"Great recipe, great taste. I used fresh mushrooms and added about ¼ cup of water as the liquid. Instead of spooning over rice in individual servings, I mixed the entire dish with 1 cup cooked white rice in a big bowl. It was delicious."

Italian Green Bean Chicken

Submitted by: **Kristy**

"This flavorful dish features simmered chicken and green beans in a simple tomato sauce."

AROUND-THE-WORLD CUISINE ▶

Prep Time: 10 minutes

Cook Time: 25 minutes

Average Rating: ★★★★☆

What other cooks have done:

"My family thought this was very good. I added cooked linguine to the pot and served the dish with Parmesan cheese and garlic bread. Delicious!"

1 pound green beans, rinsed and trimmed
2 tablespoons olive oil
3 cloves garlic, chopped
1 pound skinless, boneless chicken breast halves, cubed
2 (14.5 ounce) cans diced tomatoes
2 tablespoons minced fresh basil

1. Place green beans in a steamer over 1 inch of boiling water and cover. Steam until beans are tender.

2. Meanwhile, heat oil in a large skillet over medium-high heat. Add garlic and sauté until aromatic oils are released. Add chicken and cook until chicken is no longer pink and juices run clear.

3. Stir in tomatoes and basil and bring to a boil; reduce heat to low and simmer for 3 to 5 more minutes. Stir in steamed beans; heat through and serve. **Yield:** 6 servings.

Per serving: 177 calories, 18g protein, 10g carbohydrate, 6g fat, 4g fiber, 43mg cholesterol, 255mg sodium

Chicken Broccoli Ca—Unieng's Style

Submitted by: **unieng**

"This Indonesian-Chinese stir-fry is all that you want in a meal—delicious, fast, healthy, low in calories, and impressive. Serve it hot over white rice."

¾ pound skinless, boneless chicken breast halves, cubed
1 tablespoon oyster sauce
2 tablespoons dark soy sauce
3 tablespoons vegetable oil
2 cloves garlic, chopped
1 large onion, cut into rings
½ cup water

1 teaspoon ground black pepper
1 teaspoon white sugar
½ medium head bok choy, chopped
1 small head broccoli, chopped
1 tablespoon cornstarch
1 tablespoon water

◄ AROUND-THE-WORLD CUISINE

Prep Time: 15 minutes

Marinate Time: 15 minutes

Cook Time: 30 minutes

Average Rating: ★★★★★

What other cooks have done:

"This was so good and easy to make. I cut the broccoli into big chunks and added carrots. My family thought it was delicious. Next time, I'll add red pepper to spice it up and some unsalted peanuts."

1. In a large bowl, combine chicken, oyster sauce, and soy sauce. Marinate for 15 minutes.

2. Heat oil in a wok or large, heavy skillet over medium heat. Sauté garlic and onion in oil until soft and translucent. Increase heat to high. Add chicken and marinade; stir-fry until light golden brown, about 10 minutes. Stir in ½ cup water, pepper, and sugar. Add bok choy and broccoli; cook, stirring constantly, until soft, about 10 minutes. Stir together cornstarch and 1 tablespoon water. Pour in the cornstarch mixture and cook until sauce is thickened, about 5 minutes. **Yield:** 6 servings.

Per serving: 167 calories, 16g protein, 9g carbohydrate, 8g fat, 3g fiber, 33mg cholesterol, 419mg sodium

Ten-Minute Szechuan Chicken

Submitted by: **Michael Pusateri**

"A simple, quick recipe for Szechuan-style chicken with basic ingredients."

4 skinless, boneless chicken breasts, cubed	¼ cup water
3 tablespoons cornstarch	1 teaspoon white sugar
1 tablespoon vegetable oil	3 green onions, sliced diagonally into ½ inch pieces
4 cloves garlic, minced	
5 tablespoons low-sodium soy sauce	⅛ teaspoon cayenne pepper (or to taste)
1½ tablespoons white wine vinegar	

1. Place the chicken and cornstarch into a zip-top plastic bag or bowl and toss to coat. Heat oil in a wok or large skillet over medium-high heat. Sauté chicken and garlic in oil, stirring constantly, until lightly browned. Stir in the soy sauce, vinegar, water, and sugar. Cover and cook 3 to 5 minutes or until chicken is no longer pink and juices run clear.
2. Stir in the green onions and cayenne pepper; cook, uncovered, for about 2 more minutes. **Yield:** 4 servings.

Per serving: 206 calories, 29g protein, 10g carbohydrate, 5g fat, 1g fiber, 68mg cholesterol, 745mg sodium

Sweet-and-Sour Chicken III

Submitted by: **Sallie**

"Serve this version of the Asian-style favorite over hot cooked rice, if desired."

1 pound skinless, boneless chicken breasts, cubed	1 tablespoon cornstarch
2 tablespoons vegetable oil	¼ cup soy sauce
½ cup sliced green bell pepper	1 (8 ounce) can pineapple chunks, juice reserved
½ cup sliced red bell pepper	1 tablespoon white vinegar
1 cup sliced carrot	1 tablespoon brown sugar
1 clove garlic, minced	½ teaspoon ground ginger

1. Brown chicken in oil in a skillet over medium-high heat. Add green and red bell pepper, carrot, and garlic; stir-fry for 1 to 2 minutes.
2. In a small bowl, combine cornstarch and soy sauce. Pour into skillet. Stir in pineapple chunks and reserved liquid, vinegar, sugar, and ginger. Cook until chicken is done and sauce is thickened. **Yield:** 4 servings.

Per serving: 260 calories, 24g protein, 21g carbohydrate, 9g fat, 2g fiber, 59mg cholesterol, 972mg sodium

Mandarin Chicken Skillet

Submitted by: **Sara**

"Sautéed chicken and mushrooms simmer in a mandarin orange mixture."

1	cup broccoli florets	⅔	cup water
1	tablespoon butter	⅓	cup thawed orange juice concentrate
2	pounds skinless, boneless chicken breasts, cubed	2	chicken bouillon cubes
1½	cups sliced mushrooms	1	(11 ounce) can mandarin orange segments, drained
1	tablespoon all-purpose flour	¼	cup sliced green onions

1. Place broccoli in a steamer over 1 inch of boiling water and cover. Steam until tender but still firm, 3 to 6 minutes. Drain and set aside.
2. Heat butter in a large skillet over medium-high heat. Sauté chicken in butter until browned. Remove from skillet and set aside.
3. Sauté mushrooms in skillet for 1 minute; remove from skillet and set aside. Stir in flour, water, orange juice concentrate, and bouillon.
4. Bring to a boil, stirring constantly. Reduce heat to medium and simmer, stirring constantly, for 4 minutes. Return chicken and mushrooms to skillet; stir in orange segments, green onions, and broccoli. Heat through and serve. **Yield:** 6 servings.

Per serving: 276 calories, 41g protein, 16g carbohydrate, 4g fat, 2g fiber, 105mg cholesterol, 575mg sodium

◄ FAMILY FAVORITE
Prep Time: 15 minutes
Cook Time: 25 minutes
Average Rating: ★★★★☆
What other cooks have done:
"I used shrimp instead of chicken for this recipe. The next day, I used the leftovers to make fajitas. Both were so good!"

30 minutes or less

Light and Spicy Fish

Submitted by: **Matt Adams**

"This recipe is easy to make and very healthy. You may substitute other firm-fleshed fish, such as ocean perch or grouper, for the snapper."

2	(6 ounce) red snapper fillets	¼	cup picante sauce
¼	teaspoon garlic powder	½	lime, juiced
	Salt and ground black pepper to taste		

1. Preheat oven to 350°F (175°C). Lightly grease a large sheet of aluminum foil.
2. Place fillets on the foil and sprinkle with garlic powder and salt and pepper to taste. Spoon picante sauce evenly over fillets and squeeze lime juice over the top. Bring the sides of the foil together and fold the seam to seal in the fish. Place foil packet on a baking sheet.
3. Bake in the preheated oven for 15 to 20 minutes or until fish flakes easily with a fork. **Yield:** 2 servings.

Per serving: 185 calories, 35g protein, 5g carbohydrate, 2g fat, 1g fiber, 62mg cholesterol, 309mg sodium

◄ 5 INGREDIENTS OR LESS
Prep Time: 5 minutes
Cook Time: 20 minutes
Average Rating: ★★★★☆
What other cooks have done:
"This recipe was great. I used salmon and made it on the grill. I put some veggies in a separate foil bag and threw both bags on the grill together. Twenty minutes later, my dinner was ready! It tasted fabulous! I just had to throw out the bags, and the dinner mess was clean!"

Cajun Red Snapper

Submitted by: **Holly**
"A spicy red snapper dish."

COMPANY IS COMING ▶

Prep Time: 5 minutes

Cook Time: 15 minutes

Average Rating: ★★★★☆

What other cooks have done:

"Make this seasoning, put it in an empty seasoning shaker, and have it ready on your spice rack to use anytime you want to liven up your meal."

1	teaspoon paprika	¼	teaspoon dried oregano
1	teaspoon ground black pepper	¼	teaspoon cayenne pepper
1	teaspoon dried thyme	2	tablespoons butter
1	teaspoon dried basil	1	tablespoon olive oil
1	teaspoon garlic powder	6	(6 ounce) red snapper fillets
½	teaspoon onion powder		Salt to taste

1. In a small bowl, mix together paprika, black pepper, thyme, basil, garlic powder, onion powder, oregano, and cayenne pepper.

2. In a small saucepan over medium heat, melt butter with oil. Brush both sides of the snapper fillets with the butter mixture, reserving remaining butter mixture. Coat both sides of the fillets with the seasoning mixture.

3. Heat a large cast-iron skillet over high heat until a drop of water sizzles in it. Drizzle half of the remaining buttered mixture on 1 side of each fish fillet. Place fillets, buttered side down, in hot skillet. Cook until the fish is browned on the bottom, about 5 minutes. Drizzle remaining butter mixture over the fish and flip the fish over. Cook until fish is browned and flakes easily with a fork, about 5 more minutes. Season to taste with salt. **Yield:** 6 servings.

Per serving: 228 calories, 35g protein, 1g carbohydrate, 9g fat, 1g fiber, 72mg cholesterol, 115mg sodium

Garlic Salmon

Submitted by: **Lili**
"A large salmon fillet, steamed in foil and cooked either in the oven or on the grill, is seasoned with minced garlic, fresh dill, lemon slices, ground black pepper, and green onions."

1 (1½ pound) salmon fillet	5 lemon slices
Salt and ground black	5 sprigs fresh dill weed
pepper to taste	2 green onions, chopped
3 cloves garlic, minced	
1 sprig fresh dill weed,	
chopped	

1. Preheat oven to 450°F (230°C). Spray 2 large pieces of aluminum foil with vegetable cooking spray.

2. Place salmon fillet on top of 1 piece of foil. Sprinkle salmon with salt and pepper to taste, garlic, and chopped dill weed. Arrange lemon slices on top of fillet and place a sprig of dill on top of each lemon slice. Sprinkle fillet with chopped green onions.

3. Cover salmon with second piece of foil and pinch foil together tightly to seal. Place on a baking sheet or in a large baking dish.

4. Bake in the preheated oven for 20 to 25 minutes or until fish flakes easily with a fork. **Yield:** 6 servings.

Per serving: 169 calories, 25g protein, 2g carbohydrate, 7g fat, 1g fiber, 51mg cholesterol, 48mg sodium

◄ COMPANY IS COMING

Prep Time: 10 minutes

Cook Time: 25 minutes

Average Rating: ★★★★★

What other cooks have done:

"This was my first time making salmon, and it couldn't have turned out better. I paired this with a creamy dill sauce that included lemon juice, green onions, and fresh dill."

Jumbo Shrimp and Asparagus

Submitted by: **Amy**

"If you don't love asparagus, this will bring you into the fold. It's fantastic."

FAMILY FAVORITE ▶

Prep Time: 20 minutes

Cook Time: 15 minutes

Average Rating: ★★★★★

What other cooks have done:

"I boiled linguine noodles with the asparagus and added both to the skillet after I cooked the shrimp. I also used low-sodium soy sauce and added crushed red pepper flakes for some kick."

2	cups water	2	teaspoons chopped fresh ginger root
2	bunches asparagus, trimmed and cut into 1 inch pieces	3	tablespoons soy sauce
2	tablespoons vegetable oil	2	teaspoons white sugar
24	large fresh shrimp, peeled, deveined, and cut in half lengthwise	1	teaspoon dry sherry
			Salt to taste

1. In a medium saucepan, bring 2 cups of water to a boil. Cook asparagus in boiling water for 3 minutes. Drain, reserving 2 tablespoons of liquid.
2. Heat oil in a large skillet over medium-high heat. Sauté shrimp until pink, about 3 to 5 minutes. Add asparagus with reserved liquid, ginger root, soy sauce, sugar, sherry, and salt to taste. Stir well and cook for 5 more minutes. **Yield:** 6 servings.

Per serving: 104 calories, 9g protein, 8g carbohydrate, 5g fat, 2g fiber, 43mg cholesterol, 529mg sodium

30 minutes or less

Spicy Grilled Shrimp

Submitted by: **Suz**

"So fast and easy to prepare, these shrimp are destined to be the hit of any barbecue. If the weather interferes, they work great under the broiler, too."

FROM THE GRILL ▶

Prep Time: 15 minutes

Cook Time: 6 minutes

Average Rating: ★★★★☆

What other cooks have done:

"These are the best spicy shrimp! I broiled them, poured the shrimp and the sauce over pasta, and topped the dish with grated Parmesan cheese."

1	clove garlic	2	teaspoons lemon juice
1	tablespoon coarse salt	2	pounds large shrimp, peeled and deveined
1	teaspoon paprika	8	lemon wedges (optional)
½	teaspoon cayenne pepper		
2	tablespoons olive oil		

1. Lightly oil cold grill rack and preheat grill for medium heat.
2. In a small bowl, crush the garlic with the salt. Mix in paprika and cayenne pepper; stir in olive oil and lemon juice to form a paste. In a large bowl, toss shrimp with garlic paste until evenly coated.
3. Grill shrimp for 2 to 3 minutes per side or until pink. Transfer to a serving dish and garnish with lemon wedges, if desired. **Yield:** 6 servings.

Per serving: 164 calories, 25g protein, 3g carbohydrate, 6g fat, 1g fiber, 230mg cholesterol, 1206mg sodium

Minute Tomato Soup with Tortellini

Submitted by: **Stacey Oziel**

"I whipped this delicious soup up on a chilly day when a friend and I both craved our favorite cold weather combo—grilled cheese sandwiches and tomato soup. For the tortellini, use half of a 9 ounce package."

2	(10.75 ounce) cans condensed tomato soup	1	teaspoon dried parsley
1	tablespoon dried basil	¾	teaspoon ground black pepper
1	teaspoon dried oregano	4½	ounces cheese tortellini

1. Prepare condensed soup in a medium saucepan over medium heat according to package directions. Add basil, oregano, parsley, and pepper, stirring well. Simmer for 5 minutes. Reduce heat to low and add the tortellini. Continue to simmer for 10 more minutes or until tortellini is cooked. **Yield:** 4 servings.

Per serving: 178 calories, 6g protein, 31g carbohydrate, 4g fat, 2g fiber, 7mg cholesterol, 925mg sodium

◀ **CLASSIC COMFORT FOOD**

Prep Time: 5 minutes

Cook Time: 20 minutes

Average Rating: ★★★★☆

What other cooks have done:

"This was one of the fastest, easiest, and tastiest recipes I've made in a while. Keep an eye on the tortellini so it doesn't fall apart. I cooked this for my dorm hall, and everyone loved it."

Hobart's Chicken and Red Bean Soup

Submitted by: **Rodney**

"This is a delicious and quick recipe for a 'stay-at-home' meal that will please the whole family."

CROWD-PLEASER ▶

Prep Time: 15 minutes

Cook Time: 30 minutes

Average Rating: ★★★★☆

What other cooks have done:

"Great with grilled cheese sandwiches. I recommend adding another can of beans—either white beans or garbanzo. Delicious!"

1 (14.5 ounce) can diced tomatoes
1 (15 ounce) can tomato sauce
4 cups water
¼ cup diced onion
1 pound cooked chicken, cubed
1 (16.5 ounce) can red kidney beans, drained and rinsed
1 cup chopped broccoli
1 cup diced carrots
1 teaspoon salt
½ teaspoon ground black pepper
½ teaspoon Cajun seasoning
Pinch garlic powder

1. In a large saucepan over medium–high heat, combine diced tomatoes, tomato sauce, water, and onion. Bring to a boil; stir in cooked chicken, beans, broccoli, carrots, salt, pepper, Cajun seasoning, and garlic powder. Boil 5 minutes; reduce heat and simmer 20 more minutes. **Yield:** 6 servings.

Per serving: 190 calories, 20g protein, 17g carbohydrate, 5g fat, 5g fiber, 43mg cholesterol, 931mg sodium

Asparagus-Zucchini Rice

Submitted by: **JBurley**

"This is a great side dish that's fast, flexible, and easy. I serve it with fish, but it would also go great with chicken. You can use it with any style of rice. Try different vegetables, too!"

½	tablespoon butter	¼	teaspoon dried thyme
1	onion, chopped	⅛	teaspoon garlic powder
10	spears fresh asparagus, trimmed and cut into 2 inch pieces		Pinch cayenne pepper
			Salt and ground black pepper to taste
1	zucchini, sliced	2	cups water
½	teaspoon dried oregano	1	cup uncooked long-grain white rice
½	teaspoon dried basil		

1. In a medium saucepan over medium heat, melt butter; sauté onion in butter for about 2 minutes. Stir in asparagus and zucchini; sauté 5 minutes or until tender. Season with oregano, basil, thyme, garlic powder, cayenne pepper, and salt and black pepper to taste. Cook and stir until vegetables are coated with the seasonings.

2. Pour water into the vegetable mixture and stir in rice. Reduce heat, cover, and simmer 20 minutes until the rice is tender. **Yield:** 4 servings.

Per serving: 210 calories, 5g protein, 43g carbohydrate, 2g fat, 3g fiber, 4mg cholesterol, 24mg sodium

◄ COMPANY IS COMING

Prep Time: 15 minutes

Cook Time: 27 minutes

Average Rating: ★★★★☆

What other cooks have done:

"This side dish is easy and makes good-size portions, but I would recommend using chicken, vegetable, or beef broth instead of water for more depth of flavor. The spices are strong, but they complement the veggies. I added fresh mushrooms and topped it with Parmesan cheese."

Peerless Spears

One of our favorite harbingers of spring is asparagus. These delectable stalks with their vivid color and delicate flavor are good hot or cold, dressed up or down.

Asparagus comes in several sizes, ranging in diameter from thinner than a drinking straw to fatter than your thumb. Cooks of the world have been debating for ages over which is more delicious—thin asparagus or thick. While some people prefer the smaller spears for their delicacy and tenderness, others prefer the fatter ones for their more robust flavor and meaty texture that they can really sink their teeth into.

Whatever diameter you choose, make sure that the spears you buy are uniform in size. Look for asparagus with tightly closed tips and firm, brightly colored stalks. Yellowed or khaki-tinged spears with soggy tips are a sign that the stalks are old, bitter, or stringy.

Asparagus begins to lose its sweetness as soon as it's picked, so try to cook it as soon as possible after you buy it. If you do plan to store it in your refrigerator for a few days after you get it home, treat it like a bouquet of flowers: trim a small amount from the bottoms of the stalks with a sharp knife and place the stalks in a tall glass with a little water in the bottom. Cover the top loosely with a plastic bag and store in the refrigerator. This will keep the stalks firm and crisp until you are ready to cook them.

For more information, visit **Allrecipes.com**

Delicious Applesauce

Submitted by: **Sherice**

"This applesauce truly is delicious. My grandma makes it all the time!"

5 INGREDIENTS OR LESS ▶

Prep Time: 10 minutes

Cook Time: 30 minutes

Average Rating: ★★★★☆

What other cooks have done:

"I mashed the apples rather than shredding them, and the chunks gave the applesauce a good texture. I added some chopped walnuts for an added crunch, and it was delicious."

2	apples, peeled, cored, and shredded	¼	cup water
1	teaspoon ground cinnamon	3	tablespoons brown sugar
			Ice cream (optional)

1. Place shredded apples in a medium saucepan over medium-low heat. Sprinkle with cinnamon and add water; cook 30 minutes or until the apple bits become soft and mushy.
2. Stir in brown sugar and mix well. Serve with ice cream, if desired. **Yield:** 2 servings.

Per serving: 161 calories, 0g protein, 42g carbohydrate, 1g fat, 4g fiber, 0mg cholesterol, 9mg sodium

20 minutes or less

Lemon Pepper Green Beans

Submitted by: **Annette Byrdy**

"These green beans are easy and delicious. They are a bit tangy and spicy, and the almonds add a nice crunch. My family's favorite!"

5 INGREDIENTS OR LESS ▶

Prep Time: 5 minutes

Cook Time: 10 minutes

Average Rating: ★★★★☆

What other cooks have done:

"I used a little less lemon pepper and added ground black pepper and salt. This would be good with a number of veggies; next time, I'm trying broccoli."

1	pound green beans, rinsed and trimmed	¼	cup sliced almonds
2	tablespoons butter	2	teaspoons lemon pepper

1. Place green beans in a steamer over 1 inch of boiling water and cover. Steam until beans are tender but still firm, about 10 minutes; drain.
2. Meanwhile, melt butter in a skillet over medium heat. Sauté almonds until lightly browned. Season with lemon pepper. Stir in green beans and toss to coat. **Yield:** 4 servings.

Per serving: 81 calories, 2g protein, 6g carbohydrate, 6g fat, 3g fiber, 10mg cholesterol, 198mg sodium

Microwaved Potatoes Lyonnaise

Submitted by: **Jon Craig**

"In just minutes, you'll be serving up this savory dish of potatoes and onions microwaved with garlic, spices, and herbs."

3	large potatoes, peeled and cubed	½	teaspoon salt
2	small onions, sliced	⅛	teaspoon dried oregano
2	tablespoons butter or margarine	⅛	teaspoon ground black pepper
2	cloves garlic, minced	⅛	teaspoon paprika

1. In a 3 quart microwave-safe casserole dish, combine all ingredients.
2. Heat in microwave on high until butter melts, about 1 minute; stir. Cook 10 more minutes, stirring occasionally. **Yield:** 6 servings.

Per serving: 98 calories, 2g protein, 15g carbohydrate, 4g fat, 1g fiber, 0mg cholesterol, 380mg sodium

◄ **COVERED-DISH FAVORITE**

Prep Time: 10 minutes

Cook Time: 11 minutes

Average Rating: ★★★★☆

What other cooks have done:

"I used 4 tablespoons of butter and a little more salt and pepper than the recipe called for. I was also pretty generous with the onions and garlic. The potatoes came out of the microwave just as my dinner was coming out of the oven. Perfect!"

Zucchini Sauté

Submitted by: **Denyse**

"You can use any veggies you like in this versatile vegetable sauté. Serve over pasta, if desired."

1	tablespoon olive oil	1	tomato, diced
½	red onion, diced	1	clove garlic, minced
	Salt and ground black pepper to taste	1	teaspoon dry Italian seasoning
4	zucchini, halved and sliced		
½	pound fresh mushrooms, sliced		

1. Heat oil in a large skillet over medium heat. Sauté onion with salt and pepper for 2 minutes. Stir in zucchini and mushrooms and cook until zucchini begins to soften. Add tomato, garlic, and Italian seasoning. Cook until heated through. **Yield:** 6 servings.

Per serving: 68 calories, 3g protein, 9g carbohydrate, 3g fat, 3g fiber, 0mg cholesterol, 99mg sodium

◄ **FAMILY FAVORITE**

Prep Time: 15 minutes

Cook Time: 15 minutes

Average Rating: ★★★★★

What other cooks have done:

"Easy recipe. I sautéed the garlic with the onion instead of waiting, added spaghetti squash with the zucchini and mushrooms, and threw in scallions when I added the tomatoes. I used canned diced tomatoes with garlic, onion, and olive oil and drained the liquid before adding. I didn't have Italian seasoning, so I used parsley, oregano, and basil."

Blueberry Scones

Submitted by: **Linda Letellier**

"A good basic scone recipe with blueberries added—yummy!"

HOLIDAY GIFT GIVING ▶

Prep Time: 15 minutes

Cook Time: 20 minutes

Average Rating: ★★★★☆

What other cooks have done:

"I've successfully made this recipe with other ingredients—chocolate chips, cheese, corn, raisins—but blueberry still rules. I drop spoonfuls of batter onto a baking sheet, and they turn out soft and delicious. Very highly recommended."

2	cups all-purpose flour	¼	cup butter, chilled
¼	cup packed brown sugar	1	cup fresh blueberries
1	tablespoon baking powder	¾	cup half-and-half
¼	teaspoon salt	1	egg

1. Preheat oven to 375°F (190°C).

2. Combine flour, brown sugar, baking powder, and salt. Cut butter into flour mixture. Add blueberries and toss to mix.

3. In a separate bowl, beat together half-and-half and egg and slowly pour into dry ingredients, stirring just until dough forms. Turn dough out and knead 3 or 4 times or just until dough comes together. (Don't overhandle.)

4. Divide dough in half. On a lightly floured surface, shape each half into a 6 inch round. Cut each round into 6 wedges and place on an ungreased baking sheet.

5. Bake in the preheated oven for 20 minutes. Serve warm. **Yield:** 1 dozen scones.

Per scone: 160 calories, 3g protein, 23g carbohydrate, 6g fat, 1g fiber, 34mg cholesterol, 224mg sodium

Restaurant-Quality Maple Oatmeal Scones

Submitted by: **Holly**

"Great with a cup of coffee or tea. You can substitute chopped dried pears for the dried cherries, if desired."

¾	cup dried cherries	1	tablespoon cornstarch
1	egg	2½	teaspoons baking powder
¾	cup buttermilk	½	teaspoon baking soda
¾	teaspoon vanilla extract	⅜	teaspoon salt
2	tablespoons real maple syrup	¾	cup white sugar
½	teaspoon maple-flavored extract	¾	cup unsalted butter, cut into pieces
3	cups all-purpose flour	1	egg white, lightly beaten
½	cup rolled oats	1	teaspoon white sugar

◀ RESTAURANT FARE

Prep Time: 20 minutes

Cook Time: 20 minutes

Average Rating: ★★★★☆

What other cooks have done:

"This is by far the best scone recipe I have found. You can substitute raisins soaked in orange juice for the cherries."

1. Preheat oven to 425°F (220°C). Line a large heavy-duty baking sheet with parchment paper.

2. Place cherries in a small bowl and cover with boiling water; let stand 5 minutes. Drain and pat dry with paper towels.

3. In a small bowl, stir together the egg, buttermilk, vanilla, maple syrup, and maple extract.

4. Place the flour, oats, cornstarch, baking powder, baking soda, salt, and ¾ cup sugar in a food processor bowl. Process briefly to blend ingredients. Drop in pieces of butter and pulse to cut in. Stop when you have a coarse, grainy mixture.

5. Remove mixture to a large mixing bowl. Make a well in the center. Stir in buttermilk mixture. Blend in cherries. Stir with a fork to make a soft dough.

6. Turn dough out onto a lightly floured surface and knead just until dough comes together. Divide the dough into 3 equal pieces. Pat each piece into an 8 to 10 inch circle, ½ to ¾ inch thick. Cut each circle into eight wedges. Place on prepared baking sheet. Brush tops with egg white and sprinkle evenly with 1 teaspoon sugar.

7. Bake in the preheated oven for 15 to 18 minutes or until golden brown. **Yield:** 2 dozen scones.

Per scone: 167 calories, 3g protein, 25g carbohydrate, 6g fat, 1g fiber, 25mg cholesterol, 128mg sodium

Berry Cornmeal Muffins

Submitted by: **Shelley Albeluhn**

"Very refreshing, fruity, and delicious. These muffins will bring a smile to anyone's day. Share them with someone you love."

FREEZER FRESH ▶

Prep Time: 15 minutes

Cook Time: 25 minutes

Average Rating: ★★★★★

What other cooks have done:

"This is a good alternative to cornbread or sweetbread. I used an 8x8 inch pan and baked it for about 25 to 30 minutes. Then I sliced and served it like regular cornbread."

1	cup all-purpose flour	1	(8 ounce) container
¾	cup cornmeal		strawberry-flavored
½	cup white sugar		yogurt
2½	teaspoons baking powder	¼	cup butter, melted
¼	teaspoon salt	1	egg, lightly beaten
2	cups chopped strawberries		

1. Preheat oven to 350°F (175°C). Lightly grease a muffin pan or line with paper liners.
2. In a large bowl, sift together the flour, cornmeal, sugar, baking powder, and salt. Gently toss ½ cup flour mixture with strawberries.
3. In a small bowl, whisk together yogurt, melted butter, and egg. Add yogurt mixture to remaining flour mixture, stirring just until moistened. Fold in strawberries. Spoon batter into prepared muffin cups.
4. Bake in the preheated oven for 25 minutes or until a toothpick inserted into center of a muffin comes out clean. **Yield:** 1 dozen muffins.

Per serving: 161 calories, 3g protein, 27g carbohydrate, 5g fat, 2g fiber, 28mg cholesterol, 158mg sodium

Jacky's Fruit and Yogurt Muffins

Submitted by: **Sue Litster**

"For these moist muffins, match the type of yogurt to the type of fruit you use."

RESTAURANT FARE ▶

Prep Time: 10 minutes

Cook Time: 25 minutes

Average Rating: ★★★★★

What other cooks have done:

"This time, I used bananas, plain yogurt, a dash of maple syrup, and some chopped pecans. I can't wait to make some with mangoes, strawberries, or peaches—the combinations are endless!"

2	cups all-purpose flour	1	egg
1	cup white sugar	1	teaspoon vanilla extract
1	teaspoon baking soda	4	tablespoons butter, melted
1	teaspoon baking powder	2	cups blueberries
1	(8 ounce) container blueberry-flavored yogurt		

1. Preheat oven to 350°F (175°C). Grease a muffin pan or line with paper liners.
2. Stir together flour, sugar, baking soda, and baking powder. In a separate bowl, combine yogurt, egg, vanilla, butter, and blueberries. Add to dry ingredients, stirring just until combined. (Batter will be very thick.) Pour into prepared muffin cups.
3. Bake in the preheated oven for 25 minutes. **Yield:** 1 dozen muffins.

Per serving: 205 calories, 4g protein, 38g carbohydrate, 5g fat, 1g fiber, 28mg cholesterol, 183mg sodium

Lemon-Poppy Seed Muffins II

Submitted by: **Karen Gibson**

"These muffins are full of melt-in-your-mouth lemony goodness! If you prefer, use less lemon juice for the glaze, substituting an equal amount of milk."

⅓	cup milk	1	tablespoon lemon zest
¼	cup vegetable oil	¼	teaspoon lemon extract
⅔	cup fat-free lemon-flavored yogurt	2½	teaspoons baking powder
1	egg	½	teaspoon baking soda
1¾	cups all-purpose flour	½	teaspoon salt
¼	cup white sugar	½	cup confectioners' sugar
2	tablespoons poppy seeds	2½	teaspoons lemon juice

1. Preheat oven to 400°F (200°C). Grease the bottoms only of 12 muffin cups or 24 miniature muffin cups.

2. Beat together the milk, oil, lemon yogurt, and egg. Stir in the flour, white sugar, poppy seeds, lemon zest, lemon extract, baking powder, baking soda, and salt. Mix until just combined. Spoon batter into prepared muffin cups.

3. In a separate bowl, stir together confectioners' sugar and lemon juice; mix until smooth and of drizzling consistency. Add drops of milk if thinning is necessary. Set aside.

4. Bake muffins in the preheated oven for 16 to 18 minutes for regular muffins, 10 to 12 minutes for miniature muffins, or until golden brown. Remove to wire racks; drizzle with glaze immediately.
Yield: 1 dozen muffins or 2 dozen mini muffins.

Per muffin: 173 calories, 4g protein, 27g carbohydrate, 6g fat, 1g fiber, 18mg cholesterol, 270mg sodium

◄ OUT-OF-THE-ORDINARY

Prep Time: 13 minutes

Cook Time: 18 minutes

Average Rating: ★★★★★

What other cooks have done:

"These muffins are great. I increased the oil to ⅓ cup and the yogurt to 1 cup, and I went hog wild with the lemon zest. They came out delicious!"

Lighter Banana Muffins

Submitted by: **Shelby Mendiguren**

"This banana bread has no oil or butter of any sort because it doesn't need any. Because this bread isn't greasy, it makes great muffins without the greasy bottoms I have experienced with other recipes. You can add walnuts, if desired."

FROM THE PANTRY ▶

Prep Time: 15 minutes

Cook Time: 25 minutes

Average Rating: ★★★★☆

What other cooks have done:

"I've made banana muffins many times, and I must say that these are the ultimate! I added a few more bananas. I was impressed by the way these puffed up so well. I also made muffin tops with this recipe simply by plopping the dough in circles on a baking sheet. Scrumptious!"

2	eggs, lightly beaten	1	teaspoon salt
3	very ripe bananas, mashed	¾	cup white sugar
2	cups all-purpose flour	1	teaspoon baking soda

1. Preheat oven to 350°F (175°C). Lightly grease a muffin pan or line with paper cups.
2. In a medium bowl, combine eggs and bananas. In a separate bowl, mix together flour, salt, sugar, and baking soda. Stir banana mixture into flour mixture. Spoon batter into prepared muffin cups.
3. Bake in the preheated oven for 20 to 25 minutes or until a toothpick inserted into center of a muffin comes out clean. **Yield:** 10 muffins.

Per muffin: 197 calories, 4g protein, 43g carbohydrate, 1g fat, 2g fiber, 42mg cholesterol, 372mg sodium

Oatmeal-Blueberry Muffins

Submitted by: **Sue Snow**

"These have a great texture and stay moist and tender for days—if they haven't all been eaten before then!"

FAMILY FAVORITE ▶

Prep Time: 10 minutes

Cook Time: 25 minutes

Average Rating: ★★★★☆

What other cooks have done:

"I was hesitant to use a tablespoon of baking powder, but the baked muffins had no baking powder taste to them at all. I increased the blueberries to 2 cups and baked these at night for breakfast the next day. We all loved them."

1¼	cups quick cooking oats	1	cup milk
1	cup all-purpose flour	1	egg
⅓	cup white sugar	¼	cup vegetable oil
1	tablespoon baking powder	1	cup blueberries
½	teaspoon salt		

1. Preheat oven to 425°F (220°C). Grease a muffin pan.
2. Combine oats, flour, sugar, baking powder, and salt. Mix in milk, egg, and oil, stirring just until dry ingredients are moistened. Fold in blueberries. Spoon batter into prepared muffin cups, filling two-thirds full.
3. Bake in the preheated oven for 20 to 25 minutes. **Yield:** 1 dozen muffins.

Per muffin: 156 calories, 4g protein, 22g carbohydrate, 6g fat, 2g fiber, 19mg cholesterol, 236mg sodium

Excellent and Healthy Cornbread

Submitted by: **Maria**

"This cornbread recipe contains no oil and tastes very, very good. Serve warm with honey or butter."

1	cup unbleached flour	¾	teaspoon salt
1	cup cornmeal	1	cup plain fat-free yogurt
¼	cup white sugar	2	eggs, lightly beaten
1	teaspoon baking soda		

1. Preheat oven to 400°F (200°C). Lightly grease an 8x8 inch baking pan.

2. In a large bowl, mix together flour, cornmeal, sugar, baking soda, and salt. Stir in yogurt and eggs. Stir just until well blended, being careful not to overmix. Pour batter into prepared pan.

3. Bake in the preheated oven for 20 to 25 minutes or until center of the bread springs back when gently pressed. **Yield:** 12 servings.

Per serving: 118 calories, 4g protein, 22g carbohydrate, 1g fat, 1g fiber, 36mg cholesterol, 280mg sodium

◄ **CLASSIC COMFORT FOOD**

Prep Time: 10 minutes

Cook Time: 25 minutes

Average Rating: ★★★★☆

What other cooks have done:

"So good! We prefer our cornbread spicy as opposed to sweet, so I cut back on the sugar slightly, added ½ cup whole kernel corn, and a heaping tablespoon of crushed chilies. Also, the cornbread has a slightly tangy taste from the yogurt, which gives it some pep."

Can't Tell They're Low-Fat Brownies

Submitted by: **Roberta Tripp**

"This is my mom's brownie recipe, but I changed it to make it lower in fat. My family loves it!"

½	cup all-purpose flour	2	tablespoons vegetable oil
6	tablespoons unsweetened cocoa powder	½	teaspoon vanilla extract
1	cup white sugar	1	(4 ounce) jar pureed prunes baby food
⅛	teaspoon salt	2	eggs, lightly beaten

1. Preheat oven to 350°F (175°C). Grease an 8x8 inch pan.

2. In a medium bowl, stir together flour, cocoa, sugar, and salt. Pour in oil, vanilla, prunes, and eggs. Mix until well blended. Spread batter evenly into prepared pan.

3. Bake in the preheated oven for 30 minutes or until top is shiny and a toothpick inserted into center comes out clean. **Yield:** 2 dozen.

Per brownie: 65 calories, 1g protein, 12g carbohydrate, 2g fat, 1g fiber, 18mg cholesterol, 224mg sodium

◄ **FAMILY FAVORITE**

Prep Time: 10 minutes

Cook Time: 30 minutes

Average Rating: ★★★★☆

What other cooks have done:

"I used regular applesauce in place of the prunes and doubled the recipe for a 9x13 inch pan. The result was a moist, chewy, and slightly cakelike brownie. I absolutely loved it and will certainly make it again and again!"

Heather's Healthy Oatmeal Surprises

Submitted by: **Heather**

"These oatmeal cookies are better for you than the average cookie. Whole wheat flour, peanut butter chips, chocolate chips, cinnamon, and nutmeg also give them more flavor. If you like oatmeal cookies, I urge you to try these!"

CROWD-PLEASER ▶

Prep Time: 20 minutes

Cook Time: 10 minutes per batch

Average Rating: ★★★★★

What other cooks have done:

"Instead of chocolate chips and peanut butter chips, I added white chocolate chips, dried cranberries, and toasted pecans. These cookies have awesome flavor and a great texture."

¾ cup butter, softened
½ cup white sugar
1 cup packed brown sugar
2 egg whites
1 egg
1 teaspoon vanilla extract
1½ cups whole wheat flour
1 teaspoon baking soda
1 teaspoon ground cinnamon
⅛ teaspoon ground nutmeg
½ teaspoon salt
3 cups quick cooking oats
½ cup peanut butter chips
½ cup semisweet chocolate chips

1. Preheat oven to 350°F (175°C).
2. In a large bowl, cream together the butter, white sugar, and brown sugar until light and fluffy. Add the egg whites and egg, 1 at a time, beating well after each addition; stir in vanilla. In a separate bowl, combine the flour, baking soda, cinnamon, nutmeg, and salt; gradually stir into the creamed mixture. Stir in the oats, peanut butter chips, and chocolate chips. Drop by rounded spoonfuls onto ungreased baking sheets.
3. Bake in the preheated oven for 8 to 10 minutes. Allow cookies to cool on baking sheets for 5 minutes before removing to wire racks to cool. **Yield:** 3 dozen.

Per cookie: 144 calories, 3g protein, 20g carbohydrate, 6g fat, 2g fiber, 16mg cholesterol, 122mg sodium

Healthy Banana Cookies

Submitted by: **K. Gailbrath**

"These cookies are nutritious as well as delicious."

5 INGREDIENTS OR LESS ▶

Prep Time: 15 minutes

Stand Time: 15 minutes

Cook Time: 20 minutes per batch

Average Rating: ★★★★★

What other cooks have done:

"These cookies were moist, chewy, and sweet. I used chopped dried apricots and raisins instead of dates; I also recommend adding spices like cinnamon and nutmeg."

3 ripe bananas
2 cups rolled oats
1 cup dates, pitted and chopped
⅓ cup vegetable oil
1 teaspoon vanilla extract

1. In a large bowl, mash the bananas. Stir in oats, dates, oil, and vanilla. Mix well and let stand for 15 minutes.
2. Preheat oven to 350°F (175°C). Drop dough by teaspoonfuls onto ungreased baking sheets.
3. Bake in the preheated oven for 20 minutes or until lightly brown. Remove to wire racks to cool. **Yield:** 3 dozen.

Per cookie: 59 calories, 1g protein, 9g carbohydrate, 2g fat, 1g fiber, 0mg cholesterol, 0mg sodium

Lighter Snickerdoodles

Submitted by: **Lisa**

"A less-fattening version of an old favorite. Now you can eat even more!"

¼	cup butter	2¾	cups all-purpose flour
1¾	cups white sugar, divided	2	teaspoons cream of tartar
4	ounces low-fat cream cheese	1	teaspoon baking soda
		¼	teaspoon salt
1	egg	2	teaspoons ground cinnamon
2	egg whites		

1. In a large bowl, cream together the butter, 1½ cups white sugar, and cream cheese. Beat in the egg and egg whites until smooth. In a separate bowl, sift together the flour, cream of tartar, baking soda, and salt; stir into the creamed mixture. Cover and refrigerate dough for at least 1 hour.

2. Preheat oven to 400°F (200°C).

3. In a small dish, mix together the remaining white sugar and the cinnamon. Roll the dough into walnut-sized balls and roll the balls in the cinnamon and sugar mixture. Place the balls at least 2 inches apart on ungreased baking sheets and flatten slightly.

4. Bake in the preheated oven for 8 to 10 minutes. Remove to wire racks to cool. **Yield:** 2 dozen.

Per cookie: 142 calories, 3g protein, 26g carbohydrate, 3g fat, 1g fiber, 17mg cholesterol, 118mg sodium

◄ FAMILY FAVORITE

Prep Time: 20 minutes

Chill Time: 1 hour

Cook Time: 10 minutes per batch

Average Rating: ★★★★☆

What other cooks have done:

"I doubled the recipe and used fat-free instead of low-fat cream cheese. Our family loves soft cookies, and these are perfect. I also made some with green and red sugar for Christmas."

Best Breakfast Cookies *(pictured on facing page)*

Submitted by: **Jennifer**

"The trick is to underbake these a little bit, and the result is the soft, cakelike cookie you know and love!"

KID-FRIENDLY ▶

Prep Time: 25 minutes

Cook Time: 10 minutes per batch

Average Rating: ★★★★☆

What other cooks have done:

"Yummy! I used oat bran flour for the regular flour. I also used chocolate-covered raisins in place of the regular raisins and the apricots. I used baby food prunes as well as pumpkin puree in place of the oil. They came out really good!"

12 prunes, pitted	¼ cup vegetable oil
2 cups packed brown sugar	2 tablespoons water
2½ cups rolled oats	5 egg whites, lightly beaten
4 cups all-purpose flour	1½ teaspoons vanilla extract
1 tablespoon baking soda	¾ cup raisins
1 teaspoon baking powder	¼ cup chopped walnuts
1 teaspoon salt	⅓ cup chopped dried apricots
1½ teaspoons ground cinnamon	

1. Preheat oven to 350°F (175°C). Grease baking sheets or line with parchment paper.
2. Place prunes in bowl of a food processor. Process prunes until pureed. Set aside.
3. In a large bowl, stir together the brown sugar, oats, flour, baking soda, baking powder, salt, and cinnamon. Make a well in the center and pour in pureed prunes, oil, water, egg whites, and vanilla. Mix until well blended. Stir in the raisins, walnuts, and apricots. Scoop cookies using an ice cream scoop or roll into golf ball-sized balls. Place cookies 2 inches apart on prepared baking sheets and flatten with wet hands. (Cookies will not flatten very much while baking.)
4. Bake in the preheated oven for 10 minutes or until edges are lightly browned. (Cookies will not get crisp.) Remove to wire racks to cool.
Yield: 2½ dozen.

Per cookie: 176 calories, 4g protein, 34g carbohydrate, 3g fat, 2g fiber, 0mg cholesterol, 218mg sodium

Best Breakfast Cookies

Strawberry-Angel Food Dessert,
page 128

Honeydew-Blueberry Soup, page 121

Sunflower Chicken Salad, page 125

Cookie Salad I, page 127

No-Cook Creations

Asparagus Sandwiches

Submitted by: **Jannell Langham**

"Something different and yummy. A friend served these finger sandwiches at a baby shower. I couldn't believe they were so easy! They can be made ahead of time; just cover with plastic wrap and refrigerate."

OUT-OF-THE-ORDINARY ▶

Prep Time: 20 minutes

Average Rating: ★★★★☆

What other cooks have done:

"I made these for my friend's baby shower. They turned out pretty, and I got a lot of compliments. I used shallots in the mayonnaise mixture instead of regular onion. I am making them again for my sister's wedding shower next month, and I think I will use fresh steamed asparagus."

1 (12 ounce) can asparagus spears, drained	Pinch seasoning salt
½ cup mayonnaise	1 (16 ounce) loaf white bread
2 tablespoons finely chopped onion	

1. Set asparagus spears onto paper towels to absorb excess liquid. In a small bowl, mix together the mayonnaise, onion, and seasoning salt. Remove crusts from bread slices and spread mayonnaise mixture thinly on each slice. Place a spear onto each slice and roll up. Cut each roll in half and arrange on a serving tray. Serve immediately or cover with plastic wrap and chill until serving. **Yield:** 48 sandwich rolls.

Per roll: 43 calories, 1g protein, 5g carbohydrate, 2g fat, 0g fiber, 1mg cholesterol, 85mg sodium

Ham Salad Pitas

Submitted by: **Denise Slauson**

"These stuffed pitas are a great use for leftovers! I combined a couple of different recipes to come up with this mixture. The almonds and grapes really complement the ham. You may also use chicken or turkey if you wish."

FAMILY FAVORITE ▶

Prep Time: 15 minutes

Average Rating: ★★★★☆

What other cooks have done:

"I toasted the almonds, which strengthened their taste, so I used less. I also used yogurt cheese instead of sour cream, but if you do that, you should reduce the amount of lemon juice, or the dish will be too tart."

1 cup sour cream	½ cup seedless green grapes, halved
2 tablespoons lemon juice	
1 teaspoon prepared mustard	3 tablespoons diced green onions
1 cup chopped cooked ham	
1 cup shredded mozzarella cheese	4 pita rounds, halved
¼ cup blanched slivered almonds	

1. Combine sour cream, lemon juice, and mustard in a bowl. Add ham, cheese, almonds, grapes, and onions. Toss lightly to coat.
2. Divide ham mixture evenly between pita pockets. **Yield:** 4 servings.

Per serving: 480 calories, 25g protein, 43g carbohydrate, 23g fat, 3g fiber, 72mg cholesterol, 514mg sodium

Chicken Salad Wraps

Submitted by: **Dawn**

"Great picnic or lunch sandwich with a salsa twist. For a spicier version, add some finely chopped jalapeño peppers."

2	(10 ounce) cans chunk chicken, drained and flaked
¼	cup chopped onion
¼	cup mayonnaise

¼	cup salsa
	Salt and ground black pepper to taste
6	(10 inch) flour tortillas
12	lettuce leaves

1. In a small bowl, mix together chicken, onion, mayonnaise, salsa, and salt and pepper to taste.
2. Line each tortilla with 2 lettuce leaves. Divide chicken mixture evenly among tortillas and roll up. **Yield:** 6 servings.

Per serving: 463 calories, 27g protein, 42g carbohydrate, 15g fat, 3g fiber, 63mg cholesterol, 915mg sodium

◄ KID-FRIENDLY

Prep Time: 10 minutes

Average Rating: ★★★★★

What other cooks have done:

"I used a roasted chicken from the supermarket instead of canned chicken, and I added a third of a jalapeño pepper and an extra tablespoon of fresh salsa from the local farmer's market. Perfect! Make extra because your teenagers will put this on anything!"

Easy Snack Wraps

Submitted by: **Joan**

"So easy to make, these bite-size wraps filled with turkey, cream cheese, and veggies are a great way to fill up an appetizer tray—and your hungry guests' bellies."

1	(8 ounce) package cream cheese, softened
12	(10 inch) flour tortillas
1	head lettuce

1	(6 ounce) package sliced deli turkey
2	cups shredded carrots
2	cups minced tomato

1. Spread cream cheese evenly over tortillas. Top cream cheese with lettuce leaves. Arrange the turkey slices in even layers over lettuce. Sprinkle carrots and tomato over turkey. Roll tortillas into wraps. Cut the wraps diagonally into bite-size pieces (5 pieces per tortilla). Secure with toothpicks. **Yield:** 5 dozen.

Per serving: 67 calories, 2g protein, 9g carbohydrate, 2g fat, 1g fiber, 5mg cholesterol, 116mg sodium

◄ CROWD-PLEASER

Prep Time: 15 minutes

Average Rating: ★★★★★

What other cooks have done:

"I make these for lunch and just throw in what I have in the fridge. I recommend mixing some powdered Ranch dressing mix into the cream cheese."

Chilled Beet Soup

Submitted by: **Rosemary**
"Canned beets are great for this recipe. You can save the juice from the canned beets, freeze it, and add it in place of the chilled water or ice. Try serving the soup with a dollop of sour cream."

1½ cups sour cream	1 cup crushed ice or cold
2 tablespoons lemon juice	water
½ small onion	Sour cream (optional)
1 cup cooked beets	

1. Place 1½ cups sour cream, lemon juice, onion, and beets in a food processor or blender and puree until mixture is smooth.
2. Add ice or cold water; chill for at least 20 minutes. Serve with a dollop of sour cream on top, if desired. **Yield:** 4 servings.

Per serving: 210 calories, 4g protein, 10g carbohydrate, 18g fat, 1g fiber, 38mg cholesterol, 81mg sodium

Swan's Summer Soup

Submitted by: **Nathaniel Swan**
"This is a refreshing cold summer soup. Be sure to use the freshest and ripest ingredients for the best flavor. Serve with a loaf of fresh, crusty bread and a little bowl of extra virgin olive oil for dipping."

4 large tomatoes	¼ cup chopped fresh cilantro
1 avocado, peeled, pitted, and diced	1 tablespoon fresh lemon juice
½ cup fresh corn kernels	Salt and ground black
2 tomatoes, diced	pepper to taste

1. Juice 4 large tomatoes using a juicer or puree in a blender or food processor.
2. In a medium bowl, combine the tomato juice, avocado, corn, diced tomatoes, cilantro, and lemon juice. Season with salt and pepper to taste.
Yield: 2 servings.

Per serving: 306 calories, 8g protein, 39g carbohydrate, 18g fat, 12g fiber, 0mg cholesterol, 65mg sodium

---

PARTY FOOD ▶

Prep Time: 10 minutes

Chill Time: 20 minutes

Average Rating: ★★★★★

What other cooks have done:

"I used the juice of a whole lemon, salt, lots of pepper, and an 8 ounce container of sour cream. I added water until it was the right consistency. This was the starter for a vegetarian dinner party, and everyone loved it!"

FREEZER FRESH ▶

Prep Time: 15 minutes

Average Rating: ★★★★★

What other cooks have done:

"This soup is so good that I can barely stand it. I'm a gazpacho junkie, so this dish couldn't have been tastier. I must admit that I cheated a bit. I used commercially canned tomato juice, but that just made it quicker."

Honeydew-Blueberry Soup *(pictured on page 114)*

Submitted by: **J. Carlson**
"A cold soup of honeydew and blueberries. Top with whipped topping, if desired."

1	honeydew melon	6	oatmeal cookies
1	pint blueberries		

1. Cut the melon from the rind and into chunks. Puree in a food processor or blender until smooth. Pour into a large bowl and stir blueberries into pureed melon. Chill until cold.

2. To serve, ladle soup into individual bowls and crumble an oatmeal cookie over each serving. **Yield:** 6 servings.

Per serving: 180 calories, 2g protein, 39g carbohydrate, 3g fat, 4g fiber, 0mg cholesterol, 83mg sodium

◄ 5 INGREDIENTS OR LESS
Prep Time: 5 minutes
Chill Time: 1 hour
Average Rating: ★★★★★

What other cooks have done:
"I had my honeydew chilled in the fridge before I cut it up, so this cut down on some of the chilling time. Also, I tried this without the oatmeal cookie, and while it was very good, the cookie added a little something extra. Be sure to make the cookie crumbles large. Everyone loved this."

Chilled Cantaloupe Soup

Submitted by: **Amanda**
"This very refreshing chilled fruit soup is great for luncheons. Garnish with mint, if desired."

1	cantaloupe, peeled, seeded, and cubed	1	tablespoon fresh lime juice
2	cups orange juice, divided	¼	teaspoon ground cinnamon
			Fresh mint sprigs (optional)

1. Place cantaloupe and ½ cup orange juice in a blender or food processor; process until smooth. Transfer to a large bowl. Stir in lime juice, cinnamon, and remaining orange juice. Cover and refrigerate for at least 1 hour. Garnish with mint, if desired. **Yield:** 6 servings.

Per serving: 70 calories, 1g protein, 17g carbohydrate, 0g fat, 1g fiber, 0mg cholesterol, 9mg sodium

◄ MAKE-AHEAD
Prep Time: 10 minutes
Chill Time: 1 hour
Average Rating: ★★★★★

What other cooks have done:
"My husband cannot usually tolerate orange juice, but this is one soup that he loves, and it loves him. Besides being absolutely delicious, it is so healthy and quickly made."

Cream of Mango Soup

Submitted by: **Suzisulzer**

"A refreshing, cool, and creamy soup made with mangoes. When in season, you may add blueberries or sliced strawberries as a garnish. Fat-free sour cream may be substituted for the half-and-half."

5 INGREDIENTS OR LESS ▶

Prep Time: 10 minutes

Chill Time: 20 minutes

Average Rating: ★★★★★

What other cooks have done:

"Really delicious! I used evaporated milk because I didn't have any half-and-half, and it was still nice and creamy!"

2	mangoes, peeled, seeded, and cubed	¼	cup white sugar
1	lemon, zested and juiced	1½	cups half-and-half

1. Place the all ingredients into a blender or food processor. Cover and process until smooth and creamy. Serve chilled. **Yield:** 3 servings.

Per serving: 319 calories, 5g protein, 49g carbohydrate, 14g fat, 4g fiber, 45mg cholesterol, 54mg sodium

Chilled Strawberry Soup

Submitted by: **Michelle**

"Serve this in chilled soup bowls and garnish with fresh sliced strawberries."

MAKE-AHEAD ▶

Prep Time: 10 minutes

Chill Time: overnight

Average Rating: ★★★★☆

What other cooks have done:

"Absolutely wow! My kids each had two servings because they couldn't wait until dinner. I added ground cinnamon because it took the flavors to another level. The cinnamon gave it a nice bit of color as well."

2	cups frozen strawberries	½	cup sour cream
2	cups milk	2	tablespoons white sugar
1	cup heavy whipping cream		(or to taste)

1. Puree all ingredients in a blender or food processor until smooth. Chill overnight before serving. **Yield:** 6 servings.

Per serving: 252 calories, 4g protein, 15g carbohydrate, 20g fat, 1g fiber, 69mg cholesterol, 67mg sodium

Anytime Fruit Salad

Submitted by: **Tiffany**

"Oranges, pineapple, cottage cheese, and whipped topping combine for a refreshing, slightly sweet salad. My mom always makes this recipe, and the reason I gave it this name is because if there is ever any left, I eat it anytime."

1	(24 ounce) container cottage cheese	2	(11 ounce) cans mandarin oranges, drained
1	(12 ounce) container frozen whipped topping, thawed	1	(20 ounce) can pineapple chunks, drained
1	(6 ounce) package orange-flavored gelatin		

1. In a large bowl, combine the cottage cheese, whipped topping, and gelatin. Stir in the oranges and pineapple. Chill. **Yield:** 6 servings.

Per serving: 516 calories, 18g protein, 70g carbohydrate, 19g fat, 1g fiber, 17mg cholesterol, 540mg sodium

◄ **5 INGREDIENTS OR LESS**

Prep Time: 10 minutes

Chill Time: 20 minutes

Average Rating: ★★★★★

What other cooks have done:

"This fruit salad was light, fluffy, and delicious! I made it for my husband to take to work for a potluck, and I also sent a salad to school with my child to enjoy with her classmates. Everyone loved it!"

Red Bean Salad with Feta and Peppers

Submitted by: **Daylene**

"A tasty, nutrient-packed salad that can be eaten by itself or as a side dish. Makes a great lunch the next day. Add more lemon juice and olive oil if you like your salad to have a lot of dressing. You may use garbanzo beans in place of kidney beans if you prefer."

1	(15 ounce) can kidney beans	1	cup crumbled feta cheese
1	red bell pepper, chopped	⅓	cup chopped fresh parsley
2	cups chopped cabbage	1	clove garlic, minced
2	green onions, chopped	2	tablespoons lemon juice
		1	tablespoon olive oil

1. Rinse kidney beans under cold water. Drain well.
2. In a large salad bowl, combine beans, red bell pepper, cabbage, onions, feta, parsley, garlic, lemon juice, and olive oil. Cover and refrigerate until serving. **Yield:** 4 servings.

Per serving: 244 calories, 12g protein, 24g carbohydrate, 12g fat, 9g fiber, 33mg cholesterol, 789mg sodium

◄ **MEATLESS MAIN DISH**

Prep Time: 12 minutes

Average Rating: ★★★★★

What other cooks have done:

"A very tasty salad. I have made it a few times, and the only changes I made were to add two more cloves of garlic and a small red onion instead of two green onions. I used flavored feta cheese, too."

Sweet Pepper-Balsamic Bean Salad

Submitted by: **Kathy Miller**

"Marinated beans that pack a punch! If you refrigerate this salad overnight, it gets more tasty. You can vary the recipe by substituting black beans for the kidney beans, if desired."

1 cup chopped yellow bell pepper
1 (15 ounce) can kidney beans, drained and rinsed
1 (7 ounce) jar roasted red bell peppers, drained
12 cherry tomatoes, halved
2 tablespoons chopped fresh parsley
3 tablespoons balsamic vinegar
1 tablespoon Worcestershire sauce
1 teaspoon white sugar
1 teaspoon dried basil
1 teaspoon chopped garlic
½ head lettuce

1. In a large bowl, combine yellow pepper, beans, roasted red bell peppers, and tomatoes.

2. In a jar with a tight-fitting lid, combine the parsley, vinegar, Worcestershire sauce, sugar, basil, and garlic; shake well. Pour over vegetables; toss gently. Cover and let stand at room temperature for 30 minutes or refrigerate overnight.

3. To serve, place leaves of lettuce on individual salad plates and top with bean mixture. **Yield:** 4 servings.

Per serving: 144 calories, 8g protein, 28g carbohydrate, 1g fat, 9g fiber, 0mg cholesterol, 1127mg sodium

The No-Cook Kitchen

When you're too busy to cook—or it's too hot outside to turn on the oven—bringing home take-out doesn't seem out of the question, but fast food just isn't the same as something homemade. If you have leftovers waiting in the fridge, dinner is just a microwave away. Crisp salads full of veggies and chilled summer soups are also easy to throw together. Pick up a rotisserie chicken or cooked, peeled shrimp from the grocery for use in salads and soups. And your choices don't end there!

Can Do

If you're looking for a quick side dish or main-dish salad, crank up that can opener. There's not much nutritional difference between fresh, frozen, and canned vegetables, but opening up a can of beans can get you out of the kitchen quicker than cooking up a batch of fresh beans. Canned chicken or tuna can also make quick work of a main-dish salad or hearty sandwich. Keep recipes for chicken salad and tuna salad on hand for a tasty, oven-free option.

The Art of the Sandwich

Usually when someone says "sandwich," a boring combo of cold cuts and limp slices of bread comes to mind. Next time, take full advantage of the range of breads offered by your grocery's bakery section. Chicken salad on a croissant makes for a more interesting meal than chicken salad on plain ol' bread. Along with croissants, the next time you go grocery shopping, keep an eye out for breads and rolls that use whole grains or other extra ingredients that add flavor. Pick up a package of tortillas, too. Wraps give sandwich meats a fun spin and can work healthy veggies into your meal. Instead of dreading lunch or dinner, your family will look forward to a no-cook meal.

For more information, visit **Allrecipes.com**

Cashew-Avocado Chicken Salad

Submitted by: **Cathy**

"Try this chicken salad when you really want a treat! This recipe makes sandwiches, but it can be served over lettuce as an alternative."

4	boneless chicken breast halves, cooked and shredded	1	avocado, peeled, pitted, and diced
⅓	cup Ranch salad dressing		Salt and ground black pepper to taste
1½	tablespoons chopped fresh dill weed	12	slices bread, toasted
1	cup cashews	12	slices precooked bacon
		6	slices Swiss cheese

1. In a large bowl, mix the cooked chicken, dressing, dill weed, cashews, and avocado. Season with salt and pepper to taste. Cover and chill at least 30 minutes.

2. Spread even amounts of the chicken mixture onto 6 slices of toasted bread. Top each with 2 slices bacon and 1 slice Swiss cheese. Top with remaining bread slices to make sandwiches. **Yield:** 6 servings.

Per serving: 871 calories, 40g protein, 36g carbohydrate, 63g fat, 4g fiber, 115mg cholesterol, 1181mg sodium

◄ RESTAURANT FARE

Prep Time: 20 minutes

Chill Time: 30 minutes

Average Rating: ★★★★★

What other cooks have done:

"I like this as a salad served on greens with baguette slices on the side. I serve it with cherry tomatoes and black olives as a garnish. You can adjust the ingredients to suit your own tastes."

---

10 minutes or less

Sunflower Chicken Salad *(pictured on page 115)*

Submitted by: **Brenda Loop**

"Kids love this easy chicken salad with grapes and sunflower seeds."

2	cups cubed cooked chicken	½	cup mayonnaise
1	cup cubed Cheddar cheese		Salt and ground black pepper to taste
¼	cup sunflower seeds		
¼	cup thinly sliced celery	4	croissants or lettuce leaves (optional)
¼	cup seedless green grapes, halved		
¼	cup seedless red grapes, halved		

1. In a large bowl, combine the chicken, cheese, sunflower seeds, celery, green grapes, red grapes, mayonnaise, and salt and pepper to taste. Mix together and serve on croissants or lettuce leaves, if desired. **Yield:** 4 servings.

Per serving: 531 calories, 30g protein, 7g carbohydrate, 43g fat, 1g fiber, 105mg cholesterol, 421mg sodium

◄ FAMILY FAVORITE

Prep Time: 10 minutes

Average Rating: ★★★★☆

What other cooks have done:

"Absolutely delicious—and this opinion comes from someone who doesn't (or didn't) like chicken salad! This would also be good with toasted pecans."

Almond Chicken Salad

Submitted by: **Linda W.**
"This is a great summer salad that can be prepared ahead of time so you can enjoy the day."

MAKE-AHEAD ▶

Prep Time: 20 minutes

Average Rating: ★★★★★

What other cooks have done:

"I added mandarin orange segments for a bit of moisture and sweetness, and they were a nice addition."

4	green onions, thinly sliced	2	tablespoons white sugar
1	large carrot, shredded	2	tablespoons distilled white vinegar
1	red bell pepper, cut into ½ inch pieces	1½	tablespoons sesame oil
½	pound sugar snap peas, halved	1	tablespoon teriyaki sauce
2	cups chopped cooked chicken	1	tablespoon powdered mustard
½	cup fresh cilantro leaves		Pita rounds or lettuce leaves
½	cup blanched slivered almonds, toasted		

1. In a large bowl, mix together the onions, carrot, red bell pepper, peas, chicken, cilantro, and almonds. Set aside.
2. In a small bowl, whisk together the sugar, vinegar, sesame oil, teriyaki sauce, and mustard until smooth. Pour over salad mixture and toss until coated. Serve in pita pockets or on a bed of lettuce leaves. **Yield:** 4 servings.

Per serving: 341 calories, 27g protein, 20g carbohydrate, 17g fat, 5g fiber, 54mg cholesterol, 236mg sodium

Turkey Salad

Submitted by: **Gloria Burris**
"Spread it on crackers! Make it into a sandwich! This melt-in-your-mouth appetizer will have your whole party jumping! It's great during the holidays or anytime."

HOLIDAY FARE ▶

Prep Time: 20 minutes

Chill Time: overnight

Average Rating: ★★★★★

What other cooks have done:

"This is really good and simple! I didn't have a red bell pepper, so I used green. It still needed something red, so I added ½ cup of fresh chopped cranberries and served it over leaf lettuce."

¾	pound cooked turkey meat	2	tablespoons prepared Dijon-style mustard
2	stalks celery	1	tablespoon cider vinegar
2	green onions	1	teaspoon white sugar
½	red bell pepper	¼	teaspoon salt
3	tablespoons mayonnaise		

1. Place cooked turkey meat, celery, green onions, and red bell pepper in a blender or food processor. Finely chop using the pulse setting.
2. Transfer the turkey mixture to a medium bowl. Mix in mayonnaise, prepared Dijon-style mustard, cider vinegar, sugar, and salt. Cover and refrigerate overnight before serving. **Yield:** 24 servings.

Per serving: 40 calories, 4g protein, 1g carbohydrate, 2g fat, 0g fiber, 12mg cholesterol, 79mg sodium

20 minutes or less

Apple Coleslaw

Submitted by: **Aunt Mamie**

"This is our favorite coleslaw recipe—a yummy combo of fruit and veggies in a sweet dressing."

3	cups chopped cabbage	2	green onions, finely chopped
1	unpeeled red apple, cored and chopped	⅓	cup mayonnaise
1	unpeeled Granny Smith apple, cored and chopped	⅓	cup packed brown sugar
1	carrot, grated	1	tablespoon lemon juice (or to taste)
½	cup finely chopped red bell pepper		

1. In a large bowl, combine cabbage, red apple, green apple, carrot, red bell pepper, and green onions. In a small bowl, mix together mayonnaise, brown sugar, and lemon juice. Pour dressing over salad and toss until blended. **Yield:** 6 servings.

Per serving: 138 calories, 1g protein, 25g carbohydrate, 5g fat, 3g fiber, 3mg cholesterol, 105mg sodium

◄ COMPANY IS COMING

Prep Time: 15 minutes

Average Rating: ★★★★

What other cooks have done:

"This recipe was very good and quick. I cheated by using a bag of coleslaw mix, and I left out the onions and peppers. Next time, I will try adding some celery and grapes."

30 minutes or less

Cookie Salad I *(pictured on page 116)*

Submitted by: **JT**

"This is my mom's recipe. Serve this treat as parfaits, a salad, or a pie. To serve as a pie, pour into a graham cracker or cookie crust and chill before serving."

2	(3.4 ounce) packages instant vanilla pudding mix	2	(11 ounce) cans mandarin oranges, drained
2	cups buttermilk	½	(11.5 ounce) package fudge stripe cookies
1	(12 ounce) container frozen whipped topping, thawed	1	(12 ounce) container frozen whipped topping, thawed
1	(20 ounce) can pineapple chunks, drained		Mandarin orange slices

1. In a large bowl, mix together pudding mix and buttermilk. Beat with an electric mixer for 2 minutes. Fold in the whipped topping. Mix in the pineapple chunks and mandarin oranges. Chill 10 minutes or until ready to serve.
2. Crush cookies. Sprinkle a layer of cookie crumbs in the bottoms of 16 parfait glasses. In each glass, layer ¼ cup pudding mixture, a sprinkling of cookie crumbs, and 2 tablespoons whipped topping. Repeat layers. Top with additional mandarin orange slices. **Yield:** 16 servings.

Per serving: 495 calories, 7g protein, 72g carbohydrate, 22g fat, 2g fiber, 7mg cholesterol, 303mg sodium

◄ PARTY FOOD

Prep Time: 12 minutes

Chill Time: 10 minutes

Average Rating: ★★★★

What other cooks have done:

"This recipe is a favorite in my family. It's also excellent with sliced bananas or freshly cut strawberries. I have also used frozen strawberries with good results."

Strawberry-Angel Food
Dessert *(pictured on page 114)*

Submitted by: **Kelli**

"Angel food cake pieces are topped with sweetened cream cheese, whipped topping, and strawberries in a glaze in this chilled, layered dessert."

1 (10 inch) angel food cake	1 quart fresh strawberries, sliced
2 (8 ounce) packages cream cheese, softened	1 (13.5 ounce) jar strawberry glaze
1 cup white sugar	
1 (8 ounce) container frozen whipped topping, thawed	

1. Crumble cake into a 9x13 inch dish or trifle dish. Press cake down.
2. In a large bowl, cream together cream cheese and sugar until fluffy. Fold in whipped topping. Spread cream cheese mixture over cake.
3. In a bowl, combine strawberries and glaze until strawberries are evenly coated. Spread over cream cheese layer. Serve immediately or chill until ready to serve. **Yield:** 18 servings.

Per serving: 260 calories, 3g protein, 36g carbohydrate, 11g fat, 1g fiber, 27mg cholesterol, 242mg sodium

Biscuit Tortoni

Submitted by: **Mary Ann**

"Bursting with flavor, this dessert is a great finale for a dinner party or cookout. To serve, spoon into individual old-fashioned ice cream dishes or custard cups."

5 ounces amarettini cookies

3 tablespoons dark rum	1 cup heavy whipping cream, chilled
½ cup chopped blanched almonds, toasted	3 tablespoons brandy
¾ cup semisweet chocolate chips	1 quart vanilla ice cream, softened

1. Crush the cookies into ½ inch pieces by wrapping in a tea towel and tapping lightly with a rolling pin or mallet. (Do not crush into small pieces.) Place cookie pieces in a medium bowl and sprinkle with rum. Toss with almonds and chocolate chips. Set aside.
2. In a large bowl, beat cream with an electric mixer until thickened. Pour in brandy and beat until soft peaks form. Spoon whipped cream over cookie mixture. In same large bowl, beat ice cream just until smooth (with a flat whip). Fold cookie and cream mixture into ice cream. Freeze overnight or until firm. **Yield:** 8 servings.

Per serving: 472 calories, 7g protein, 42g carbohydrate, 30g fat, 2g fiber, 70mg cholesterol, 77mg sodium

No-Bake Rum Balls

Submitted by: **Refugio L.**
"A holiday favorite! Try using brandy in place of the rum."

2½	cups crushed vanilla wafers	¼	cup rum
1	cup confectioners' sugar		Additional confectioners'
2	tablespoons cocoa powder		sugar
1	cup chopped walnuts		
3	tablespoons dark corn syrup		

1. In a medium bowl, mix together the vanilla wafers, 1 cup sugar, and cocoa. Stir in the chopped walnuts, corn syrup, and rum. Mix until well blended.
2. Form dough into 2 inch balls and roll in additional confectioners' sugar. Store in an airtight container. **Yield:** 3 dozen.

Per candy: 103 calories, 1g protein, 14g carbohydrate, 5g fat, 1g fiber, 0mg cholesterol, 41mg sodium

◄ HOLIDAY GIFT GIVING

Prep Time: 15 minutes

Average Rating: ★★★★★

What other cooks have done:
"I was putting a little care package together for a family that is moving, and I decided to make some Christmas cookies since I won't be seeing them during the holidays. Well, these rum balls were the easiest and best-tasting treats in the package."

Cookie Balls

Submitted by: **Annette**
"Only three ingredients! Decorate with chocolate jimmies or colored sprinkles immediately after dipping."

1	pound chocolate sandwich cookies, crushed	1	pound vanilla-flavored candy coating, melted
1	(8 ounce) package cream cheese, softened		

1. In a large mixing bowl, combine crushed cookies and cream cheese to form a stiff dough. Roll into balls and dip with a fork into melted candy coating. Let rest on wax paper 15 minutes or until set. **Yield:** 3 dozen.

Per candy: 149 calories, 2g protein, 17g carbohydrate, 9g fat, 0g fiber, 9mg cholesterol, 106mg sodium

◄ KID-FRIENDLY

Prep Time: 20 minutes

Stand Time: 15 minutes

Average Rating: ★★★★★

What other cooks have done:
"This recipe was good, but I altered it by adding 1 cup melted chocolate to the cream cheese mixture, and I let it cool so that it would be easier to work with. I used a melon baller to make the balls and then dipped the balls into chocolate rather than vanilla candy coating. Be sure to let the chocolate-covered balls rest on a wire rack so that they won't form a chocolate 'heel.'"

Creamy Orange Fudge

Submitted by: **Karen**

"White chocolate, cream cheese, confectioners' sugar, and orange extract are the only ingredients in this no-cook orange-flavored fudge."

2   (8 ounce) packages cream cheese, softened
2   pounds white chocolate, melted and slightly cooled
6¾   cups confectioners' sugar
1   tablespoon orange extract

1. Beat cream cheese and melted chocolate until well blended. Add confectioners' sugar and beat until mixture is smooth. Stir in orange extract. Spread in an 8x8 inch dish and let set before cutting into squares. Store in refrigerator. **Yield:** 3 dozen.

Per candy: 254 calories, 2g protein, 34g carbohydrate, 13g fat, 0g fiber, 15mg cholesterol, 63mg sodium

Easy Devonshire Cream

Submitted by: **Sandie Tarp**

"A wonderful topping for scones, or use as a dip for fruit."

1   (3 ounce) package cream cheese, softened
1   tablespoon white sugar
Pinch salt
1   cup whipping cream

1. In a medium bowl, cream together cream cheese, sugar, and salt. Beat in cream until soft peaks form. Chill until serving. **Yield:** 16 servings.

Per serving: 73 calories, 1g protein, 1g carbohydrate, 7g fat, 0g fiber, 26mg cholesterol, 46mg sodium

Chewy Chocolate Candies

Submitted by: **Diane Blanchard**

"These will remind you of a famous chocolate candy. Let the dough rest for a few minutes after kneading to make rolling easier."

2 tablespoons butter, melted	3 cups confectioners' sugar, divided
2 (1 ounce) squares unsweetened chocolate, melted and cooled	¾ cup powdered milk
½ cup light corn syrup	1 teaspoon vanilla extract

1. In a medium mixing bowl, stir together butter and chocolate. Beat in corn syrup, 2 cups confectioners' sugar, powdered milk, and vanilla. (Dough will be stiff.)

2. Sprinkle a work surface with the remaining 1 cup confectioners' sugar. Turn dough out onto work surface and knead until remaining sugar is incorporated. Shape into small logs and wrap in wax paper. **Yield:** 25 servings.

Per candy: 108 calories, 2g protein, 22g carbohydrate, 2g fat, 0g fiber, 3mg cholesterol, 37mg sodium

◄ PARTY FOOD

Prep Time: 45 minutes

Average Rating: ★★★★★

What other cooks have done:

"I made these candies to put in baskets at a party, and they didn't last the evening before they were all gone!"

Blueberry Salad

Submitted by: **Robin**

"This dessert salad can be changed around to suit your taste."

2 (3 ounce) packages raspberry-flavored gelatin	1 (8 ounce) package cream cheese, softened
2 cups hot water	½ cup white sugar
1 (20 ounce) can crushed pineapple, drained	1 cup sour cream
1 (21 ounce) can blueberry pie filling	1 teaspoon vanilla extract

1. Combine gelatin and hot water; stir until dissolved. Stir in pineapple and blueberry pie filling. Pour into a 9x13 inch dish and chill 30 minutes or until firm.

2. Cream together cream cheese and sugar. Beat in sour cream and vanilla. Spread over firm gelatin. Chill until serving. **Yield:** 15 servings.

Per serving: 214 calories, 3g protein, 33g carbohydrate, 9g fat, 1g fiber, 23mg cholesterol, 95mg sodium

◄ COVERED-DISH FAVORITE

Prep Time: 10 minutes

Chill Time: 30 minutes

Average Rating: ★★★★★

What other cooks have done:

"This recipe is absolutely delicious and easy to make! It tastes like a blueberry cheesecake and has a surprise tang from the pineapple. Next time I make it, I'll pour the fruit and gelatin mix into a couple of prebaked graham cracker pie crusts. I recommend using some fresh blueberries for decorating the top of the dessert."

Easy Berry Parfait

Submitted by: **Amy Frey**

"This is a quick and easy way to top off any meal with the light taste of sweet berries. You can use fresh seasonal berries, but the frozen ones work just as well. Top with a few berries and mint leaves for garnish."

⅓   cup blueberries
⅓   cup strawberries
1   (8 ounce) container frozen whipped topping, thawed
½   cup raspberries
½   cup blackberries
1   pint vanilla frozen yogurt

1. In a blender, combine blueberries, strawberries, and whipped topping. Blend until smooth. Transfer to a mixing bowl and fold in raspberries and blackberries. Layer the berry mixture with the frozen yogurt in 6 dessert glasses, finishing with a berry layer. Serve immediately. **Yield:** 6 servings.

Per serving: 186 calories, 3g protein, 24g carbohydrate, 7g fat, 2g fiber, 3mg cholesterol, 38mg sodium

Banana Split Ice Cream Pie

Submitted by: **Star Pooley**

"Who doesn't love a good old-fashioned banana split? How about a pie that combines all the ingredients of this favorite! Almonds may be used in place of walnuts."

2   bananas, sliced
1   (9 inch) prepared chocolate cookie crumb crust
1   quart strawberry ice cream, softened
1   (20 ounce) can crushed pineapple, drained
1   cup whipping cream
¼   cup chopped walnuts
¼   cup maraschino cherries (optional)

1. Arrange bananas over bottom of crust. Spread ice cream in an even layer over bananas. Top with drained pineapple. Whip the cream and spread over top. Sprinkle with nuts.
2. Place pie in freezer for 4 hours or overnight until firm. Garnish with cherries, if desired. **Yield:** 8 servings.

Per serving: 402 calories, 4g protein, 45g carbohydrate, 25g fat, 2g fiber, 49mg cholesterol, 217mg sodium

Avocado Pie

Submitted by: **Sally Owens**

"This deliciously unusual pie is easy to make and requires no baking! Garnish with whipped topping."

2   avocados, peeled, pitted, and pureed
½   cup lemon juice
1   (14 ounce) can sweetened condensed milk

1   (9 inch) prepared graham cracker crust
    Frozen whipped topping

1. In a medium mixing bowl, combine avocado, lemon juice, and condensed milk. Blend well and pour into graham cracker crust. Chill 30 minutes or overnight before serving. Garnish with whipped topping. **Yield:** 8 servings.

Per serving: 288 calories, 4g protein, 34g carbohydrate, 17g fat, 3g fiber, 6mg cholesterol, 198mg sodium

◄ **OUT-OF-THE-ORDINARY**

Prep Time: 10 minutes

Chill Time: 30 minutes

Average Rating: ★★★★☆

What other cooks have done:

"Everyone declared this pie a winner and went back for seconds. This definitely has a lemony taste, so you may want to cut back if you don't like tartness."

Double-Layer Pumpkin Pie

Submitted by: **Joyce**

"Rich and creamy, this decadent pumpkin pie will earn raves as the centerpiece of your holiday dessert table."

½   (8 ounce) package cream cheese, softened
1   tablespoon milk
1   tablespoon white sugar
1½ cups frozen whipped topping, thawed
1   (9 inch) prepared graham cracker crust
1   cup cold milk

2   (3.4 ounce) packages instant vanilla pudding mix
1   (15 ounce) can unsweetened pumpkin
1   teaspoon ground cinnamon
½   teaspoon ground ginger
¼   teaspoon ground cloves

1. In a large bowl, whisk together cream cheese, 1 tablespoon milk, and sugar until smooth. Gently stir in whipped topping. Spread in bottom of crust.

2. Pour 1 cup cold milk into a large bowl and thoroughly mix in pudding mix, pumpkin, cinnamon, ginger, and cloves. When thickened, spread over cream cheese layer.

3. Refrigerate 4 hours or overnight until set. **Yield:** 8 servings.

Per serving: 356 calories, 4g protein, 51g carbohydrate, 16g fat, 2g fiber, 18mg cholesterol, 693mg sodium

◄ **HOLIDAY FARE**

Prep Time: 20 minutes

Chill Time: overnight

Average Rating: ★★★★★

What other cooks have done:

"This is a great recipe—a much lighter version of pumpkin pie. Use ⅓-less-fat cream cheese and fat-free, sugar-free pudding mix for an even lighter take on a holiday classic."

Mississippi Mud Pie I

Submitted by: **Holly**
"Very easy and deliciously creamy!"

What other cooks have done:

"This recipe was a hit at a family gathering I took it to. It makes two 8 inch pies. I made one with a chocolate cookie crust and one with a vanilla cookie crust."

2   cups graham cracker crumbs
¼   cup white sugar
½   cup butter, softened
1   (12 ounce) container frozen whipped topping, thawed and divided
¾   cup white sugar
1   (8 ounce) package cream cheese, softened
1   (3.9 ounce) package instant chocolate pudding mix
1   (3.4 ounce) package instant butterscotch pudding mix
3   cups milk

1. Thoroughly blend graham cracker crumbs, ¼ cup sugar, and butter. Press firmly in bottom of a 9x13 inch pan.
2. Blend together half the whipped topping, ¾ cup sugar, and softened cream cheese. Spread mixture on top of crust.
3. Whip together puddings and milk and spread on top of cream cheese mixture. Top with remaining whipped topping. Chill 30 minutes or overnight until ready to serve. **Yield:** 12 servings.

Per serving: 438 calories, 5g protein, 53g carbohydrate, 24g fat, 1g fiber, 46mg cholesterol, 510mg sodium

Appetizers & Beverages

Fig and Olive Tapenade

Submitted by: **Anne**

"This is an easy gourmet appetizer. I've brought it to several parties, and it is always a hit! I often add some chopped green olives to the olive mixture and a little more balsamic vinegar. Goat cheese may be used in place of the cream cheese. Serve with slices of French bread or crackers."

COMPANY IS COMING ▶

Prep Time: 15 minutes

Cook Time: 15 minutes

Chill Time: overnight

Average Rating: ★★★★★

What other cooks have done:

"Not reading the recipe correctly, I pureed the ingredients. Although it was a fantastic spread, I'll remember to finely chop the ingredients next time so it has the consistency of chutney instead."

⅓ cup finely chopped walnuts
1 cup finely chopped dried figs
½ cup water
1 tablespoon olive oil
2 tablespoons balsamic vinegar
1 teaspoon dried rosemary
1 teaspoon dried thyme
¼ teaspoon cayenne pepper
⅔ cup chopped kalamata olives
2 cloves garlic, minced
Salt and ground black pepper to taste
1 (8 ounce) package cream cheese

1. Preheat oven to 350°F (175°C).

2. Place walnuts in a single layer on a baking sheet. Bake in the preheated oven for 10 minutes or until lightly browned and fragrant.

3. Meanwhile, combine figs and water in a saucepan over medium heat. Bring to a boil and cook until figs are tender and liquid has reduced. Remove from heat and stir in the olive oil, balsamic vinegar, rosemary, thyme, and cayenne pepper. Add olives and garlic and mix well. Season with salt and black pepper to taste. Cover and refrigerate overnight.

4. To serve, unwrap cream cheese and place on a serving platter. Spoon tapenade over cheese and sprinkle with walnuts. **Yield:** 6 servings.

Per serving: 355 calories, 5g protein, 27g carbohydrate, 27g fat, 5g fiber, 41mg cholesterol, 522mg sodium

Roasted Tomato Salsa I

Submitted by: **Katherine**

"This chunky, smoky salsa tastes amazing with tortilla chips. Roasted tomatoes, garlic, onion, and jalapeño are blended with cilantro and cumin to create one of the tastiest and easiest Mexican-inspired recipes you'll ever try."

12	roma (plum) tomatoes	1	teaspoon ground cumin
2	cloves garlic, unpeeled	¼	teaspoon salt
1	small onion, quartered	3	tablespoons fresh lime juice
1	jalapeño pepper	¼	cup chopped fresh cilantro
1½	tablespoons olive oil		

1. Preheat broiler.
2. In a medium baking dish, place tomatoes, garlic, onion, and jalapeño pepper. Drizzle with olive oil.
3. Checking often, broil in the preheated oven for 5 to 10 minutes or until outsides of vegetables are charred.
4. Remove vegetables from oven. Remove and discard tomato cores, jalapeño stem, and garlic skins.
5. In a food processor, coarsely chop the charred vegetables. Transfer to a medium bowl and mix in cumin, salt, lime juice, and cilantro.
Yield: 24 servings.

Per serving: 17 calories, 0g protein, 2g carbohydrate, 1g fat, 0g fiber, 0mg cholesterol, 28mg sodium

◄ HOT & SPICY

Prep Time: 20 minutes

Cook Time: 10 minutes

Average Rating: ★★★★☆

What other cooks have done:

"Great salsa! The first time I made it, I thought that the charred skin was to be removed from all the veggies before blending. I tried it both ways and found the charred skin adds a lot of flavor. I core the tomatoes and remove the stem and seeds from the jalapeño, cut them in two, and place them skin side up in the baking dish before broiling; it's faster and not as messy. I use this sauce as a side dish with chicken or beef, too."

Creamy Veggie Fondue

Submitted by: **Al P.**

"This is my spin on a popular cheese fondue. Have fun with it and incorporate the cheeses and veggies you like. Serve with veggies and breadsticks."

CROWD-PLEASER ▶

Prep Time: 15 minutes

Cook Time: 20 minutes

Average Rating: ★★★★★

What other cooks have done:

"I could have eaten the whole thing by myself! I served it with cubed French bread, broccoli and cauliflower florets, fresh mushrooms, and green peppers. Fabulous!"

¼ cup white wine
1 (8 ounce) package shredded Cheddar cheese
1 (8 ounce) package shredded Monterey Jack cheese
1 (8 ounce) package cream cheese, softened
¼ cup chopped green onions
¼ cup frozen chopped spinach, thawed and drained
1 teaspoon powdered mustard
1 teaspoon cayenne pepper
1 teaspoon garlic powder
1 teaspoon coarsely ground black pepper
¼ cup milk

1. In a medium saucepan over medium heat, mix together white wine, Cheddar cheese, Monterey Jack cheese, and cream cheese. Cook, stirring frequently, until melted, about 10 minutes.

2. Stir in green onions, spinach, powdered mustard, cayenne pepper, garlic powder, and black pepper. Add milk. Continue cooking until all ingredients are well blended, about 10 minutes.

3. Transfer mixture to a double boiler or fondue pot to keep warm while serving. **Yield:** 32 servings.

Per serving: 83 calories, 4g protein, 1g carbohydrate, 7g fat, 0g fiber, 21mg cholesterol, 104mg sodium

White Pizza Dip

Submitted by: **Juliet**

"This is a delicious garlic dip. Stir your favorite pizza toppings into the mixture before baking to add extra flavor."

FAMILY FAVORITE ▶

Prep Time: 5 minutes

Cook Time: 30 minutes

Average Rating: ★★★★★

What other cooks have done:

"I've made this numerous times, all to rave reviews. Pepperoni, sausage, crushed red pepper flakes, mushrooms, and artichoke hearts make great additions. I've also used crunchy breadsticks and pita rounds cut into triangles as dippers."

1 (1.2 ounce) package herb and garlic soup mix
1 cup sour cream
1 cup ricotta cheese
1 cup shredded mozzarella cheese, divided
1 (16 ounce) loaf French bread, sliced

1. Preheat oven to 350°F (175°C).

2. In a medium mixing bowl, combine soup mix, sour cream, ricotta cheese, and ¾ cup mozzarella cheese. Transfer mixture to a 1 quart casserole dish. Sprinkle remaining mozzarella cheese over the top of the mixture.

3. Bake in the preheated oven, uncovered, for 30 minutes. Serve hot with bread slices. **Yield:** 10 servings.

Per serving: 248 calories, 10g protein, 28g carbohydrate, 11g fat, 2g fiber, 26mg cholesterol, 548mg sodium

Mary's Roasted Red Pepper Dip

Submitted by: **Doreen**

"This is a huge hit with kids as well as adults, and it is very easy to make. Serve this flavorful dip with tortilla chips. Roasted red peppers and two kinds of cheese create the perfect combination. Adjust the amounts of onion and garlic to taste."

1	(7 ounce) jar roasted red bell peppers, drained and diced
¾	pound shredded Monterey Jack cheese
1	(8 ounce) package cream cheese, softened
1	cup mayonnaise
1	clove garlic, minced
1	tablespoon minced onion
2	tablespoons prepared Dijon-style mustard

1. Preheat oven to 350°F (175°C).
2. In a small baking dish, combine all ingredients.
3. Bake in the preheated oven for 20 minutes or until bubbly and lightly browned. Serve warm. **Yield:** 32 servings.

Per serving: 116 calories, 3g protein, 1g carbohydrate, 11g fat, 0g fiber, 21mg cholesterol, 224mg sodium

◄ **PARTY FOOD**

Prep Time: 10 minutes

Cook Time: 20 minutes

Average Rating: ★★★★★

What other cooks have done:

"I added more onion, garlic, and mustard. I also snuck in a few tablespoons of grated Parmesan cheese. I topped it off with sliced roasted red peppers, which looked pretty, and served it with assorted crackers and veggies."

Honey-Mustard Dipping Sauce

Submitted by: **Michele O'Sullivan**

"A tasty honey-mustard sauce for chicken fingers, egg rolls, chow mein noodles, ham sandwiches—there's no limit to this sauce."

½	cup cold water
1	teaspoon cornstarch
¼	cup honey
2	tablespoons thinly sliced green onions
1	tablespoon lemon juice
4	teaspoons prepared Dijon-style mustard
¼	teaspoon onion powder

1. Combine water and cornstarch in a medium saucepan and stir to dissolve. Stir in honey. Heat to boiling, stirring constantly. Reduce heat and simmer until sauce thickens, about 15 minutes.
2. Remove sauce from heat. Stir in green onions, lemon juice, mustard, and onion powder. Serve warm or chilled. **Yield:** 8 servings.

Per serving: 38 calories, 0g protein, 10g carbohydrate, 0g fat, 0g fiber, 0mg cholesterol, 64mg sodium

◄ **KID-FRIENDLY**

Prep Time: 15 minutes

Cook Time: 20 minutes

Average Rating: ★★★★☆

What other cooks have done:

"My husband and I made chicken in our fondue pot for Valentine's Day. I made this sauce to accompany it. The only change I made was not adding the green onions because I didn't have them. The sauce was yummy!"

Hot Corn Dip *(pictured on page 149)*

Submitted by: **Corinne Doubiago**

"This mixture of corn, diced tomatoes, cream cheese, and spices is a great hot appetizer. I crave it all the time! Serve with tortilla chips."

COVERED-DISH FAVORITE ▶

Prep Time: 10 minutes

Cook Time: 30 minutes

Average Rating: ★★★★★

What other cooks have done:

"This is addictive! I added only half of the diced tomatoes and threw in some Southwestern-style salsa for more kick. Very good."

- 1 (15.25 ounce) can white corn, drained
- 1 (15.25 ounce) can yellow corn, drained
- 1 (10 ounce) can diced tomatoes and green chiles, drained
- 1 (8 ounce) package cream cheese, diced and softened
- ½ teaspoon chili powder
- ½ teaspoon garlic powder
- Chopped fresh cilantro to taste

1. Preheat oven to 350°F (175°C).
2. In a medium baking dish, mix all ingredients.
3. Bake in the preheated oven for 30 minutes or until hot and bubbly.
Yield: 48 servings.

Per serving: 29 calories, 1g protein, 3g carbohydrate, 2g fat, 0g fiber, 5mg cholesterol, 78mg sodium

Ben's Seafood Dip

Submitted by: **Benjamin Jones**

"A must-have at get-togethers! This chunky seafood dip is so easy, you'll find yourself making several batches at a time. Imitation crabmeat may be substituted for shrimp."

PARTY FOOD ▶

Prep Time: 15 minutes

Cook Time: 1 minute

Chill Time: 30 minutes

Average Rating: ★★★★☆

What other cooks have done:

"Wonderful! This is a very creamy, smooth dip. I topped it with chopped nuts after it had set for an extra dash of pizzazz. A great recipe for supermarket shrimp and fresh vegetables."

- 1 (8 ounce) package cream cheese
- 1 (.25 ounce) envelope unflavored gelatin
- 1 (10.75 ounce) can condensed cream of mushroom soup
- ¾ cup chopped celery
- ¾ cup chopped green onions
- ¾ cup water chestnuts, drained
- 1½ cups cooked shrimp, peeled and deveined

1. Place the cream cheese and gelatin in a medium microwave-safe bowl and microwave on high for 1 minute or until melted. Stir until creamy.
2. Stir in the cream of mushroom soup, celery, green onions, water chestnuts, and shrimp. Chill for 30 minutes before serving or until cold. **Yield:** 48 servings.

Per serving: 29 calories, 2g protein, 1g carbohydrate, 2g fat, 0g fiber, 11mg cholesterol, 66mg sodium

Pepperoni Dip I

Submitted by: **Barbara**

"Serve this pizza-like dip with pita chips, bagel rounds, or tortilla chips."

1	(8 ounce) package cream cheese, softened	½	cup pepperoni, diced
½	cup sour cream	¼	cup chopped onion
⅛	teaspoon garlic powder	¼	cup chopped green bell pepper
¼	teaspoon dried oregano	1	cup shredded mozzarella cheese
1	cup pizza sauce		

1. Preheat oven to 350°F (175°C).
2. In a small bowl, combine cream cheese, sour cream, garlic powder, and oregano. Spread cream cheese mixture into a 9 inch pie plate. Spread pizza sauce evenly over the cream cheese mixture. Arrange the pepperoni, onion, and green bell pepper over the sauce.
3. Bake in the preheated oven for 10 minutes.
4. Remove dip from the oven and sprinkle with mozzarella cheese.
5. Return dip to the oven and bake until the mozzarella cheese has melted. **Yield:** 8 servings.

Per serving: 252 calories, 9g protein, 5g carbohydrate, 22g fat, 1g fiber, 59mg cholesterol, 517mg sodium

◄ FAMILY FAVORITE

Prep Time: 15 minutes

Cook Time: 15 minutes

Average Rating: ★★★★★

What other cooks have done:

"I didn't layer; I just mixed it all together, topping it with the mozzarella cheese. Fantastic dip! We served it with French bread and butter crackers. I can't wait to make it for the upcoming holidays."

Chili-Cheese Dip III

Submitted by: **Kathy Rogers**

"This quick, easy chili-cheese dip is a little different from most and is sure to be a favorite!"

2	(8 ounce) packages cream cheese, softened	1	(13.5 ounce) package nacho-flavored tortilla chips
1	(15 ounce) can chili without beans		
4	cups shredded Cheddar cheese		

1. Spread cream cheese on the bottom of a microwave-safe dish. Spread chili over cream cheese. Top with a layer of shredded Cheddar cheese. Microwave on high for 5 minutes or until the Cheddar cheese melts. Serve with nacho tortilla chips. **Yield:** 15 servings.

Per serving: 374 calories, 14g protein, 19g carbohydrate, 28g fat, 2g fiber, 70mg cholesterol, 570mg sodium

◄ 5 INGREDIENTS OR LESS

Prep Time: 5 minutes

Cook Time: 5 minutes

Average Rating: ★★★★★

What other cooks have done:

"I bake mine; I like the cheese to get just slightly browned. I have made this with a Monterey Jack and Cheddar mixture, which was very good. Spreading a little sour cream over the chili before topping with cheese is also tasty."

Mexican-Style Dip

Submitted by: **Lynn**

"This Tex-Mex recipe was a big hit when I took it to work. The dip was gone in an hour—with many requests for the recipe!"

PARTY FOOD ▶

Prep Time: 15 minutes

Cook Time: 23 minutes

Average Rating: ★★★★★

What other cooks have done:

"This dip was great and extremely easy to make. I recommend serving it with corn chips or some sort of dipping chip. (The dip is really deep, and you really only get the full effect with all layers on your chip.) We tried it with refried beans on top of the cream cheese and loved it."

1	(8 ounce) package cream cheese, softened	⅔	cup water
1	pound extra-lean ground beef	½	cup salsa
1	(1.25 ounce) package taco seasoning mix	¼	cup chopped jalapeño pepper
		2	cups shredded Mexican-style cheese

1. Preheat oven to 350°F (175°C). Lightly grease a 9 inch pie plate.

2. Spread cream cheese evenly into the bottom of the pie plate.

3. Brown ground beef in a large skillet. Drain excess fat. Mix in the taco seasoning and water. Cook, stirring constantly, 2 to 4 minutes. Remove skillet from heat and mix in salsa and jalapeño. Pour the beef mixture over the cream cheese in the pie plate. Sprinkle Mexican-style cheese over the beef mixture.

4. Bake in the preheated oven for 10 minutes or until the cheese has melted. **Yield:** 12 servings.

Per serving: 238 calories, 13g protein, 5g carbohydrate, 18g fat, 0g fiber, 64mg cholesterol, 683mg sodium

Cheese Ball

Submitted by: **Lesslie**

"This is a great appetizer with a cheesy yet sweet flavor."

MAKE-AHEAD ▶

Prep Time: 10 minutes

Chill Time: overnight

Average Rating: ★★★★★

What other cooks have done:

"I drained the pineapple until there was almost no liquid left. Though I didn't have any, some cheesecloth would have helped with draining the pineapple. I will definitely use some when I make this again."

2	(8 ounce) packages cream cheese	1	tablespoon chopped green bell pepper
1	(8 ounce) can crushed pineapple, drained	¼	tablespoon seasoning salt
1	tablespoon diced onion	1	cup chopped pecans
			Butter crackers

1. Mix together the cream cheese, pineapple, onion, bell pepper, and seasoning salt.

2. Form into a ball and roll in chopped pecans. Chill overnight. Serve with butter crackers. **Yield:** 20 servings.

Per serving: 127 calories, 2g protein, 3g carbohydrate, 12g fat, 1g fiber, 25mg cholesterol, 101mg sodium

Special Deviled Eggs

Submitted by: **Sara**

"Horseradish sauce and sweet relish set these deviled eggs apart from the rest!"

6	eggs	1	tablespoon prepared
¼	cup mayonnaise		mustard
2	tablespoons finely chopped		Paprika to taste
	onion		Salt and ground black
3	tablespoons sweet pickle		pepper to taste
	relish		
1	tablespoon prepared		
	horseradish		

1. Place eggs in a medium saucepan and cover with cold water. Bring water to a boil; immediately remove from heat. Cover and let stand for 10 to 12 minutes. Remove eggs to cool; peel and cut lengthwise.
2. Remove yolks from eggs. In a medium bowl, mash yolks and mix with mayonnaise, onion, sweet pickle relish, horseradish, and mustard.
3. Return yolk mixture to egg halves. Garnish with paprika and salt and pepper to taste. Chill until ready to serve. **Yield:** 6 servings.

Per serving: 154 calories, 7g protein, 4g carbohydrate, 12g fat, 0g fiber, 218mg cholesterol, 213mg sodium

◄ **COVERED-DISH FAVORITE**

Prep Time: 10 minutes

Cook Time: 12 minutes

Cool Time: 20 minutes

Average Rating: ★★★★☆

What other cooks have done:

"This egg recipe is wonderful. We thoroughly enjoyed this tangy, creamy version of an old standby. Be sure to squeeze excess moisture from the pickle relish so your filling will maintain a nice creaminess rather than a runny consistency."

Lemon Macaroon Tartlets

Submitted by: **Andrea**

"This no-plate finger food is often requested for its looks and taste. Enjoy!"

2	cups flaked coconut	1	(3.4 ounce) package instant
½	cup white sugar		lemon pudding mix
¼	cup plus 2 tablespoons	1	(8 ounce) container frozen
	all-purpose flour		whipped topping, thawed
1	teaspoon vanilla extract	1	cup flaked coconut
2	egg whites		

1. Preheat oven to 400°F (200°C). Grease 2 miniature muffin pans.
2. In a mixing bowl, combine 2 cups coconut, sugar, flour, vanilla, and egg whites; stir well. Divide mixture evenly among prepared muffin cups, pressing mixture into bottom and up sides of cups. (Use cooking spray on hands to prevent mixture from sticking to your hands.)
3. Bake in the preheated oven until edges are browned. Cool 2 minutes in pans on a wire rack. Remove from pans and cool completely on wire rack.
4. Prepare pudding mix according to package directions. Spoon pudding into tartlet shells. Top each tartlet evenly with whipped topping and sprinkle evenly with 1 cup coconut. **Yield:** 2 dozen.

Per tartlet: 110 calories, 1g protein, 16g carbohydrate, 5g fat, 1g fiber, 0mg cholesterol, 81mg sodium

◄ **PARTY FOOD**

Prep Time: 20 minutes

Cook Time: 20 minutes

Average Rating: ★★★★★

What other cooks have done:

"A nice, fresh-tasting summertime treat. To get a more intense lemon flavor, I added lemon zest to the pudding mixture and topped the whipped topping with both coconut and lemon zest for added taste and presentation."

Snicky Snackies

Submitted by: **Kevin Ryan**

"Caramel pretzels make crunchy, salty, and sweet snacks!"

KID-FRIENDLY ▶

Prep Time: 10 minutes

Cook Time: 30 minutes

Average Rating: ★★★★★

What other cooks have done:

"This recipe was great, but you need a really big pan for combining all the ingredients. I had to separate the mixture into two pans. Also, parchment paper works much better than wax paper for cooling. This recipe is a great twist on caramel corn."

2 cups mini twist pretzels
2 cups mixed nuts
1 cup unsalted butter
2 cups packed dark brown sugar
½ cup light corn syrup
Pinch salt

1. Preheat oven to 250°F (120°C).

2. Combine pretzels and nuts in a 9x13 inch baking dish. Set aside.

3. In a large saucepan, combine the butter, sugar, corn syrup, and salt. Stir over medium heat until sugar dissolves. Bring to a boil and cook until very thick and at hard ball stage or until a candy thermometer reaches 260°F (125°C). Pour over pretzel mixture and mix all together.

4. Bake in the preheated oven for 20 minutes, stirring after 10 minutes. Remove from oven and spread on wax paper to cool. **Yield:** 20 servings.

Per serving: 350 calories, 4g protein, 48g carbohydrate, 17g fat, 2g fiber, 25mg cholesterol, 495mg sodium

Cheese Blintzes

Submitted by: **Michele Murray**

"Mom's Cheese Blintzes are a party favorite. These blintzes can be made ahead and frozen in an airtight container. Do not thaw them before baking."

FREEZER FRESH ▶

Prep Time: 23 minutes

Cook Time: 10 minutes

Average Rating: ★★★★★

What other cooks have done:

"I served these as dessert for my husband's Super Bowl party. After eating so many spicy and salty things, the men loved these, and several asked for the recipe. They're easy and fun to make, and they're just yummy!"

1 (16 ounce) loaf white bread, sliced
¼ cup white sugar
2 teaspoons ground cinnamon
2 (8 ounce) packages cream cheese, softened
2 tablespoons milk
1 teaspoon vanilla extract
½ cup butter, melted
1 (8 ounce) container sour cream

1. Preheat oven to 350°F (175°C). Grease a baking sheet.

2. Trim crusts from bread and roll the slices flat.

3. In a small bowl, combine sugar and cinnamon.

4. In a large bowl, mix softened cream cheese, milk, and vanilla until smooth. Spread cream cheese mixture onto each slice of flattened bread. Roll up each bread slice evenly. Dip each roll in melted butter and then in the sugar-cinnamon mixture. Cut rolls into 1 inch slices. Arrange blintzes on prepared baking sheet.

5. Bake in the preheated oven for 10 minutes. Serve with sour cream. **Yield:** 9 servings.

Per serving: 534 calories, 10g protein, 35g carbohydrate, 40g fat, 1g fiber, 106mg cholesterol, 552mg sodium

Greek Saganaki *(pictured on page 151)*

Submitted by: **Elizabeth Chorley**
"Serve this pan-fried feta cheese with slices of ripe red tomatoes and lemon."

16 ounces feta cheese
2 eggs
2 teaspoons finely chopped fresh oregano
1 cup all-purpose flour
5 tablespoons olive oil

4 large ripe tomatoes, thickly sliced
Freshly ground black pepper to taste
2 lemons, cut into wedges

1. Slice feta into about 16 slices. In a small bowl, beat eggs with oregano. Dip each slice of feta in egg, shake off excess, and coat in flour.
2. Heat olive oil in a frying pan over medium-high heat. Quickly cook feta slices in batches in olive oil until golden, turning once. Remove and pat dry with paper towels.
3. Arrange feta on a plate with tomato slices. Season with pepper to taste and garnish with lemon wedges. **Yield:** 8 servings.

Per serving: 320 calories, 12g protein, 19g carbohydrate, 22g fat, 2g fiber, 103mg cholesterol, 657mg sodium

◄ AROUND-THE-WORLD CUISINE
Prep Time: 10 minutes
Cook Time: 15 minutes
Average Rating: ★★★★★
What other cooks have done:
"My local grocery store was out of feta cheese, so I tried this with queso blanco instead. It turned out great! Very quick and easy to make and a real hit for a brunch I served last week. Can't wait to try this tasty recipe with feta."

Dill-Wrapped Cream Cheese

Submitted by: **Jan**
"Easy, easy, easy! Dill-sprinkled cream cheese is wrapped in crescent roll dough and baked until golden. Serve this extra special appetizer with apple slices and crackers."

1 (8 ounce) can refrigerated crescent roll dough
1 (8 ounce) package cream cheese

1 teaspoon dried dill weed

1. Preheat oven to 350°F (175°C). Lightly grease a baking sheet.
2. Unroll dough on a lightly floured surface and press seams together. Sprinkle top of block of cream cheese with enough dill to cover. Place cream cheese, dill side down, in center of dough. Sprinkle with more dill to cover. Bring sides of dough up around cheese block; press edges together to seal.
3. Bake in the preheated oven for about 15 minutes. Serve warm. **Yield:** 6 servings.

Per serving: 277 calories, 6g protein, 16g carbohydrate, 21g fat, 0g fiber, 41mg cholesterol, 404mg sodium

◄ 5 INGREDIENTS OR LESS
Prep Time: 5 minutes
Cook Time: 15 minutes
Average Rating: ★★★★☆
What other cooks have done:
"This is a great recipe. I make individual rolls instead of one big one. I let the cream cheese soften and mix the dill in with it. I spoon a teaspoon of filling onto each roll, roll them up, and pinch the sides together. I have used both fresh and dried dill, depending on what I had on hand."

Asiago Toasted Cheese Puffs

Submitted by: **Alison Brune**
"A rich and tasty appetizer. People will request the recipe every time you make it!"

COMPANY IS COMING ▶

Prep Time: 15 minutes

Cook Time: 3 minutes

Average Rating: ★★★★★

What other cooks have done:

"I didn't have French bread in the house, so I used hot dog buns. They worked out fine, although I'm sure they would be much more delicious made with the specified bread. Next time, I'll add more mayo and cut back on the thyme."

1	cup grated Asiago cheese	1	teaspoon dried parsley
1	teaspoon pressed garlic		Pinch salt
⅓	cup mayonnaise		Pinch ground black pepper
1	teaspoon dried oregano	1	(16 ounce) loaf French
1	teaspoon dried thyme		bread, thinly sliced

1. Preheat broiler.
2. In a small bowl, combine the Asiago, garlic, mayonnaise, oregano, thyme, parsley, salt, and pepper. If the mixture does not hold together well, add more mayonnaise, if desired. Arrange the bread slices in a single layer on a baking sheet. Spread the Asiago mixture on the slices.
3. Broil in the preheated oven for 3 minutes or until the cheese is melted and lightly browned. Serve immediately. **Yield:** 12 servings.

Per serving: 181 calories, 6g protein, 20g carbohydrate, 9g fat, 1g fiber, 12mg cholesterol, 408mg sodium

Feta Cheese Foldovers

Submitted by: **Christine L.**
"Golden puffed pastries are filled with a feta cheese mixture. These can be made ahead and popped into the oven after your guests arrive."

HOLIDAY FARE ▶

Prep Time: 20 minutes

Cook Time: 20 minutes

Average Rating: ★★★★★

What other cooks have done:

"This is an appetizer that looks more difficult to make than it is. It's really very easy to put together, and the pastries have a nice taste. I used feta with sun-dried tomatoes and basil for extra flavor."

8	ounces feta cheese, crumbled	1	(17.3 ounce) package frozen puff pastry, thawed
3	tablespoons finely chopped green onions	1	egg yolk, beaten with 1 teaspoon water
1	egg, lightly beaten		

1. Preheat oven to 375°F (190°C).
2. In a small bowl, blend feta cheese, green onions, and egg. Cut pastry into 12 (3 inch) squares. Place a mounded tablespoon of feta mixture in the center of each square. Moisten edges with water and fold pastry over filling to form a triangle. Firmly press edges together with a fork to seal. Lightly brush pastries with the egg yolk mixture. Place pastries on a baking sheet.
3. Bake in the preheated oven for 20 minutes or until golden brown. Serve warm or at room temperature. **Yield:** 12 servings.

Per serving: 287 calories, 6g protein, 19g carbohydrate, 20g fat, 1g fiber, 52mg cholesterol, 319mg sodium

Basil Pesto Bread

Submitted by: **Kristie Behrens**

"I freeze this simple pesto in ice cube trays and put the cubes in freezer bags. You can easily take out and thaw what you need. Enjoy!"

3	cups fresh basil leaves	1	(16 ounce) loaf Italian bread
½	cup olive oil		
2	cloves garlic, peeled	3	roma (plum) tomatoes, thinly sliced
¼	cup pine nuts, toasted		
¼	cup grated Parmesan cheese	1	(8 ounce) package mozzarella cheese, sliced

1. Preheat broiler.

2. In a blender or food processor, puree the basil leaves, olive oil, and garlic. Add pine nuts and Parmesan cheese. Continue processing until desired consistency is reached.

3. Slice Italian bread to desired thickness. Spread a layer of pesto on each slice. Top with tomato slices and mozzarella cheese slices.

4. Place bread slices in a single layer on a large baking sheet. Broil in the preheated oven for 5 minutes or until cheese is bubbly and lightly browned. **Yield:** 16 servings.

Per serving: 196 calories, 7g protein, 16g carbohydrate, 12g fat, 1g fiber, 9mg cholesterol, 262mg sodium

◀ **PARTY FOOD**

Prep Time: 25 minutes

Cook Time: 5 minutes

Average Rating: ★★★★★

What other cooks have done:

"Thank you for such a simple and delicious recipe! If you don't have time, you can just buy pesto at the grocery store. You can easily eat this alone as a light meal. It makes a great appetizer—just cut it into small pieces!"

Garlic Pita Bread Bites

Submitted by: **Lisa Rebbechi**

"Great and easy to make—as well as delicious. Everyone goes crazy about these when I make them."

1	(10 ounce) package pita rounds	1	teaspoon Italian seasoning
3	tablespoons butter	2	tablespoons grated Parmesan cheese
1	teaspoon crushed garlic		

1. Preheat oven to 350°F (175°C).

2. Split pita rounds and roughly cut into approximately 2 inch pieces. Arrange on a large baking sheet.

3. In a small saucepan over medium heat, melt butter and mix in garlic and Italian seasoning. Pour the mixture over pita bread pieces. Sprinkle slices with Parmesan cheese.

4. Bake in the preheated oven for 10 minutes or until lightly browned. **Yield:** 20 servings.

Per serving: 56 calories, 2g protein, 8g carbohydrate, 2g fat, 0g fiber, 5mg cholesterol, 102mg sodium

◀ **CROWD-PLEASER**

Prep Time: 15 minutes

Cook Time: 12 minutes

Average Rating: ★★★★★

What other cooks have done:

"Very easy. I usually just cut up pita bread to serve with dips, but this was way yummier, looked nicer, and held the dips better. I didn't have Parmesan cheese, and they still tasted great."

Hot and Spicy Pecans *(pictured on page 151)*

Submitted by: **Diane Kester**

"These pecans aren't too hot, but you can leave out the red pepper if you like them milder. These make a great appetizer for the holidays or anytime."

2	tablespoons butter, melted	¼	teaspoon salt
1	tablespoon Worcestershire sauce	¼	teaspoon garlic powder
¼	teaspoon cayenne pepper	2	cups pecan halves
		1	tablespoon chili powder

1. Preheat oven to 300°F (150°C).

2. In a medium bowl, mix butter, Worcestershire sauce, cayenne pepper, salt, and garlic powder. Stir in the pecans and gently toss with chili powder to coat. Spread coated pecans on a baking sheet.

3. Bake in the preheated oven for 30 minutes, stirring approximately every 10 minutes. **Yield:** 16 servings.

Per serving: 118 calories, 2g protein, 3g carbohydrate, 12g fat, 2g fiber, 4mg cholesterol, 66mg sodium

HOLIDAY GIFT GIVING ▶

Prep Time: 10 minutes

Cook Time: 30 minutes

Average Rating: ★★★★★

What other cooks have done:

"I increased the cayenne pepper and made it with whole almonds instead of pecans. Big hit!"

Potato Chips *(pictured on page 151)*

Submitted by: **Jessica**

"Make your own potato chips using your microwave. A tasty, healthy, and easy alternative to store-bought potato chips, not to mention economical! Use a mandoline to make slicing the potato into paper-thin slices a breeze."

1	tablespoon vegetable oil	½	teaspoon salt (or to taste)
1	potato, sliced paper-thin (peel optional)		

1. Pour vegetable oil into a heavy-duty, zip-top plastic bag. Add potato slices and shake well to coat.

2. Lightly coat a large dinner plate with oil or cooking spray. Arrange potato slices in a single layer on the plate.

3. Microwave in batches on high for 3 to 5 minutes or until lightly browned. (If not browned, chips will not become crisp.) Remove chips from plate and toss with salt or other seasonings to taste. Let cool. Repeat process with remaining potato slices. (You will not need to keep oiling the plate.) **Yield:** 4 servings.

Note: Cooking times may vary depending on wattage of microwave ovens. We tested this recipe using a 1100-watt microwave.

Per serving: 54 calories, 1g protein, 6g carbohydrate, 3g fat, 1g fiber, 0mg cholesterol, 293mg sodium

CLASSIC COMFORT FOOD ▶

Prep Time: 30 minutes

Cook Time: 5 minutes per batch

Average Rating: ★★★★★

What other cooks have done:

"Fabulous! Make sure you put enough oil on the plate so the chips don't stick. I seasoned mine with popcorn seasonings, and they were delicious!"

Hot Corn Dip, page 140

Easy Raspberry Lemonade,
page 164

Greek Saganaki,
page 145

Potato Chips, page 148, and Hot and Spicy Pecans,
page 148

Cappuccino Cooler, page 163

Cinnamon Snack Mix

Submitted by: **Sara**

"Toss together this crunchy and delicious snack mix for your next slumber party. It's so yummy you may need to make two batches."

5	cups honey graham cereal	¾	cup sliced almonds
3	cups teddy bear-shaped graham cracker cookies	1	cup golden raisins
		⅓	cup butter
2	cups crushed ramen noodles	⅓	cup honey
		1	teaspoon orange juice

1. Preheat oven to 375°F (190°C).
2. In a large bowl, mix honey graham cereal, bear-shaped graham cracker cookies, crushed ramen noodles, almonds, and golden raisins.
3. Melt butter in a small saucepan over low heat and stir in honey and orange juice. Spread over the honey graham cereal mixture and toss to coat. Spread mixture on a large baking sheet.
4. Bake in the preheated oven for 10 minutes. **Yield:** 24 servings.

Per serving: 158 calories, 2g protein, 25g carbohydrate, 6g fat, 1g fiber, 7mg cholesterol, 233mg sodium

◄ **FAMILY FAVORITE**

Prep Time: 10 minutes

Cook Time: 12 minutes

Average Rating: ★★★★★

What other cooks have done:

"Huge hit! Easy enough for my daughter to participate and tasty enough to be made many times in the future! I used cereal wheat squares in place of the ramen noodles and added a dash of cinnamon to the butter mixture. Also, you can mix and match a variety of cereals."

Honey-Nut Granola

Submitted by: **Karen Miscall–Bannon**

"Yummy, crunchy breakfast treat that's good on ice cream, too."

4	cups rolled oats	½	cup honey
1	cup sliced almonds	1	teaspoon vanilla extract
1	cup chopped pecans	1	tablespoon ground cinnamon
1	cup sunflower seeds		
⅓	cup canola oil		

1. Preheat oven to 300°F (150°C).
2. In a large bowl, stir together oats, almonds, pecans, and sunflower seeds. In a separate bowl, mix together oil, honey, vanilla, and cinnamon; stir well. Combine oat mixture and honey mixture. Spread on 2 ungreased baking sheets.
3. Bake in the preheated oven for 10 minutes; remove from oven and stir. Return to oven and continue baking about 10 more minutes or until golden. Remove from oven and let cool completely before serving or storing in an airtight container. **Yield:** 20 servings.

Per serving: 233 calories, 6g protein, 21g carbohydrate, 15g fat, 4g fiber, 0mg cholesterol, 1mg sodium

◄ **HOLIDAY GIFT GIVING**

Prep Time: 10 minutes

Cook Time: 20 minutes

Cool Time: 30 minutes

Average Rating: ★★★★★

What other cooks have done:

"This is the best granola recipe. I always double the recipe because we eat it up so fast. I cut the fat by using applesauce in place of oil. Smells great when baking and makes a nice gift, too. I just put it in a canning jar and decorate the top with pretty fabric and decorative cord."

Over-the-Top Nachos

Submitted by: **Charlie**
"These nachos can be served as a great appetizer, snack, or quick lunch. Serve with sour cream, salsa, and guacamole."

Prep Time: 10 minutes

Cook Time: 15 minutes

Average Rating: ★★★★☆

What other cooks have done:

"I cooked the meat with some taco seasoning, and I melted 3 ounces of cream cheese with the beans for ease of spreading. I topped everything with sour cream, guacamole, chopped roma tomatoes, minced green onions, and sliced black olives. Messy but yummy!"

1 pound ground beef
1 onion, finely diced
  Salt and ground black pepper to taste
1 (14.5 ounce) package tortilla chips
1 (16 ounce) can refried beans
2 cups shredded Cheddar cheese, divided
1 jalapeño pepper, sliced

1. In a large skillet over medium heat, brown ground beef, onion, and salt and pepper to taste; drain.
2. Arrange chips on a microwave-safe platter. Spread beans over the chips. Layer with half of the cheese, all of the ground beef mixture, and remaining cheese. Arrange jalapeño slices on top.
3. Microwave on medium-high for 5 minutes or until cheese has melted. Serve immediately. **Yield:** 6 servings.

Per serving: 837 calories, 33g protein, 57g carbohydrate, 54g fat, 9g fiber, 119mg cholesterol, 918mg sodium

Asparagus Rolantina

Submitted by: **J.L.**
"Asparagus spears rolled in prosciutto and cheese are topped with a crunchy breadcrumb and grated cheese crust. I recommend using pencil-thin asparagus."

Prep Time: 10 minutes

Cook Time: 22 minutes

Average Rating: ★★★★☆

What other cooks have done:

"This is a pretty starter, but it's also great as a light main meal with a few extra vegetables. Varying the cheese also works—try a medium Cheddar, for example. I've tried using bundles of baby carrots, too, but they need to be blanched first, or they'll be too raw."

1 pound fresh asparagus spears, trimmed
4 (½ ounce) slices prosciutto
4 slices Swiss cheese
  Freshly ground black pepper to taste
¼ cup butter, melted
1 cup Italian-style breadcrumbs
½ cup grated Parmesan cheese

1. Preheat oven to 350°F (175°C).
2. Cook asparagus in a large pot of boiling water for 1 to 2 minutes.
3. Lay 1 slice of prosciutto on a plate. Layer a slice of cheese on top of the prosciutto. Place 3 to 4 asparagus spears at 1 end of the cheese and prosciutto and sprinkle with pepper to taste. Roll the cheese and prosciutto up over the asparagus and secure with a toothpick. Repeat procedure with remaining asparagus, prosciutto, and cheese. Place asparagus rolls in a casserole dish. Pour melted butter over the asparagus. Sprinkle with breadcrumbs and Parmesan cheese.
4. Bake in the preheated oven for 15 to 20 minutes or until cheese is melted and breadcrumbs are crisp. **Yield:** 4 servings.

Per serving: 471 calories, 24g protein, 27g carbohydrate, 29g fat, 4g fiber, 83mg cholesterol, 1562mg sodium

Baked Cheese Olives

Submitted by: **Anita**

"Rich, cheesy dough surrounding a savory olive makes a great pick-up appetizer or snack. You can freeze the unbaked dough-wrapped olives and bake them right out of the freezer, extending the baking time by a few minutes."

1	cup shredded Cheddar cheese	⅛	teaspoon cayenne pepper
2	tablespoons butter, softened	24	pimento-stuffed green olives
½	cup all-purpose flour		

1. Preheat oven to 400°F (200°C).
2. In a small mixing bowl, combine cheese and butter. Stir flour and cayenne pepper into the cheese mixture. Blend well. Wrap a tablespoon of dough around each green olive. Arrange the wrapped olives on a baking sheet.
3. Bake in the preheated oven for 15 minutes or until golden brown.
Yield: 8 servings.

Per serving: 123 calories, 5g protein, 6g carbohydrate, 9g fat, 0g fiber, 22mg cholesterol, 356mg sodium

◄ FREEZER FRESH

Prep Time: 15 minutes

Cook Time: 15 minutes

Average Rating: ★★★★☆

What other cooks have done:

"I added a small amount of olive juice to the cheese and flour mixture so it would be easier to wrap around the olives. I also added paprika. Great recipe!"

Bacon and Date Appetizer

Submitted by: **Cinn**

"An easy, quick appetizer that I first tasted at a Native American wedding ceremony. Dates are stuffed with almonds and wrapped in bacon."

1	(8 ounce) package pitted dates	4	ounces almonds
		1	pound sliced bacon

1. Preheat broiler.
2. Slit dates. Place 1 almond inside each date. Wrap dates with bacon, securing with toothpicks.
3. Broil in the preheated oven for 10 minutes or until bacon is evenly brown and crisp. **Yield:** 6 servings.

Per serving: 631 calories, 11g protein, 31g carbohydrate, 53g fat, 5g fiber, 51mg cholesterol, 554mg sodium

◄ PARTY FOOD

Prep Time: 20 minutes

Cook Time: 10 minutes

Average Rating: ★★★★★

What other cooks have done:

"I use the microwave when making large batches for a party. The microwave really does a great job with bacon, and paper towels absorb the extra grease."

Santa Fe Veggie Quesadillas

Submitted by: **Hydeeho**

"I've made this quick and colorful appetizer for many great dinner parties. Serve with fresh salsa, guacamole, and sour cream—or serve the quesadillas by themselves. Thawed and drained frozen veggies may be substituted for canned. Look for the combination of corn, red bell pepper, and black beans in your grocery store's frozen food section."

FAMILY FAVORITE ▶

Prep Time: 10 minutes

Cook Time: 5 minutes

Average Rating: ★★★★★

What other cooks have done:

"Simple, tasty, and so easy to make. We cut the tortilla in half and folded each half over while it was on the griddle so that it was more like a true quesadilla. I served them with salsa and sour cream. I reheated the leftover ones in the toaster oven the next day for about four or five minutes, and they tasted just as good."

1 tablespoon oil	½ cup whole kernel corn, drained
1 (12 inch) flour tortilla	½ cup diced red bell pepper
¾ cup shredded Cheddar/ Monterey Jack cheese blend	½ cup black beans, drained
	1 green onion, chopped

1. Heat oil in a large skillet over medium heat. Place the tortilla in the skillet and flip it once to ensure an even coating of oil on both sides.

2. Heat the tortilla on 1 side for 1 minute. Beginning at the center of the tortilla, sprinkle the cheese blend evenly over tortilla until the tortilla's entire surface is covered. Top the cheese with corn, red bell pepper, black beans, and green onion. When the cheese is completely melted, carefully slide the tortilla from the pan onto a cutting board. Slice into 8 wedges and serve warm. **Yield:** 4 servings.

Per serving: 219 calories, 9g protein, 27g carbohydrate, 8g fat, 4g fiber, 18mg cholesterol, 435mg sodium

Fresh from the Freezer

Frozen foods are the height of convenience—all the washing, trimming and chopping has been done for you, so all you need to do is heat and eat. Basic frozen ingredients, such as vegetables, fruits, and meats, can help you get fresh, tasty, and nutritious meals on the table, pronto! Even better, frozen fruits and vegetables are often more nutritious than their fresh counterparts. Food intended for freezing always gets processed and quickly frozen within hours of being picked, whereas fresh produce may sit in storage or on the shelves for days, weeks, or even months before you finally get it home and cook it. And while nutrients in fresh foods deplete the longer they sit on the shelf, freezing preserves the majority of those nutrients, even when the foods are frozen for an extended period of time.

The Thaw Laws

Thawing foods at room temperature will compromise the safety of your food. Instead, follow these methods.

• In the refrigerator: This is the slowest thawing technique. Small frozen items may thaw overnight in the refrigerator, while larger items will take significantly longer.

• Under cold running water: Place the frozen food in a leak-proof bag and place it under cold running water.

• In a microwave on the defrost setting: Plan to cook the food immediately after it has thawed in a microwave because some areas of the food may have begun cooking during the defrost cycle.

For more information, visit **Allrecipes.com**

Tasty Spinach Treats

Submitted by: **Kristen**

"I created these delicious spinach cups to take to a potluck dinner, and they disappeared! They're a cinch to make and taste good either right out of the oven or cooled."

1 tablespoon butter
½ cup finely chopped onion
1 (10 ounce) package frozen chopped spinach, thawed and drained
¾ cup mayonnaise
1 (8 ounce) package shredded mozzarella cheese

1½ teaspoons ground nutmeg
Salt and ground black pepper to taste
1 (12 ounce) can refrigerated buttermilk biscuit dough

1. Preheat oven to 375°F (190°C). Lightly grease 20 miniature muffin cups.

2. Melt butter in a medium saucepan over medium heat. Stir in the onion and cook until tender and lightly browned.

3. In a medium bowl, mix together onion, spinach, mayonnaise, mozzarella cheese, nutmeg, and salt and pepper to taste.

4. Unroll buttermilk biscuit dough and separate each biscuit into 2 halves. Place a biscuit dough half into each muffin cup, extending dough slightly beyond the rim of cup edge. Fill the biscuit dough cups with desired amounts of the onion and spinach mixture.

5. Bake in the preheated oven for 12 minutes or until biscuit dough and filling are lightly browned. **Yield:** 10 servings.

Per serving: 304 calories, 9g protein, 18g carbohydrate, 23g fat, 2g fiber, 26mg cholesterol, 603mg sodium

◀ **COVERED-DISH FAVORITE**

Prep Time: 30 minutes

Cook Time: 17 minutes

Average Rating: ★★★★☆

What other cooks have done:

"This is the most requested dish in my house. I've made these with broccoli and Cheddar cheese and with sautéed mushrooms and mozzarella cheese."

Spicy Seafood Shell Appetizers

Submitted by: **Mary Beth Blum**

"Making these shells stuffed with a spicy, cheesy seafood mixture is extremely fast and easy, and they are very tasty."

1½ cups mayonnaise
⅔ cup grated Parmesan cheese
⅔ cup shredded Swiss cheese
⅓ cup chopped onion
2 teaspoons Worcestershire sauce
10 drops hot pepper sauce
1 (4 ounce) can small shrimp, drained
1 (6 ounce) can crabmeat, drained and flaked
2 (2.1 ounce) packages frozen mini phyllo shells
Paprika to taste

1. Preheat oven to 400°F (200°C). Lightly grease baking sheets.

2. In a medium bowl, mix together mayonnaise, Parmesan cheese, Swiss cheese, onion, Worcestershire sauce, and hot pepper sauce. Gently stir in shrimp and crabmeat.

3. Fill phyllo shells with seafood mixture. Arrange stuffed shells on prepared baking sheets.

4. Bake in the preheated oven for 7 to 10 minutes or until lightly browned. Sprinkle with paprika before serving. **Yield:** 3 dozen.

Per serving: 97 calories, 3g protein, 2g carbohydrate, 9g fat, 0g fiber, 16mg cholesterol, 157mg sodium

Artichoke and Crabmeat Triangles

Submitted by: **Barbara Gilhuly**

"This is an easy recipe. It is an old favorite of mine that I once used as a dip. I like the English muffins base—it gives a nice crispy texture."

1	(14 ounce) can artichoke hearts, drained	⅓	cup chopped onion
1	pound crabmeat	¾	cup grated Parmesan cheese
1	cup mayonnaise	1	(12 ounce) package English muffins

1. Preheat oven to 375°F (190°C).
2. In a bowl, combine artichoke hearts, crabmeat, mayonnaise, onion, and cheese. Mix thoroughly.
3. Split each English muffin in half and spread the crabmeat mixture on top of each muffin half. Cut each muffin half into quarters. Arrange the muffin bites on baking sheets.
4. Bake in the preheated oven for 12 minutes or until golden brown. Serve hot. **Yield:** 4 dozen.

Per appetizer: 83 calories, 3g protein, 4g carbohydrate, 5g fat, 0g fiber, 10mg cholesterol, 127mg sodium

◄ **RESTAURANT FARE**

Prep Time: 15 minutes

Cook Time: 12 minutes per batch

Average Rating: ★★★★★

What other cooks have done:

"I wrapped the filling with phyllo dough. I was asked for the recipe numerous times."

Chicken Puffs

Submitted by: **Jen Sandoval**

"A rich, creamy chicken mixture is rolled in croissants and baked to form delicious puffs. Wonderful for get-togethers!"

2	skinless, boneless chicken breast halves, cubed	2	(3 ounce) packages cream cheese
3	tablespoons chopped onion	6	tablespoons butter
3	cloves garlic, peeled and minced	3	(10 ounce) cans refrigerated crescent roll dough

1. Preheat oven to 325°F (165°C).
2. In a medium saucepan over medium heat, sauté chicken, onion, and garlic. Cook until onions are tender and chicken is lightly browned.
3. In a medium bowl, blend chicken mixture, cream cheese, and butter with an electric mixer until creamy.
4. Unroll crescent roll dough and form into 12 rectangles. Place approximately 1 tablespoon of chicken mixture on each rectangle. Fold into balls. Arrange balls on a lightly greased large baking sheet.
5. Bake in the preheated oven for 12 minutes or until golden brown. **Yield:** 1 dozen.

Per serving: 398 calories, 11g protein, 28g carbohydrate, 26g fat, 0g fiber, 42mg cholesterol, 663mg sodium

◄ **FAMILY FAVORITE**

Prep Time: 20 minutes

Cook Time: 25 minutes

Average Rating: ★★★★☆

What other cooks have done:

"One thing I can suggest to make them easier is to not worry about the shape of your finished puff. By the time they rise in the oven, they are all pretty symmetrical. Just be careful not to get the filling on the outside and be sure to pinch the seals together."

Sausage Flowers

Submitted by: **Teresa**

"Won ton cups are filled with a flavorful cheese and sausage mixture and then baked. Topped with a dollop of sour cream and a sprinkling of chopped green onions, these lovely appetizers will be the first to disappear! Impressive, yet easy to make!"

1	pound ground Italian sausage	24	(3.5 inch square) won ton wrappers
½	cup shredded Monterey Jack cheese	1⅓	cups sour cream
½	cup shredded colby cheese	1	bunch green onions, chopped
1	cup salsa		

1. Preheat oven to 350°F (175°C). Lightly grease a miniature muffin pan.

2. Cook ground Italian sausage in a large, deep skillet over medium-high heat until evenly browned. Drain and remove from heat.

3. Stir Monterey Jack cheese and colby cheese into the warm sausage to melt. Stir in salsa.

4. Gently press won ton wrappers into the prepared muffin cups so that the edges extend past cup edges. Place a heaping tablespoon of the sausage mixture into each won ton wrapper.

5. Bake in the preheated oven for 10 minutes or until won ton edges begin to brown.

6. Transfer baked won tons to a serving platter. Dollop each with approximately 1 tablespoon sour cream. Sprinkle with chopped green onions. **Yield:** 24 servings.

Per serving: 143 calories, 5g protein, 7g carbohydrate, 11g fat, 1g fiber, 26mg cholesterol, 267mg sodium

Jet Swirl Pizza Appetizers

Submitted by: **Julie Anne**

"Similar to meat-filled calzones, these cheesy little swirls were invented during football season. The name was inspired by our favorite team."

1	(10 ounce) can refrigerated pizza crust dough	¼	pound provolone cheese, sliced
¼	pound Genoa salami, thinly sliced	½	cup shredded mozzarella cheese
¼	pound pepperoni, sliced		

1. Preheat oven to 350°F (175°C). Lightly grease a large baking sheet.
2. Roll pizza crust dough into an approximately 10x14 inch rectangle on prepared baking sheet. Layer with Genoa salami, pepperoni, and provolone cheese. Sprinkle with mozzarella cheese to within ½ inch of dough edge. Roll up, jellyroll style. Seal the edge with a fork.
3. Bake in the preheated oven for 25 minutes or until golden brown. Slice into 1 inch pieces to serve. **Yield:** 5 servings.

Per serving: 457 calories, 23g protein, 28g carbohydrate, 27g fat, 1g fiber, 63mg cholesterol, 1502mg sodium

◀ PARTY FOOD

Prep Time: 10 minutes

Cook Time: 25 minutes

Average Rating: ★★★★★

What other cooks have done:

"I made two batches: one with just pepperoni and cheese and one with just crumbled sausage and cheese. I also sprinkled a bit of garlic powder and oregano on the dough before adding the toppings. I served them warm with heated pizza sauce for dipping. They turned out magnificent!"

Mini Ham and Cheese Rolls

Submitted by: **Tara Laine Hoffman**

"These are fantastic for either a Super Bowl party or a luncheon tea. They are addictive, so be sure to make an extra batch."

2	tablespoons dried minced onion	24	dinner rolls
1	tablespoon prepared mustard	½	pound chopped ham
2	tablespoons poppy seeds	½	pound thinly sliced Swiss cheese
½	cup butter or margarine, melted		

1. Preheat oven to 325°F (165°C).
2. In a small bowl, combine onion, mustard, poppy seeds, and butter.
3. Split each dinner roll. Layer ham and cheese on the bottom halves of each roll. Arrange the sandwiches on a large baking sheet. Drizzle the poppy seed mixture over the sandwiches.
4. Bake in the preheated oven for 20 minutes or until cheese has melted. Serve sandwiches warm. **Yield:** 24 servings.

Per serving: 146 calories, 7g protein, 7g carbohydrate, 10g fat, 1g fiber, 25mg cholesterol, 277mg sodium

◀ FAMILY FAVORITE

Prep Time: 15 minutes

Cook Time: 20 minutes

Average Rating: ★★★★★

What other cooks have done:

"These are very yummy. I use sliced ham, Swiss cheese, and frozen (pre-cooked) rolls in a throw-away pan. You can just slice them open, insert the ham and cheese, and put them back into the pan before drizzling them with the butter mixture. This way, you won't lose any of the butter mixture. These are great for parties."

Chai Tea Mix

Submitted by: **Jo**

"You can spice up this instant chai tea mix even further by adding nutmeg, allspice, and white pepper."

HOLIDAY GIFT GIVING ▶

Prep Time: 20 minutes

Average Rating: ★★★★★

What other cooks have done:

"This is great! I love it. I doubled the cardamom and ginger and added pepper and nutmeg because I like it spicy!"

1 cup fat-free dry milk powder
1 cup powdered non-dairy coffee creamer
1 cup French vanilla-flavored powdered non-dairy coffee creamer
2½ cups white sugar
1½ cups unsweetened instant tea
2 teaspoons ground ginger
2 teaspoons ground cinnamon
1 teaspoon ground cloves
1 teaspoon ground cardamom

1. In a large bowl, combine milk powder, non-dairy creamer, French vanilla-flavored creamer, sugar, and instant tea. Stir in ginger, cinnamon, cloves, and cardamom. In a blender or food processor, blend 1 cup mixture at a time until mixture is the consistency of fine powder.
2. To serve, stir 2 heaping tablespoons of Chai Tea Mix into a mug of hot water. **Yield:** 16 servings.

Per serving: 223 calories, 4g protein, 44g carbohydrate, 4g fat, 0g fiber, 2mg cholesterol, 66mg sodium

Hot Buttered Apple Cider

Submitted by: **Karen**

"This is a wonderful drink on a cold night or morning. You will have extra spiced butter for your next batch!"

5 INGREDIENTS OR LESS ▶

Prep Time: 5 minutes

Cook Time: 20 minutes

Average Rating: ★★★★★

What other cooks have done:

"This was pure heaven! My husband has now made a rule to always keep this beverage on our menu, regardless of the weather!

1 (17.5 ounce) bottle apple cider
½ cup pure maple syrup
½ cup butter, softened
½ teaspoon ground nutmeg
½ teaspoon ground allspice

1. In a saucepan over medium-low heat, heat apple cider with maple syrup for 20 minutes or until steaming hot.
2. In a small bowl, combine butter, nutmeg, and allspice. Mix well.
3. Pour cider into mugs and top with a teaspoon of spiced butter.
Yield: 8 servings.

Per serving: 183 calories, 0g protein, 20g carbohydrate, 12g fat, 0g fiber, 31mg cholesterol, 125mg sodium

Drew's World-Famous Triple-Rush Hot Chocolate

Submitted by: **Drew E. Sprague**

"A triple rush of all my favorite things in one great winter drink! Serve with marshmallows and a dash of chocolate sprinkles."

½	cup semisweet chocolate chips	¼	teaspoon ground cinnamon
½	cup milk		Dash hot chili powder
1	teaspoon instant coffee granules	½	cup cold milk

1. Combine the chocolate chips and milk in a microwave-safe dish and microwave on high, stirring every 20 to 30 seconds, for 5 minutes or until melted and smooth. Mix in the coffee granules, cinnamon, and hot chili powder; stir until the instant coffee has dissolved. Stir in the cold milk. Strain into mugs. Thin with additional milk, if desired. **Yield:** 2 servings.

Per serving: 266 calories, 6g protein, 33g carbohydrate, 15g fat, 3g fiber, 10mg cholesterol, 71mg sodium

◄ CLASSIC COMFORT FOOD

Prep Time: 5 minutes

Cook Time: 5 minutes

Average Rating: ★★★★★

What other cooks have done:

"Hot chocolate for the true chocoholic. This was so rich—just the way we like it. For summertime, I'll put this mixture in my blender with some ice cream. What a great shake this would make!"

Cappuccino Cooler *(pictured on page 152)*

Submitted by: **Susan**

"The combination of coffee, chocolate ice cream, chocolate syrup, and whipped cream makes this a perfect pick-me-up drink!"

1½	cups cold coffee	Crushed ice
1½	cups chocolate ice cream	Whipped cream
¼	cup chocolate syrup	Chocolate shavings

1. In a blender, combine coffee, ice cream, and chocolate syrup. Blend until smooth. Pour over crushed ice into glasses. Garnish each serving with a dollop of whipped cream and chocolate shavings. **Yield:** 2 to 3 servings.

Per serving: 333 calories, 5g protein, 52g carbohydrate, 13g fat, 2g fiber, 37mg cholesterol, 101mg sodium

◄ FAMILY FAVORITE

Prep Time: 5 minutes

Average Rating: ★★★★★

What other cooks have done:

"I love this recipe! I used different kinds of ice cream, and it turned out just as good."

Basic Fruit Smoothie

Submitted by: **Janelle**

"This is a great smoothie consisting of fruit, fruit juice, and ice. I like to use whatever fresh fruits I crave that day. Mangoes, papayas, kiwi fruit, and any kind of berry make a great smoothie. Experiment with your favorites!"

5 INGREDIENTS OR LESS ▶

Prep Time: 10 minutes

Average Rating: ★★★★★

What other cooks have done:

"We enjoyed trying this basic smoothie recipe in different ways. Our family likes to add a couple of teaspoons of vanilla, and we sprinkle it with cinnamon just to give it an extra kick."

1 quart strawberries, hulled
1 banana, broken into chunks
2 peaches

1 cup orange-mango or peach-mango juice
2 cups ice

1. In a blender, combine strawberries, banana, and peaches. Blend until fruit is pureed. Blend in the juice. Add ice and blend to desired consistency. Pour into glasses and serve. **Yield:** 4 servings.

Per serving: 113 calories, 2g protein, 27g carbohydrate, 1g fat, 4g fiber, 0mg cholesterol, 16mg sodium

minutes or less

Easy Raspberry Lemonade *(pictured on page 150)*

Submitted by: **Tori Hermansen**

"We came up with this recipe for my brother's wedding reception. We wanted to serve something that was easy and quick to fix, yet good at the same time. After a few tries, we ended up with this recipe . . . and a lot of compliments."

CROWD-PLEASER ▶

Prep Time: 5 minutes

Average Rating: ★★★★★

What other cooks have done:

"This gave ordinary lemonade a kick! I used lemon-lime club soda. I put the mixture into a soda bottle so it would not go flat."

1 (12 ounce) can frozen raspberry lemonade concentrate
3 cups water
¾ teaspoon lime juice
1 (12 ounce) bottle lemon-lime carbonated beverage

1 cup crushed ice
Fresh raspberries
Fresh mint

1. In a large punch bowl or pitcher, combine raspberry lemonade concentrate, water, and lime juice. Stir in lemon-lime beverage and crushed ice. Pour into glasses and garnish each with a fresh raspberry and mint. **Yield:** 8 servings.

Per serving: 60 calories, 1g protein, 15g carbohydrate, 0g fat, 1g fiber, 0mg cholesterol, 5mg sodium

Easy Entrées

Beef, Portuguese Style

Submitted by: **Darlene Camara**

"This is a recipe that I got from my mother-in-law. The gravy is close to the one they use in Portuguese restaurants."

COMPANY IS COMING ▶

Prep Time: 10 minutes

Cook Time: 18 minutes

Average Rating: ★★★★☆

What other cooks have done:

"I thought this was fantastic! I used cube steak, and it still tasted great! I can't wait to try it with a better cut of meat. I used beef broth instead of water and added some pimentos on a whim."

¾	cup red wine	½	teaspoon salt
¼	cup water	6	(4 ounce) beef tenderloin
10	cloves garlic, chopped		steaks
1	tablespoon chile paste	⅓	cup vegetable oil
½	teaspoon white pepper		

1. In a medium bowl, combine red wine, water, garlic, chile paste, white pepper, and salt. Add beef and turn to coat evenly.
2. In a large, heavy skillet over medium heat, fry 3 steaks for 2 minutes on each side; set steaks aside and drain pan liquids into the red wine mixture. Repeat with remaining steaks.
3. Add oil to skillet and reduce heat to medium-low. Fry steaks in batches of 3 for 2 more minutes on each side. Drain oil and return all steaks and marinade to pan. Boil for 2 minutes. **Yield:** 6 servings.

Per serving: 463 calories, 21g protein, 4g carbohydrate, 39g fat, 0g fiber, 81mg cholesterol, 273mg sodium

Pan-Fried Steak with Marsala Sauce

Submitted by: **Lynne**

"A very fast and easy recipe for a delicious steak with a superb sauce."

HOLIDAY FARE ▶

Prep Time: 10 minutes

Cook Time: 15 minutes

Average Rating: ★★★★★

What other cooks have done:

"This was very good. It's a great sauce, and it's wonderful with mushrooms. I added them at the same time I added the broth and Marsala."

1	tablespoon vegetable oil	2	cloves garlic, minced
4	beef chuck steaks, well	½	cup Marsala wine
	trimmed (about 1½	½	cup beef broth
	pounds)	3	tablespoons butter
	Salt and ground black	½	teaspoon fresh rosemary,
	pepper to taste		chopped

1. Heat oil in a large, heavy skillet over high heat until hot. Season steaks with salt and pepper to taste. Add steaks to skillet and immediately reduce heat to medium high. Cook for 4 minutes. Turn steaks and cook for 4 to 6 more minutes or to desired degree of doneness. Remove steaks; set aside and cover with aluminum foil to keep warm.
2. Remove skillet from heat. Sauté garlic for 1 to 2 minutes in the hot skillet. Return skillet to medium-low heat and add Marsala and beef broth. Boil for 3 minutes. Remove pan from heat and whisk in butter and rosemary. Serve sauce over steaks. **Yield:** 4 servings.

Per serving: 339 calories, 33g protein, 5g carbohydrate, 18g fat, 0g fiber, 120mg cholesterol, 366mg sodium

Chicken-Fried Steak, Cuban Style

Submitted by: **Roxie**
"Delicious and tasty chicken-fried steaks are perked up with a zesty Latin touch."

3	cups dry breadcrumbs	2	eggs
1	tablespoon fresh oregano	4	(4 ounce) cube steaks
1	teaspoon ground cumin	2	cups vegetable oil
	Salt and ground black pepper to taste	1	lemon, sliced

1. In a shallow dish, combine breadcrumbs, oregano, cumin, and salt and pepper to taste. Beat eggs in another shallow dish. Dip each steak in beaten eggs and then in the breadcrumb mixture. Make sure to cover each steak well with the breadcrumb mixture.
2. In a large, deep skillet, pour oil to a depth of 1 inch and heat over medium-high heat.
3. Cook steaks in hot oil, turning once, for 20 minutes or to desired degree of doneness (brown for well done and golden brown for medium). Serve with lemon slices. **Yield:** 4 servings.

Per serving: 578 calories, 28g protein, 63g carbohydrate, 24g fat, 4g fiber, 134mg cholesterol, 763mg sodium

◄ CLASSIC COMFORT FOOD

Prep Time: 10 minutes

Cook Time: 20 minutes

Average Rating: ★★★★★

What other cooks have done:

"I love chicken-fried steak, but this is the first time I have ever attempted to make it myself. The spices in the breading mixture added a nice background taste but were not over powering. I really loved the slight lemon flavor the garnish gave. We ended up topping ours with fresh squeezed lemon because we liked it so much."

Awesome Korean Steak *(pictured on page 186)*

Submitted by: **Michael Patten**
"This quick-cooking Korean steak recipe has been handed down from a Korean lady to my Mum and then to me. Serve over rice, shredded cabbage, or with fried vegetables."

½	cup soy sauce	5	tablespoons mirin (Japanese sweet wine)
5	tablespoons white sugar		
2½	tablespoons sesame seeds	2	pounds thinly sliced round steak
2	tablespoons sesame oil		
3	shallots, thinly sliced		Toasted sesame seeds (optional)
2	cloves garlic, crushed		

1. In a large bowl, stir together the soy sauce, sugar, sesame seeds, sesame oil, shallots, garlic, and mirin. Add the meat and stir to coat. Cover and marinate overnight in refrigerator.
2. Heat a large skillet over medium heat. Fry the meat for 5 to 10 minutes or until no longer pink. Sprinkle with toasted sesame seeds, if desired. **Yield:** 6 servings.

Per serving: 376 calories, 20g protein, 22g carbohydrate, 22g fat, 1g fiber, 69mg cholesterol, 1261mg sodium

◄ MAKE-AHEAD

Prep Time: 20 minutes

Marinate Time: overnight

Cook Time: 10 minutes

Average Rating: ★★★★★

What other cooks have done:

"I make coleslaw to go with this. I shred half a head of Chinese cabbage and add 2 finely sliced shallots, half a grated white radish, and 1 grated carrot. I dress up the mixture with ¼ cup light olive oil, ¼ cup superfine sugar, ½ cup white vinegar, and 1 teaspoon sesame oil."

Steak and Rice

Submitted by: **Christine Ropeter**
"A meal in itself, this spicy beef and pepper combo served over a bed of rice is an instant favorite and economical, too."

COVERED-DISH FAVORITE ▶

Prep Time: 15 minutes

Cook Time: 30 minutes

Average Rating: ★★★★★

What other cooks have done:

"I had just gotten a bunch of tomatoes from my landlady that I wanted to use since they were so sweet. The combination of the spices, tomatoes, and beef was perfect. My husband and I loved it."

2	cups water	¼	cup soy sauce
1	cup white rice	½	teaspoon garlic powder
2	tablespoons vegetable oil	½	teaspoon ground black pepper
1½	pounds round steak, sliced into 2 inch strips	½	teaspoon ground ginger
1	green bell pepper, sliced into strips	1	beef bouillon cube
1	(29 ounce) can diced tomatoes	¼	cup cornstarch
		2	cups water

1. In a saucepan, bring 2 cups of water to a boil. Stir in 1 cup of rice. Cover and reduce heat to a simmer. Simmer for 20 minutes.
2. Meanwhile, heat oil in a large frying pan over medium-high heat. Add meat and cook until medium-rare; add bell pepper and continue cooking until meat is browned.
3. Reduce heat and add tomatoes, soy sauce, garlic powder, black pepper, and ginger. Cover and simmer 10 minutes.
4. Dissolve bouillon cube and cornstarch in 2 cups water and stir well before adding to simmering beef. Cover and simmer 10 minutes, stirring occasionally, until sauce resembles the consistency of gravy. Remove from heat and serve over rice. **Yield:** 5 servings.

Per serving: 497 calories, 35g protein, 44g carbohydrate, 19g fat, 3g fiber, 83mg cholesterol, 1449mg sodium

Steak Mix-Up

Submitted by: **Kim**

"Combine sliced sirloin with peppers, onions, and tomatoes in a creamy sauce to make an easy, filling dish. Try serving over rice."

2	tablespoons vegetable oil	1	onion, chopped
1½	pounds top sirloin, cut into 2 inch strips	1	green bell pepper, chopped
		2	roma (plum) tomatoes, diced
	Salt and ground black pepper to taste	1	(10.75 ounce) can condensed cream of mushroom soup
	Garlic powder to taste		
1	teaspoon onion powder	1	cup milk

1. Heat oil in a large skillet over medium heat. Add beef, salt, black pepper, garlic powder, and onion powder. Sauté for 5 to 10 minutes or until meat is well browned. Add onion and sauté for 5 more minutes. Stir in bell pepper, tomato, soup, and milk. Mix well, reduce heat to low, and simmer for 10 to 15 minutes, stirring often. **Yield:** 4 servings.

Per serving: 572 calories, 37g protein, 16g carbohydrate, 40g fat, 2g fiber, 120mg cholesterol, 656mg sodium

◄ ONE-DISH MEAL

Prep Time: 15 minutes

Cook Time: 30 minutes

Average Rating: ★★★★★

What other cooks have done:

"This recipe was not only tasty and easy to make, it also reheated very well. I served it over tricolored pasta (which added some more color) and used half a can of cream of potato and half a can of cream of mushroom soup."

30 minutes or less

Thit Bo Sao Dau

Submitted by: **Maryellen**

"This is a wonderful Vietnamese stir-fry dish with beef and green beans."

1	clove garlic, minced	3	tablespoons vegetable oil, divided
¼	teaspoon ground black pepper	½	onion, thinly sliced
1	teaspoon cornstarch	2	cups fresh green beans, washed and trimmed
1	teaspoon vegetable oil		
1	pound sirloin tips, thinly sliced	¼	cup chicken broth
		1	teaspoon soy sauce

1. In a large mixing bowl, combine garlic, black pepper, cornstarch, and 1 teaspoon vegetable oil. Add beef and mix well.

2. Heat 2 tablespoons oil in a large wok or skillet over high heat for 1 minute. Add beef; cook and stir for about 2 minutes or until beef begins to brown. Transfer beef to a large bowl and set aside.

3. Heat remaining 1 tablespoon oil in wok. Add onion; cook, stirring constantly, until tender. Mix in green beans and broth. Cover and reduce heat to medium. Simmer for 4 to 5 minutes or until beans are tender-crisp. Stir in soy sauce and beef. Cook, stirring constantly, for 1 to 2 minutes or until heated through. **Yield:** 4 servings.

Per serving: 376 calories, 23g protein, 6g carbohydrate, 29g fat, 2g fiber, 76mg cholesterol, 202mg sodium

◄ AROUND-THE-WORLD CUISINE

Prep Time: 15 minutes

Cook Time: 15 minutes

Average Rating: ★★★★★

What other cooks have done:

"We really enjoyed this dish. I added a scant quarter teaspoon of red chile pepper flakes, and it perked things up quite nicely. I served it with jasmine rice, and the flavors really complimented each other."

Taco Bake I

Submitted by: **Leslie**

"This is a wonderful Tex-Mex dish to serve to guests or to your family. Try it with tortilla chips."

5 INGREDIENTS OR LESS ▶

Prep Time: 10 minutes

Cook Time: 30 minutes

Average Rating: ★★★★☆

What other cooks have done:

"This is a very easy dish that takes almost no time. We liked it quite a bit. I crushed tortilla chips over mine."

1½	pounds lean ground beef	1	(16 ounce) jar salsa
1	(1.25 ounce) package taco seasoning mix	2	cups shredded Monterey Jack cheese
1	(16 ounce) can refried beans		

1. Preheat oven to 350°F (175°C). Grease a 9x13 inch baking dish.
2. In a large, heavy skillet over medium-high heat, brown ground beef. Drain beef and mix in taco seasoning.
3. Spoon browned meat into prepared dish. Spoon refried beans over meat; add salsa. Top with shredded cheese.
4. Bake in the preheated oven for 20 minutes. **Yield:** 8 servings.

Per serving: 413 calories, 26g protein, 15g carbohydrate, 27g fat, 4g fiber, 93mg cholesterol, 939mg sodium

30 minutes or less

Chili Casserole

Submitted by: **Sarah**

"This is a great dish when you do not have much time to make dinner but want something that has substance and will fill you up."

KID-FRIENDLY ▶

Prep Time: 10 minutes

Cook Time: 30 minutes

Average Rating: ★★★★☆

What other cooks have done:

"This recipe was easy and very yummy! I put extra cheese in the casserole. I served it with a dollop of sour cream on each serving and with cornbread."

1½	pounds ground beef	¼	cup taco sauce
½	cup chopped onion	1	(15.25 ounce) can sweet whole kernel corn
3	stalks celery, chopped		
1	(15 ounce) can chili	1	(8 ounce) package egg noodles
1	(14.5 ounce) can peeled and diced tomatoes, undrained	¼	cup shredded Cheddar cheese

1. Preheat oven to 350°F (175°C). Grease a 9x13 inch baking dish.
2. In a large skillet over medium-high heat, sauté beef and onion for 5 to 8 minutes or until meat is browned and onion is tender; drain. Add the celery, chili, tomatoes, taco sauce, and corn. Heat thoroughly, reduce heat to low, and allow to simmer.
3. Meanwhile, prepare the noodles according to package directions. When cooked, place them in prepared dish. Pour the meat mixture over the noodles, stirring well. Top with the cheese.
4. Bake in the preheated oven for 20 minutes or until cheese is melted and bubbly. **Yield:** 6 servings.

Per serving: 669 calories, 32g protein, 52g carbohydrate, 38g fat, 7g fiber, 149mg cholesterol, 843mg sodium

Hamburger Casserole

Submitted by: **Sara**

"This is a quick and easy way to make dinner for the family. It's a hamburger casserole with Mexican flair. Try it with shredded cheese sprinkled on top."

1	pound ground beef	1	(15.25 ounce) can sweet whole kernel corn, drained
1	onion, chopped		
1	stalk celery, chopped		
8	ounces egg noodles	¼	cup salsa
1	(15 ounce) can chili	1	(1 ounce) package taco seasoning mix
1	(14.5 ounce) can peeled and diced tomatoes		

1. Preheat oven to 300°F (150°C).

2. In a large skillet over medium heat, combine ground beef, onion, and celery; sauté for 10 minutes or until the meat is browned and the onion is tender. Drain and set aside.

3. Meanwhile, cook noodles according to package directions. Drain; add to meat mixture. Stir in chili, tomatoes, corn, salsa, and taco seasoning. Mix well and place mixture into a 10x15 inch baking dish.

4. Bake in the preheated oven for 20 minutes or until thoroughly heated. **Yield:** 6 servings.

Per serving: 553 calories, 25g protein, 56g carbohydrate, 26g fat, 7g fiber, 112mg cholesterol, 1073mg sodium

◄ **FAMILY FAVORITE**

Prep Time: 15 minutes

Cook Time: 30 minutes

Average Rating: ★★★★★

What other cooks have done:

"I used a can of sloppy joe mix and rotini noodles. My can of diced tomatoes had green chiles in it, so I skipped the salsa. I served it with tortilla chips and fresh asparagus sautéed in olive oil and garlic."

Salisbury Steak

Submitted by: **Kelly Berenger**

"This recipe has been in my family for years. It's easy to cook but tastes like it took hours to make. I usually make extra sauce to pour over mashed potatoes."

1	(10.5 ounce) can condensed French onion soup, divided	1	tablespoon all-purpose flour
		¼	cup ketchup
1½	pounds ground beef	¼	cup water
½	cup dry breadcrumbs	1	tablespoon Worcestershire sauce
1	egg		
¼	teaspoon salt	½	teaspoon powdered mustard
⅛	teaspoon ground black pepper		

1. In a large bowl, mix ⅓ cup condensed French onion soup, ground beef, breadcrumbs, egg, salt, and black pepper. Shape into 6 patties.

2. In a large skillet over medium-high heat, brown patties. Drain fat.

3. In a small bowl, blend flour and remaining soup until smooth. Mix in ketchup, water, Worcestershire sauce, and mustard. Add to skillet. Cover; cook for 20 minutes, stirring occasionally. **Yield:** 6 servings.

Per serving: 441 calories, 23g protein, 14g carbohydrate, 32g fat, 1g fiber, 132mg cholesterol, 836mg sodium

◄ **FREEZER FRESH**

Prep Time: 15 minutes

Cook Time: 30 minutes

Average Rating: ★★★★★

What other cooks have done:

"I make these with mashed potatoes and corn whenever I need something easy and comforting. I have also made a double batch, except for the sauce, and have frozen one for later, which works really well. Just make the sauce when you are ready to serve the dish or use a beef gravy mix for your sauce."

Veal Forestière

Submitted by: **Bobbi**

"Breaded veal cutlets with a Marsala mushroom sauce are easy and delicious!"

RESTAURANT FARE ▶

Prep Time: 15 minutes

Cook Time: 30 minutes

Average Rating: ★★★★★

What other cooks have done:

"This is an easy and very quick recipe! I added some fresh rosemary and thyme with the garlic and shallots. I also substituted port wine for the Marsala wine, as that's what I had on hand. My husband loved it! I served it with green beans and sautéed baby bok choy."

6	(12 ounce) veal cutlets, pounded thin	½	cup Marsala wine
¼	cup all-purpose flour	½	cup veal or beef stock
3	tablespoons butter	1	(10 ounce) can artichoke hearts, drained and sliced
1	tablespoon minced garlic		Salt and ground black pepper to taste
1	tablespoon minced shallots		
8	ounces cremini mushrooms, sliced		

1. Lightly dredge veal cutlets in flour and shake off the excess. Melt butter in a large skillet over medium-high heat. Add cutlets and cook 1 to 2 minutes per side or until browned and nearly cooked through. Remove and set aside.
2. Sauté garlic and shallots in skillet until shallots are tender. Stir in mushrooms and cook until mushrooms begin to sweat. Pour in wine; cook 2 to 3 more minutes, stirring to scrape up browned bits. Add stock and simmer 5 to 10 minutes or until liquid begins to reduce.
3. Return veal to pan; add artichokes, and cook until heated through. Season with salt and pepper to taste. To serve, arrange the veal on plates and spoon the sauce over veal. **Yield:** 6 servings.

Per serving: 259 calories, 18g protein, 19g carbohydrate, 11g fat, 3g fiber, 71mg cholesterol, 596mg sodium

30 *minutes or less*

Autumn Spice Ham Steak

Submitted by: **Sarah**

"Pumpkin pie spice can be used in place of cinnamon when garnishing this ham steak smothered in maple-flavored apples and spices."

HOLIDAY FARE ▶

Prep Time: 10 minutes

Cook Time: 15 minutes

Average Rating: ★★★★☆

What other cooks have done:

"I removed the ham steaks, added ½ tablespoon of additional butter, and cooked the apples with the syrup. After the apples were nice and caramelized, I returned the ham to the pan."

1½	tablespoons butter	½	cup maple-flavored pancake syrup
1	(2 pound) ham steak	1	teaspoon ground cinnamon
1	red apple, cored and thinly sliced		
1	green apple, cored and thinly sliced		

1. Melt butter in a large skillet over medium-high heat. Add ham and cook, turning once, 10 minutes or until browned. Lay sliced apples over the ham. Pour syrup over apples. Reduce heat to medium and simmer, stirring occasionally, until apples are cooked through.
2. Sprinkle with cinnamon and serve immediately. **Yield:** 4 servings.

Per serving: 800 calories, 61g protein, 37g carbohydrate, 45g fat, 2g fiber, 225mg cholesterol, 205mg sodium

Barbecued Ham

Submitted by: **Suzanne**

"This easy-to-prepare ham is complemented by a flavorful barbecue sauce made from scratch."

1	tablespoon vegetable oil	¼	cup prepared mustard
2	tablespoons chopped onion	3	tablespoons brown sugar
½	cup ketchup	1	tablespoon Worcestershire sauce
¼	cup water	1	(1 pound) cooked ham, thinly sliced and chopped
¼	cup vinegar		

1. Heat oil in a skillet over medium heat; sauté onion until brown. In a bowl, blend together ketchup, water, vinegar, mustard, brown sugar, and Worcestershire sauce. Add mixture to skillet with onions and ham and simmer 5 to 10 minutes or until hot. **Yield:** 4 servings.

Per serving: 395 calories, 32g protein, 21g carbohydrate, 21g fat, 1g fiber, 107mg cholesterol, 645mg sodium

◀ FROM THE PANTRY

Prep Time: 15 minutes

Cook Time: 15 minutes

Average Rating: ★★★★☆

What other cooks have done:

"I made the recipe as is but added a little more ham. The sauce is a perfect consistency for serving with rice or noodles."

Ham and Fruit Stir-Fry

Submitted by: **Caity-O**

"Ham, pineapple, apple, and brown sugar are all stir-fried together in pineapple juice. This is wonderful served over couscous."

1	tablespoon olive oil	1	apple, cored and chopped
1	(2 pound) ham steak, cubed	1	tablespoon brown sugar
1	onion, chopped		Salt and ground black pepper to taste
1	(20 ounce) can pineapple chunks with juice, divided		

1. Heat oil in a large skillet over medium heat. Sauté ham and onion in the skillet for 5 minutes. Add half of the juice from the can of pineapple and simmer until juice is absorbed by the ham, about 1 to 2 minutes.

2. Stir in the pineapple chunks, apple, and brown sugar. Pour in remaining pineapple juice as needed to prevent mixture from getting too thick. Stir all ingredients together and allow to heat through, about 5 minutes. Season with salt and pepper to taste. **Yield:** 3 servings.

Per serving: 770 calories, 85g protein, 37g carbohydrate, 30g fat, 3g fiber, 212mg cholesterol, 8161mg sodium

◀ OUT-OF-THE-ORDINARY

Prep Time: 15 minutes

Cook Time: 12 minutes

Average Rating: ★★★★☆

What other cooks have done:

"Wow! So unique yet so popular. I was a little apprehensive about the apples at first, but all the fruit fit perfectly with the pineapple-flavored ham. Next time, I might add some mushrooms."

Pork Chops with Raspberry Sauce

Submitted by: **Coppertopped**

"Succulent herbed boneless pork loin chops paired with a tangy raspberry sauce are heaven on a plate! This is a special family dish that's also perfect for company. I paired it with mashed potatoes and julienned steamed carrots. My husband can't wait to have it again."

COMPANY IS COMING ▶

Prep Time: 15 minutes

Cook Time: 15 minutes

Average Rating: ★★★★★

What other cooks have done:

"This was delicious and so easy. I started making mashed potatoes first. While that was cooking, I seasoned the pork chops and started cooking them. Then I made the sauce and heated up some canned corn. Dinner was on the table so fast! The combination of the sage and thyme with the raspberry sauce was great. A definite keeper and one I would use for company."

½	teaspoon dried thyme, crushed	1	tablespoon butter
½	teaspoon dried sage, crushed	1	tablespoon olive oil
¼	teaspoon salt	¼	cup seedless raspberry jam
¼	teaspoon ground black pepper	2	tablespoons orange juice
4	(4 ounce) boneless pork loin chops	2	tablespoons white wine vinegar
		4	sprigs fresh thyme (optional)

1. Preheat oven to 200°F (95°C).

2. In a small bowl, combine thyme, sage, salt, and pepper. Rub evenly over pork chops.

3. Melt butter and olive oil in a nonstick skillet. Cook pork chops for 4 to 5 minutes on each side, turning once. Remove from skillet and keep warm in preheated oven.

4. In the skillet, combine raspberry jam, orange juice, and vinegar. Bring to a boil and cook for 2 to 3 minutes or until sauce is reduced to desired consistency. (Sauce will thicken as it cools.) Spoon sauce onto a serving plate and top with pork chops. Garnish with sprigs of thyme, if desired. **Yield:** 4 servings.

Note: You may substitute 1½ teaspoons minced fresh herbs for ½ teaspoon dried herbs.

Per serving: 321 calories, 23g protein, 15g carbohydrate, 18g fat, 0g fiber, 73mg cholesterol, 224mg sodium

Skillet Chops with Mushroom Gravy

Submitted by: **Kathy Statham**
"Serve this comforting dish with mashed potatoes and a tossed salad."

½ cup dry breadcrumbs
2 tablespoons grated Parmesan cheese
4 (4 ounce) pork chops
1 tablespoon vegetable oil
1 (10.75 ounce) can condensed cream of mushroom soup
½ cup milk

1. Combine breadcrumbs and Parmesan cheese in a large zip-top plastic bag. Add chops, 2 at a time, and shake to coat.
2. Heat oil in a large skillet over medium-high heat and cook chops until brown on both sides, about 2 minutes per side. Remove chops from skillet and reduce heat to medium.
3. Add soup and milk to skillet, stirring to scrape up any browned bits. (Adjust amount of milk to reach desired thickness.) Bring to a gentle boil, increasing heat slightly if necessary. When mixture is bubbling, return chops to skillet. Cover and reduce heat to low. Simmer for 20 minutes or until chops are cooked through. **Yield:** 4 servings.

Per serving: 347 calories, 28g protein, 17g carbohydrate, 18g fat, 1g fiber, 63mg cholesterol, 754mg sodium

◄ FROM THE PANTRY
Prep Time: 10 minutes
Cook Time: 30 minutes
Average Rating: ★★★★★
What other cooks have done:
"I use this recipe all the time with one variation—I use brown gravy mix and add a 4 ounce can of mushrooms. You can double the gravy if you're serving mashed potatoes."

Pork Chops with Blue Cheese Gravy *(pictured on page 190)*

Submitted by: **Toni**
"This recipe makes the most delicious creamy gravy to serve over pork chops."

2 tablespoons butter
1 tablespoon vegetable oil
4 (½ inch thick) pork chops
½ teaspoon ground black pepper (or to taste)
½ teaspoon garlic powder (or to taste)
1 cup whipping cream
2 ounces blue cheese, crumbled
Additional blue cheese (optional)

1. Melt butter in a large skillet over medium heat; add oil. Season the pork chops with pepper and garlic powder. Fry the chops in butter until no longer pink and the juices run clear, about 16 to 18 minutes. Turn occasionally to brown evenly.
2. Remove chops and keep warm. Add whipping cream to skillet, stirring to loosen any browned bits. Stir in blue cheese. Cook, stirring constantly, until sauce thickens, about 5 minutes. Pour sauce over warm chops. Sprinkle with additional blue cheese, if desired. **Yield:** 4 servings.

Per serving: 403 calories, 16g protein, 2g carbohydrate, 37g fat, 0g fiber, 138mg cholesterol, 296mg sodium

◄ RESTAURANT FARE
Prep Time: 10 minutes
Cook Time: 25 minutes
Average Rating: ★★★★★
What other cooks have done:
"For all you blue cheese lovers out there, this is the recipe for you! The pork chops were the most tender of any I've cooked, and the blue cheese sauce was excellent. The sauce would be fantastic over steak, too."

Indonesian Pork Satay

Submitted by: **Debbie**

"Serve with dipping sauce on the side. Chicken, beef, or lamb can also be used."

MAKE-AHEAD ▶

Prep Time: 15 minutes

Marinate Time: overnight

Cook Time: 15 minutes

Average Rating: ★★★★★

What other cooks have done:

"I didn't separate out the pork. Instead, I placed everything in a stew pot and cooked it for about 25 to 30 minutes. I served it with couscous."

2 cloves garlic, chopped	2 teaspoons crushed coriander seed
½ cup chopped green onions	
1 tablespoon chopped fresh ginger root	1 teaspoon crumbled dried red chile pepper
1 cup roasted salted peanuts	½ cup chicken broth
2 tablespoons lemon juice	½ cup melted butter
2 tablespoons honey	1½ pounds pork tenderloin, cubed
½ cup soy sauce	

1. In a blender or food processor, blend garlic, green onions, ginger, peanuts, lemon juice, honey, soy sauce, coriander, and red pepper. Puree until almost smooth. Add broth and butter; blend.
2. Place pork cubes in a heavy-duty, zip-top plastic bag and pour soy sauce mixture over meat. Marinate overnight in refrigerator.
3. Preheat broiler.
4. Remove pork from bag. Pour marinade into a saucepan; bring to a boil and cook for 5 minutes. Set aside ¼ cup of marinade to brush onto pork as it cooks. Boil remaining marinade for several more minutes and set aside to cool; reserve to use as dipping sauce.
5. Thread cubes onto skewers, if desired, and broil in the preheated oven 4 minutes. Turn pork and brush with cooked marinade. Broil 4 more minutes or until brown. **Yield:** 8 servings.

Per serving: 328 calories, 20g protein, 11g carbohydrate, 24g fat, 2g fiber, 71mg cholesterol, 1268mg sodium

30 minutes or less

Peach Pork Picante *(pictured on page 189)*

Submitted by: **Christine Johnson**

"This one-skillet dish is just peachy! Salsa, seasoning, pork, and peach preserves all add up to one fruity, tangy treat."

FROM THE PANTRY ▶

Prep Time: 10 minutes

Cook Time: 15 minutes

Average Rating: ★★★★★

What other cooks have done:

"I used kitchen scissors to cut up the pork. Also, I doubled the peach preserves because I used hot salsa and wanted a sweeter taste. I served it over white rice."

1 pound boneless pork loin, cubed	1 cup salsa
	¼ cup peach preserves
1 (1.25 ounce) package taco seasoning mix	Hot cooked rice
	Chopped fresh cilantro (optional)
1 tablespoon olive oil	

1. Season pork with taco seasoning. Heat oil in a large skillet over medium-high heat. Add pork and sauté 5 minutes or until browned. Add salsa and peach preserves; mix well. Cover and reduce heat. Let simmer for about 10 minutes and serve over rice. Sprinkle with chopped cilantro, if desired. **Yield:** 4 servings.

Per serving: 223 calories, 16g protein, 15g carbohydrate, 11g fat, 1g fiber, 45mg cholesterol, 558mg sodium

Thai Pork Loin

Submitted by: **Henry Stollard**
"Thinly sliced pork loin combines with butter, wine, and fresh cilantro for a quick and savory dish."

1 pound thinly sliced pork loin	1 cup chicken stock
Salt and ground black pepper to taste	1 cup dry white wine
1 tablespoon unsalted butter	3 tablespoons chopped fresh cilantro
1 tablespoon extra virgin olive oil	

1. Season pork with salt and pepper to taste.
2. In a large skillet, heat butter and olive oil over medium heat. Add pork to hot skillet and cook until browned, turning once. Add chicken stock and cook until liquid thickens.
3. Stir in dry white wine, scraping the bottom of the pan to loosen browned bits. Reduce heat and simmer until liquid is reduced by half. Remove from heat and allow to cool slightly. Stir in cilantro. Spoon sauce over pork and serve. **Yield:** 4 servings.

Per serving: 332 calories, 23g protein, 1g carbohydrate, 21g fat, 0g fiber, 79mg cholesterol, 602mg sodium

◄ AROUND-THE-WORLD CUISINE
Prep Time: 15 minutes
Cook Time: 30 minutes
Average Rating: ★★★★★
What other cooks have done:
"This is one of my favorite quick and easy dishes. I make it all the time. If I don't have cilantro, it's also great with one bunch of green onions, thinly sliced."

---

30 *minutes or less*

Pork in Olive Oil Marinade

Submitted by: **Marlies Monika**
"Serve this light Mediterranean meal with French bread."

5 tablespoons olive oil, divided	¼ cup red wine vinegar
1½ pounds pork tenderloin, cut into bite-size pieces	2 tablespoons port wine
2 cloves garlic, minced	Pinch salt
4 sprigs fresh cilantro, chopped	Pinch ground black pepper
	Pinch cayenne pepper

1. Heat 2 tablespoons olive oil in a large, heavy skillet over high heat. Sauté pork until evenly browned and fully cooked. Transfer to a bowl and sprinkle with garlic and cilantro; keep warm.
2. In a small bowl, combine 3 tablespoons olive oil, vinegar, and port. Season with salt, black pepper, and cayenne. Whisk until consistency is creamy. Stir into cooked pork and serve immediately. **Yield:** 4 servings.

Per serving: 337 calories, 28g protein, 2g carbohydrate, 23g fat, 0g fiber, 80mg cholesterol, 154mg sodium

◄ RESTAURANT FARE
Prep Time: 15 minutes
Cook Time: 10 minutes
Average Rating: ★★★★★
What other cooks have done:
"After browning the pork, I added a bit of sherry (didn't have port wine) to the skillet to deglaze it. Then I added the drippings in with the olive oil and vinegar that I tossed with the pork pieces. Didn't have fresh cilantro, so I used dried, and it still tasted wonderful!"

Sweet-and-Sour Smoked Sausage

Submitted by: **Andrea Evans**

"My brother created this recipe when he first got married; it's one of my favorites. I love to serve it with corn, mashed potatoes, and croissant rolls. You can find sweet-and-sour sauce in the Asian food section of your local supermarket."

HOT & SPICY ▶

Prep Time: 15 minutes

Cook Time: 30 minutes

Average Rating: ★★★★★

What other cooks have done:

"Very easy and different. Also good on torpedo or hoagie rolls as a sandwich."

1½ pounds smoked sausage, sliced
1 green bell pepper, sliced into strips
1 red bell pepper, sliced into strips
1 onion, thinly sliced
2 tablespoons butter

Salt and ground black pepper to taste
2 tablespoons sweet-and-sour sauce
Pinch cayenne pepper
Dash hot pepper sauce (or to taste)

1. Place the sausage in a large skillet over medium–high heat. Sauté for 5 to 10 minutes, turning often, or until well browned. Drain and set sausage aside.

2. In the same skillet over medium heat, combine the green bell pepper, red bell pepper, onion, and butter and sauté for 10 minutes or until all vegetables are tender. Add the sausage and stir together well. Season with salt and ground black pepper to taste.

3. Add the sweet-and-sour sauce, cayenne pepper, and hot pepper sauce. Reduce heat to low and simmer for 5 to 10 minutes, allowing all the flavors to blend. **Yield:** 5 servings.

Per serving: 600 calories, 31g protein, 10g carbohydrate, 48g fat, 1g fiber, 105mg cholesterol, 2120mg sodium

Sausage Gravy I

Submitted by: **Rene**

"My mother learned how to make this while we lived in Nashville many years ago, and it is now a family favorite. Good, old-fashioned sausage gravy is her most requested recipe from family and friends alike. Serve over biscuits or toast."

6	slices bacon	½	teaspoon salt
1	pound ground pork sausage	¼	teaspoon ground black pepper
¼	cup all-purpose flour		
3	cups milk		

1. Cook bacon in a large skillet over medium-high heat. Reserve bacon for another use. In the same skillet, brown sausage. Set aside, leaving the drippings in the skillet.
2. Reduce heat to medium; add flour to the skillet and stir constantly until mixture just turns golden brown.
3. Gradually whisk milk into skillet. When the mixture is smooth, thickened, and begins to bubble, return the sausage to skillet. Season with salt and pepper. Reduce heat and simmer for about 15 minutes.
Yield: 8 servings.

Per serving: 343 calories, 10g protein, 8g carbohydrate, 30g fat, 0g fiber, 51mg cholesterol, 598mg sodium

◄ CLASSIC COMFORT FOOD

Prep Time: 5 minutes

Cook Time: 30 minutes

Average Rating: ★★★★★

What other cooks have done:

"This is an excellent, tasty recipe. I made it for the first time three years ago for our family Christmas breakfast, and it was an instant hit. Now, it's part of our yearly menu. Try making it a couple of hours ahead of time and putting it in a slow-cooker until ready to serve."

Down-Home Casserole

Submitted by: **Lillian Merkel**

"This recipe is my mother's, and everyone loves it. She is 86 and a wonderful cook. I am submitting it in her name. This is good home-cooking."

6	slices bacon	2	carrots, chopped
4	potatoes, peeled and thinly sliced	1	onion, chopped
1	large head fresh broccoli, chopped	1	pound kielbasa sausage, cut into 1 inch pieces
½	cup chopped celery		Salt and ground black pepper to taste

1. In a large, heavy skillet over medium-high heat, cook bacon until crisp, about 10 minutes. Remove the bacon, reserving drippings in the skillet.
2. Add potatoes, broccoli, celery, carrots, and onion to the skillet. Reduce heat to medium and sauté for 5 minutes. Place the kielbasa over vegetables, allowing juices to trickle down over the vegetables.
3. Sauté for 5 to 10 more minutes or until vegetables reach desired tenderness. Season with salt and pepper to taste. Crumble the reserved bacon, return it to the skillet, and stir to combine. **Yield:** 5 servings.

Per serving: 585 calories, 20g protein, 28g carbohydrate, 44g fat, 6g fiber, 83mg cholesterol, 1267mg sodium

◄ FAMILY FAVORITE

Prep Time: 20 minutes

Cook Time: 25 minutes

Average Rating: ★★★★☆

What other cooks have done:

"I cooked the potatoes for about 10 minutes in the microwave before adding them to the skillet. Also, I used a little more bacon and seasoned it all with some garlic and onion powder. Very tasty meal! We loved it and wanted more when it was all gone. Some of us sprinkled a little cheese over our bowl, but the dish was good without it, too."

Smoked Sausage and Zucchini Sauté

Submitted by: **Amy Franklin**

"This quick and easy main dish is a good way to use up extra zucchini from the summer garden. My mother used to make this to keep the kitchen from getting too hot from the oven. Serve over cooked rice."

FAMILY FAVORITE ▶

Prep Time: 20 minutes

Cook Time: 15 minutes

Average Rating: ★★★★☆

What other cooks have done:

"The perfect summertime dinner. I served it on a bed of brown rice cooked with chicken broth and green onions."

1 pound smoked sausage, cut into 1 inch pieces	½ teaspoon garlic salt
1 tablespoon butter or margarine	¼ teaspoon dried oregano
2 zucchini, cut lengthwise, then in half	¼ teaspoon ground black pepper
1 tablespoon instant minced onion	2 tomatoes, chopped

1. In a skillet over medium heat, brown the sausage. Remove sausage from skillet and set aside. Add butter, zucchini, and onion to the skillet and cook until zucchini is tender-crisp. Return the browned sausage to the skillet and add garlic salt, oregano, and pepper. Cook until all ingredients are hot. Add chopped tomatoes and serve immediately. **Yield:** 4 servings.

Per serving: 501 calories, 27g protein, 11g carbohydrate, 39g fat, 2g fiber, 77mg cholesterol, 2346mg sodium

S.O.P.P.

Submitted by: **Jennifer**

"S.O.P.P. stands for sausage, onions, potatoes, and peppers. This is a simple stir-fry that tastes delicious and is easy to whip up for your family."

5 INGREDIENTS OR LESS ▶

Prep Time: 20 minutes

Cook Time: 25 minutes

Average Rating: ★★★★☆

What other cooks have done:

"I use this recipe with cooked, sliced Italian sausage. I add a little red pepper oil to a pan, sauté the peppers and onion, add the meat to brown, and then toss with cooked rotini noodles and a little more oil. Excellent!"

2 tablespoons vegetable oil	1 onion, sliced
6 potatoes, peeled and cubed	2 green bell peppers, chopped
2 pounds smoked sausage, sliced	

1. Heat oil in a large skillet over medium heat. Place the potatoes in the skillet. Cover and simmer, stirring occasionally, until potatoes are almost tender and lightly browned, about 10 minutes.
2. Stir in the sausage, onion, and bell pepper. Cover and cook for about 15 more minutes or until onion and bell pepper reach desired tenderness. **Yield:** 5 servings.

Per serving: 892 calories, 44g protein, 35g carbohydrate, 63g fat, 5g fiber, 123mg cholesterol, 2736mg sodium

Classy Chicken *(pictured on page 2)*

Submitted by: **Monica deRegt**

"This is an elegant, easy-to-make chicken dish bursting with flavors of sun-dried tomatoes and creamy white wine sauce. My husband calls this the classiest meal I serve because it's exactly like what you order in a fancy restaurant. It pairs nicely with roasted baby potatoes and steamed broccoli and it's also delicious served over fettuccine."

⅓ cup sliced sun-dried tomatoes
1 cup all-purpose flour
4 skinless, boneless chicken breast halves
  Salt and ground black pepper to taste
2 tablespoons butter or margarine
½ cup chicken broth
½ cup dry white wine
1 tablespoon prepared Dijon-style mustard
1 zucchini, cut in half lengthwise, then sliced diagonally
1 clove garlic
1 teaspoon dill weed
⅓ cup sour cream
⅓ cup chicken broth
¼ teaspoon salt
  Ground black pepper (optional)

◄ COMPANY IS COMING

Prep Time: 15 minutes

Cook Time: 25 minutes

Average Rating: ★★★★★

What other cooks have done:

"This is a terrific meal. I made two minor changes. I used olive oil instead of butter and added a lot more zucchini. This is indeed a very pretty and appetizing meal. It is also very fast. I served this over whole wheat couscous. I can't wait to have company over for dinner so I can serve this."

1. Place sun-dried tomatoes in a small bowl and cover with hot water. Set aside.

2. Place the flour in a shallow dish. Season chicken with salt and pepper to taste; dredge in flour. Shake off excess flour. Heat the butter in a large skillet over medium-high heat. Brown the chicken breasts on each side, about 3 minutes per side.

3. Pour ½ cup chicken broth and white wine into the skillet, scraping the pan to loosen any browned bits. Stir in the mustard. Cover and cook for a few minutes until chicken springs back when touched but is not cooked through. Drain sun-dried tomatoes. Add the zucchini and sun-dried tomatoes; season with garlic and dill weed. Cover and cook until the zucchini is tender and the chicken is no longer pink and juices run clear, about 5 to 10 minutes.

4. Remove the chicken to a platter and remove the pan from the heat. Stir sour cream and ⅓ cup broth into the pan liquid. Season with ¼ teaspoon salt and serve chicken with sauce. Sprinkle with pepper, if desired **Yield:** 4 servings.

Per serving: 346 calories, 30g protein, 31g carbohydrate, 9g fat, 2g fiber, 76mg cholesterol, 375mg sodium

Lemon-Mushroom-Herb Chicken

Submitted by: **Valerie Serao**

"Easy chicken and herbs in a creamy lemon and mushroom sauce. The sauce is excellent over rice—my kids can't get enough!"

FAMILY FAVORITE ▶

Prep Time: 15 minutes

Cook Time: 25 minutes

Average Rating: ★★★★★

What other cooks have done:

"If you've never tried capers, the flavor reminds me somewhat of Dijon mustard. Toward the end of cooking, I uncovered the pan, letting the sauce simmer so it would be a little thicker. Serve over brown rice along with sides of sugar snap peas and cottage cheese."

1	cup all-purpose flour
½	tablespoon dried thyme
2	tablespoons dried basil
1	tablespoon dried parsley
1	teaspoon paprika
1	teaspoon salt
½	teaspoon ground black pepper
1	teaspoon garlic powder
4	skinless, boneless chicken breast halves
½	cup butter
1	(10.75 ounce) can condensed cream of mushroom soup
1	(10.5 ounce) can condensed chicken broth
¼	cup dry white wine
1	lemon, juiced
1	tablespoon chopped fresh parsley
2	tablespoons capers
1	tablespoon grated lemon zest

1. In a shallow dish or bowl, combine the flour, thyme, basil, parsley, paprika, salt, ground black pepper, and garlic powder. Dredge chicken in the mixture to coat, patting off any excess flour.

2. Melt butter in a large skillet over medium heat and cook chicken until no longer translucent. In a medium bowl, mix together the cream of mushroom soup, chicken broth, wine, and lemon juice; pour over chicken.

3. Cover skillet and simmer 20 minutes or until chicken is no longer pink and juices run clear. Garnish with parsley, capers, and lemon zest. **Yield:** 4 servings.

Per serving: 579 calories, 36g protein, 37g carbohydrate, 32g fat, 4g fiber, 132mg cholesterol, 2021mg sodium

Chicken Catch-a-Cola

Submitted by: **Benjamin Lankheet**

"The idea of using a cola beverage came to me after fixing redeye gravy, which uses coffee for flavor. Here, you get the cola flavor with a little sweetness. You will be very pleasantly surprised by the great taste of this dish."

⅓ cup seasoned dry
    breadcrumbs
1 teaspoon paprika
½ teaspoon salt
¼ teaspoon ground black
    pepper
4 skinless, boneless chicken
    breast halves, pounded to
    ½ inch thickness

1 tablespoon butter
1 cup cola-flavored
    carbonated beverage
3 ounces deli ham slices
1 cup sliced fresh mushrooms
½ cup cooking sherry
1 tablespoon balsamic vinegar
½ cup sour cream

1. Combine breadcrumbs, paprika, salt, and pepper in a zip-top plastic bag. Place chicken breasts in the bag and shake to coat.
2. Melt butter in a large skillet over medium heat. Add chicken breasts and cook for 4 minutes on each side or until brown. Remove chicken to a plate and keep warm. Pour the cola into the skillet and stir to loosen any browned bits from the pan. Add ham, mushrooms, sherry, and balsamic vinegar. Reduce heat to medium-low and simmer, uncovered, until the liquid has reduced by half.
3. Stir sour cream into the skillet and return chicken breasts to the pan. Cover and simmer for 5 more minutes or until chicken is no longer pink and juices run clear or until a meat thermometer inserted into thickest part of chicken registers 170°F (75°C). Remove chicken to serving plates and spoon sauce over each serving. **Yield:** 4 servings.

Per serving: 377 calories, 36g protein, 22g carbohydrate, 15g fat, 1g fiber, 109mg cholesterol, 873mg sodium

◄ FROM THE PANTRY
Prep Time: 15 minutes
Cook Time: 25 minutes
Average Rating: ★★★★★

What other cooks have done:
"This really turned out great! I added some chopped onion to the chicken for an extra kick. And I think that next time I will add some cornstarch to the sauce to thicken it. It was wonderful served over egg noodles."

Aussie Chicken *(pictured on facing page)*

Submitted by: **Rebecca**

"This recipe is very similar to a chicken dish served at a local well-known restaurant. A friend of mine was kind enough to share it. It includes chicken breasts topped with mushrooms, bacon, and cheese cooked in a yummy honey-mustard sauce."

RESTAURANT FARE ▶

Prep Time: 15 minutes

Chill Time: 30 minutes

Cook Time: 25 minutes

Average Rating: ★★★★★

What other cooks have done:

"This was very good. I only coated the chicken with the honey mustard mixture. Then I put a piece of cheese on top of the chicken to hold the mushrooms and bacon in place."

4	skinless, boneless chicken breast halves, pounded to ½ inch thickness	1	tablespoon dried onion flakes
2	teaspoons seasoning salt	1	tablespoon vegetable oil
6	slices bacon, cut in half	1	cup sliced fresh mushrooms
½	cup prepared mustard	2	cups shredded Colby-Monterey Jack cheese
½	cup honey	2	tablespoons chopped fresh parsley (optional)
¼	cup light corn syrup		
¼	cup mayonnaise		

1. Rub chicken breasts with seasoning salt; cover and refrigerate for 30 minutes.

2. Preheat oven to 350°F (175°C).

3. In a medium bowl, combine the mustard, honey, corn syrup, mayonnaise, and dried onion flakes. Reserve half of sauce in refrigerator.

4. Place bacon in a large, deep skillet. Cook over medium-high heat until crisp. Set aside.

5. Meanwhile, heat oil in a large skillet over medium heat. Add chicken to skillet and sauté for 3 to 5 minutes per side or until browned. Remove from skillet and place the breasts into a 9x13 inch baking dish.

6. Apply honey-mustard sauce to each breast; layer each breast evenly with mushrooms and bacon. Sprinkle each breast with shredded cheese.

7. Bake in the preheated oven for 15 minutes or until cheese is melted and chicken juices run clear. Garnish with parsley, if desired, and serve with the reserved honey-mustard sauce. **Yield:** 4 servings.

Per serving: 976 calories, 47g protein, 58g carbohydrate, 64g fat, 2g fiber, 140mg cholesterol, 1714mg sodium

Aussie Chicken

Awesome Korean Steak, page 167

Smothered Mexican Lasagna, page 200

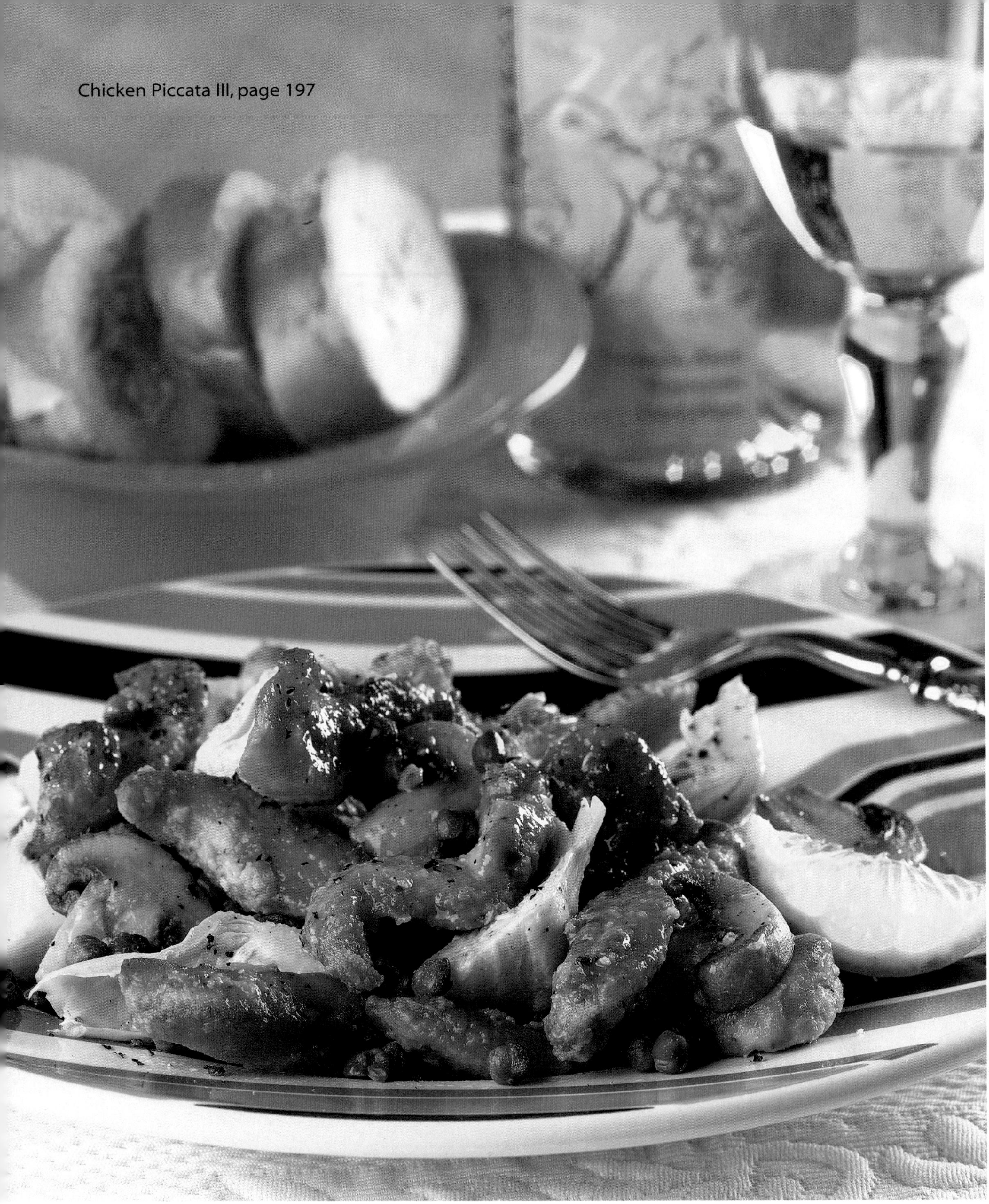

Chicken Piccata III, page 197

Peach Pork Picante, page 176

Shrimp Étouffée II, page 204

Pork Chops with Blue Cheese
Gravy, page 175

Baked Halibut Steaks, page 201

Acapulco Chicken

Acapulco Chicken *(pictured on facing page)*

Submitted by: **CapeCodLorrie**

"Easy, fast, and delicious! This perfect weeknight dish takes me less than 30 minutes, so it's a regular in our house. You can vary the heat by the kinds and amounts of chili powder and hot peppers you use. Serve over hot cooked rice in taco bowls, if desired."

2 skinless, boneless chicken breast halves, cut into bite-size pieces	½ cup chopped onion
1 tablespoon chili powder, divided	2 jalapeño peppers, seeded and minced
Salt and ground black pepper to taste	1 large tomato, cut into chunks
1 tablespoon olive oil	10 drops hot pepper sauce
1 cup chopped green bell pepper	Shredded Cheddar cheese (optional)

1. Season chicken with ½ tablespoon chili powder and salt and black pepper to taste. Heat oil in a large skillet over medium-high heat and sauté seasoned chicken for 3 to 4 minutes or until chicken is no longer pink and juices run clear. Remove from skillet with a slotted spoon and keep warm.

2. In same skillet, stir-fry bell pepper and onion until soft. Add jalapeño pepper, tomato, remaining ½ tablespoon chili powder, and hot pepper sauce. Cook, stirring occasionally, for 3 to 5 more minutes; add chicken and stir-fry for 2 more minutes. Sprinkle with cheese, if desired. **Yield:** 2 servings.

Per serving: 333 calories, 30g protein, 24g carbohydrate, 14g fat, 5g fiber, 72mg cholesterol, 635mg sodium

◄ HOT & SPICY

Prep Time: 20 minutes

Cook Time: 15 minutes

Average Rating: ★★★★★

What other cooks have done:

"I'm not a big fan of super spicy foods, so I did not use hot sauce or the jalapeño peppers. I added one can of black beans and three cloves pressed garlic. Also, instead of one fresh tomato, I used one can of diced tomatoes with chiles. I served it with Mexican rice and also had Cheddar cheese, black olives, and sour cream for garnishes. I will definitely make this again."

Mandarin Orange Chicken

Submitted by: **Tammie Bickar**

"For a pretty and tasty dish that's easy and quick, serve this with rice."

OUT-OF-THE-ORDINARY ▶

Prep Time: 20 minutes

Cook Time: 25 minutes

Average Rating: ★★★★☆

What other cooks have done:

"The sauce for this recipe is so delicious; it can also be used for pork. It would make a great egg roll dip as well. Everyone who has tasted this wants the recipe."

4	skinless, boneless chicken breast halves, pounded to ¼ inch thickness	⅓	cup orange juice
¼	cup all-purpose flour	1	(11 ounce) can mandarin oranges, drained
2	tablespoons olive oil	1	tablespoon chopped green onions
2	tablespoons butter	¼	cup chopped cashews
⅓	cup hoisin sauce		

1. Dredge chicken in flour to lightly coat.

2. Heat olive oil and butter in a medium skillet over medium heat and sauté the chicken breasts until chicken is no longer pink and juices run clear. Set aside and keep warm.

3. Stir hoisin sauce and orange juice into the skillet, scraping up the browned bits. Mix in mandarin oranges, green onions, and cashews. Return chicken to the skillet. Heat through. **Yield:** 4 servings.

Note: Hoisin sauce, also called Peking sauce, is a thick, reddish-brown sauce that is sweet and spicy and widely used in Chinese cooking. It can be found in Asian markets and in the Asian or ethnic section of many large supermarkets.

Per serving: 403 calories, 31g protein, 28g carbohydrate, 19g fat, 2g fiber, 85mg cholesterol, 536mg sodium

30 *minutes or less*

T's Easy Chicken

Submitted by: **Tracy**

"I just came up with this one day when I was fooling around in the kitchen."

FROM THE PANTRY ▶

Prep Time: 10 minutes

Cook Time: 17 minutes

Average Rating: ★★★★☆

What other cooks have done:

"I just moved, so there wasn't much in my fridge. I used balsamic vinaigrette, lemon juice, fresh mushrooms, and a whole can of diced tomatoes with the juice, and it turned out great. I served it with angel hair pasta and fresh asparagus that I picked up that day."

¼	cup olive oil	½	cup sliced fresh mushrooms
¼	cup fresh lemon juice	½	cup diced tomatoes, drained
¼	cup diced onion		
4	skinless, boneless chicken breast halves		

1. Heat oil and lemon juice in a large skillet over medium heat; add onion and sauté. When onion is tender, add chicken, mushrooms, and tomatoes.

2. Cook over medium–high heat for 5 to 7 minutes each side, stirring occasionally, or until chicken is no longer pink and juices run clear. **Yield:** 4 servings.

Per serving: 255 calories, 24g protein, 4g carbohydrate, 16g fat, 1g fiber, 61mg cholesterol, 98mg sodium

No-Fuss Chicken

Submitted by: **Don Johnson**

"Chicken breasts breaded with crushed cornflake cereal are quick, easy, and delicious. Serve with rice, if desired, and use extra mayonnaise mixture for dipping."

4	skinless, boneless chicken breasts	2	tablespoons prepared mustard
1	cup mayonnaise	¼	cup grated Parmesan cheese
		1	cup crushed cornflake cereal

1. Preheat oven to 400°F (200°C). Lightly grease a 9x13 inch dish.
2. Rinse chicken and pat dry. In a small bowl, mix together the mayonnaise, mustard, and cheese. Brush mixture onto chicken pieces to coat.
3. Place cereal crumbs in a shallow dish or bowl; roll chicken in crumbs to coat and place coated chicken in prepared dish.
4. Bake in the preheated oven, uncovered, for 20 to 25 minutes or until chicken is no longer pink and juices run clear. **Yield:** 4 servings.

Per serving: 643 calories, 33g protein, 21g carbohydrate, 47g fat, 0g fiber, 106mg cholesterol, 762mg sodium

◄ **5 INGREDIENTS OR LESS**

Prep Time: 15 minutes

Cook Time: 25 minutes

Average Rating: ★★★★★

What other cooks have done:

"I made this with my 10-year-old daughter. It was moist and flavorful, yet still crispy due to the cornflake crumbs. I used seasoned salt, onion powder, and some basil flakes in the cornflake crumbs for color. Everyone loved it."

Cream Cheese Chicken

Submitted by: **Jenny**

"A nice alternative to everyday chicken, this dish is great for special occasions."

1	teaspoon butter	1	cup packed brown sugar
8	ounces fresh mushrooms, sliced	½	cup prepared Dijon-style mustard
2	(3 ounce) packages cream cheese, softened	½	cup chopped walnuts
6	skinless, boneless chicken breast halves		

1. Preheat oven to 450°F (230°C).
2. Melt butter in a skillet over medium heat. Sauté mushrooms until tender. Reduce heat to low and stir in cream cheese until melted. Remove from heat.
3. Pound chicken breasts thin with a meat mallet. Spread with mushroom mixture and roll up. In a small bowl, mix together brown sugar and Dijon mustard. Press mustard mixture onto chicken. Roll chicken in chopped nuts. Place in a baking dish.
4. Bake in the preheated oven, uncovered, for 15 to 20 minutes or until chicken is no longer pink and juices run clear. **Yield:** 6 servings.

Per serving: 472 calories, 33g protein, 42g carbohydrate, 21g fat, 1g fiber, 101mg cholesterol, 688mg sodium

◄ **COVERED-DISH FAVORITE**

Prep Time: 15 minutes

Cook Time: 26 minutes

Average Rating: ★★★★★

What other cooks have done:

"I spread out a long sheet of wax paper on my counter before I started working, and I'm glad I did—it was a mess, and it was nice to just throw away the paper!"

Honey Chicken

Submitted by: **Sarah**

"This is a great marinade. Chicken breasts are bathed in a tangy citrus and honey marinade and baked to perfection."

MAKE-AHEAD ▶

Prep Time: 10 minutes

Marinate Time: overnight

Cook Time: 25 minutes

Average Rating: ★★★★★

What other cooks have done:

"We didn't have regular orange juice, so we squeezed our own. We made drumsticks instead of breasts and were very happy with the results."

¾ cup orange juice	½ teaspoon ground black pepper
2 tablespoons fresh lemon juice	1 teaspoon curry powder
¼ cup olive oil	½ teaspoon paprika
½ cup honey	4 skinless, boneless chicken breast halves
1 teaspoon salt	

1. Combine orange juice, lemon juice, oil, honey, salt, pepper, curry powder, and paprika. Mix well. Add chicken breasts and toss to coat. Cover and marinate overnight in refrigerator.
2. Preheat oven to 350°F (175°C). Lightly grease a 9x13 inch dish.
3. Remove chicken from marinade, discarding any remaining marinade, and place in prepared dish.
4. Bake in the preheated oven, uncovered, for 20 to 25 minutes or until chicken is no longer pink and juices run clear. **Yield:** 4 servings.

Per serving: 404 calories, 28g protein, 41g carbohydrate, 15g fat, 1g fiber, 68mg cholesterol, 661mg sodium

Chicken Provolone

Submitted by: **ashbeth**

"This is great for large dinner parties and church dinners. I've also used skinless, boneless chicken thighs, and it turned out great every time!"

CROWD-PLEASER ▶

Prep Time: 15 minutes

Cook Time: 30 minutes

Average Rating: ★★★★★

What other cooks have done:

"This had a pleasing, subtle white wine flavor that wasn't overpowering. This is a very simple dish with no frills that I would serve company."

8 skinless, boneless chicken breast halves	1¼ cups white wine
4 slices provolone cheese, halved	¼ cup melted butter
2 (10.75 ounce) cans condensed cream of chicken soup	1 (16 ounce) package herb-seasoned stuffing mix

1. Preheat oven to 350°F (175°C). Grease a 9x13 inch baking dish.
2. Arrange chicken in a single layer in prepared dish. Top each breast half with a half slice of provolone cheese.
3. In a medium bowl, blend cream of chicken soup and white wine. Pour over the chicken.
4. In a separate medium bowl, mix the butter and stuffing mix. Top the chicken with the stuffing mixture.
5. Bake in the preheated oven, uncovered, for 30 minutes or until chicken is no longer pink and juices run clear. **Yield:** 8 servings.

Per serving: 551 calories, 40g protein, 49g carbohydrate, 17g fat, 4g fiber, 100mg cholesterol, 1642mg sodium

Chicken Piccata III *(pictured on page 188)*

Submitted by: **Sharon**
"This variation on the original uses mushrooms and artichoke hearts for a tasty twist. Yum! Serve over pasta or rice. White wine or water may be substituted for chicken broth."

½ cup all-purpose flour	3 tablespoons lemon juice
½ teaspoon paprika	¾ cup chicken broth
Salt and ground black pepper to taste	½ teaspoon garlic powder
1 pound skinless, boneless chicken breast halves, cut into thin strips	1 (14 ounce) can artichoke hearts, drained and quartered
¼ cup vegetable oil	Capers (optional)
4 ounces fresh mushrooms, sliced	Lemon wedges (optional)

1. In a shallow bowl, mix together flour, paprika, and salt and pepper to taste. Dredge chicken pieces in the seasoned flour.

2. Heat oil in a large skillet over medium heat and sauté chicken until light golden brown, about 2 minutes. Remove chicken from skillet and set aside.

3. Add mushrooms, lemon juice, and chicken broth to skillet. Simmer until a smooth, light sauce develops. Season with garlic powder. Return chicken to the skillet and simmer until chicken is no longer pink and juices run clear. Stir in artichoke hearts and remove from heat. Garnish with capers and lemon wedges, if desired. **Yield:** 4 servings.

Per serving: 445 calories, 33g protein, 38g carbohydrate, 18g fat, 5g fiber, 69mg cholesterol, 883mg sodium

◄ COMPANY IS COMING

Prep Time: 20 minutes

Cook Time: 15 minutes

Average Rating: ★★★★★

What other cooks have done:
"Pretty easy to make and tasted very good. I ended up using chicken breast halves pounded to about ¼ inch thickness rather than strips. Also, I added capers at the end because I always think that capers are part of piccata."

Basil Chicken over Angel Hair *(pictured on page 1)*

Submitted by: **Wendy Mercadante**
"A tasty chicken and pasta dish."

FAMILY FAVORITE ▶

Prep Time: 15 minutes

Cook Time: 20 minutes

Average Rating: ★★★★☆

What other cooks have done:

"I marinated the chicken in olive oil, minced dried onion, Italian seasoning, and fresh garlic. I also used a red onion in the recipe, and I used a drained can of garlic and onion diced tomatoes instead of fresh tomatoes."

1	(8 ounce) package dried angel hair pasta	¼	cup chopped fresh
2	teaspoons olive oil	½	teaspoon salt
½	cup finely chopped onion	⅛	teaspoon hot pepper sauce
1	clove garlic, chopped	¼	cup freshly grated Parmesan cheese
2½	cups chopped tomatoes		Fresh basil (optional)
2	cups cooked, cubed chicken		

1. Bring a large pot of lightly salted water to a boil; cook angel hair pasta about 8 to 10 minutes or until al dente. Drain and set aside.
2. Meanwhile, in a large skillet, heat oil over medium-high heat. Sauté onion and garlic until tender. Stir in tomatoes, chicken, basil, salt, and hot pepper sauce. Reduce heat to medium and cover skillet. Simmer for 10 minutes, stirring frequently, or until mixture is hot and tomatoes are soft. Toss mixture with hot cooked angel hair pasta. Top with Parmesan cheese. Garnish with fresh basil, if desired. **Yield:** 4 servings.

Per serving: 372 calories, 29g protein, 39g carbohydrate, 11g fat, 4g fiber, 57mg cholesterol, 580mg sodium

Chicken I Hate You!

Submitted by: **Kate Lacey**
"Why the name? One time, my husband came home late from work without calling me. When he asked me, 'What's for dinner?' I said, 'Chicken I hate you!'—and a new dish was born! It's great."

FROM THE PANTRY ▶

Prep Time: 20 minutes

Cook Time: 25 minutes

Average Rating: ★★★★☆

What other cooks have done:

"The night I made this, my husband walked in the door 45 minutes later than expected. He, too, asked me what was for dinner and when I told him the name, he turned ghostly white! Perfect reaction to a wonderful and easy to prepare dinner."

1	tablespoon vegetable oil	1	(16 ounce) can Italian-style diced tomatoes, drained
1	pound skinless, boneless chicken breast halves, cut into chunks	1	(4.5 ounce) jar sliced mushrooms, drained
1	(4.5 ounce) package Alfredo sauce egg noodles mix	1	tablespoon grated Parmesan cheese
1	(10 ounce) can asparagus spears, drained		

1. Heat oil in a large skillet over medium-high heat. Add chicken and sauté until chicken is no longer pink and juices run clear.
2. Meanwhile, prepare Alfredo noodles according to package directions; when finished, stir in cooked chicken, asparagus, tomatoes, and mushrooms. Sprinkle with cheese and serve. **Yield:** 4 servings.

Per serving: 337 calories, 35g protein, 27g carbohydrate, 10g fat, 3g fiber, 102mg cholesterol, 1165mg sodium

Chicken and Shrimp

Submitted by: **Gail**

"Elegant, easy, and delicious."

5	tablespoons olive oil, divided	1¼	teaspoons salt, divided
1	(8 ounce) package sliced fresh mushrooms	4	skinless, boneless chicken breast halves, cut into 1 inch cubes
1	onion, chopped	¼	cup dry white wine
2	cloves garlic, chopped	1¼	cups water
1	pound large shrimp, peeled and deveined		Ground black pepper to taste
3	tablespoons all-purpose flour, divided		

1. Heat 1 tablespoon oil in a large skillet over medium-high heat. Sauté mushrooms until golden; remove from skillet with a slotted spoon and set aside.

2. Add another 2 tablespoons oil to skillet. Sauté onion, garlic, and shrimp until shrimp turn pink. Remove from skillet and set aside with mushrooms.

3. In a shallow dish or bowl, mix 2 tablespoons flour with ¾ teaspoon salt. Dredge chicken in flour to coat. Add 1 tablespoon oil to skillet and sauté chicken in oil for 3 to 5 minutes or until chicken is no longer pink and juices run clear. Set chicken aside with shrimp and mushrooms.

4. Heat 1 tablespoon oil in skillet and stir in 1 tablespoon flour. Cook about 30 seconds, stirring constantly, until brown. Stir in wine, ½ teaspoon salt, and water. Boil for 1 minute.

5. Reduce heat to medium-low and return chicken, shrimp, and mushrooms to skillet. Simmer for about 10 minutes. Season with pepper to taste and serve. **Yield:** 6 servings.

Per serving: 425 calories, 40g protein, 23g carbohydrate, 15g fat, 0g fiber, 143mg cholesterol, 652mg sodium

◄ CROWD-PLEASER

Prep Time: 15 minutes

Cook Time: 25 minutes

Average Rating: ★★★★★

What other cooks have done:

"I loved the sauce, so next time, I'll make more. Serve this over hot cooked pasta or with French bread to soak up the sauce. This recipe is a keeper."

Smothered Mexican Lasagna

(pictured on page 187)

Submitted by: **Brenda Britten**

"Great-tasting and easy Mexican lasagna. Tastes like it was hard work."

COVERED-DISH FAVORITE ▶

Prep Time: 20 minutes

Cook Time: 28 minutes

Average Rating: ★★★★★

What other cooks have done:

"I added a layer of refried beans mixed with salsa and a layer of reduced-fat Mexican-four cheese blend. So the layers were: tortilla, refried bean mix, half of ricotta cheese mix, meat, half of Mexican cheese, another ricotta cheese layer, and, finally, more Mexican cheese on top. I served it with fat-free tortilla chips and corn."

1½ pounds ground turkey
1 bunch green onions, chopped
1 (1.25 ounce) package taco seasoning mix
1 cup water
1 (14.5 ounce) can diced tomatoes, undrained
1 (4.5 ounce) can diced green chile peppers, undrained
1 (15 ounce) container ricotta cheese
2 eggs
6 (10 inch) flour tortillas
2 cups shredded Mexican four-cheese blend (optional)
Diced tomatoes (optional)
1 (8 ounce) container sour cream
¼ cup salsa

1. Preheat oven to 400°F (200°C).

2. Place ground turkey in a large, deep skillet. Cook over medium-high heat 8 minutes or until evenly brown. Stir in green onions, taco seasoning mix, water, diced tomatoes with juice, and green chiles with juice. Reduce heat to medium.

3. In a medium bowl, mix together ricotta and eggs. Place 2 tortillas in the bottom of a 9x13 inch pan. Spread a third of the ricotta mixture on tortillas. Spoon a third of the meat mixture over the cheese. Repeat layers until all is used. Top with shredded cheese, if desired.

4. Bake in the preheated oven for 20 minutes or until sauce is bubbly. Sprinkle with diced tomato before serving, if desired. Serve sour cream and salsa on the side. **Yield:** 6 servings.

Per serving: 737 calories, 41g protein, 69g carbohydrate, 32g fat, 5g fiber, 199mg cholesterol, 1500mg sodium

Baked Halibut Steaks *(pictured on page 191)*

Submitted by: **Dakota Kelly**

"An Italian-style vegetable and feta cheese topping is the perfect enhancement to delicious baked halibut."

1	teaspoon olive oil	¼	teaspoon salt
1	cup diced zucchini	¼	teaspoon ground black
½	cup minced onion		pepper
1	clove garlic, peeled and	4	(6 ounce) halibut steaks
	minced	⅓	cup crumbled feta cheese
2	cups diced fresh tomatoes		
2	tablespoons chopped fresh		
	basil		

1. Preheat oven to 450°F (230°C). Lightly grease a 9x13 inch dish.
2. Heat olive oil in a medium saucepan over medium heat and stir in zucchini, onion, and garlic. Cook, stirring constantly, 5 minutes or until tender. Remove from heat and add tomatoes, basil, salt, and pepper.
3. Arrange halibut steaks in a single layer in the prepared baking dish. Spoon zucchini mixture evenly over steaks. Top with feta cheese.
4. Bake in the preheated oven for 15 minutes or until fish flakes easily with a fork. **Yield:** 4 servings.

Per serving: 261 calories, 39g protein, 7g carbohydrate, 8g fat, 2g fiber, 66mg cholesterol, 386mg sodium

◄ **COMPANY IS COMING**

Prep Time: 15 minutes

Cook Time: 20 minutes

Average Rating: ★★★★★

What other cooks have done:

"This meal was extremely easy to make, and the fish turned out moist and cooked to perfection. The colors of the ingredients added to a nice presentation. Definitely a dish to make any night of the week."

30 *minutes or less*

Capers and Halibut

Submitted by: **Barbara Tantrum**

"This is a very easy seared halibut with a buttery wine and caper sauce. It takes hardly any time at all to make, but it's sure to leave a lasting impression."

1	tablespoon olive oil	3	tablespoons capers, with
2	(8 ounce) halibut steaks		liquid
½	cup white wine		Salt and ground black
1	teaspoon chopped garlic		pepper to taste
¼	cup butter		

1. Heat the olive oil in a large skillet over medium–high heat. Sear steaks on all sides until nicely browned. Remove and set aside.
2. Pour wine into pan, stirring to scrape up any browned bits. Let the wine reduce by half, about 5 minutes. Stir in the garlic, butter, and capers. Season with salt and pepper to taste. Simmer for 1 minute.
3. Return the steaks to the pan and coat them with sauce. Cook 5 minutes or until fish flakes easily with a fork. Serve fish immediately with the sauce from the pan poured over it. **Yield:** 2 servings.

Per serving: 557 calories, 47g protein, 2g carbohydrate, 35g fat, 0g fiber, 134mg cholesterol, 741mg sodium

◄ **OUT-OF-THE-ORDINARY**

Prep Time: 10 minutes

Cook Time: 15 minutes

Average Rating: ★★★★★

What other cooks have done:

"Don't let those capers scare you. This was a wonderful meal with a delicious taste. Very easy. Try grilling halibut steaks while basting with the sauce."

Lemon-Orange Orange Roughy

Submitted by: **Brian Ehrler**

"Orange roughy fillets with a citrus twist. Very quick to prepare."

1 tablespoon olive oil	1 orange, juiced
4 (4 ounce) orange roughy fillets	1 lemon, juiced
	½ teaspoon lemon pepper

1. Heat oil in a large skillet over medium-high heat. Arrange fillets in the skillet and drizzle with orange juice and lemon juice. Sprinkle with lemon pepper. Cook, turning once, for 5 minutes or until fish flakes easily with a fork. **Yield:** 4 servings.

Per serving: 133 calories, 17g protein, 8g carbohydrate, 4g fat, 2g fiber, 22mg cholesterol, 129mg sodium

Pan-Seared Red Snapper

Submitted by: **Katie**

"This is great for a gourmet taste on a tight schedule. Also, my husband, who isn't a fish fan, requests this recipe. Drizzle sauce over fish and serve with vegetables."

2 (6 ounce) red snapper fillets	1 tablespoon honey
1 lemon, juiced	1 teaspoon ground ginger
2 tablespoons rice wine vinegar	1 tablespoon olive oil
1 teaspoon prepared Dijon-style mustard	¼ cup chopped green onions

1. Rinse snapper under cold water and pat dry. In a shallow bowl, mix together lemon juice, rice vinegar, mustard, honey, and ginger.
2. Heat oil in a nonstick skillet over medium heat. Dip snapper fillets in marinade to coat and place in skillet, skin side up. Cook for 2 to 3 minutes on each side or until fish flakes easily with a fork. Remove fish from skillet and pour remaining marinade and green onions into skillet. Reduce heat and simmer for 2 to 3 minutes. Pour sauce over fish and serve immediately. **Yield:** 2 servings.

Per serving: 225 calories, 24g protein, 16g carbohydrate, 9g fat, 3g fiber, 41mg cholesterol, 139mg sodium

---

5 INGREDIENTS OR LESS ▶

Prep Time: 15 minutes

Cook Time: 5 minutes

Average Rating: ★★★★★

What other cooks have done:

"I used a large naval orange (juiced) and ¼ cup bottled lemon juice. It took a little longer to cook because the juices thickened up and stuck to the fish nicely. I served it with brown rice, green beans, and tomato slices seasoned with vinegar."

FAMILY FAVORITE ▶

Prep Time: 10 minutes

Cook Time: 9 minutes

Average Rating: ★★★★☆

What other cooks have done:

"I love this recipe but decided to play with it the second time around. I replaced the green onions with about ⅛ cup chopped shallots and marinated the snapper for about 5 minutes in the sauce. It came out excellent!"

Moroccan Salmon Cakes with Garlic Mayonnaise

Submitted by: **Emily**

"This is a great alternative to the standard salmon patty recipe and uses couscous, spinach, and cumin for an exotic flavor."

½	cup mayonnaise	2	egg yolks, lightly beaten
1	clove garlic, crushed	2	cloves garlic, crushed
⅛	teaspoon paprika	1	teaspoon ground cumin
½	cup couscous	½	teaspoon ground black pepper
⅔	cup orange juice	½	teaspoon salt
1	(14.75 ounce) can red salmon, drained	3	tablespoons olive oil
1	(10 ounce) package frozen chopped spinach, thawed, drained, and squeezed dry		

1. In a small stainless steel or glass bowl, stir together mayonnaise, garlic, and paprika. Set aside.

2. Prepare couscous according to package directions using ⅔ cup orange juice in place of water.

3. In a mixing bowl, combine the cooked couscous, red salmon, drained spinach, egg yolks, garlic, cumin, pepper, and salt. Form into patties.

4. Heat the olive oil in a large skillet over medium heat and fry patties until golden brown, turning once, about 8 to 10 minutes. Serve with garlic mayonnaise. **Yield:** 4 servings.

Per serving: 620 calories, 28g protein, 26g carbohydrate, 47g fat, 4g fiber, 188mg cholesterol, 950mg sodium

◄ **COMPANY IS COMING**

Prep Time: 20 minutes

Cook Time: 15 minutes

Average Rating: ★★★★★

What other cooks have done:

"I used pink salmon instead of red and mustard instead of paprika, but the recipe still turned out super."

Salmon with Dill

Submitted by: **John Bragg**

"This is a simple recipe for salmon. With just a hint of seasoning, you can bring out the delicious taste of the salmon. Serve with tartar sauce and lemon."

4	(4 ounce) salmon fillets or steaks	1	teaspoon onion powder
¼	teaspoon salt	1	teaspoon dried dill weed
½	teaspoon ground black pepper	2	tablespoons butter

1. Preheat oven to 400°F (200°C).

2. Rinse salmon and arrange in a 9x13 inch baking dish. Sprinkle salt, pepper, onion powder, and dill over fish. Dot butter evenly over fish.

3. Bake in the preheated oven for 20 to 25 minutes or until salmon flakes easily with a fork. **Yield:** 4 servings.

Per serving: 262 calories, 23g protein, 1g carbohydrate, 18g fat, 0g fiber, 83mg cholesterol, 272mg sodium

◄ **FROM THE PANTRY**

Prep Time: 10 minutes

Cook Time: 25 minutes

Average Rating: ★★★★★

What other cooks have done:

"This was great. I didn't have any onion powder, so I substituted a small amount of garlic powder and added two green onions and a sprig of finely chopped fresh lemon thyme. Delicious."

Steamed Tuna Fish

Submitted by: **Janice Laughton**

"Ginger, sherry, garlic, and soy sauce flavor tender steamed tuna."

FAMILY FAVORITE ▶

Prep Time: 20 minutes

Cook Time: 10 minutes

Average Rating: ★★★★★

What other cooks have done:

"I made this dish with asparagus, and I just could not get enough of the sauce! I put it on everything. It was excellent. However, I recommend searing the tuna instead of steaming it and using just a touch less ginger."

8	(4 ounce) fresh tuna steaks	½	cup minced fresh ginger root
½	cup soy sauce	3	cloves garlic, minced
½	cup sherry	1	teaspoon salt
½	cup vegetable oil	1	teaspoon ground black pepper
1	bunch green onions, finely chopped		

1. Place tuna steaks in a steamer basket over 1 inch of boiling water and cover. Steam 6 to 8 minutes or until fish flakes easily with a fork.
2. Meanwhile, in a medium saucepan, combine soy sauce, sherry, vegetable oil, green onions, ginger, garlic, salt, and pepper. Bring to a boil.
3. Remove tuna steaks from steamer and place on a serving dish. Pour sauce over tuna steaks and serve immediately. **Yield:** 8 servings.

Per serving: 281 calories, 28g protein, 7g carbohydrate, 15g fat, 1g fiber, 51mg cholesterol, 1339mg sodium

Shrimp Étouffée II *(pictured on page 190)*

Submitted by: **Kay**

"This is a very easy shrimp étouffée recipe that uses your microwave! I usually add four dashes of hot pepper sauce to the dish, but bring the hot stuff to the table in case someone wants a zestier dinner."

ONE-DISH MEAL ▶

Prep Time: 23 minutes

Cook Time: 19 minutes

Average Rating: ★★★★★

What other cooks have done:

"My husband and I loved this easy and tasty recipe. I cooked all the chopped ingredients on the stovetop until tender. Then I added the shrimp and remaining ingredients and cooked it for about 10 minutes. Perfect. I did add a few dashes of Worcestershire sauce, a bay leaf, and about 2 tablespoons of water during the last 10 minutes."

¼	cup butter or margarine	3	to 5 tablespoons tomato paste
½	cup chopped onion	1	pound peeled and deveined shrimp
½	cup chopped green onions		Salt to taste
½	cup chopped green bell pepper	¼	teaspoon hot pepper sauce to taste
4	cloves garlic, minced	¼	teaspoon cayenne pepper
½	cup celery, diced		Hot cooked rice
½	cup chopped fresh parsley		Addtional chopped fresh parsley
1	(10.75 ounce) can condensed cream of chicken soup		

1. In a 2 quart microwave-safe dish, combine butter, onion, green onion, bell pepper, garlic, and celery. Microwave on high for 8 to 9 minutes.
2. Stir in parsley, soup, tomato paste, shrimp, salt, hot pepper sauce, and cayenne. Microwave on high for 5 minutes. Microwave for 5 more minutes until mixture thickens and shrimp turn pink. Serve over hot cooked rice. Garnish with additional parsley. **Yield:** 4 servings.

Per serving: 197 calories, 15g protein, 9g carbohydrate, 11g fat, 2g fiber, 119mg cholesterol, 703mg sodium

New Orleans Barbecued Shrimp

Submitted by: **Carl V. Tibbetts**

"Be sure to cover the table with old newspapers to gather the shells and make cleanup easy. Make sure to have warmed French bread to dunk in the sauce!"

1	pound unpeeled shrimp	2	teaspoons ground black
½	cup butter		pepper
½	cup zesty Italian dressing	⅛	teaspoon garlic powder
1	tablespoon lemon juice	1	loaf French bread

1. Preheat oven to 350°F (175°C).
2. Wash shrimp and drain well.
3. Melt butter in a 1 quart casserole dish. Add Italian dressing, lemon juice, black pepper, and garlic powder.
4. Add shrimp to the casserole dish. Stir gently to cover the shrimp with the mixture. Cover and bake in the preheated oven, stirring occasionally, for 25 to 30 minutes or until shrimp turn pink.
5. Serve the hot shrimp on a large platter with French bread and sauce on the side. **Yield:** 2 servings.

Per serving: 871 calories, 47g protein, 8g carbohydrate, 72g fat, 1g fiber, 469mg cholesterol, 1808mg sodium

◀FAMILY FAVORITE
Prep Time: 10 minutes
Cook Time: 30 minutes
Average Rating: ★★★★★
What other cooks have done:
"I used minced garlic instead of powder and added some hot pepper sauce for extra kick. Do not skip the fresh French bread dipped in the leftover sauce—it was as good as the shrimp!"

30 minutes or less

Broiled Lemon and Garlic Tiger Prawns

Submitted by: **Steve Jensen**

"This is a family favorite for movie night at home; it's quick and easy and kids like the 'finger food' style."

1½	pounds tiger prawns, peeled and deveined	1½	tablespoons lemon juice
1	cup butter	3	tablespoons grated Parmesan cheese
1	teaspoon minced garlic		

1. Preheat broiler.
2. With a sharp knife, remove tails from prawns and butterfly them from the underside. Arrange prawns on broiler pan.
3. In a small saucepan, sauté butter with garlic and lemon juice. Pour ¼ cup butter mixture in a small bowl and brush onto prawns. Reserve remaining sauce to serve with shrimp. Sprinkle Parmesan cheese over prawns.
4. Place broiler pan on top rack and broil prawns in the preheated oven for 4 to 5 minutes or until prawns turn pink. Serve with reserved butter mixture for dipping. **Yield:** 6 servings.

Per serving: 396 calories, 24g protein, 2g carbohydrate, 33g fat, 0g fiber, 85mg cholesterol, 359mg sodium

◀KID-FRIENDLY
Prep Time: 15 minutes
Cook Time: 10 minutes
Average Rating: ★★★★★
What other cooks have done:
"These were absolutely fantastic! I made them as a side dish using large prawns, which reduced the broiling time a little. They turned out great!"

Portobello Mushroom Stroganoff

Submitted by: **Chordata**

"This is a rich and meaty vegetarian stroganoff made with portobello mushrooms and served over egg noodles. It is quick to make and tastes delicious."

COVERED-DISH FAVORITE ▶

Prep Time: 15 minutes

Cook Time: 20 minutes

Average Rating: ★★★★★

What other cooks have done:

"Excellent results! I took a little liberty and substituted beef broth. I added some chanterelle mushrooms as well."

8	ounces dried egg noodles	1½	cups sour cream
3	tablespoons butter	3	tablespoons all-purpose
1	large onion, chopped		flour
¾	pound portobello	¼	cup chopped fresh parsley
	mushrooms, sliced		Salt and ground black
1½	cups vegetable broth		pepper to taste

1. Bring a large pot of lightly salted water to a boil. Add noodles and cook 7 minutes or until al dente. Drain and set aside.

2. While noodles cook, melt butter in a large, heavy skillet over medium heat. Add onion and cook, stirring until softened. Increase heat to medium-high and add sliced mushrooms. Cook until the mushrooms are limp and browned. Remove to a bowl and set aside.

3. In the same skillet, stir in vegetable broth, being sure to stir in any browned bits off the bottom of the pan. Bring to a boil and cook until the mixture has reduced by one-third. Reduce heat to low and return the mushrooms and onion to the skillet.

4. Remove the pan from the heat. Stir together the sour cream and flour; blend into the mushrooms. Return skillet to the burner and continue cooking over low heat, just until the sauce thickens. Stir in the parsley and season with salt and pepper to taste. Serve over cooked egg noodles. **Yield:** 4 servings.

Per serving: 514 calories, 14g protein, 52g carbohydrate, 30g fat, 4g fiber, 107mg cholesterol, 527mg sodium

Eggless Tofu-Spinach Quiche

Submitted by: **Rachel Cross**

"The tofu gives this quiche a good texture. I've brought it to potlucks where friends aren't vegetarian . . . no one ever knew! It's always a hit!"

½	pound tofu, drained	1	teaspoon minced garlic
⅓	cup 1% milk	¼	cup diced onion
½	teaspoon salt (or to taste)	⅔	cup shredded Cheddar cheese
½	teaspoon ground black pepper	½	cup shredded Swiss cheese
1	(10 ounce) package frozen chopped spinach, thawed and drained	1	(9 inch) unbaked pie crust

1. Preheat oven to 350°F (175°C).

2. In a blender, combine tofu and milk; process until smooth, adding more milk if necessary. Blend in salt and pepper.

3. In a medium bowl, combine spinach, garlic, onion, Cheddar cheese, Swiss cheese, and tofu mixture. Mix well; pour into pie crust.

4. Bake in preheated oven for 30 minutes or until set and golden brown on top. Let stand 5 minutes before cutting. **Yield:** 6 servings.

Per serving: 285 calories, 13g protein, 18g carbohydrate, 19g fat, 3g fiber, 22mg cholesterol, 496mg sodium

◀ **MEATLESS MAIN DISH**

Prep Time: 15 minutes

Cook Time: 30 minutes

Stand Time: 5 minutes

Average Rating: ★★★★☆

What other cooks have done:

"Outstanding recipe; it was a big hit. We also enjoyed slices of it cold on a picnic."

Garbanzo Stir-Fry

Submitted by: **June**

"This garbanzo bean and veggie stir-fry is great because you can add as many or as few ingredients as you like."

2	tablespoons olive oil	1	(15 ounce) can garbanzo beans, drained and rinsed
1	tablespoon chopped fresh oregano	1	large zucchini, halved and sliced
1	tablespoon chopped fresh basil	½	cup sliced mushrooms
1	clove garlic, crushed Ground black pepper to taste	1	tablespoon chopped fresh cilantro
		1	tomato, chopped

1. Heat oil in a large skillet over medium heat. Stir in oregano, basil, garlic, and pepper. Add garbanzo beans and zucchini, stirring well to coat. Cook, covered, for 10 minutes, stirring occasionally.

2. Stir in mushrooms and cilantro and cook, stirring occasionally, until tender. Place the chopped tomato on top of the mixture. Cover and let the tomatoes steam for a few minutes. (Do not overcook.) Serve immediately. **Yield:** 4 servings.

Per serving: 213 calories, 6g protein, 30g carbohydrate, 8g fat, 6g fiber, 0mg cholesterol, 325mg sodium

◀ **ONE-DISH MEAL**

Prep Time: 15 minutes

Cook Time: 30 minutes

Average Rating: ★★★★☆

What other cooks have done:

"We had this in warmed pita bread with some finely shredded pizza cheese (mozzarella and Cheddar blend)."

Chickpea Curry

Submitted by: **Aminah A. Rahman**

"Using canned chickpeas allows for a fast, convenient dish."

AROUND-THE-WORLD CUISINE ▶

Prep Time: 10 minutes

Cook Time: 30 minutes

Average Rating: ★★★★★

What other cooks have done:

"I would never have thought that I could make something that tasted so much like it came from a restaurant. It was so simple—don't let the list of spices make you think that it's more difficult than it is! I added thawed and drained chopped leaf spinach at the end with the cilantro. Very tasty and filling over rice."

2	tablespoons vegetable oil	1	teaspoon ground coriander
2	onions, minced		Salt to taste
2	cloves garlic, minced	1	teaspoon cayenne pepper
2	teaspoons fresh ginger root, finely chopped	1	teaspoon ground turmeric
6	whole cloves	2	(15 ounce) cans chickpeas (garbanzo beans), undrained
2	(2 inch) cinnamon sticks, crushed	1	cup chopped fresh cilantro, divided
1	teaspoon ground cumin		

1. Heat oil in a large skillet over medium heat and sauté onions until tender.

2. Stir in garlic, ginger, cloves, cinnamon, cumin, coriander, salt, cayenne, and turmeric. Cook for 1 minute, stirring constantly, over medium heat. Mix in garbanzo beans and their liquid. Continue to cook and stir until all ingredients are well blended and heated through. Remove from heat. Stir in cilantro just before serving, reserving 1 tablespoon for garnish. **Yield:** 8 servings.

Per serving: 178 calories, 6g protein, 29g carbohydrate, 5g fat, 6g fiber, 0mg cholesterol, 398mg sodium

30 *minutes or less*

Butter Bean Burgers

Submitted by: **Silverwolf**

"Serve these as a sandwich with your favorite toppings. They're great!"

KID-FRIENDLY ▶

Prep Time: 15 minutes

Cook Time: 11 minutes

Average Rating: ★★★★★

What other cooks have done:

"These were really good. I didn't have butter beans or lima beans in the house, so I used black beans instead. I added cayenne pepper to the mixture for a little kick and topped the burger with taco sauce. Nice, healthy lunch!"

1	(15 ounce) can butter beans, drained	½	cup shredded Cheddar cheese
1	small onion, chopped	¼	teaspoon garlic powder
1	tablespoon finely chopped jalapeño pepper		Salt and ground black pepper to taste
6	saltine crackers, crushed		Vegetable oil
1	egg, beaten		

1. In a medium bowl, mash butter beans. Mix in onion, jalapeño pepper, crushed crackers, egg, cheese, garlic powder, and salt and black pepper to taste. Divide into 4 equal parts and shape into patties.

2. Heat oil in a large skillet over medium–high heat; pour oil into a skillet to depth of ¼ inch. Fry patties until golden, about 5 minutes on each side. **Yield:** 4 servings.

Per serving: 298 calories, 11g protein, 19g carbohydrate, 20g fat, 4g fiber, 68mg cholesterol, 632mg sodium

Pizza, Pasta & More

Veggie Ranch Pizza

Submitted by: **Darlene**

"Delicious and loaded with fresh veggies, this is pizza for people who want a change from tomato sauce. Use your favorite fresh veggies and pizza crust. Use light dressing and reduced-fat cheese for a healthier meal."

1 (12 inch) prebaked pizza crust	½ cup chopped broccoli
1 cup Ranch-style salad dressing	½ cup chopped onion
2 cups shredded Cheddar cheese	½ cup chopped red bell pepper
½ cup shredded carrot	½ cup sliced fresh mushrooms
½ cup chopped cauliflower	1 pound mozzarella cheese, shredded

1. Preheat oven to 350°F (175°C).
2. Place pizza crust on a pizza pan or baking sheet and spread dressing evenly over crust. Sprinkle with Cheddar cheese, carrot, cauliflower, broccoli, onion, red bell pepper, and mushrooms. Top with mozzarella cheese.
3. Bake in the preheated oven for 10 to 15 minutes or until the vegetables are tender and cheese is melted and lightly browned. **Yield:** 10 servings.

Per serving: 490 calories, 21g protein, 19g carbohydrate, 36g fat, 1g fiber, 65mg cholesterol, 922mg sodium

20 minutes or less

Allie's Mushroom Pizza

Submitted by: **AllieA**

"A simple mushroom-spinach pizza that tastes much better than takeout."

1 (12 inch) prebaked pizza crust	8 ounces shredded mozzarella cheese
3 tablespoons olive oil	1 cup sliced fresh mushrooms
1 teaspoon sesame oil	
1 cup fresh spinach, rinsed and dried	

1. Preheat oven to 350°F (175°C). Place pizza crust on a pizza pan or baking sheet.
2. In a small bowl, mix together olive oil and sesame oil. Brush onto pizza crust, covering entire surface. Stack the spinach leaves; cut lengthwise into ½ inch strips; scatter strips evenly over crust. Top pizza with shredded mozzarella and sliced mushrooms.
3. Bake in the preheated oven for 8 to 10 minutes or until cheese is melted and edges of crust are crisp. **Yield:** 8 servings.

Per serving: 275 calories, 14g protein, 26g carbohydrate, 13g fat, 1g fiber, 21mg cholesterol, 425mg sodium

Goat Cheese and Tomato Pizza

Submitted by: **Jennifer Tune**

"This homemade pizza substitutes goat cheese for mozzarella. You can use store-bought sauce if you're in a hurry. You can always add other ingredients—artichoke hearts make a great addition!"

1	(6 ounce) can tomato paste
¾	cup water
¼	cup olive oil
2	roma (plum) tomatoes, diced
1	tablespoon Italian seasoning
½	teaspoon garlic salt
⅛	teaspoon cayenne pepper
½	teaspoon ground black pepper
2	(6.5 ounce) packages dry pizza crust mix
6	roma (plum) tomatoes, thinly sliced
4	ounces goat cheese

1. Preheat oven to 425°F (220°C). Lightly grease a baking sheet.
2. In a small saucepan, mix tomato paste with water and oil; stir in diced tomato. Add Italian seasoning, garlic salt, cayenne pepper, and black pepper. Simmer, uncovered, over low heat for 15 minutes.
3. Meanwhile, prepare pizza dough according to package directions. Roll into a 10x14 inch rectangle on prepared baking sheet. Bake in the preheated oven for 2 to 3 minutes. Remove from oven.
4. When sauce is done, spread ¾ cup or desired amount of sauce over crust. Store remaining sauce in an airtight container in the refrigerator for another use. Arrange sliced tomatoes over pizza and top with small chunks of goat cheese. Bake in the preheated oven for 15 more minutes or until crust is golden brown. **Yield:** 8 servings.

Per serving: 304 calories, 10g protein, 40g carbohydrate, 12g fat, 3g fiber, 11mg cholesterol, 611mg sodium

◄ OUT-OF-THE-ORDINARY

Prep Time: 15 minutes

Cook Time: 30 minutes

Average Rating: ★★★★☆

What other cooks have done:

"I added red and green peppers as well as a hot chile pepper for a great contrast against the creamy mildness of the goat cheese."

Pizza Without the Red Sauce

(pictured on page 226)

Submitted by: **aimee**

"I do not like red sauce, but pizza is one of my favorite foods. So I came up with this good alternative to traditional pizza. It still has a light tomato taste."

FAMILY FAVORITE ▶

Prep Time: 15 minutes

Cook Time: 10 minutes

Average Rating: ★★★★★

What other cooks have done:

"My family has been enjoying home-made pizza every Saturday night for years. When I added this one to the tradition, even the 14-year-old skeptic liked it! Now, this pizza is a regular hit. My friend uses the sauce (the first seven ingredients) on baked pierogi and to make garlic bread. Delicious and highly recommended!"

2 tablespoons butter, melted	1 cup firmly packed fresh spinach, torn
1 tablespoon olive oil	1 small tomato, sliced
3 tablespoons minced garlic	½ small sweet onion, sliced
2 tablespoons sun–dried tomato pesto	1 fresh jalapeño pepper, seeded and chopped
3 teaspoons fresh basil leaves	1 (4 ounce) package feta cheese, crumbled
3 teaspoons fresh oregano	
1 tablespoon grated Parmesan cheese	
1 (14 ounce) prebaked pizza crust	

1. Preheat oven to 450°F (230°C).

2. In a small bowl, combine butter, olive oil, garlic, pesto, basil, oregano, and Parmesan cheese. Spread mixture evenly over pizza crust.

3. Arrange spinach, tomato, onion, and jalapeño on pizza. Top with crumbled feta cheese.

4. Bake in the preheated oven for about 10 minutes or until cheese begins to brown. **Yield:** 8 servings.

Per serving: 237 calories, 9g protein, 23g carbohydrate, 13g fat, 2g fiber, 28mg cholesterol, 579mg sodium

Muffaletta Pizza

Submitted by: **Steve**

"A terrific variation on an old New Orleans favorite. We serve it as an appetizer to guests. The olive salad mixture may be used right away, but it's best when chilled overnight. Adjust the ingredients to taste."

8 jumbo pitted black olives
8 pitted green olives
2 tablespoons chopped celery
2 tablespoons chopped red onion
2 cloves garlic, chopped
6 fresh basil leaves, chopped
1 tablespoon chopped fresh parsley
3 tablespoons olive oil, divided
½ teaspoon dried oregano
    Salt and freshly ground black pepper to taste
1 (12 inch) prebaked pizza crust
½ teaspoon garlic powder or to taste
    Salt to taste
2 ounces shredded mozzarella cheese
2 ounces shredded provolone cheese
2 ounces grated Parmesan cheese
2 ounces thinly sliced hard salami, cut into strips
2 ounces thinly sliced mortadella, cut into strips
4 ounces thinly sliced prosciutto, cut into strips

◄ OUT-OF-THE-ORDINARY

Prep Time: 30 minutes

Cook Time: 10 minutes

Average Rating: ★★★★★

What other cooks have done:

"I only used ¼ pound of prosciutto and that was plenty. The pizza looked great and tasted excellent. Everyone oohed and aahed."

1. In a medium bowl, mix black olives, green olives, celery, red onion, garlic, basil, parsley, 2 tablespoons olive oil, oregano, and salt and pepper to taste. Cover and chill in the refrigerator until ready to use or overnight.

2. Preheat oven to 500°F (260°C).

3. Sprinkle pizza crust with remaining tablespoon olive oil, garlic powder, and salt to taste. Place directly on the oven rack and bake in the preheated oven for about 5 minutes. Do not allow crust to become overly browned or crisp. Remove from oven and allow to cool.

4. Preheat broiler.

5. In a medium bowl, mix together mozzarella cheese, provolone cheese, Parmesan cheese, hard salami, mortadella, and prosciutto. Stir in the olive mixture. Blend the mixtures well.

6. Spread the blended mixture over the prepared pizza crust. Place pizza crust on a baking sheet.

7. Broil in the preheated oven for 5 minutes or until cheeses are melted and meats are lightly browned. Cut into 3 inch squares and serve immediately. **Yield:** 6 servings.

Per serving: 516 calories, 23g protein, 38g carbohydrate, 30g fat, 1g fiber, 49mg cholesterol, 1634mg sodium

Arrabbiata Sauce *(pictured on page 228)*

Submitted by: **Ellen**

"Spicy and delicious, this sauce is ideal on penne pasta."

CLASSIC COMFORT FOOD ▶

Prep Time: 15 minutes

Cook Time: 20 minutes

Average Rating: ★★★★☆

What other cooks have done:

"I was looking for a smoother arrabbiata sauce. So, after the ingredients were combined, I put them in the blender to puree them into a smooth consistency. I then added a splash of milk to make it a bit more creamy and simmered as directed."

1 teaspoon olive oil	1 tablespoon lemon juice
1 cup chopped onion	½ teaspoon Italian seasoning
4 cloves garlic, minced	¼ teaspoon ground black pepper
½ cup red wine	2 (14.5 ounce) cans peeled and diced tomatoes
1 tablespoon white sugar	Hot cooked pasta
1 tablespoon chopped fresh basil	Freshly grated Parmesan cheese
1 teaspoon crushed red pepper flakes	Chopped fresh parsley
2 tablespoons tomato paste	

1. Heat oil in a large skillet or saucepan over medium heat. Sauté onion and garlic in oil for 5 minutes.

2. Stir in wine, sugar, basil, red pepper flakes, tomato paste, lemon juice, Italian seasoning, black pepper, and tomatoes; bring to a boil. Reduce heat to medium and simmer, uncovered, about 15 minutes.

3. Ladle sauce over the hot cooked pasta of your choice. Sprinkle with Parmesan cheese and chopped parsley. **Yield:** 6 servings.

Per serving: 75 calories, 2g protein, 12g carbohydrate, 1g fat, 2g fiber, 0mg cholesterol, 258mg sodium

30 minutes or less

Angel Hair with Feta and Sun-Dried Tomatoes

Submitted by: **Nicole Faust Hunt**

"My husband begs me to make this dish. It's a surprisingly delicious mixture of flavors. Feel free to tailor the ingredient amounts to your taste. This is how we like it, but it is quite flexible."

MEATLESS MAIN DISH ▶

Prep Time: 20 minutes

Cook Time: 10 minutes

Average Rating: ★★★★☆

What other cooks have done:

"I used bow tie pasta both times I made this dish. The pasta was easy to mix with the other ingredients and held up well. The second time I made this, I added grilled chicken to the pasta."

1 (16 ounce) package angel hair pasta	1 cup grated Parmesan cheese
¼ cup olive oil	1 bunch fresh cilantro, chopped
4 cloves garlic, crushed	Salt and ground black pepper to taste
3 ounces sun-dried tomatoes, softened and chopped	
1 (8 ounce) package tomato-basil feta cheese, crumbled	

1. Bring a large pot of lightly salted water to a boil. Add pasta and cook for 6 to 8 minutes or until al dente; drain. Return pasta to pot.

2. Meanwhile, combine olive oil, garlic, tomatoes, feta, and Parmesan cheese. Stir in cilantro and season with salt and pepper to taste. Add to pasta and toss to coat. Serve warm. **Yield:** 8 servings.

Per serving: 383 calories, 17g protein, 39g carbohydrate, 18g fat, 4g fiber, 35mg cholesterol, 888mg sodium

Champagne Shrimp and Pasta

Submitted by: **Tricia Flasck**

"A friend of mine gave me this recipe, and it has become a family favorite. It's elegant enough for company yet very simple to make, especially if you purchase shrimp that has already been peeled."

8	ounces angel hair pasta	2	roma (plum) tomatoes, diced
1	tablespoon extra virgin olive oil	1	cup heavy cream, divided
1	cup sliced fresh mushrooms	3	tablespoons chopped fresh parsley
1	pound medium shrimp, peeled and deveined		Salt and ground black pepper to taste
1½	cups champagne		Freshly grated Parmesan cheese
¼	teaspoon salt		
2	tablespoons minced shallots		

1. Bring a large pot of lightly salted water to a boil. Add pasta and cook for 6 to 8 minutes or until al dente; drain.

2. Meanwhile, heat oil in a large skillet over medium–high heat. Sauté mushrooms in oil until tender. Remove mushrooms from pan and set aside.

3. Combine shrimp, champagne, and ¼ teaspoon salt in the pan and heat over high heat. When liquid just begins to boil, remove shrimp from pan with a slotted spoon. Add shallots and tomatoes to champagne; boil until liquid is reduced to ½ cup, about 8 minutes. Stir in ¾ cup cream; boil until slightly thick, about 1 to 2 minutes. Return shrimp and mushrooms to skillet and heat through.

4. Toss hot cooked pasta with remaining ¼ cup cream, parsley, and salt and pepper to taste. To serve, spoon shrimp with sauce over pasta and top with Parmesan cheese. **Yield:** 4 servings.

Per serving: 598 calories, 32g protein, 38g carbohydrate, 29g fat, 3g fiber, 254mg cholesterol, 463mg sodium

◄ COMPANY IS COMING

Prep Time: 15 minutes

Cook Time: 20 minutes

Average Rating: ★★★★★

What other cooks have done:

"I added three cloves of chopped garlic to this and substituted green onions for the shallots, which I had a hard time finding at my market."

Cavatelli and Broccoli

Submitted by: **linda m**
"This is a quick meal to make. Serve with garlic bread."

3	heads fresh broccoli, cut into florets	1	teaspoon salt
½	cup olive oil	1	teaspoon crushed red pepper flakes
3	cloves garlic, minced	2	tablespoons grated Parmesan cheese
1½	pounds cavatelli pasta		

1. In a large pot of boiling water, cook broccoli for about 5 minutes. Drain. Rinse under cold water and set aside.
2. Heat olive oil in a large skillet over medium heat. Sauté garlic until lightly golden, being careful not to burn it. Add the broccoli. Sauté for about 10 minutes or until broccoli is tender-crisp.
3. Meanwhile, bring a large pot of lightly salted water to a boil; add pasta and cook for 8 to 10 minutes or until al dente. Drain and place in a large serving bowl. Toss with the broccoli and season with salt and red pepper flakes. Sprinkle with Parmesan cheese and serve.
Yield: 12 servings.

Per serving: 312 calories, 10g protein, 47g carbohydrate, 10g fat, 4g fiber, 0mg cholesterol, 232mg sodium

Cavatelli with Broccoli and Sausage

Submitted by: **Susan**
"Hot and spicy crowd-pleaser!"

1	(16 ounce) package cavatelli pasta	1	pound frozen broccoli
1	pound spicy Italian sausage	½	teaspoon crushed red pepper flakes
½	cup olive oil	¼	cup grated Parmesan cheese
4	cloves garlic, minced		

1. Bring a large pot of lightly salted water to a boil. Add pasta and cook for 5 minutes; add broccoli and cook for 3 to 5 more minutes or until pasta is al dente; drain.
2. Meanwhile, in a medium skillet over medium heat, cook sausage until no longer pink; drain and set aside.
3. Heat olive oil in a small skillet over medium heat and sauté garlic until golden.
4. In a large serving bowl, toss together the sausage, garlic, cavatelli, broccoli, red pepper flakes, and Parmesan. Serve immediately. **Yield:** 8 servings.

Per serving: 552 calories, 19g protein, 46g carbohydrate, 33g fat, 4g fiber, 46mg cholesterol, 491mg sodium

Chicken and Bow Tie Pasta

Submitted by: **Stacey Philhower**

"Easy and delicious chicken and bow tie pasta with a white cream sauce."

4 skinless, boneless chicken breast halves

1 (12 ounce) package farfalle (bow tie) pasta

1 (14 ounce) can chicken broth

1 head broccoli, cut into florets

1 medium red bell pepper, thinly sliced

2 cloves garlic, minced
Salt and ground black pepper to taste

2 (8 ounce) containers chive-and-onion cream cheese

¼ cup freshly grated Parmesan cheese

1. Place chicken in a saucepan and add water to cover. Boil for 20 minutes. Allow to cool; shred meat.

2. Meanwhile, bring a large pot of lightly salted water to a boil. Add pasta and cook for 8 to 10 minutes or until al dente; drain.

3. In a large skillet over medium-high heat, combine chicken broth, broccoli, bell pepper, garlic, and salt and black pepper to taste. Cover and simmer for 8 to 10 minutes or until broccoli is tender-crisp. Stir in cream cheese until smooth. Mix in chicken and pasta until evenly coated. Top with Parmesan cheese. **Yield:** 4 servings.

Per serving: 900 calories, 48g protein, 75g carbohydrate, 43g fat, 6g fiber, 182mg cholesterol, 1699mg sodium

◄ FAMILY FAVORITE

Prep Time: 15 minutes

Cook Time: 30 minutes

Average Rating: ★★★★★

What other cooks have done:

"I changed a few things to speed up the cooking time. I cut up the chicken, browned it, and added chicken broth and frozen mixed veggies instead of fresh. It was easy and still tasted great."

Bow Tie Medley

Submitted by: **Kristie**

"This is a great recipe for a flavorful vegetarian pasta dish."

What other cooks have done:

"I used angel hair pasta and dried basil and cooked all the tomatoes rather than reserving any for the top. I also increased the amount of mushrooms and used two zucchini instead of one zucchini and one yellow squash. Delicious!"

1	(16 ounce) package farfalle (bow tie) pasta	5	roma (plum) tomatoes, chopped, divided
1	tablespoon olive oil	¼	cup fresh basil leaves
½	red onion, chopped	1	teaspoon dried oregano
4	cloves garlic, minced	1	teaspoon salt
1	zucchini, chopped	1	teaspoon ground black pepper
1	yellow squash, chopped	¼	cup olive oil
½	cup sliced fresh mushrooms	1	cup finely grated Parmesan cheese
½	red bell pepper, cut into strips		

1. Bring a large pot of lightly salted water to a boil. Add pasta and cook for 8 to 10 minutes or until al dente; drain.

2. Heat 1 tablespoon olive oil in a large skillet over medium heat. Sauté onion, garlic, zucchini, yellow squash, mushrooms, bell pepper, and half of the chopped tomatoes until tender. Season with basil, oregano, salt, and black pepper. Add pasta and ¼ cup olive oil. Mix well and heat through. Sprinkle with Parmesan and remaining chopped tomatoes before serving. **Yield:** 12 servings.

Per serving: 239 calories, 9g protein, 31g carbohydrate, 9g fat, 2g fiber, 7mg cholesterol, 355mg sodium

Giacomina's Authentic Pasta Asciutta

Submitted by: **Joe**

"To add a pesto flavor, sprinkle with ¼ cup finely chopped fresh basil and toss gently to coat. A quick tip to keep your cheese mold-free is to store it in a tightly covered container with a few sugar cubes."

What other cooks have done:

"I blanched fresh green beans for three minutes. Then I boiled small new potatoes for six minutes while the onion sautéed in butter until golden. I added a bucketful of garlic and used whole wheat penne instead of fettuccine. What a wonderful blend of flavors!"

6	potatoes, peeled and cubed	12	cloves garlic, halved
1	pound fresh green beans, washed and trimmed	1	onion, chopped
1	(16 ounce) package fettuccine pasta	½	cup butter
¾	cup olive oil	1	cup grated Parmesan cheese Salt and ground black pepper to taste

1. Bring a large pot of lightly salted water to a boil. Add potatoes and cook until tender, being careful not to overcook. Drain and set aside.

2. Meanwhile, steam green beans for 10 to 12 minutes or until tender-crisp. Set aside.

3. Bring a large pot of lightly salted water to a boil. Add pasta and cook for 8 to 10 minutes or until al dente; drain.

4. In a heavy skillet, heat oil over medium-low heat and add garlic and onion. Sauté until golden and crisp. Add butter and heat until melted.

5. Add potatoes, green beans, garlic and onion mixture, and Parmesan to pasta; toss gently. Season with salt and pepper to taste. **Yield:** 8 servings.

Per serving: 641 calories, 16g protein, 65g carbohydrate, 37g fat, 6g fiber, 41mg cholesterol, 362mg sodium

20 minutes or less

Famous Restaurant Alfredo Sauce

Submitted by: **GOODNIGHTGRACIE2**
"This is a much sought-after recipe from a popular chain restaurant. My nephew worked there as a cook and gave it to me."

1	(16 ounce) package fettuccine pasta	¾ cup half-and-half
½	cup butter	Pinch garlic salt (or to taste)
¾	cup cream cheese	Lemon pepper to taste

1. Bring a large pot of lightly salted water to a boil. Add pasta and cook for 8 to 10 minutes or until al dente; drain.
2. Combine the butter, cream cheese, and half-and-half in a saucepan. Season with garlic salt and lemon pepper to taste. Bring to a low boil over medium-low heat. Cook, stirring constantly, until thickened slightly. Serve over pasta. **Yield:** 4 servings.

Per serving: 821 calories, 20g protein, 86g carbohydrate, 46g fat, 4g fiber, 127mg cholesterol, 470mg sodium

◄ **FROM THE PANTRY**

Prep Time: 5 minutes

Cook Time: 15 minutes

Average Rating: ★★★★☆

What other cooks have done:

"I made sure to use the double boiler so I could melt the cream cheese completely, which is the key to keeping this sauce from getting lumpy. I used milk instead of half-and-half, and the consistency was good. Keep adding a dash each of garlic salt and lemon pepper until the flavor suits you. I also added three tablespoons of freshly grated Parmesan cheese."

Pasta with Scallops, Zucchini, and Tomatoes

Submitted by: **Lisa Stinger**
"This is my family's favorite summer meal!"

FAMILY FAVORITE ▶

Prep Time: 15 minutes

Cook Time: 15 minutes

Average Rating: ★★★★☆

What other cooks have done:

"Definitely use fresh basil. I also added shrimp. After the pasta was cooked, I sautéed shrimp in a couple tablespoons of olive oil and minced garlic. I tossed the pasta in with the sauce and let it simmer for five minutes to soak in the flavors. It's a gorgeous dish and so tasty."

1	(16 ounce) package fettuccine pasta	4	roma (plum) tomatoes, chopped
¼	cup olive oil	1	pound bay scallops
3	cloves garlic, minced	1	cup chopped fresh basil
2	zucchini, diced	2	tablespoons grated Parmesan cheese
½	teaspoon salt		
½	teaspoon crushed red pepper flakes		

1. Bring a large pot of lightly salted water to a boil. Add pasta and cook for 8 to 10 minutes or until al dente; drain.
2. Meanwhile, heat oil in a large skillet. Add garlic; cook until tender. Add zucchini, salt, and red pepper flakes and sauté for 10 minutes. Add chopped tomatoes, bay scallops, and basil; simmer for 5 minutes or until scallops are opaque.
3. Pour sauce over cooked pasta and top with grated Parmesan cheese. **Yield:** 4 servings.

Per serving: 671 calories, 37g protein, 92g carbohydrate, 18g fat, 6g fiber, 39mg cholesterol, 535mg sodium

Carrie's Artichoke and Sun-Dried Tomato Pasta

Submitted by: **Carrie**
"Prawns and chicken are excellent additions to this versatile pasta dish with a wine-based sauce."

COMPANY IS COMING ▶

Prep Time: 15 minutes

Cook Time: 20 minutes

Average Rating: ★★★★★

What other cooks have done:

"I used olive oil instead of butter, doubled the amount of crushed garlic, and added the whole jar of sun-dried tomatoes. I also substituted chopped chicken breast for mushrooms."

1	(9 ounce) package fresh fettuccine pasta	1	(2.25 ounce) can sliced black olives, drained
4	tablespoons butter	1	cup dry white wine
3	cloves garlic, crushed	2	tablespoons lemon juice
½	medium onion, chopped	1	ripe tomato, chopped
1	(8 ounce) package sliced mushrooms	1	cup Parmesan cheese
1	(12 ounce) jar marinated artichoke hearts	1	teaspoon ground black pepper
⅔	(8 ounce) jar sun-dried tomatoes packed in oil		

1. Bring a large pot of lightly salted water to a boil. Add pasta and cook for 8 to 10 minutes or until al dente; drain.

2. Meanwhile, melt butter in a large saucepan over medium heat. Sauté garlic, onion, and mushrooms until tender. Stir in artichoke hearts, sun-dried tomatoes, olives, wine, and lemon juice. Bring to a boil; cook until liquid is reduced by a third, about 4 minutes.
3. Toss pasta with sauce. Top with tomato and Parmesan cheese. Add pepper and serve. **Yield:** 4 servings.

Per serving: 632 calories, 24g protein, 60g carbohydrate, 31g fat, 9g fiber, 97mg cholesterol, 1084mg sodium

Fettuccine with Mushroom, Ham, and Rosé Sauce

Submitted by: **Chris and Carolyn**
"This thick, creamy, and heavenly entrée is not your everyday pasta dish!"

1	(16 ounce) package fettuccine pasta	2	teaspoons dried basil
¼	cup butter	2	teaspoons dried parsley
½	cup finely diced onion	1	teaspoon crushed red pepper
3	cloves garlic, minced	6	slices ham, chopped
2	(8 ounce) packages fresh sliced mushrooms	1½	cups heavy whipping cream
2	teaspoons dried oregano	1	cup spaghetti sauce

1. Bring a large pot of lightly salted water to a boil. Add pasta and cook for 8 to 10 minutes or until al dente; drain.
2. Meanwhile, in a large sauté pan, melt the butter over medium heat. Add the onion and garlic and cook until softened. Stir in the sliced mushrooms, oregano, basil, parsley, and red pepper. Cook, stirring occasionally, until the liquid from the mushrooms has evaporated. Add the ham and cook for another 4 to 5 minutes.
3. Pour in the heavy cream and bring to a boil. Slowly stir in the spaghetti sauce, blending well with the cream. Cook, stirring occasionally, until the sauce has reduced by a third and is thick.
4. Place fettuccine on plates and ladle even portions of sauce over top. **Yield:** 4 servings.

Per serving: 969 calories, 28g protein, 98g carbohydrate, 53g fat, 9g fiber, 178mg cholesterol, 978mg sodium

◄ HOT & SPICY
Prep Time: 15 minutes
Cook Time: 20 minutes
Average Rating: ★★★★★

What other cooks have done:
"This is a great recipe and very easy. I leave out the red pepper because it's a little spicy for my taste. I also leave out the mushrooms. Don't feel like you have to use chunks of ham. Since I don't bake ham very often, I've used deli-sliced sandwich ham several times, and it's just as good. This is also excellent with bow tie pasta."

Scallop Scampi

Submitted by: **Nikki Medina**

"Here's a healthy and delicious recipe with lots of taste. If you like a thicker sauce, you can add a teaspoon of cornstarch at the end."

4 tablespoons butter	1 (10 ounce) can chicken broth
3 cloves garlic, minced	1 pound bay scallops
1 large onion, minced	1 (16 ounce) package linguine pasta
½ cup dry white wine	1 tablespoon chopped fresh parsley (optional)
1 teaspoon salt	
¼ teaspoon ground black pepper	
½ cup grated Romano cheese, divided	

1. Melt butter in a large skillet over medium heat; sauté garlic and onion until translucent. Add wine, salt, pepper, and ¼ cup cheese.
2. Add chicken broth and scallops; increase heat and boil rapidly for 7 to 8 minutes.
3. Meanwhile, bring a large pot of lightly salted water to a boil. Add pasta and cook for 8 to 10 minutes or until al dente; drain.
4. Remove scallop mixture from heat and add parsley, if desired. Top linguine with scallop mixture. Sprinkle with remaining cheese; serve.
Yield: 8 servings.

Per serving: 359 calories, 19g protein, 45g carbohydrate, 11g fat, 2g fiber, 22mg cholesterol, 765mg sodium

Creamy Pesto Shrimp

Submitted by: **Loretta Buffa**

"One of our family's favorites, this dish is also great when made with crab meat instead of shrimp."

1 (16 ounce) package linguine pasta	1 cup grated Parmesan cheese
½ cup butter	⅓ cup pesto
2 cups heavy cream	1 pound large shrimp, peeled and deveined
½ teaspoon ground black pepper	

1. Bring a large pot of lightly salted water to a boil. Add pasta and cook for 8 to 10 minutes or until al dente; drain.
2. Meanwhile, melt butter in a large skillet over medium heat. Stir in cream and pepper. Cook, stirring constantly, for 6 to 8 minutes.
3. Stir Parmesan cheese into cream sauce until thoroughly mixed.

Blend in the pesto and cook for 3 to 5 minutes or until thickened.
4. Stir in the shrimp and cook about 5 minutes or until shrimp turn pink. Serve over the hot linguine. **Yield:** 8 servings.

Per serving: 679 calories, 28g protein, 45g carbohydrate, 44g fat, 2g fiber, 212mg cholesterol, 539mg sodium

20 minutes or less

Linguine and Clam Sauce

Submitted by: **Peg**

"This is a very easy and tasty recipe; my family loves it. Try serving it with a green salad and garlic bread, if desired."

1	(16 ounce) package linguine pasta	4	cloves garlic, crushed
¼	cup olive oil	2	tablespoons chopped fresh parsley
¼	cup butter		Salt and ground black pepper to taste
2	(6.5 ounce) cans minced clams, drained, with juice reserved	2	tablespoons grated Parmesan cheese

1. Bring a large pot of lightly salted water to a boil. Add pasta and cook for 8 to 10 minutes or until al dente; drain.
2. Meanwhile, in a small saucepan over medium heat, heat oil, butter, reserved clam juice, garlic, and parsley; stir and simmer for 5 minutes.
3. Add clams and salt and pepper to taste. Pour over pasta. Toss with Parmesan cheese and serve. **Yield:** 5 servings.

Per serving: 625 calories, 32g protein, 71g carbohydrate, 24g fat, 3g fiber, 76mg cholesterol, 220mg sodium

◀ FROM THE PANTRY

Prep Time: 10 minutes

Cook Time: 10 minutes

Average Rating: ★★★★★

What other cooks have done:

"I got rave reviews from my dinner guests last night. I squeezed about a quarter of a lemon into the sauce and added some white wine. I also added two and a half pounds of live littleneck clams to the sauce while simmering. I placed thinly sliced lemons around the edge of the bowl, and they made the presentation lovely."

Shrimp and Mushroom Linguine with Creamy Cheese Herb Sauce *(pictured on facing page)*

Submitted by: **Karyn**

"This recipe is a 'gift from the gods.' You can substitute veggies for the shrimp."

1	(8 ounce) package linguine pasta	2	cloves garlic, minced
½	pound fresh mushrooms, sliced	1	(3 ounce) package cream cheese
½	pound frozen, peeled shrimp, thawed	2	tablespoons chopped fresh parsley
2	tablespoons butter	¾	teaspoon dried basil
½	cup butter	⅔	cup water

1. Bring a large pot of lightly salted water to a boil. Add pasta and cook for 8 to 10 minutes or until al dente; drain.
2. Meanwhile, sauté mushrooms and shrimp in 2 tablespoons butter until mushrooms are tender and cooked.
3. Melt ½ cup butter in a large pan; add garlic. Stir in the cream cheese, breaking it up with a spoon as it melts. Stir in the parsley and basil. Simmer for 10 minutes. Stir in water and mix until smooth.
4. Add the cooked shrimp and mushrooms and heat through. Toss with the cooked linguine and serve. **Yield:** 4 servings.

Per serving: 552 calories, 23g protein, 44g carbohydrate, 33g fat, 3g fiber, 196mg cholesterol, 432mg sodium

Anchovy Linguine

Submitted by: **Dennis Valentine**

"A very simple dish prepared in minutes. Serve with French or Italian bread."

1	(16 ounce) package linguine pasta	3	(2 ounce) cans anchovy filets, drained and chopped
6	tablespoons olive oil	1	cup water
4	cloves garlic, minced		
2	tablespoons chopped fresh parsley		

1. Bring a large pot of lightly salted water to a boil. Add pasta and cook for 8 to 10 minutes or until al dente; drain.
2. Meanwhile, heat oil in a skillet over medium heat; sauté garlic in oil until brown. Stir in parsley and chopped anchovies. Add water and simmer for 2 to 3 minutes.
3. Toss pasta with anchovy sauce and serve. **Yield:** 6 servings.

Per serving: 438 calories, 17g protein, 55g carbohydrate, 17g fat, 3g fiber, 19mg cholesterol, 831mg sodium

Shrimp and Mushroom Linguine with Creamy
Cheese Herb Sauce

Pizza Without the Red Sauce, page 212

Lamb Lover's Pilaf, page 238

Cheese Ravioli with Three Pepper Topping,
page 234

Arrabbiata Sauce, page 214

Linguine with Scampi

Submitted by: **Shannon Cooper**

"A wonderfully easy and quick scampi recipe!"

1 (12 ounce) package linguine pasta
¾ cup butter
1 pound shrimp, peeled and deveined
4 cloves garlic, minced
2 tablespoons lemon juice
3 tablespoons chopped fresh parsley
Salt and ground black pepper to taste

1. Preheat oven to 400°F (200°C).
2. Bring a large pot of lightly salted water to a boil. Add pasta and cook for 8 to 10 minutes or until al dente; drain.
3. Meanwhile, put butter in a 9x13 inch glass baking dish and place in oven until butter melts.
4. Add shrimp, garlic, and lemon juice to melted butter; stir to blend. Return dish to oven and bake shrimp for 3 minutes. Mix in parsley and continue baking until shrimp are just cooked through, about 2 more minutes. Season with salt and pepper to taste.
5. Place pasta in a large serving bowl. Spoon shrimp mixture over pasta and toss to combine. Serve immediately. **Yield:** 4 servings.

Per serving: 701 calories, 30g protein, 63g carbohydrate, 38g fat, 3g fiber, 266mg cholesterol, 557mg sodium

◄ FAMILY FAVORITE

Prep Time: 10 minutes

Cook Time: 17 minutes

Average Rating: ★★★★★

What other cooks have done:

"Simple shrimp recipes are the best. This one is great as is and even simpler if you just cook the shrimp on the stovetop. I melt the butter in a skillet, add the garlic and shrimp, and toss in the parsley. Finally, I add the cooked pasta to the pan."

Cajun Shrimp Orecchiette

Submitted by: **Dawn Drouin**

"This dish is very spicy—add Cajun seasoning to suit your taste."

2 cups uncooked orecchiette pasta
⅓ cup butter
½ cup chopped shallots
3 cloves garlic, chopped
¼ cup chopped green onions
1½ tablespoons Cajun seasoning (or to taste)
1 tablespoon cracked black pepper
1 cup white wine
1 cup diced roma (plum) tomatoes
1 pound medium shrimp, peeled and deveined
1 cup baby spinach

1. Bring a large pot of lightly salted water to a boil. Add pasta and cook for 9 to 11 minutes or until almost al dente; drain.
2. Meanwhile, melt butter in a medium skillet over medium heat. Stir in shallots, garlic, and green onions. Season with Cajun seasoning and pepper and cook about 2 minutes. Mix in wine, tomatoes, and shrimp. Continue to cook and stir until shrimp are opaque. Mix in the pasta and spinach. Cover and simmer 3 to 5 minutes or until pasta is al dente and spinach has wilted. **Yield:** 6 servings.

Per serving: 327 calories, 20g protein, 28g carbohydrate, 12g fat, 2g fiber, 143mg cholesterol, 583mg sodium

◄ HOT & SPICY

Prep Time: 15 minutes

Cook Time: 18 minutes

Average Rating: ★★★★☆

What other cooks have done:

"This was great. I added sautéed mushrooms to the sauce and about ⅓ cup Alfredo sauce to thicken it up a bit. Very good flavor and a nice mix of ingredients."

Orzo and Rice

Submitted by: **Carol**

"This filling side dish that's great with chicken is a real family favorite in our house."

5 INGREDIENTS OR LESS ▶

Prep Time: 5 minutes

Cook Time: 30 minutes

Average Rating: ★★★★★

What other cooks have done:

"This is so simple and so good! My family loves this side dish combination of pasta and rice. I prefer to add more bouillon for a little more flavor."

2	tablespoons butter	1	chicken bouillon cube
½	cup uncooked orzo pasta	2	cups hot water
½	cup long-grain white rice		

1. In a large, heavy saucepan, melt butter over medium heat; add orzo and brown until golden.

2. Add rice, bouillon, and water; bring to a boil. Reduce heat to medium-low and cover.

3. Simmer for about 20 to 25 minutes or until all water is absorbed. **Yield:** 5 servings.

Per serving: 192 calories, 5g protein, 32g carbohydrate, 5g fat, 1g fiber, 13mg cholesterol, 282mg sodium

Greek Penne and Chicken

Submitted by: **Jennifer**

"This is one of my favorite 'standby' recipes. I keep the ingredients on hand to make a quick, delicious, satisfying meal."

RESTAURANT FARE ▶

Prep Time: 20 minutes

Cook Time: 15 minutes

Average Rating: ★★★★★

What other cooks have done:

"The best chicken pasta we've had! I simmered the chicken strips in chicken broth and white wine with the onion, garlic, and lemon juice. Toward the end, I added marinated artichoke hearts and some sliced mushrooms to the chicken."

1	(16 ounce) package penne pasta	1	roma (plum) tomato, chopped
1½	tablespoons butter	½	cup crumbled feta cheese
½	cup chopped red onion	3	tablespoons chopped fresh parsley
2	cloves garlic, minced	2	tablespoons lemon juice
1	pound skinless, boneless chicken breast halves, cut into bite-size pieces	1	teaspoon dried oregano
1	(14 ounce) can artichoke hearts in water		Salt and ground black pepper to taste

1. Bring a large pot of lightly salted water to a boil. Add pasta and cook for 8 to 10 minutes or until al dente; drain.

2. Meanwhile, in a large skillet over medium-high heat, melt butter; add onion and garlic and cook for 2 minutes. Add chopped chicken and continue cooking, stirring occasionally, until golden brown, about 6 to 8 minutes. Reduce heat to medium-low.

3. Drain and chop artichoke hearts. Add chopped artichoke, chopped tomato, feta cheese, parsley, lemon juice, oregano, and drained penne pasta to the large skillet. Cook until heated through, about 2 to 3 minutes.

4. Season with salt and pepper to taste. Serve warm. **Yield:** 4 servings.

Per serving: 705 calories, 48g protein, 100g carbohydrate, 13g fat, 9g fiber, 94mg cholesterol, 1070mg sodium

Death by Garlic

Submitted by: **Terry Stirling**

"This is a very flavorful dish that my brothers named Death by Garlic. Warning: If one person has this, you'd better all have some! I like to brown kielbasa sausage, toss it in, and sprinkle feta cheese on top."

1	(16 ounce) package penne pasta	½	teaspoon crushed red pepper flakes
10	cloves garlic, minced	3	tablespoons chopped fresh parsley
½	cup olive oil	⅓	cup grated Romano cheese
½	teaspoon salt		

1. Bring a large pot of lightly salted water to a boil. Add pasta and cook for 8 to 10 minutes or until al dente; drain.
2. In a skillet over medium heat, brown garlic in oil. Add salt, red pepper flakes, and parsley and remove from heat.
3. Toss penne pasta with garlic mixture. Sprinkle with Romano cheese and serve. **Yield:** 4 servings.

Per serving: 697 calories, 19g protein, 86g carbohydrate, 32g fat, 4g fiber, 10mg cholesterol, 418mg sodium

◄ **FAMILY FAVORITE**

Prep Time: 10 minutes

Cook Time: 15 minutes

Average Rating: ★★★★☆

What other cooks have done:

"This is our favorite dish, but without the kielbasa, it isn't nearly as good. We use more than the 10 cloves of garlic, and it's wonderful. Try different pasta shapes—the garlic sticks well to rotini or farfalle pasta."

Creamy Smoked Salmon Pasta

Submitted by: **Dinah**

"This is a lighter version of pasta carbonara. For people who want the flavor but not the bacon, smoked salmon is the perfect substitute!"

1	(16 ounce) package penne pasta	½	cup grated Romano cheese
6	tablespoons butter	1	cup frozen green peas, thawed and drained
½	onion, finely chopped	½	cup canned mushrooms, drained
2	tablespoons all-purpose flour	10	ounces smoked salmon, chopped
2	teaspoons garlic powder		
2	cups skim milk		

1. Bring a large pot of lightly salted water to a boil. Add pasta and cook for 8 to 10 minutes or until al dente; drain.
2. Meanwhile, melt butter in a large skillet over medium heat. Sauté onion in butter until tender.
3. Stir flour and garlic powder into the butter and onions. Gradually stir in milk. Heat to just below boiling; gradually stir in cheese until the sauce is smooth. Stir in peas and mushrooms and cook over low heat for 4 minutes.
4. Toss in smoked salmon and cook for 2 more minutes. Serve over pasta. **Yield:** 8 servings.

Per serving: 398 calories, 20g protein, 50g carbohydrate, 14g fat, 3g fiber, 40mg cholesterol, 553mg sodium

◄ **COMPANY IS COMING**

Prep Time: 15 minutes

Cook Time: 20 minutes

Average Rating: ★★★★☆

What other cooks have done:

"This is a great recipe, but I tweaked it a bit so I could use ingredients I had on hand. I used fresh garlic and mushrooms. I didn't have any Romano cheese, so I stirred some cream cheese and goat cheese into the mixture. I also used fresh basil fettuccine."

Chicken Caesar Pasta

Submitted by: **Barbara**

"An interesting twist on a classic. My family's new favorite."

CROWD-PLEASER ▶

Prep Time: 15 minutes

Cook Time: 20 minutes

Average Rating: ★★★★☆

What other cooks have done:

"I served the dressing, croutons, and Parmesan cheese on the side to avoid making it soggy in case we had leftovers. I also used precooked chicken to speed things up a bit."

1	(16 ounce) package penne pasta	¼	cup red wine vinegar
1	tablespoon butter	½	cup grated Parmesan cheese
6	skinless, boneless chicken breast halves, cut into 1 inch cubes	1	head romaine lettuce, rinsed, drained, and shredded
½	teaspoon ground black pepper	1	roma (plum) tomato, chopped
¼	teaspoon salt		Croutons (optional)
1	(8 ounce) bottle Caesar salad dressing		Parmesan cheese curls (optional)

1. Bring a large pot of lightly salted water to a boil. Add pasta and cook for 8 to 10 minutes or until al dente; drain.

2. Meanwhile, melt butter in a large skillet over medium heat. Season chicken with pepper and salt; add chicken to skillet. Cook for about 5 minutes or until chicken is no longer pink and juices run clear. Remove skillet from heat.

3. In a bowl, mix together salad dressing, vinegar, and ½ cup Parmesan cheese. Toss dressing with chicken, lettuce, and pasta. Place in large serving bowl and sprinkle with tomato. Garnish with croutons and Parmesan curls, if desired. **Yield:** 8 servings.

Per serving: 456 calories, 32g protein, 45g carbohydrate, 16g fat, 3g fiber, 69mg cholesterol, 593mg sodium

Penne with Chicken and Pesto

Submitted by: **Mary**

"I sometimes substitute chicken broth for half the heavy cream to reduce calories. I also use additional Parmesan."

FAMILY FAVORITE ▶

Prep Time: 12 minutes

Cook Time: 20 minutes

Average Rating: ★★★★★

What other cooks have done:

"Very good and super easy to make! I used a packaged pesto mix and made the pesto before boiling the pasta. It came out just fine. The sauce is rich and tasty. I think next time I may marinate the chicken in garlic powder for a few hours before cooking."

1	(16 ounce) package penne pasta	2	cloves garlic, minced
2	tablespoons butter		Salt and ground black pepper to taste
2	tablespoons olive oil	1¼	cups heavy cream
4	skinless, boneless chicken breast halves, cut into thin strips	¼	cup pesto
		3	tablespoons grated Parmesan cheese

1. Bring a large pot of lightly salted water to a boil. Add pasta and cook for 8 to 10 minutes or until al dente; drain.

2. Meanwhile, heat butter and olive oil in a large skillet over medium heat. Sauté chicken and garlic in oil until chicken is almost cooked. Reduce heat and stir in salt and pepper to taste, cream, pesto, and

Parmesan cheese. Cook until chicken is no longer pink and juices run clear. Stir in cooked pasta. **Yield:** 8 servings.

Per serving: 498 calories, 24g protein, 43g carbohydrate, 26g fat, 2g fiber, 97mg cholesterol, 179mg sodium

30 minutes or less

Portobello Mushroom Ravioli with Prawns

Submitted by: **Michelle Campbell**

"This is a sinfully rich pasta with portobello mushrooms, prawns, and capers in a white wine, butter, and garlic sauce."

1	(12 ounce) package fresh cheese-filled ravioli	7	large portobello mushrooms, sliced
¼	cup butter	2	tablespoons butter
3	cloves garlic, minced	2	tablespoons white wine
2	tablespoons olive oil	½	lemon, juiced
3	tablespoons capers		Freshly ground black pepper to taste
½	cup white wine	2	tablespoons freshly grated Parmesan cheese
20	large prawns, peeled and deveined		

1. Bring a large pot of lightly salted water to a boil. Add pasta and cook for 8 to 10 minutes or until al dente; drain.

2. Meanwhile, in a large saucepan, melt ¼ cup butter over medium heat. Sauté garlic in butter for 1 to 2 minutes. Stir in olive oil and capers. Add ½ cup white wine and prawns and bring to a boil.

3. Reduce heat and simmer for 2 to 3 minutes, letting wine reduce. Stir in sliced mushrooms, 2 tablespoons butter, and 2 tablespoons wine. (Sauce should be thick, but still liquid after cooking for 2 to 3 more minutes.) Stir in lemon juice and add pepper to taste.

4. To serve, divide ravioli between 4 plates; place 5 prawns on each plate. Evenly distribute sauce between the 4 plates and top with Parmesan cheese. **Yield:** 4 servings.

Per serving: 571 calories, 26g protein, 43g carbohydrate, 32g fat, 6g fiber, 82mg cholesterol, 570mg sodium

◀ **COMPANY IS COMING**

Prep Time: 15 minutes

Cook Time: 15 minutes

Average Rating: ★★★★★

What other cooks have done:

"I removed the prawns with a slotted spoon after they turned pink and set them aside while the rest of the sauce reduced. I returned them to the sauce at the end to warm them before serving. Also, I was out of capers, so I used a tablespoon of crushed, chopped soft green peppercorns. Worked great!"

Cheese Ravioli with Three Pepper Topping (*pictured on page 227*)

Submitted by: **Amanda**

"I cooked this one day for myself as a nice change from tomato sauces."

"Yum—that sums it up. This was a wonderful change from tomato-based pasta sauces, just as the description states. I doubled the recipe and added about 1 teaspoon roasted minced garlic to the onion and pepper mixture while it was cooking because I'm a garlic junkie. It was light and fresh tasting."

16	ounces cheese-filled ravioli	2	cups vegetable or chicken broth, divided
3	tablespoons olive oil	¼	teaspoon crushed red pepper flakes
1	small onion, diced		
1	green bell pepper, sliced		Freshly ground black pepper
½	red bell pepper, sliced		Freshly grated Parmesan cheese
½	yellow bell pepper, sliced		

1. Bring a large pot of lightly salted water to a boil. Add pasta and cook for 8 to 10 minutes or until al dente; drain.
2. Meanwhile, heat oil in large skillet over medium heat. Sauté onion and bell peppers until tender. Add 1 cup of the broth. Season with red pepper flakes and simmer for 5 minutes. Stir in remaining broth; cook until most of broth has evaporated. Spoon bell pepper mixture over ravioli. Sprinkle with black pepper and Parmesan cheese. **Yield:** 6 servings.

Per serving: 265 calories, 10g protein, 28g carbohydrate, 13g fat, 3g fiber, 30mg cholesterol, 461mg sodium

Chicken, Sausage, and Zucchini Pasta

Submitted by: **Mary**

"I just threw this together one night, and we all loved it!"

"This was very good. I cooked the sausages whole before slicing them, and I may do that next time with the chicken as well. I used a 26 ounce jar of sauce, which was plenty. With a loaf of Italian bread and a salad topped with Parmesan cheese, this was a very nice meal."

1	(16 ounce) package rotini pasta	1	teaspoon Italian seasoning
4	(3.5 ounce) links Italian sausage, sliced		Salt and ground black pepper to taste
2	skinless, boneless chicken breast halves, cubed	1	(14.5 ounce) can diced tomatoes
1	onion, chopped	1¾	cups spaghetti sauce
1	clove garlic, minced	1	(4.5 ounce) jar sliced mushrooms
1	green bell pepper, diced	3	zucchini, thickly sliced

1. Bring a large pot of lightly salted water to a boil. Add pasta and cook for 8 to 10 minutes or until al dente; drain.
2. Meanwhile, in a Dutch oven, cook sausage until brown. Add chicken and cook until no longer pink and juices run clear. Stir in onion, garlic, green bell pepper, Italian seasoning, and salt and black pepper to taste. Cover and simmer until vegetables are tender. Stir in tomatoes, spaghetti sauce, mushrooms, and zucchini. Simmer until zucchini is tender-crisp.
3. Toss cooked pasta with sauce. Serve warm. **Yield:** 6 servings.

Per serving: 608 calories, 31g protein, 70g carbohydrate, 23g fat, 7g fiber, 69mg cholesterol, 1056mg sodium

Pasta with Peas and Sausage

Submitted by: **Elaina**

"Delicious and creamy. Something different for pasta."

1	(16 ounce) package rigatoni pasta	12	ounces frozen green peas
2	tablespoons olive oil	1½	cups heavy cream
1	clove garlic, minced	¼	cup butter
1	pound sweet Italian sausage, casings removed	2	tablespoons grated Parmesan cheese

1. Bring a large pot of lightly salted water to a boil. Add pasta and cook for 8 to 10 minutes or until al dente; drain.

2. Meanwhile, heat oil in a skillet over medium heat; add garlic and briefly sauté. Add sausage and cook until brown. Add frozen peas and simmer for 5 minutes. Slowly add heavy cream and butter to skillet; bring to a slight boil. Cook for 5 minutes. Toss with cooked pasta and top with Parmesan cheese. **Yield:** 4 servings.

Per serving: 1206 calories, 38g protein, 98g carbohydrate, 75g fat, 8g fiber, 217mg cholesterol, 1020mg sodium

◄ KID-FRIENDLY

Prep Time: 10 minutes

Cook Time: 20 minutes

Average Rating: ★★★★★

What other cooks have done:

"I didn't have any heavy cream, so I used half-and-half. I also added a little water with some beef bouillon in order to increase the liquid. This turned out great and was very flavorful. It's simple but delicious!"

Cajun Pasta Fresca

Submitted by: **Nicole**

"If you like food with a little kick and you are a pasta fan, this recipe is for you!"

1	(16 ounce) package vermicelli pasta	1	tablespoon chopped fresh parsley
2	tablespoons olive oil	1	tablespoon Cajun seasoning
1	teaspoon minced garlic	½	cup shredded mozzarella cheese
13	roma (plum) tomatoes, chopped, juice reserved	½	cup grated Parmesan cheese
1	tablespoon salt		

1. Bring a large pot of lightly salted water to a boil. Add pasta and cook for 8 to 10 minutes or until al dente; drain.

2. Meanwhile, heat oil in a large skillet over medium heat; briefly sauté garlic in oil. Stir in tomatoes and their juice and sprinkle with salt. When tomatoes are bubbly, mash slightly with a fork. Stir in parsley. Reduce heat and simmer for 5 more minutes.

3. Toss hot pasta with tomato sauce, Cajun seasoning, mozzarella cheese, and Parmesan cheese. **Yield:** 8 servings.

Per serving: 304 calories, 13g protein, 47g carbohydrate, 8g fat, 3g fiber, 9mg cholesterol, 1211mg sodium

◄ CROWD-PLEASER

Prep Time: 10 minutes

Cook Time: 15 minutes

Average Rating: ★★★★☆

What other cooks have done:

"This was a fantastically fresh alternative to ordinary pasta sauce. I added some extra veggies (zucchini, spinach, and mushrooms) and it made a tasty primavera. Bravo!"

Pepper Rice and Confetti Beef

Submitted by: **Johnnie Burgess**
"This mouth-watering dish is too quick and easy not to become your favorite weeknight meal."

FAMILY FAVORITE ▶

Prep Time: 15 minutes

Cook Time: 20 minutes

Average Rating: ★★★★☆

What other cooks have done:

"I seasoned the beef and bell peppers with a fajita seasoning packet while cooking them on the stove. I threw the green onions in with the beef mixture during the last five minutes of cooking, and I doubled the honey-mustard sauce."

1½ cups chicken broth
1½ cups uncooked white rice
1 tablespoon vegetable oil
½ pound beef sirloin, thinly sliced
½ red bell pepper, thinly sliced
½ yellow bell pepper, thinly sliced
½ green bell pepper, thinly sliced
Salt and ground black pepper to taste
2 tablespoons prepared Dijon-style mustard
2 tablespoons honey
½ cup chopped green onion

1. In a medium saucepan, bring chicken broth to a boil. Add rice and stir. Reduce heat; cover and simmer for 20 minutes.
2. Meanwhile, heat oil in a large skillet over medium heat; add beef and bell peppers to skillet. Cook until beef is evenly browned. Season with salt and black pepper to taste. Remove from heat.
3. Stir Dijon mustard and honey into the beef mixture. Stir green onions into rice. Serve peppers and beef over rice. **Yield:** 4 servings.

Per serving: 424 calories, 17g protein, 69g carbohydrate, 9g fat, 2g fiber, 30mg cholesterol, 690mg sodium

Cheesy Chicken and Rice Casserole

Submitted by: **Lee**
"This is a quick and easy dish that even the kids like! If you are in a big hurry, use cooked chicken and instant rice. This can be made ahead of time and refrigerated—just add the bread topping right before cooking."

5 INGREDIENTS OR LESS ▶

Prep Time: 15 minutes

Cook Time: 29 minutes

Average Rating: ★★★★☆

What other cooks have done:

"I used crushed buttery round crackers with a little melted butter mixed in for the topping instead of the bread. I stirred in about three-fourths of the cheese with the chicken mixture, along with about 1 teaspoon garlic powder. My whole family enjoyed this, including my picky five-year-old. Overall, a good dish for a quick weeknight supper, especially if you have cooked rice and chicken on hand!"

4 skinless, boneless chicken breast halves, cut into bite-size pieces
Salt and ground black pepper to taste
2 cups cooked white rice
1 (10.75 ounce) can condensed cream of chicken soup
2 cups shredded Cheddar cheese
3 slices soft white bread, cubed

1. Preheat oven to 350°F (175°C).
2. Season chicken with salt and pepper to taste and place in a microwave-safe dish. Cover and microwave on high for 5 to 6 minutes. Turn and cook for another 2 to 3 minutes or until chicken is no longer pink and juices run clear. Let cool.

3. In a 9x13 inch baking dish, combine chicken, rice, and soup; mix well. Sprinkle with cheese and top with bread cubes.
4. Bake in the preheated oven for 20 minutes or until cheese is melted and bubbly and bread is crunchy. **Yield:** 5 servings.

Per serving: 465 calories, 38g protein, 30g carbohydrate, 20g fat, 1g fiber, 107mg cholesterol, 903mg sodium

Broccoli, Rice, Cheese, and Chicken Casserole

Submitted by: **Heather**
"This is a delicious twist to the traditional broccoli, rice, and cheese casserole, and it's very easy to make. You can also cut this in half. I use one can cream of mushroom soup when I make half."

2 cups water	¼ cup butter
2 cups uncooked instant white rice	1 cup milk
2 (10 ounce) cans chunk chicken, drained	1 (16 ounce) package frozen chopped broccoli
1 (10.75 ounce) can condensed cream of mushroom soup	1 small white onion, chopped
1 (10.75 ounce) can condensed cream of chicken soup	1 pound processed cheese

1. Preheat oven to 375°F (190°C).
2. In a medium saucepan, bring 2 cups water to a boil. Add instant rice. Cover and remove from heat. Let stand for 5 minutes.
3. In a 9x13 inch baking dish, mix the prepared rice, chicken, cream of mushroom soup, cream of chicken soup, butter, milk, broccoli, onion, and processed cheese.
4. Bake in the preheated oven for 28 minutes or until cheese is melted. Stir halfway through cooking to help cheese melt evenly.
Yield: 8 servings.

Per serving: 543 calories, 32g protein, 33g carbohydrate, 31g fat, 3g fiber, 101mg cholesterol, 1682mg sodium

◄ FROM THE PANTRY
Prep Time: 15 minutes
Cook Time: 30 minutes
Stand Time: 5 minutes
Average Rating: ★★★★☆
What other cooks have done:
"If you're in a hurry, this is the casserole for you. I did, however, make some changes. I used 2 cups of shredded Cheddar instead of processed cheese. I also used cream of broccoli soup instead of cream of mushroom. Curry powder, black pepper, and paprika added a kick."

Lamb Lover's Pilaf *(pictured on page 227)*

Submitted by: **Casey Stewart**
"If you like those restaurants with tapestries on the walls, pillows on the floor, and little brass tables, you will enjoy this take on Moroccan lamb pilaf. Boneless lamb, celery, bulgur wheat, and onion are graced with hints of cinnamon, allspice, and chicken broth. Raisins and slivered almonds top off this lovely dish."

2	tablespoons vegetable oil, divided		2	stalks celery, minced
1½	pounds boneless lamb stew meat, cut into ½ inch strips		1	cup dry bulgur wheat
			1½	cups chicken broth
½	teaspoon Greek-style seasoning		1	pinch ground cinnamon
			1	pinch ground allspice
1	onion, chopped		¼	cup raisins
			¼	cup slivered almonds

1. Heat 1 tablespoon of oil in a large skillet over medium-high heat. Season lamb strips with Greek seasoning and sauté in oil until browned. Remove from skillet and set aside.
2. Reduce heat to medium and heat remaining tablespoon of oil. Sauté onion and celery in oil until soft; add bulgur wheat and continue cooking, stirring often, for an additional 2 minutes.
3. Stir in reserved lamb, broth, cinnamon, and allspice. Reduce heat to low and simmer for 10 minutes, covered, until liquid has been absorbed. Top with raisins and almonds and serve. **Yield:** 6 servings.

Per serving: 304 calories, 22g protein, 27g carbohydrate, 13g fat, 6g fiber, 54mg cholesterol, 339mg sodium

Sandwiches & Soups

Open-Faced Broiled Roast Beef Sandwich

Submitted by: **HellSwitch**
"The combination of ingredients in this sandwich blows my mind every time I make it. Eat it with a knife and fork."

2	hoagie rolls, split	2	tomatoes, thinly sliced
2	tablespoons mayonnaise	½	red onion, thinly sliced
2	teaspoons prepared coarse-ground mustard	4	slices provolone cheese
1	pound deli-sliced roast beef		Salt and ground black pepper to taste

1. Preheat broiler.
2. Cut rolls in half and toast in a toaster or oven. Place on a baking sheet. Spread each half with mayonnaise and mustard. Layer evenly with roast beef, tomato, red onion, provolone, and salt and pepper to taste.
3. Broil in the preheated oven 3 to 6 inches from heat source for 2 to 4 minutes or until cheese is bubbly. **Yield:** 4 servings.

Per serving: 398 calories, 34g protein, 23g carbohydrate, 19g fat, 2g fiber, 78mg cholesterol, 1641mg sodium

Dan's Meat Wrap

Submitted by: **Dan Lisee**
"You can use different meats for a variation of this great deli-style wrap."

1	(10 inch) flour tortilla	½	cup chopped tomato
4	slices roast beef	¼	cup chopped onion
½	cup shredded Cheddar-Monterey Jack cheese blend	4	black olives
½	cup shredded lettuce	2	tablespoons Italian-style salad dressing

1. Place tortilla on a plate. Top tortilla with roast beef and cheese. Microwave on high for 45 seconds or until cheese is melted. Sprinkle with lettuce, tomato, onion, and olives. Top with Italian dressing. Roll up. **Yield:** 1 serving.

Per serving: 779 calories, 40g protein, 56g carbohydrate, 44g fat, 6g fiber, 109mg cholesterol, 1778mg sodium

Sesame-Lime Steak Wraps

Submitted by: **Linda W.**

"Thinly sliced beef is marinated in an Asian-inspired lime-sesame sauce, cooked, and then wrapped in tortillas with red leaf lettuce."

½	pound eye of round, thinly sliced	1	teaspoon sesame oil	
¼	cup lime juice	1	teaspoon finely chopped fresh ginger root	
¼	cup honey	4	leaves red leaf lettuce, rinsed, dried, and torn	
1	tablespoon vegetable oil	4	(8 inch) flour tortillas	
2	teaspoons toasted sesame seeds			
2	teaspoons reduced-sodium soy sauce			

1. Place sliced beef in a shallow bowl. In a jar, combine lime juice, honey, oil, sesame seeds, soy sauce, sesame oil, and ginger. Seal lid tightly and shake until well combined. Pour over beef; cover and marinate in refrigerator for 30 minutes.

2. Heat a nonstick skillet over high heat until very hot. Add beef and marinade to pan and sauté until steak is evenly brown. Remove beef with a slotted spoon. Boil marinade until reduced by half, stirring frequently to prevent burning, about 5 minutes. Return beef to pan and mix well; set aside to cool slightly.

3. Place lettuce leaves on tortillas and top evenly with beef slices. Fold up bottom third of each tortilla and tightly roll from the side. **Yield:** 4 servings.

Per serving: 402 calories, 16g protein, 47g carbohydrate, 17g fat, 2g fiber, 35mg cholesterol, 353mg sodium

◀ FAMILY FAVORITE

Prep Time: 15 minutes

Marinate Time: 30 minutes

Cook Time: 15 minutes

Average Rating: ★★★★☆

What other cooks have done:

"This has a fantastic flavor. I added some chopped cilantro, which went well with the lime juice. This would be a great marinade for chicken, too."

Pork Sausage and Cabbage Pitas

Submitted by: **Holly**

"I've made this very quick, simple, one-dish meal for years. You can vary the crushed red pepper depending on how spicy you like it."

ONE-DISH MEAL ▶

Prep Time: 10 minutes

Cook Time: 30 minutes

Average Rating: ★★★★★

What other cooks have done:

"I loved this! I used a teaspoon of red pepper, and it was just spicy enough. I served it on a hard roll with mustard, and it was delicious."

1½	pounds ground pork sausage	1	tablespoon white sugar
1	medium head cabbage, shredded		Salt to taste
		½	cup water
1	small onion, chopped	⅓	cup sour cream
1	tablespoon crushed red pepper flakes	1	(8 ounce) package pita rounds, halved

1. In a wok or skillet over medium-high heat, brown pork sausage; drain and set aside.

2. Combine shredded cabbage, onion, crushed red pepper flakes, sugar, salt, and water in skillet. Cover and steam for approximately 20 minutes, stirring occasionally, or until cabbage is tender.

3. Return pork sausage to skillet with cabbage mixture and add sour cream; mix well. Serve stuffed inside pita halves. **Yield:** 6 servings.

Per serving: 648 calories, 20g protein, 32g carbohydrate, 50g fat, 4g fiber, 83mg cholesterol, 1480mg sodium

30 minutes or less

BLT Wraps *(pictured on page 3)*

Submitted by: **Karen**

"I love wraps, but I'm allergic to mayonnaise, so I designed this wrap to be held together with melted cheese instead. For a good variation, substitute taco meat and grilled onions for the bacon."

KID-FRIENDLY ▶

Prep Time: 15 minutes

Cook Time: 15 minutes

Average Rating: ★★★★★

What other cooks have done:

"I skipped the cheese and used Ranch dressing instead. I also used an Italian herb wheat wrap for extra flavor. This was really good."

1	pound thick-sliced bacon, cut into 1 inch pieces	½	head iceberg lettuce, shredded
4	(6 inch) flour tortillas	1	tomato, diced
1	cup shredded Cheddar cheese		

1. Place bacon in a large, deep skillet. Cook over medium-high heat until evenly brown. Drain and set aside.

2. Place 1 tortilla on a microwave-safe plate. Sprinkle tortilla with one-fourth of cheese. Microwave on high for 1 to 2 minutes or until cheese is melted. Immediately top with one-fourth each of bacon, lettuce, and tomato. Fold sides of tortilla over; roll up. Repeat with remaining ingredients. Cut each wrap in half before serving. **Yield:** 4 servings.

Per serving: 735 calories, 23g protein, 19g carbohydrate, 63g fat, 1g fiber, 107mg cholesterol, 1337mg sodium

Gourmet Chicken Sandwich *(pictured on page 262)*

Submitted by: **Lisa Clarke**

"Sautéed chicken breasts are topped with a mayonnaise/mustard/rosemary spread and graced by two slices of rosemary and onion focaccia bread. These sandwiches are great when you want a quick supper but not something from the freezer. They remind me of an expensive sandwich from an upscale deli. The spread and the chicken can be made in advance, and the chicken can be eaten hot or cold."

Ground black pepper to taste
4 skinless, boneless chicken breast halves, pounded to ¼ inch thickness
1 tablespoon olive oil
1 teaspoon minced garlic
¼ cup mayonnaise
4 teaspoons prepared Dijon-style mustard
2 teaspoons chopped fresh rosemary
1 (8 inch) round rosemary and onion focaccia bread

1. Sprinkle pepper to taste on 1 side of chicken. Heat oil in a large skillet over medium-high heat; brown garlic in oil; add chicken, peppered side down. Sauté chicken until chicken is no longer pink and juices run clear, about 12 minutes, turning once during cooking.
2. In a small bowl, combine the mayonnaise, mustard, and rosemary. Split focaccia bread in half horizontally. Spread mayonnaise mixture evenly on cut sides of bread. Layer bottom slice of bread with chicken. Cover with top slice of bread; cut into wedges and serve. **Yield:** 4 servings.

Per serving: 370 calories, 31g protein, 16g carbohydrate, 19g fat, 1g fiber, 73mg cholesterol, 478mg sodium

◄ COMPANY IS COMING
Prep Time: 10 minutes
Cook Time: 15 minutes
Average Rating: ★★★★★

What other cooks have done:
"Loved this! I had leftover chicken thighs already cooked, so I just warmed those up and used them. The focaccia I used had plenty of garlic in it, and the spread was perfectly sweet and tangy. I used creamy mayonnaise-mustard blend, which was the only mustard I had, and added honey to taste. I will be making this many times as summer comes and we want a warm, but not hot, meal."

In the Bag

Making your own lunch helps you have more structured days by letting you establish a lunch routine that's workable and healthful. It really doesn't take much effort to get a bag packed with goodies ready to go to fuel you for the rest of the day. Preparing your own lunch can be economical, time saving, and, of course, your meal will taste great!

The Brown Bag Nutrition Breakdown
Your lunch should provide you with enough energy for the remainder of your day, so be sure to include some form of protein, plenty of carbohydrates and fiber, and as little fat as possible. Protein activates two neurotransmitters located within the brain that will help promote alertness and will help you focus on tasks you often perform during a busy weekday. You want some carbohydrates, but be careful—a lunch of pure carbs (just pasta, for example) can cause the neurotransmitter serotonin to become activated, promoting sleepiness. A great example of a well-balanced lunch is the good ol' sandwich.

Variety is the Spice of Lunch
Fruits and vegetables should be small and easy to eat, like grapes, cherries, blueberries, baby carrots, cucumber slices, bell pepper wedges, and lightly steamed broccoli florets. Beyond sliced bread, try crackers, pita bread, cornbread, mini bagels, tortillas, or even pasta salad. For protein, there's good ol' peanut butter, hummus, sliced cheese, cold cuts, tuna salad, or a thermos full of chili.

Awaken All the Senses
Choose foods that represent an array of textures, colors, aromas, and flavors. Try to pair soft and smooth textures with crunchy and chewy ones, and choose foods with vivid and contrasting colors. Make sure that rich flavors are accompanied by refreshing ones and that a salty meal has a touch of sweetness thrown in. With a hearty and nutritious lunch, you can even feel good about adding a cookie or a brownie to the bag!

For more information, visit **Allrecipes.com**

Buffalo Chicken Sandwiches

Submitted by: **Lisa**

"Let this spicy Buffalo wings sandwich take flight right into your lunch box."

HOT & SPICY ▶

Prep Time: 10 minutes

Cook Time: 15 minutes

Average Rating: ★★★★☆

What other cooks have done:

"This was great even without being put in a sandwich. The chicken was a delicious meal with a side dish of rice and a vegetable."

4	skinless, boneless chicken breast halves	2	teaspoons paprika
1	(2 ounce) bottle hot pepper sauce	1	red onion, sliced into rings
1	(5 ounce) bottle green hot pepper sauce	8	French baguette slices
		4	slices tomato
		4	leaves lettuce

1. Preheat broiler. Line a broiler pan with foil.

2. Place chicken in prepared pan. Pour hot pepper sauce and green hot pepper sauce over chicken; sprinkle with paprika. Top with onion.

3. Broil in the preheated oven for 15 minutes or until chicken is no longer pink and juices run clear.

4. Place each breast half on a baguette slice; top each with tomato and lettuce and cover with another baguette slice. Serve. **Yield:** 4 servings.

Per serving: 506 calories, 39g protein, 72g carbohydrate, 6g fat, 5g fiber, 68mg cholesterol, 2171mg sodium

Roast Chicken Pita Pockets

Submitted by: **Irene Chua**

"Chicken sandwiches with all the fixings are great for snacks or meals. If you can't find honey-roasted chicken, substitute any other kind of roasted chicken."

HOT & SPICY ▶

Prep Time: 15 minutes

Cook Time: 5 minutes

Average Rating: ★★★★☆

What other cooks have done:

"I didn't have roasted chicken, so I used 3 boneless chicken breasts and sliced them thin while still partially frozen. This was a tasty change from the usual pita fillings, and if you like sloppy joes, you will like this."

1	pita round, halved	½	cup mayonnaise
2	honey-roasted skinless, boneless chicken breast halves, chopped	½	cup ketchup
		½	cup chili sauce
2	cups shredded lettuce	1	dash hot pepper sauce
1	large onion, chopped	1	teaspoon lemon juice
½	cup shredded Cheddar cheese	¼	teaspoon ground black pepper

1. Preheat oven to 250°F (120°C).

2. Heat pita halves in the preheated oven until slightly browned.

3. Meanwhile, in a large bowl, combine chicken, lettuce, onion, cheese, mayonnaise, ketchup, chili sauce, hot pepper sauce, lemon juice, and black pepper. Mix well.

4. Fill each hot pita half evenly with chicken mixture. Serve hot. **Yield:** 2 servings.

Per serving: 909 calories, 38g protein, 64g carbohydrate, 55g fat, 3g fiber, 118mg cholesterol, 3423mg sodium

Slaw-mmin' Wraps

Submitted by: **juleskicks2**
"This nutritious, balanced meal that's a snap to throw together works great with leftover chicken."

2	tablespoons olive oil	3	tablespoons mayonnaise
1	onion, chopped	2	tablespoons prepared
2	cloves garlic, crushed		Dijon-style mustard
½	(16 ounce) package	1	teaspoon ground cumin
	broccoli coleslaw mix	4	cloves garlic, minced
1	cup shredded cabbage	½	teaspoon onion powder
¾	cup diced, cooked chicken	½	teaspoon lemon pepper
	Salt and ground black		Salt and ground black
	pepper to taste		pepper to taste
1	(15 ounce) can garbanzo	4	(10 inch) flour tortillas
	beans, undrained		

1. Heat oil in a large, heavy skillet over medium–high heat. Sauté onion and 2 cloves crushed garlic for 3 minutes or until onions are soft and translucent. Stir in the broccoli coleslaw mix and cook until tender. Add the cabbage and chicken and toss for 1 to 2 minutes. Remove from heat and season with salt and pepper to taste.

2. In a blender, combine garbanzo beans, mayonnaise, mustard, cumin, 4 cloves minced garlic, onion powder, lemon pepper, and salt and pepper to taste. Blend until smooth and creamy.

3. Microwave tortillas on high for a few seconds for easier folding. Spread each tortilla evenly with garbanzo bean mixture; dollop each tortilla with slaw mixture. Wrap tortillas and serve. **Yield:** 4 servings.

Per serving: 594 calories, 21g protein, 74g carbohydrate, 24g fat, 10g fiber, 26mg cholesterol, 1023mg sodium

◄ OUT-OF-THE-ORDINARY

Prep Time: 10 minutes

Cook Time: 10 minutes

Average Rating: ★★★★★

What other cooks have done:

"I didn't have broccoli coleslaw, so I cut up red and green bell peppers and used them instead. Also, I used more chicken and added a few dashes of onion and garlic powder to the sauté. Finally, I didn't have garbanzo beans, so I used a can of northern beans—very good!"

Turkey and Provolone Sandwiches

Submitted by: **Jennifer Gatlin**

"Hoagie rolls baked with slices of turkey, provolone cheese, and a mushroom and onion mixture are topped with olives, tomato, and lettuce. This is a favorite meal with my family. I make it using the turkey and cheese from our local grocery store deli. If desired, spread mustard and mayonnaise on top half of bread before assembling sandwich."

FAMILY FAVORITE ▶

Prep Time: 15 minutes

Cook Time: 10 minutes

Average Rating: ★★★★★

What other cooks have done:

"I made mine on sourdough sandwich rolls, which I buttered and baked for five minutes by themselves before adding the toppings."

1	tablespoon butter	1	pound sliced provolone cheese
6	large mushrooms, sliced		
1	small onion, chopped	¼	cup sliced black olives
6	hoagie rolls, split lengthwise	6	slices tomato
1	pound deli-sliced turkey meat	6	leaves iceberg lettuce

1. Preheat oven to 400°F (200°C). Line a baking sheet with parchment paper.

2. Melt butter in a small skillet over medium heat. Sauté mushrooms and onion in skillet until tender; set aside. Place bottom halves of bread on prepared baking sheet. Top each half evenly with turkey, mushroom and onion mixture, and cheese.

3. Bake in the preheated oven for about 5 minutes or until cheese is melted. Remove from oven and top each sandwich with olives, tomato, and lettuce. Place top half of bread on each sandwich and serve. **Yield:** 6 servings.

Per serving: 577 calories, 40g protein, 40g carbohydrate, 29g fat, 3g fiber, 88mg cholesterol, 1966mg sodium

Tuna Pita Melts

Submitted by: **Glori Butero**

"This is a quick and easy twist on your average tuna melt, and it looks and tastes delicious."

6	(6 inch) whole pita rounds	¼	teaspoon salt
2	(6 ounce) cans tuna, drained	1	large tomato, sliced into thin wedges
2	tablespoons mayonnaise	1	cup shredded Cheddar cheese
2	tablespoons dill pickle relish		
½	teaspoon dried dill		

1. Preheat oven to 400°F (200°C).
2. Place whole pita rounds in a single layer on a baking sheet. Bake in the preheated oven for 5 minutes or until lightly toasted.
3. Meanwhile, in a medium bowl, mix together tuna, mayonnaise, relish, dill, and salt. Spread tuna mixture evenly onto each pita round. Arrange tomato wedges over the tuna and sprinkle with shredded Cheddar cheese.
4. Bake in the preheated oven for 5 minutes or until cheese has melted. **Yield:** 6 servings.

Per serving: 363 calories, 26g protein, 36g carbohydrate, 13g fat, 2g fiber, 44mg cholesterol, 682mg sodium

◄ FROM THE PANTRY

Prep Time: 10 minutes

Cook Time: 15 minutes

Average Rating: ★★★★★

What other cooks have done:

"I love tuna, so this made a great lunch. I never thought of using pita bread, and it was a really nice change. I'm not crazy about relish in my tuna, so I omitted it but added some chopped red onion along with garlic and onion powders and black pepper."

Quick Breakfast in a Pita

Submitted by: **Elsie**

"I make these sandwiches for myself when I'm rushed. This recipe is great for using leftovers and is very versatile. You can add any seasonings you like."

1	pita round, halved	Salt and ground black
1	medium potato, diced	pepper to taste
2	eggs	

1. Preheat oven to 350°F (175°C). Place pita halves in oven to warm.
2. Cook diced potatoes in boiling water until done; drain.
3. Heat a medium skillet coated with cooking spray over high heat. Add potatoes and sauté until lightly browned, about 5 minutes. Reduce heat to medium and add eggs. Mix gently until eggs are firm, about 45 seconds. Season with salt and pepper to taste. Stuff warm pita halves with potato and egg mixture. Serve immediately. **Yield:** 2 servings.

Per serving: 206 calories, 11g protein, 30g carbohydrate, 5g fat, 2g fiber, 212mg cholesterol, 231mg sodium

◄ 5 INGREDIENTS OR LESS

Prep Time: 5 minutes

Cook Time: 15 minutes

Average Rating: ★★★★★

What other cooks have done:

"I cook my potatoes with garlic, onion, and a touch of olive oil. I also add bacon, cheese, and avocado."

Easy Eggplant Pita

Submitted by: **Nikki**
"Adjust the amount of garlic powder in this yummy veggie pita to your taste."

1	tablespoon olive oil	4	pita rounds, halved
1	small eggplant, diced	1	cup shredded mozzarella cheese
¼	cup fresh sliced mushrooms		
1	green bell pepper, chopped	½	cup Ranch-style salad dressing (optional)
½	onion, chopped		
¼	teaspoon garlic powder		

1. Heat olive oil in a large skillet over medium-high heat. Combine eggplant, mushrooms, green bell pepper, onion, and garlic powder in skillet and cook until vegetables are brown and softened.
2. Stuff hot vegetable mixture into pita halves. Sprinkle mozzarella cheese into the pockets. Top pitas with Ranch dressing, if desired. **Yield:** 8 servings.

Per serving: 236 calories, 7g protein, 24g carbohydrate, 13g fat, 3g fiber, 15mg cholesterol, 359mg sodium

Curried Cream of Any Veggie Soup

Submitted by: **Dick**
"This low-calorie vegetable soup works well with broccoli, mushrooms, potatoes, and celery."

1	tablespoon vegetable oil	2	tablespoons all-purpose flour
1	onion, chopped		
1	clove garlic, minced	2	cups fat-free milk
1	tablespoon curry powder		Salt and ground black pepper to taste
4	cups chicken broth		
4	cups chopped mixed vegetables		

1. Heat oil in a large saucepan over medium heat. Add onion and garlic and sauté until tender. Stir in curry and cook, stirring constantly, for 2 minutes. Add broth and vegetables and bring to a boil. Simmer 15 minutes or until tender.
2. Dissolve flour in milk and stir into soup. Simmer until thickened. Season with salt and pepper to taste. **Yield:** 6 servings.

Per serving: 159 calories, 8g protein, 24g carbohydrate, 5g fat, 5g fiber, 2mg cholesterol, 826mg sodium

Cream of Broccoli Soup I

Submitted by: **William Anatooskin**

"For a richer, creamier soup, use half-and-half instead of milk."

4	cups water	2½	cups milk
4	cups broccoli florets	¼	teaspoon ground nutmeg
2	tablespoons butter or margarine	¼	teaspoon ground black pepper
1	onion, chopped	½	cup shredded sharp Cheddar cheese
1	large stalk celery, chopped		
⅓	cup all-purpose flour		
2	tablespoons chicken bouillon granules		

1. In a medium pot, combine water and broccoli florets and bring to a boil; reduce heat and cook for about 3 minutes. Drain, reserving all of the water.
2. In a food processor or blender, process half the cooked broccoli until fairly smooth. Set aside with remaining broccoli.
3. In a heavy saucepan, melt butter; add onion and celery and cook for 3 to 4 minutes or until soft. Stir in flour; cook, stirring constantly, for 1 to 2 minutes. Add reserved water and chicken bouillon granules and bring to a boil, stirring constantly. Reduce heat to medium; simmer, stirring constantly, until thickened.
4. Stir in milk, nutmeg, pepper, and broccoli and heat through. Sprinkle with Cheddar cheese and serve. **Yield:** 6 servings.

Per serving: 202 calories, 10g protein, 16g carbohydrate, 12g fat, 3g fiber, 28mg cholesterol, 912mg sodium

◄ FAMILY FAVORITE

Prep Time: 20 minutes

Cook Time: 25 minutes

Average Rating: ★★★★★

What other cooks have done:

"Not only was it easy to make, it was delicious to eat. I cut down on the onion, used half-and-half, and increased the butter to ⅓ cup. The nutmeg added a nice flavor and aroma."

Curried Carrot Soup

Submitted by: **Doug Mathews**

"Quick, easy, and light, this soup is the only way to get my niece to eat carrots. You can garnish with golden raisins or a dollop of sour cream."

2	tablespoons vegetable oil	2	pounds carrots, chopped
1	onion, chopped	4	cups vegetable broth
1	tablespoon curry powder	2	cups water (or as needed)

1. Heat oil in a large pot over medium heat. Sauté onion in oil until tender and translucent. Stir in curry powder. Add chopped carrots and stir until carrots are coated. Add the vegetable broth and simmer until carrots are soft, about 20 minutes.
2. Transfer carrots and broth to a blender and puree until smooth. Pour back into pot and thin with water to your preferred consistency. **Yield:** 6 servings.

Per serving: 129 calories, 3g protein, 20g carbohydrate, 6g fat, 5g fiber, 0mg cholesterol, 723mg sodium

◄ KID-FRIENDLY

Prep Time: 15 minutes

Cook Time: 30 minutes

Average Rating: ★★★★☆

What other cooks have done:

"We love this recipe. It's even better the next day. I add more onion and more curry than is suggested to make it spicier. It's nice served with caramelized onions, sour cream, and croutons."

Creamy Potato and Leek Soup

Submitted by: **Michele Hodge**

"I like to take a potato masher and roughly mash some of the potatoes, which helps to thicken the soup. I also like to use seasoned chicken broth. You can use heavy cream or half-and-half, depending on how rich you want the soup to be."

RESTAURANT FARE ▶

Prep Time: 15 minutes

Cook Time: 20 minutes

Average Rating: ★★★★★

What other cooks have done:

"Instead of leeks, try this with kale. I added a few links of Italian sausage and about ¾ teaspoon ground black pepper to the simmering potatoes."

6	potatoes, peeled and cubed	2	leeks, chopped
1	(14 ounce) can chicken broth	2	teaspoons butter
		1½	cups heavy whipping cream

1. In a medium pot over medium heat, combine the potatoes and broth and simmer for 20 minutes or until potatoes are tender.

2. Meanwhile, in a skillet over medium heat, sauté the leeks in butter for 5 to 10 minutes or until tender. Add the leeks and cream to the potatoes and stir well. Mash potatoes with a potato masher to slightly thicken the soup, if desired. Ladle into bowls to serve. **Yield:** 4 servings.

Per serving: 513 calories, 8g protein, 42g carbohydrate, 36g fat, 5g fiber, 122mg cholesterol, 400mg sodium

30 minutes or less

Creamy Mushroom Soup

Submitted by: **Lori**

"This fresh and creamy soup is easy to make and filled with hearty chopped mushrooms."

HOLIDAY FARE ▶

Prep Time: 10 minutes

Cook Time: 15 minutes

Average Rating: ★★★★★

What other cooks have done:

"I tried a wide selection of mushrooms and saved some of the mushrooms for a garnish. Great presentation!"

¼	cup butter	1	(14 ounce) can chicken broth
1	cup chopped shiitake mushrooms	1	cup half-and-half
1	cup chopped portobello mushrooms		Salt and ground black pepper to taste
2	shallots, chopped		Pinch ground cinnamon (optional)
2	tablespoons all-purpose flour		

1. Melt the butter in a large saucepan over medium-high heat. Sauté the shiitake mushrooms, portobello mushrooms, and shallots for about 5 minutes or until soft. Mix in the flour until smooth. Gradually stir in the chicken broth. Cook, stirring constantly, 5 minutes or until thick and bubbly.

2. Stir in the half-and-half and season with salt and pepper to taste; sprinkle with cinnamon, if desired. Heat through but do not boil. **Yield:** 4 servings.

Per serving: 247 calories, 5g protein, 14g carbohydrate, 20g fat, 1g fiber, 53mg cholesterol, 593mg sodium

Curry-Pumpkin Soup

Submitted by: **Mary Ingram**

"This is a wonderfully soothing soup—a perfect choice for a holiday party or dinner. Adjust the amount of curry and soy sauce for spiciness. You can add sautéed chopped sweet onions and substitute heavy cream for the half-and-half for a flavor twist."

2	tablespoons pumpkin seeds (optional)	1	(29 ounce) can unsweetened pumpkin
2	tablespoons butter	1½	cups half-and-half
3	tablespoons all-purpose flour	2	tablespoons soy sauce
2	tablespoons curry powder	1	tablespoon white sugar
4	cups vegetable broth		Salt and ground black pepper to taste

1. Preheat oven to 375°F (190°C).

2. Arrange pumpkin seeds, if desired, in a single layer on a baking sheet. Toast in the preheated oven for about 10 minutes or until seeds begin to brown.

3. Melt butter in a large pot over medium heat. Stir in flour and curry powder until smooth. Cook, stirring constantly, until mixture begins to bubble. Gradually whisk in broth and cook until thickened. Stir in pumpkin and half-and-half. Add soy sauce, sugar, and salt and pepper to taste. Bring just to a boil; remove from heat. Sprinkle with toasted pumpkin seeds, if desired. **Yield:** 8 servings.

Per serving: 157 calories, 4g protein, 17g carbohydrate, 9g fat, 4g fiber, 25mg cholesterol, 1071mg sodium

◄ COMPANY IS COMING

Prep Time: 10 minutes

Cook Time: 20 minutes

Average Rating: ★★★★☆

What other cooks have done:

"I especially like adding an extra tablespoon of curry powder or using curry paste. Also, I add about 2 cups of cooked brown rice at the end."

Carrot Soup

Submitted by: **Tricia**

"Serve this creamy soup with a nice green salad and cornbread."

2½	cups sliced carrots	1	teaspoon cayenne pepper
1½	cups vegetable broth, divided	1	cup half-and-half
1	tablespoon butter		Salt and ground black pepper to taste
1	tablespoon all-purpose flour		Milk or water (as needed)
1	tablespoon chopped fresh parsley		
1	tablespoon chopped fresh basil		

1. Steam carrots until tender.
2. In a blender or food processor, combine cooked carrots and ¾ cup broth. Blend until smooth. Set aside.
3. In a medium saucepan, melt butter over medium heat. Stir in flour, parsley, basil, and cayenne pepper. Add half-and-half. Cook, stirring constantly, until slightly thickened and bubbly. Stir in carrot mixture and remaining broth. Season with salt and black pepper to taste. Thin with milk or water, if desired. **Yield:** 2 servings.

Per serving: 307 calories, 7g protein, 27g carbohydrate, 21g fat, 5g fiber, 60mg cholesterol, 913mg sodium

30 minutes or less

Creamy Corn Soup

Submitted by: **Abby**

"This soup is delicious—especially if you are fighting off a cold. Try adding a chopped green chile pepper or some small slices of chicken."

½	onion, chopped	2	(11 ounce) cans whole kernel corn
1	clove garlic, minced		
¼	cup chopped fresh parsley	2½	tablespoons cream cheese
1	tablespoon butter	1	teaspoon garlic salt
3	tablespoons all-purpose flour	1	teaspoon ground black pepper
2½	cups milk		Cayenne pepper to taste
1	cup chicken broth		

1. In a large pot over medium heat, combine the onion, garlic, parsley, and butter. Sauté for about 5 minutes or until onions are tender.
2. Add flour, stirring well to form a paste. Whisk in milk and broth. Add corn and cream cheese and heat through. Add garlic salt, black pepper, and cayenne pepper to taste; stir well. **Yield:** 6 servings.

Per serving: 158 calories, 5g protein, 16g carbohydrate, 8g fat, 2g fiber, 22mg cholesterol, 538mg sodium

Spinach-Tortellini Soup

Submitted by: **Nicole**

"This is a recipe I got from a friend who's in culinary school. It's really simple and tastes even better the next day."

1	(10 ounce) package frozen chopped spinach	¼	tablespoon dried basil
2	(14 ounce) cans chicken broth	¼	tablespoon garlic powder Salt and ground black pepper to taste
1	(9 ounce) package fresh cheese tortellini		

1. In a large pot over high heat, combine the spinach and chicken broth. Bring to a boil and reduce heat to low. Stir in tortellini and simmer for 10 minutes or until the tortellini is cooked to desired tenderness. Season with basil, garlic powder, and salt and pepper to taste. Ladle into bowls to serve. **Yield:** 4 servings.

Per serving: 246 calories, 13g protein, 34g carbohydrate, 8g fat, 4g fiber, 28mg cholesterol, 1170mg sodium

◄ **FROM THE PANTRY**

Prep Time: 10 minutes

Cook Time: 15 minutes

Average Rating: ★★★★☆

What other cooks have done:

"I used vegetable broth because I'm a vegetarian. I made sure to drain the spinach before adding it to the pot, and I also threw in chopped carrots and fresh tomatoes for more flavor and color. Don't forget to take the pot off the heat as soon as the pasta is al dente; otherwise, the pasta will fall apart."

Cabbage Patch Soup

Submitted by: **Anne**

"This is primarily a vegetable soup with cabbage as the main ingredient. You could substitute vegetable broth for the chicken broth, if desired. Also, try adding a dash of hot pepper sauce for a little kick."

1	tablespoon olive oil	1	cup sliced carrots
3	tablespoons bacon bits	1	teaspoon salt
1	onion, chopped	¼	teaspoon ground black pepper
1	tablespoon all-purpose flour		
3	(14 ounce) cans chicken broth	1	bay leaf
2	cups shredded cabbage	1	cup frozen green peas
		¾	cup sour cream

1. Heat the oil in a large saucepan over medium heat. Sauté the bacon bits and onion in the oil for about 5 minutes or until onion is tender. Stir in the flour to coat well and quickly pour in the chicken broth. Stir constantly for 3 minutes or until somewhat thickened.
2. Add the cabbage, carrots, salt, pepper, and bay leaf. Reduce heat to low and simmer for 20 minutes. Stir in the peas and sour cream just before serving. Allow to heat through and remove bay leaf. **Yield:** 6 servings.

Per serving: 172 calories, 9g protein, 12g carbohydrate, 10g fat, 3g fiber, 15mg cholesterol, 1201mg sodium

◄ **FAMILY FAVORITE**

Prep Time: 15 minutes

Cook Time: 30 minutes

Average Rating: ★★★★☆

What other cooks have done:

"The house smelled so good while this was cooking that we could hardly wait the 20 minutes it took to simmer. We added a cup of chopped cooked chicken. Along with garlic bread, this soup made a quick, hearty, and delicious meal."

Delicious Ham and Potato Soup

Submitted by: **ELLIE11**

"The great thing about this recipe for ham and potato soup is that you can add additional ingredients, and it still turns out great."

CLASSIC COMFORT FOOD ▶

Prep Time: 20 minutes

Cook Time: 25 minutes

Average Rating: ★★★★★

What other cooks have done:

"Comfort food at its best! A wonderful recipe to use up leftover ham. I added some frozen peas and diced carrots to get some veggies into my family."

3½	cups peeled and diced potatoes	½	teaspoon salt (or to taste)
⅓	cup diced celery	1	teaspoon ground white or black pepper (or to taste)
⅓	cup finely chopped onion	5	tablespoons butter
¾	cup diced cooked ham	5	tablespoons all-purpose flour
3¼	cups water	2	cups milk
2	tablespoons chicken bouillon granules		

1. In a large pot, combine the potatoes, celery, onion, ham, and water. Bring to a boil and cook over medium heat until potatoes are tender, about 10 to 15 minutes. Stir in the bouillon granules, salt, and pepper.
2. In a medium saucepan, melt butter over medium-low heat. Whisk in flour and cook, stirring constantly, until thick, about 1 minute. Slowly stir in milk, being careful to prevent lumps from forming. Continue stirring over medium-low heat for 4 to 5 minutes or until thick.
3. Stir the milk mixture into the soup and cook until heated through. Serve immediately. **Yield:** 8 servings.

Per serving: 199 calories, 7g protein, 20g carbohydrate, 10g fat, 2g fiber, 34mg cholesterol, 292mg sodium

Tuscan Soup

Submitted by: **Dianne Brown**

"Tuscan soup with spicy sausage, potatoes, and spinach."

AROUND-THE-WORLD CUISINE ▶

Prep Time: 15 minutes

Cook Time: 25 minutes

Average Rating: ★★★★★

What other cooks have done:

"I substituted heavy whipping cream for the evaporated milk and added a couple cloves of garlic and a can of cannellini beans for an even heartier soup. Topped with grated Romano cheese, it's a new family favorite."

3	(3.5 ounce) links spicy Italian sausage	1	bunch fresh spinach, washed and chopped
1	onion, chopped	¼	cup evaporated milk
6	cups chicken broth		Salt and ground black pepper to taste
3	large potatoes, cubed		

1. Remove casings from sausage and crumble sausage into a skillet. Add onion and cook over medium heat until meat is no longer pink. Drain.
2. Place meat in a large pot; add broth and potatoes. Boil until potatoes are cooked.
3. Add spinach. Continue boiling until spinach is lightly cooked.
4. Remove soup from heat; stir in evaporated milk and salt and pepper to taste. **Yield:** 4 servings.

Per serving: 454 calories, 24g protein, 34g carbohydrate, 25g fat, 6g fiber, 57mg cholesterol, 1739mg sodium

Quick and Easy 20-Minute Chicken Posole

Submitted by: **Veronica Oyama**

"Prepare this recipe for unexpected guests or take it to a potluck party."

1	tablespoon olive oil	1	(7 ounce) can chopped green chile peppers, drained
1	large onion, thinly sliced		
2	cloves garlic, minced		
2	teaspoons dried oregano	1	(2.25 ounce) can sliced black olives, drained
½	teaspoon ground cumin		
2	(14 ounce) cans chicken broth	¾	pound skinless, boneless chicken breast, cubed
1	(15 ounce) can white hominy		

1. In a large pot over medium heat, combine oil, onion, garlic, oregano, and cumin. Cook, covered, 5 minutes or until onions are tender.
2. Stir in broth, hominy, chile peppers, and olives. Bring to a boil and reduce heat to medium. Stir in chicken. Cover and cook until chicken is no longer pink, about 5 to 10 minutes. **Yield:** 6 servings.

Per serving: 183 calories, 16g protein, 16g carbohydrate, 6g fat, 3g fiber, 33mg cholesterol, 1234mg sodium

◄ COVERED-DISH FAVORITE

Prep Time: 10 minutes

Cook Time: 20 minutes

Average Rating: ★★★★★

What other cooks have done:

"I was looking for a more traditional posole, so I made a few changes—I omitted the green chiles and olives, added about one-third of a can of red enchilada sauce, and topped it with chopped cabbage and radishes. This is most definitely a make-again recipe."

Quick and Easy Chicken Noodle Soup *(pictured on page 261)*

Submitted by: **Vincenza**

"When you don't have time to make your soup totally from scratch, this is a very easy, very good substitute."

1	tablespoon butter	1	cup sliced carrots
½	cup chopped onion	1½	teaspoons chopped fresh basil
½	cup chopped celery		
4	(14 ounce) cans chicken broth	1½	teaspoons chopped fresh oregano
1	(14 ounce) can vegetable broth	¼	teaspoon salt
1	cup diced, cooked chicken	¼	teaspoon ground black pepper
1½	cups egg noodles		

1. Melt butter in a large pot over medium heat. Cook onion and celery in butter until just tender, about 5 minutes. Add chicken broth, vegetable broth, chicken, noodles, carrots, basil, oregano, salt, and pepper. Bring to a boil; reduce heat and simmer 20 minutes or until soup is hot. **Yield:** 6 servings.

Per serving: 164 calories, 11g protein, 12g carbohydrate, 8g fat, 1g fiber, 35mg cholesterol, 1563mg sodium

◄ CLASSIC COMFORT FOOD

Prep Time: 10 minutes

Cook Time: 27 minutes

Average Rating: ★★★★★

What other cooks have done:

"I really like the flavor of this soup. Instead of using egg noodles, I used spaghetti noodles broken into pieces."

Chicken and Rice Soup I

Submitted by: **Nell Marsh**
"Creamy chicken soup with rice."

FAMILY FAVORITE ▶

Prep Time: 15 minutes

Cook Time: 30 minutes

Average Rating: ★★★★★

What other cooks have done:

"Instead of boiling the chicken, I cubed it and browned it in olive oil. I then made the roux in the same pan. I also added ½ teaspoon each of crushed rosemary, thyme, and marjoram."

¾	cup chopped celery	3	cups milk, divided
¾	cup finely diced onion	1½	cups chopped, cooked
1	cup uncooked white rice		chicken
2	chicken bouillon cubes		Additional milk (if needed)
2½	cups water		Ground black pepper to
½	cup butter, melted		taste
¼	cup all-purpose flour		

1. In a large pot, combine celery, onion, rice, bouillon cubes, and water. Cook about 20 minutes or until most of the water is absorbed by the rice. Remove from heat.
2. Meanwhile, combine butter and flour in a medium skillet over medium heat. Add 2 cups milk, stirring to make a smooth sauce.
3. Add milk mixture to rice mixture. Add chicken and remaining 1 cup milk and heat through. Add more milk to thin soup, if needed. Add pepper to taste and serve hot. **Yield:** 8 servings.

Per serving: 317 calories, 12g protein, 29g carbohydrate, 17g fat, 1g fiber, 59mg cholesterol, 481mg sodium

Crabmeat and Corn Soup

Submitted by: **William Anatooskin**
"A very tasty chowder-type recipe. Delicious anytime."

FREEZER FRESH ▶

Prep Time: 15 minutes

Cook Time: 30 minutes

Average Rating: ★★★★★

What other cooks have done:

"This was so easy to make and perfect for the extra imitation crab we had (that I never know what to do with). It turned out thick and hearty and would be the perfect base for any other seafood. Thanks for the great recipe."

¼	cup butter, melted	1	pound fresh crabmeat
¼	cup all-purpose flour	½	teaspoon ground white
2	cups whole milk		pepper
2	cups half-and-half	½	teaspoon seasoning salt
1¾	cups whole kernel corn	1	tablespoon soy sauce
1	cup chopped green onions	¼	cup chopped parsley

1. In a large, heavy pot, combine butter and flour and stir gently until blended. (Do not burn or let darken.) Gradually add milk, stirring constantly; add half-and-half, stirring gently. Add corn and green onions and cook for a few minutes until tender.
2. Add crabmeat, pepper, seasoning salt, and soy sauce and simmer until very hot and small bubbles form around the edge. (Do not let boil.) Top with parsley and serve hot. **Yield:** 8 servings.

Note: To use fresh corn, cut the kernels off 4 cobs. Scrape cobs for juices, and add kernels and juices to soup. Cook until corn is tender.

Per serving: 265 calories, 16g protein, 17g carbohydrate, 16g fat, 1g fiber, 80mg cholesterol, 532mg sodium

Cajun Crab Soup

Submitted by: **Doreen**
"This rich, delicious soup is modeled after a great soup that I had in a restaurant in Bethany Beach, Delaware."

½   cup unsalted butter
1   onion, chopped
2   cloves garlic, minced
¼   cup all-purpose flour
2   cups clam juice
2   cups chicken broth
1   (10 ounce) package frozen white corn
1   teaspoon salt
½   teaspoon ground white pepper
¼   teaspoon dried thyme
¼   teaspoon cayenne pepper
2   cups heavy whipping cream
1   pound lump crabmeat, drained
4   green onions, chopped

1. Melt butter in a large saucepan over medium heat. Sauté onion and garlic in butter until onion is tender. Whisk in flour and cook for 2 minutes. Stir in clam juice and chicken broth; bring to a boil. Mix in corn and season with salt, white pepper, thyme, and cayenne pepper. Reduce heat and simmer 15 minutes.

2. Stir in cream, crabmeat, and green onions. Heat through but do not boil. **Yield:** 8 servings.

Per serving: 428 calories, 16g protein, 15g carbohydrate, 35g fat, 1g fiber, 165mg cholesterol, 886mg sodium

◀ RESTAURANT FARE

Prep Time: 15 minutes

Cook Time: 30 minutes

Average Rating: ★★★★★

What other cooks have done:

"I was making this for a party and had lots of other food prep work to do, so I took this recipe through the first step several hours ahead of time, transferring the simmered mixture to a slow cooker set on low to keep it hot. Just before the guests arrived, I added the cream, crabmeat, and onions. Couldn't have been happier with the results."

Neptune's Favorite Crab Bisque

Submitted by: **Elizabeth**

"This lovely crab bisque is simple, quick, and absolutely delectable! Garnish with chervil or parsley."

1	(10.75 ounce) can condensed cream of mushroom soup	2	cups milk
		1	cup whipping cream
1	(10.75 ounce) can cream of asparagus soup	1	(6 ounce) can lump crabmeat
		1¼	cups white wine

1. In a large pot, combine mushroom soup, asparagus soup, milk, and cream. Simmer over medium heat, stirring frequently, until almost boiling; reduce heat.
2. Flake crabmeat and add to soup. Simmer 5 more minutes; add white wine. **Yield:** 5 servings.

Note: For a "seafood bisque," add lobster, clams, mussels, or any seafood combination.

Per serving: 314 calories, 13g protein, 16g carbohydrate, 18g fat, 1g fiber, 72mg cholesterol, 961mg sodium

Creamy Scallop Chowder

Submitted by: **Shirley**

"For this wonderful soup featuring white wine, onions, and tender scallops, you may use either ocean or bay scallops."

1	pound scallops, rinsed and drained	1	cup milk
2	tablespoons butter	½	cup dry white wine
1	bunch green onions, minced	1	teaspoon salt
			Pinch ground white pepper
4	ounces fresh mushrooms, sliced	½	cup shredded Swiss cheese
2	tablespoons all-purpose flour	2	tablespoons chopped fresh parsley

1. Cut any large scallops in half. In a small pot, melt butter over medium-low heat. Sauté onions and mushrooms in butter until tender.
2. Stir in flour. Pour in milk and stir over medium heat until thickened and bubbly. Add scallops, wine, salt, and white pepper. Heat until thickened. Top with Swiss cheese and parsley and serve. **Yield:** 4 servings.

Per serving: 290 calories, 23g protein, 14g carbohydrate, 14g fat, 2g fiber, 61mg cholesterol, 884mg sodium

Cheesy Vegetable Chowder

Submitted by: **Candice**

"If you love cheese and vegetables, you'll love this soup!"

7	cups water	2	(15 ounce) cans sweet peas
9	chicken bouillon cubes, crumbled	2	cups chopped fresh green beans
6	potatoes, cubed	½	cup butter
2	cloves garlic, minced	½	cup all-purpose flour
1	large white onion, chopped	3	cups milk
1	bunch celery, chopped	1	pound processed cheese, cubed
3	cups chopped carrots		
2	(15.25 ounce) cans whole kernel corn		

1. In a large pot over medium heat, combine water, bouillon, potatoes, and garlic. Bring to a boil; stir in onion, celery, and carrots. Reduce heat to low and simmer 15 minutes.
2. Stir in corn, peas, and green beans and continue to cook.
3. Meanwhile, in a medium saucepan over medium heat, melt butter. Whisk in flour and let cook for 10 seconds to form a roux. Whisk in milk, a little at a time, and cook, stirring constantly, until mixture is thick and bubbly. Stir in cheese until melted. Pour this mixture into the large pot and stir well. Heat through and serve. **Yield:** 32 servings.

Per serving: 158 calories, 6g protein, 18g carbohydrate, 7g fat, 3g fiber, 19mg cholesterol, 754mg sodium

◄ CROWD-PLEASER

Prep Time: 15 minutes

Cook Time: 30 minutes

Average Rating: ★★★★★

What other cooks have done:

"My husband and I loved this soup. I added a few tasty vegetables, including chunks of zucchini, green onions, and lima beans. I also added tomato sauce and some basil, oregano, and parsley."

Cowboy Stew I *(pictured on page 262)*

Submitted by: **LaDonna**

"This is nice and thick and yummy. Sour cream is also good on this. Garnish with shredded Cheddar cheese."

1½	pounds ground beef	1	(15 ounce) can tomato sauce
1	onion, chopped	1	(4 ounce) can diced green chiles
1	(14.75 ounce) can cream-style corn		Sour cream (optional)
1	(15 ounce) can chili		Shredded Cheddar cheese (optional)
1	(15 ounce) can pork and beans		

1. Brown ground beef and onion until done. Drain.
2. Meanwhile, combine corn, chili, pork and beans, tomato sauce, and green chiles in a large pot; simmer 10 minutes. Add beef and onion and simmer 20 minutes or until hot. Top with sour cream, if desired, and sprinkle with cheese, if desired, and serve. **Yield:** 6 to 8 servings.

Per serving: 307 calories, 25g protein, 30g carbohydrate, 10g fat, 5g fiber, 40mg cholesterol, 694mg sodium

◄ CLASSIC COMFORT FOOD

Prep Time: 5 minutes

Cook Time: 30 minutes

Average Rating: ★★★★☆

What other cooks have done:

"This is one of the first recipes I made after discovering this site, and I still find it delicious and easy to make. It's a hearty chili that can be assembled in a hurry from mostly canned ingredients."

Rae's Vegetarian Chili

Submitted by: **Rae Arsenault**

"This is a low-fat, high-protein recipe. For vegans, simply leave out the cheese. The variety of beans adds a nice touch of color, and it can be made as mild or spicy as you like."

MEATLESS MAIN DISH ▶

Prep Time: 10 minutes

Cook Time: 25 minutes

Average Rating: ★★★★☆

What other cooks have done:

"I sautéed half a medium onion with the garlic and omitted the cheese. I also used spicy pinto beans, extra hot sauce, and crushed red pepper flakes. (Some like it hot!)"

2	tablespoons olive oil
4	cloves garlic, minced
1	(28 ounce) can diced tomatoes, undrained
1	(8 ounce) can tomato sauce
1	(6 ounce) can tomato paste
1	(12 ounce) can or bottle beer
¼	cup chili powder (or to taste)
1	tablespoon powdered mustard
1	teaspoon dried oregano
	Freshly ground black pepper to taste
1	teaspoon ground cumin
⅛	teaspoon hot pepper sauce
1	(15 ounce) can pinto beans, rinsed and drained
1	(15 ounce) can garbanzo beans, drained
1	(15 ounce) can black beans, rinsed and drained
1	(15 ounce) can kidney beans, rinsed and drained
1	(16 ounce) can cannellini beans, rinsed and drained
1	(15.25 ounce) can whole kernel corn, rinsed and drained
2	cups shredded Cheddar cheese (optional)

1. Heat oil in a large pot over medium heat; add garlic and sauté 1 to 2 minutes.

2. Add diced tomatoes, tomato sauce, tomato paste, beer, chili powder, powdered mustard, oregano, black pepper to taste, cumin, and hot pepper sauce. Stir in the pinto beans, garbanzo beans, black beans, kidney beans, cannellini beans, and corn. Bring the mixture to a boil; reduce heat and let simmer for 20 minutes. Top each serving with cheese, if desired. **Yield:** 8 servings.

Per serving: 535 calories, 26g protein, 73g carbohydrate, 16g fat, 19g fiber, 30mg cholesterol, 1370mg sodium

Quick and Easy Chicken Noodle Soup,
page 255

Gourmet Chicken Sandwich, page 243

Cowboy Stew I, page 259

Fresh Tomato Salad, page 285

Yum-Yum Corn, page 270

Whipped Sweet Potato
Casserole, page 274

Simple Sides & Salads

Asparagus Parmesan

Submitted by: **jen947**

"In this quick and easy side, asparagus is sautéed and topped off with Parmesan cheese."

5 INGREDIENTS OR LESS ▶

Prep Time: 5 minutes

Cook Time: 12 minutes

Average Rating: ★★★★☆

What other cooks have done:

"This recipe is awesome. I alter it slightly to decrease fat. I steam the asparagus for three minutes, drain, and sauté it in 1 tablespoon oil and 1 tablespoon butter for five minutes. Then I sprinkle it with fresh Parmesan cheese. Wonderful!"

1	tablespoon butter	¾	teaspoon grated Parmesan cheese
¼	cup olive oil		Salt and ground black pepper to taste
1	pound fresh asparagus spears, trimmed		

1. Melt butter with olive oil in a large skillet over medium heat. Add asparagus spears and cook, stirring occasionally, for 10 minutes or to desired firmness. Drain off excess oil. Sprinkle asparagus with Parmesan cheese and salt and pepper to taste. Serve. **Yield:** 5 servings.

Per serving: 138 calories, 2g protein, 4g carbohydrate, 13g fat, 2g fiber, 6mg cholesterol, 31mg sodium

Georgian Green Beans

Submitted by: **Sara K**

"Scrumptious and tangy green beans from Georgia are a great side dish with any meat."

CROWD-PLEASER ▶

Prep Time: 15 minutes

Cook Time: 25 minutes

Average Rating: ★★★★☆

What other cooks have done:

"I substituted veggie broth for the chicken broth so that my vegetarian friends could enjoy it as well. Even those that are not green bean eaters enjoyed it."

2	pounds fresh green beans, trimmed	1½	teaspoons red wine vinegar
3	tablespoons unsalted butter, divided	3	tablespoons chicken broth
1	large red onion, quartered and thinly sliced		Salt and ground black pepper to taste
2	cloves garlic, peeled and minced	3	tablespoons finely chopped cilantro

1. Bring a large pot of lightly salted water to a boil. Add green beans and cook for 3 minutes. Remove from heat and rinse with cold water until no longer hot. Drain and pat dry.

2. Melt 1 tablespoon butter in a medium skillet over medium heat. Stir in the onion and garlic and sauté until onion is tender. Melt remaining butter in the skillet and add green beans. Stir in the vinegar and broth. Season with salt and pepper to taste. Mix in cilantro. Cover, reduce heat, and simmer for 15 minutes or until green beans are tender. **Yield:** 10 servings.

Per serving: 66 calories, 2g protein, 8g carbohydrate, 4g fat, 3g fiber, 9mg cholesterol, 65mg sodium

Snappy Green Beans

Submitted by: **Casey**

"This is a nice little alternative to plain green beans. If you want it extra 'snappy,' add more vinegar!"

6   slices bacon
1   cup chopped onion
3   tablespoons distilled white
      vinegar

1   (14.5 ounce) can cut green
      beans, drained

1. Place bacon in a large, deep skillet. Cook over medium-high heat until evenly brown. Drain, crumble, and set aside, reserving drippings.
2. Sauté onion in drippings; add vinegar and sauté until onions are tender. Add green beans and cook until heated through. Crumble bacon over green beans and serve. **Yield:** 4 servings.

Per serving: 266 calories, 5g protein, 7g carbohydrate, 24g fat, 3g fiber, 28mg cholesterol, 605mg sodium

◄ **5 INGREDIENTS OR LESS**

Prep Time: 5 minutes

Cook Time: 20 minutes

Average Rating: ★★★★★

What other cooks have done:

"I used fresh green beans, garlic-flavored red wine vinegar, and precooked bacon. I also added some minced garlic. I steamed everything together in the microwave and served it after it had cooled."

Lemon Green Beans with Walnuts

Submitted by: **Karen David**

"Steamed green beans tossed with butter, lemon zest, lemon juice, and toasted walnuts. This is also excellent with asparagus. Pecans can be substituted for walnuts."

½   cup chopped walnuts
1   pound fresh green beans,
      trimmed and cut into
      2 inch pieces
2½ tablespoons unsalted butter,
      melted

1   lemon, juiced and zested
      Salt and ground black
      pepper to taste

1. Preheat oven to 375°F (190°C).
2. Arrange nuts in a single layer on a baking sheet. Toast in the preheated oven until lightly browned, about 5 to 10 minutes. Set aside.
3. Place green beans in a steamer over 1 inch of boiling water and cover. Steam for 8 to 10 minutes or until tender but still bright green.
4. Place cooked beans in a large bowl and toss with butter, lemon juice, and lemon zest. Season with salt and pepper to taste. Transfer beans to a serving dish and sprinkle with toasted walnuts. Serve immediately. **Yield:** 4 servings.

Per serving: 202 calories, 5g protein, 13g carbohydrate, 17g fat, 6g fiber, 19mg cholesterol, 9mg sodium

◄ **HOLIDAY FARE**

Prep Time: 15 minutes

Cook Time: 20 minutes

Average Rating: ★★★★☆

What other cooks have done:

"I loved the lemon flavor with green beans. Before roasting the walnuts, I quickly dipped the walnuts in some melted honey. It really added more flavor to them."

Green Beans with Cherry Tomatoes

Submitted by: **STARNETSA**

"These beans are briefly boiled and tossed with cherry tomatoes in a buttery basil sauce to make the most yummy green beans ever! We serve this dish at Easter dinner every year, but it's a delicious accent to any meal."

HOLIDAY FARE ▶

Prep Time: 10 minutes

Cook Time: 18 minutes

Average Rating: ★★★★☆

What other cooks have done:

"I served this at Thanksgiving dinner, and everyone loved it! I've also added sprinkled Parmesan cheese on top, and it brings out a lot of flavor."

1½ pounds fresh green beans, trimmed and cut into 2 inch pieces	¾ teaspoon garlic salt
	¼ teaspoon ground black pepper
1½ cups water	1½ teaspoons chopped fresh basil
¼ cup butter	
1 tablespoon white sugar	2 cups cherry tomato halves

1. Place beans and water in a large saucepan. Cover and bring to a boil. Reduce heat to low and simmer until tender, about 10 minutes. Drain and set aside.
2. Melt butter in a skillet over medium heat. Stir in sugar, garlic salt, pepper, and basil. Add tomatoes and cook, stirring gently, just until soft. Pour the tomato mixture over the green beans and toss gently to blend. **Yield:** 6 servings.

Per serving: 122 calories, 3g protein, 13g carbohydrate, 8g fat, 4g fiber, 21mg cholesterol, 318mg sodium

Caramelized Red Bell Peppers and Onions

Submitted by: **Crow**

"This divine combination of sweet red peppers and sweet red onions goes very well with lamb. For a little variety, add ¼ cup raisins before serving."

COMPANY IS COMING ▶

Prep Time: 15 minutes

Cook Time: 30 minutes

Average Rating: ★★★★☆

What other cooks have done:

"Absolutely yummy! I didn't have red wine, so I used white and added a cup of halved mushrooms and a pinch of garlic powder. I spooned the whole thing over some baked chicken breasts."

2 red bell peppers, cut into strips	¼ cup red wine (optional)
	Pinch salt
2 red onions, cut into strips	Pinch ground black pepper
1 tablespoon olive oil	Pinch dried basil
1 teaspoon butter	

1. In a hot saucepan over medium heat, combine red bell pepper, onion, oil, and butter; sauté for 2 minutes. Reduce heat to medium-low and continue cooking, stirring occasionally, until the onion and bell pepper soften.
2. Stir red wine into the vegetables, if desired, and cook for 20 minutes or until wine evaporates. Season with salt, black pepper, and basil. **Yield:** 4 servings.

Per serving: 88 calories, 1g protein, 9g carbohydrate, 5g fat, 2g fiber, 3mg cholesterol, 111mg sodium

Roasted Garlic Cauliflower

Submitted by: **SHELLERY**

"My 11-year-old son loves this wonderful roasted cauliflower. Add more spices and herbs to suit your taste."

3 tablespoons olive oil	Salt and ground black
2 tablespoons minced garlic	pepper to taste
1 large head cauliflower, chopped	1 bunch fresh parsley, chopped
⅓ cup grated Parmesan cheese	

1. Preheat the oven to 450°F (230°C). Grease a large casserole dish.
2. Place the olive oil and garlic in a large zip-top plastic bag. Add cauliflower and shake to coat. Pour into the prepared casserole dish.
3. Bake in the preheated oven for 25 minutes, stirring after 10 minutes. Increase oven temperature to broil. Top cauliflower with Parmesan cheese, salt and pepper to taste, and parsley; broil for 3 to 5 minutes or until golden brown. **Yield:** 6 servings.

Per serving: 128 calories, 6g protein, 9g carbohydrate, 9g fat, 4g fiber, 4mg cholesterol, 152mg sodium

◄ FAMILY FAVORITE

Prep Time: 15 minutes

Cook Time: 30 minutes

Average Rating: ★★★★★

What other cooks have done:

"I added some grated carrot, sliced mushrooms, and chopped leeks. I also stirred in the Parmesan cheese and parsley before baking and stirred every 10 minutes while it baked. When cooked, I sprinkled mozzarella cheese over the top before broiling. It was fabulous!"

Candied Carrots

Submitted by: **Denyse**

"My family's favorite vegetable. This is great for the holidays, too!"

1 pound carrots, cut into 2 inch pieces	¼ cup packed brown sugar
	Pinch salt
2 tablespoons butter, diced	Pinch ground black pepper

1. Bring a large pot of water to a boil. Add carrots and reduce heat to a high simmer. Cook about 20 minutes. Do not allow the carrots to become mushy. Drain.
2. Reduce heat to low and return the carrots to the pan. Stir in butter, brown sugar, salt, and pepper. Cook for 3 to 5 minutes or until sugar is bubbly. Serve hot. **Yield:** 4 servings.

Per serving: 152 calories, 1g protein, 25g carbohydrate, 6g fat, 4g fiber, 16mg cholesterol, 201mg sodium

◄ 5 INGREDIENTS OR LESS

Prep Time: 10 minutes

Cook Time: 30 minutes

Average Rating: ★★★★★

What other cooks have done:

"Outstanding. I used baby carrots because that is what I had on hand. I also added some ginger for an extra bite and decreased the sugar."

Yum-Yum Corn *(pictured on page 264)*

Submitted by: **Sharon Durham**

"Corn baked with an irresistible combination of butter, cream cheese, and garlic. Every time I make this for other people, they ask for the recipe. Just one taste and everyone says 'yum!' It's especially a favorite with my kids."

KID-FRIENDLY ▶

Prep Time: 10 minutes

Cook Time: 30 minutes

Average Rating: ★★★★☆

What other cooks have done:

"This recipe works with any vegetable. I made it using canned peas, and it was fabulous. A favorite in my house!"

2	(16 ounce) packages frozen whole kernel corn	1	clove garlic, pressed
½	cup butter, melted	1	teaspoon white sugar
1	(8 ounce) package cream cheese, softened		Salt to taste
		1½	teaspoons fresh parsley

1. Preheat oven to 350°F (175°C).
2. Cook corn according to package directions. Drain. Mix in butter, cream cheese, garlic, sugar, salt, and parsley.
3. Spoon into a 2 quart casserole dish and bake in the preheated oven for 25 minutes or until bubbly. **Yield:** 10 servings.

Per serving: 258 calories, 5g protein, 24g carbohydrate, 18g fat, 3g fiber, 49mg cholesterol, 175mg sodium

20 minutes or less

Cream Corn Like No Other

Submitted by: **Diana Yockey**

"This is nothing like canned creamed corn! My husband is not a fan of corn or creamed dishes, but he thinks this is great. This is easy and quick to prepare and is an especially delicious side dish for chicken or pork. Everyone always asks for the recipe."

CLASSIC COMFORT FOOD ▶

Prep Time: 7 minutes

Cook Time: 10 minutes

Average Rating: ★★★★★

What other cooks have done:

"I made this for Christmas dinner, and it was the biggest hit. My family keeps asking me to make it. I used a provolone, mozzarella, Asiago, and Parmesan cheese blend from the grocery store, which made it even creamier."

2	(10 ounce) packages frozen whole kernel corn, thawed	¼	teaspoon freshly ground black pepper
1	cup heavy cream	1	cup whole milk
2	tablespoons butter	2	tablespoons all-purpose flour
2	tablespoons white sugar	¼	cup freshly grated Parmesan cheese
1	teaspoon salt		

1. In a skillet over medium heat, combine the corn, cream, butter, sugar, salt, and pepper. In a small bowl, whisk together the milk and flour; stir into the corn mixture. Cook, stirring, over medium heat until the mixture is thickened and corn is cooked through. Remove from heat and stir in the Parmesan cheese until melted. Serve hot.
Yield: 8 servings.

Per serving: 257 calories, 6g protein, 25g carbohydrate, 17g fat, 2g fiber, 55mg cholesterol, 416mg sodium

Tater-Dipped Eggplant

Submitted by: **Sandra Rowe**

"Eggplant is battered and breaded with instant mashed potato flakes and browned in the oven until tender. Since I tried this method, we never serve eggplant any other way."

¼	cup butter, melted	1	medium eggplant, peeled and cut into ¾ inch slices
1	egg		
1	teaspoon salt		
⅛	teaspoon ground black pepper	1	cup instant mashed potato flakes

1. Preheat oven to 450°F (230°C). Pour melted butter into a shallow baking dish.

2. In a small bowl, mix together the egg, salt, and pepper. Dip eggplant slices into the egg mixture, and then dip into the potato flakes to coat. Place the coated slices of eggplant into the hot buttered dish.

3. Bake in the preheated oven for about 20 minutes or until tender, turning once after 10 minutes. **Yield:** 4 servings.

Note: This recipe can also be made in a large skillet over medium-high heat.

Per serving: 199 calories, 4g protein, 18g carbohydrate, 13g fat, 4g fiber, 84mg cholesterol, 731mg sodium

◄ MEATLESS MAIN DISH

Prep Time: 10 minutes

Cook Time: 20 minutes

Average Rating: ★★★★☆

What other cooks have done:

"I reduced the butter to 2 tablespoons and sprayed the entire baking dish with butter-flavored cooking spray. I added Italian-style breadcrumbs to the potato flakes, and sprayed the eggplant slices with butter-flavored cooking spray before baking. I cooked it for 15 minutes each side—it was so crispy!"

Mushroom Rice

Submitted by: **Jennifer Levin**

"Rice with mushrooms, garlic, and green onion—who could beat that? My family loves this recipe, which can also be served as a main meal if you add cooked chicken. This recipe works equally well with white or brown rice, instant or otherwise."

2	teaspoons butter	2	cups chicken broth
6	mushrooms, coarsely chopped	1	cup uncooked white rice
		½	teaspoon chopped fresh parsley
1	clove garlic, minced		
1	green onion, finely chopped		Salt and ground black pepper to taste

1. Melt butter in a saucepan over medium heat. Add mushrooms, garlic, and green onion and cook until mushrooms are cooked and liquid has evaporated. Stir in chicken broth and rice. Season with parsley and salt and pepper to taste. Reduce heat, cover, and simmer for 20 minutes. **Yield:** 4 servings.

Per serving: 222 calories, 6g protein, 41g carbohydrate, 4g fat, 1g fiber, 5mg cholesterol, 1105mg sodium

◄ HOLIDAY FARE

Prep Time: 10 minutes

Cook Time: 25 minutes

Average Rating: ★★★★☆

What other cooks have done:

"A great way to jazz up white rice. I added a little extra garlic and some red pepper flakes while sautéing the veggies. This is a keeper."

Cheesy Ranch New Red Potatoes

Submitted by: **F.R.**
"My family requests these potatoes all the time. They are awesome and so easy!"

KID-FRIENDLY ▶

Prep Time: 10 minutes

Cook Time: 20 minutes

Average Rating: ★★★★★

What other cooks have done:

"These potatoes were great. Instead of cutting them in half, I quartered the potatoes prior to boiling them. After they were cooked, I put them in a casserole dish and spread the dressing on them. Then I sprinkled the cheese over the top. I stirred it together and put it in the oven. I think this was a bit easier."

12 small new red potatoes, halved	1 teaspoon ground black pepper
1 cup Ranch-style salad dressing	
1 (8 ounce) package shredded colby–Monterey Jack cheese	

1. Preheat oven to 350°F (175°C).
2. Place potatoes in a large saucepan over medium heat with water to cover. Bring to a boil and cook 10 minutes or until tender; drain.
3. Place cooked potatoes, cut side up, on an ungreased cookie sheet. Spread a spoonful of dressing on the cut side of each potato half. Sprinkle evenly with cheese and pepper.
4. Bake in the preheated oven for 5 minutes or until cheese is melted. **Yield:** 4 servings.

Per serving: 735 calories, 21g protein, 55g carbohydrate, 49g fat, 5g fiber, 46mg cholesterol, 951mg sodium

Oven-Roasted Potatoes

Submitted by: **Janet**
"This great roasted potato side dish is made with olive oil and herbs."

FROM THE PANTRY ▶

Prep Time: 10 minutes

Cook Time: 30 minutes

Average Rating: ★★★★★

What other cooks have done:

"These are so tasty and easy to throw together. I always add ¼ cup grated Parmesan cheese. I have made them several times, and last time, I used red potatoes—they looked beautiful and tasted great!"

⅛ cup olive oil	½ teaspoon dried parsley
1 tablespoon minced garlic	½ teaspoon crushed red pepper flakes
½ teaspoon dried basil	½ teaspoon salt
½ teaspoon dried marjoram	4 large potatoes, peeled and cubed
½ teaspoon dried dill weed	
½ teaspoon dried thyme	
½ teaspoon dried oregano	

1. Preheat oven to 475°F (245°C).
2. In a large bowl, combine oil, garlic, basil, marjoram, dill weed, thyme, oregano, parsley, red pepper flakes, and salt. Stir in potatoes until evenly coated. Place potatoes in a single layer in a roasting pan or on a baking sheet.
3. Bake in the preheated oven for 20 to 30 minutes, turning occasionally to brown on all sides. **Yield:** 4 servings.

Per serving: 177 calories, 3g protein, 27g carbohydrate, 7g fat, 2g fiber, 0mg cholesterol, 298mg sodium

Honey-Glazed Pea Pods and Carrots

Submitted by: **Michele O'Sullivan**

"A touch of golden honey flavors these tender pea pods and sweet carrots."

2	cups sliced carrots	½	teaspoon cornstarch
½	pound snow peas, trimmed	2	tablespoons honey
3	tablespoons butter		

1. Bring a large pot of salted water to a boil. Add carrots and cook about 10 to 12 minutes or until tender-crisp. Add snow peas and cook until tender-crisp; drain and set aside.
2. Melt butter in the same pan and stir in cornstarch. Return carrots and peas to pan and stir in honey. Cook over medium heat, stirring occasionally, until heated through. **Yield:** 6 servings.

Per serving: 106 calories, 2g protein, 13g carbohydrate, 6g fat, 2g fiber, 16mg cholesterol, 87mg sodium

◄ FAMILY FAVORITE

Prep Time: 15 minutes

Cook Time: 20 minutes

Average Rating: ★★★★☆

What other cooks have done:

"I used sweet baby carrots, so there was no need to slice or chop. I tossed in a few sliced water chestnuts. Next time, I'll try a little horseradish with this recipe."

Spinach Marie

Submitted by: **sara**

"This is a decadent blend of spinach, Cheddar and Monterey Jack cheeses, milk, and spices."

2½	cups milk	¾	pound Cheddar cheese, cubed
½	teaspoon powdered mustard		
½	teaspoon garlic salt	3	(10 ounce) packages frozen chopped spinach, thawed and drained
1	tablespoon butter		
½	cup chopped onion		
3	tablespoons melted butter	1	cup shredded Monterey Jack cheese
3	tablespoons all-purpose flour		

1. Preheat oven to 350°F (175°C).
2. In a medium saucepan over low heat, combine milk, mustard, and garlic salt. Bring to a slow boil and simmer for 2 minutes.
3. In a small saucepan, heat 1 tablespoon butter over medium heat. Sauté onion in butter until browned; stir into milk mixture.
4. In a small saucepan, combine 3 tablespoons melted butter and flour. Cook over medium-low heat until thickened; stir into milk mixture.
5. Add Cheddar cheese to the milk mixture, mixing well to melt. Stir in spinach. Pour mixture into a 9x13 inch casserole dish and sprinkle with Monterey Jack cheese.
6. Bake in the preheated oven for 10 minutes or until heated through. **Yield:** 8 servings.

Per serving: 354 calories, 20g protein, 12g carbohydrate, 26g fat, 4g fiber, 79mg cholesterol, 629mg sodium

◄ COMPANY IS COMING

Prep Time: 10 minutes

Cook Time: 30 minutes

Average Rating: ★★★★☆

What other cooks have done:

"This was fun to make. I added ½ cup cracker crumbs with the Monterey Jack and let it sit for 10 minutes after I took it out of the oven so it could thicken. It was a big hit with my picky family."

Sautéed Portobellos and Spinach

Submitted by: **Leslie**

"Tender portobello mushrooms and spinach are simmered with Parmesan cheese, wine, and seasonings for a unique, easy, and extremely tasty side dish. Excellent with a steak and baked potato dinner."

CROWD-PLEASER ▶

Prep Time: 10 minutes

Cook Time: 10 minutes

Average Rating: ★★★★★

What other cooks have done:

"This was my first time working with portobello mushrooms. I cannot believe how easy and delicious this was. I thought the spinach pieces were too small for the size of the mushrooms, so I will buy the whole-leaf spinach next time. I doubled the recipe and added several more garlic cloves."

6	tablespoons butter	½	teaspoon salt
5	large portobello mushrooms, sliced	½	teaspoon ground black pepper
2	(10 ounce) packages frozen chopped spinach, thawed and drained	2	cloves garlic, chopped
		4	tablespoons dry red wine
1	tablespoon fresh chopped basil	½	cup freshly grated Parmesan cheese

1. Melt butter in a large skillet over medium heat. Sauté mushrooms, spinach, basil, salt, pepper, and garlic until mushrooms are tender and spinach is heated through.

2. Add wine and reduce heat to low; simmer 1 minute. Stir in Parmesan cheese and serve. **Yield:** 8 servings.

Per serving: 143 calories, 6g protein, 6g carbohydrate, 11g fat, 3g fiber, 28mg cholesterol, 406mg sodium

Whipped Sweet Potato Casserole *(pictured on page 264)*

Submitted by: **Bea**

"A good recipe to try on finicky kids."

HOLIDAY FARE ▶

Prep Time: 10 minutes

Cook Time: 30 minutes

Average Rating: ★★★★★

What other cooks have done:

"This was very good—even my kids liked it! I saved time by microwaving the sweet potatoes, and it still came out great."

2	medium-size sweet potatoes, peeled and cubed	¾	cup brown sugar
		⅛	teaspoon ground nutmeg
2	tablespoons orange juice	2	tablespoons butter, cubed
		1	cup miniature marshmallows

1. Preheat oven to 350°F (175°C).

2. In a large saucepan, cook sweet potatoes in salted water over medium-high heat for about 20 minutes or until done. Drain and add orange juice, brown sugar, nutmeg, and butter. Whip until smooth. Spread into a medium-size casserole dish or 6 (4 ounce) ramekins and top evenly with marshmallows.

3. Bake in the preheated oven for about 10 minutes or until marshmallows are golden brown. **Yield:** 6 servings.

Per serving: 348 calories, 3g protein, 74g carbohydrate, 5g fat, 3g fiber, 12mg cholesterol, 84mg sodium

Smushed Apples and Sweet Potatoes

Submitted by: **Elfindancer**

"This is a simple recipe that I make as a sweet, easy side dish. It tastes a lot like apple pie—but healthier!"

2 large sweet potatoes, peeled and diced	½ teaspoon ground allspice
2 tablespoons butter	1 Granny Smith apple, peeled, cored, and sliced
¼ cup white sugar	2 tablespoons milk
1 teaspoon ground cinnamon	

1. Place the sweet potatoes in a medium saucepan with water to cover; bring to a boil. Reduce heat to medium and simmer for about 20 minutes or until tender. Remove from heat. Drain and set aside.
2. Melt butter over low heat in a small saucepan. Mix in the sugar, cinnamon, and allspice. Add the apple slices and let simmer, covered, for 5 minutes or until the apples are tender. Add apple mixture and milk to the drained sweet potatoes. Beat with an electric mixer until potatoes are mashed. **Yield:** 6 servings.

Note: As a variation, you can mix in cloves or nutmeg. This is also delicious topped with brown sugar and pecans.

Per serving: 126 calories, 1g protein, 22g carbohydrate, 4g fat, 2g fiber, 11mg cholesterol, 48mg sodium

◄ **FAMILY FAVORITE**

Prep Time: 10 minutes

Cook Time: 30 minutes

Average Rating: ★★★★★

What other cooks have done:

"The flavor is perfect. My husband, who is not a big fan of sweet potatoes, said, 'This tastes like pie!' and ate a large helping. I sprinkled brown sugar, raisins, and dried cranberries on top."

Baked Tomatoes Oregano

Submitted by: **Michele O'Sullivan**

"An excellent side dish. Tastes like pizza without the crust!"

4 large ripe tomatoes, sliced to ¼ inch thickness	2 sprigs fresh parsley, chopped
2 tablespoons grated Romano cheese	Salt and ground black pepper to taste
½ cup fresh breadcrumbs	½ teaspoon dried oregano
1 clove garlic, minced	1 tablespoon olive oil

1. Preheat oven to 400°F (200°C). Coat a shallow baking dish with cooking spray.
2. Place tomato slices close together in prepared baking dish. Sprinkle with cheese, breadcrumbs, garlic, parsley, salt and pepper to taste, and oregano. Drizzle with olive oil.
3. Bake for 20 minutes in the preheated oven or until cheese is lightly toasted. **Yield:** 4 servings.

Per serving: 110 calories, 4g protein, 14g carbohydrate, 5g fat, 3g fiber, 4mg cholesterol, 97mg sodium

◄ **COMPANY IS COMING**

Prep Time: 15 minutes

Cook Time: 20 minutes

Average Rating: ★★★★☆

What other cooks have done:

"I arranged the tomatoes in a flat oven-proof serving dish in an overlapping fashion. I added ½ cup Parmesan and mozzarella right before removing it from the oven. I only waited for the cheese to bubble and brown slightly. A great make-ahead dish for a party."

Zucchini and Corn Topped with Cheese

Submitted by: **Leanna Ramirez**

"Melted Monterey Jack and Cheddar cheeses make this colorful vegetable dish instant comfort food."

KID-FRIENDLY ▶

Prep Time: 15 minutes

Cook Time: 25 minutes

Stand Time: 5 minutes

Average Rating: ★★★★★

What other cooks have done:

"This is an absolutely fabulous recipe. I used fresh tomatoes, fresh corn, and half a yellow zucchini."

2	tablespoons vegetable oil	2	teaspoons garlic powder
6	medium-size zucchini, sliced		Salt and ground black pepper to taste
½	medium-size onion, chopped	½	pound shredded Monterey Jack cheese
1	(15.25 ounce) can whole kernel corn, drained	½	pound shredded sharp Cheddar cheese
1	(14.5 ounce) can diced tomatoes, drained		

1. Heat oil in a medium saucepan over medium heat; sauté zucchini and onion in oil for 5 to 7 minutes or until onion is tender. Stir in corn, diced tomatoes, garlic powder, and salt and pepper to taste. Cover and cook 15 minutes or until zucchini is soft.

2. Remove the saucepan from heat. Mix in the Monterey Jack cheese and Cheddar cheese. Cover and let stand until cheeses are melted, about 5 minutes. **Yield:** 8 servings.

Per serving: 329 calories, 18g protein, 18g carbohydrate, 22g fat, 3g fiber, 55mg cholesterol, 575mg sodium

Mixed Vegetable Casserole

Submitted by: **Linna**

"Vegetables in a creamy, cheesy sauce. Everyone wants the recipe after they have tried it!"

COVERED-DISH FAVORITE ▶

Prep Time: 15 minutes

Cook Time: 30 minutes

Average Rating: ★★★★☆

What other cooks have done:

"I used sour cream instead of mayonnaise, and it turned out great. This was so easy to make."

2	(14.5 ounce) cans mixed vegetables, drained	1	cup mayonnaise
1	small onion, diced	1	cup shredded white Cheddar cheese
1	(10.75 ounce) can condensed cream of chicken soup	36	buttery round crackers, crushed

1. Preheat oven to 350°F (175°C).

2. In a medium bowl, combine the mixed vegetables, onion, soup, mayonnaise, and cheese. Mix well and spread mixture into a 9x13 inch baking dish. Top with cracker crumbs.

3. Bake in the preheated oven for 30 minutes or until browned and bubbly. **Yield:** 6 servings.

Per serving: 586 calories, 14g protein, 35g carbohydrate, 43g fat, 5g fiber, 46mg cholesterol, 1435mg sodium

Cheesy Vegetables and Noodles

Submitted by: **Jennifer E.**

"With just five ingredients, you'll have a winning accompaniment to dinner tonight."

1	(8 ounce) package rigatoni pasta	2	cups cubed processed cheese
1	(10 ounce) package frozen mixed vegetables	½	teaspoon soy sauce
		½	teaspoon garlic salt

1. Bring a large pot of lightly salted water to a boil. Add pasta and cook for 8 to 10 minutes or until al dente; drain.

2. Meanwhile, prepare frozen vegetables according to package directions.

3. In a small saucepan, combine processed cheese, soy sauce, and garlic salt. Stir over medium heat until cheese is melted.

4. Combine pasta, vegetables, and cheese sauce. Stir to combine and serve. **Yield:** 5 servings.

Per serving: 429 calories, 22g protein, 46g carbohydrate, 19g fat, 4g fiber, 45mg cholesterol, 1079mg sodium

◄ FROM THE PANTRY

Prep Time: 10 minutes

Cook Time: 15 minutes

Average Rating: ★★★★☆

What other cooks have done:

"This was easy, quick, and good. I really liked the zing that the soy sauce added. I added thyme and rosemary, and I used thin spaghetti. Good recipe for when you are in a hurry!"

Blue Cheese Macaroni

Submitted by: **sara**

"This is not your average mac and cheese! Macaroni is combined with a creamy mixture of blue cheese, Parmesan cheese, and yogurt and served with green and red bell peppers."

2	cups elbow macaroni	½	cup sliced red bell pepper
2	tablespoons butter	¾	cup heavy cream
1	teaspoon salt	⅓	cup all-purpose flour
½	teaspoon ground black pepper	½	cup plain yogurt
½	cup sliced green bell pepper	1	cup crumbled blue cheese
		½	cup grated Parmesan cheese

1. Bring a large pot of lightly salted water to a boil. Add macaroni and cook for 8 to 10 minutes or until al dente; drain.

2. Meanwhile, in a medium saucepan over medium heat, combine butter, salt, black pepper, and green and red bell peppers. Simmer until heated through. Stir in cream, flour, yogurt, and cheeses.

3. Stir cooked macaroni into cheese mixture and serve hot. **Yield:** 6 servings.

Per serving: 420 calories, 15g protein, 34g carbohydrate, 25g fat, 2g fiber, 76mg cholesterol, 923mg sodium

◄ CLASSIC COMFORT FOOD

Prep Time: 10 minutes

Cook Time: 15 minutes

Average Rating: ★★★★☆

What other cooks have done:

"My husband and I love blue cheese, and we give this two thumbs up. I used evaporated skim milk instead of cream and tossed in a crushed clove of garlic with the peppers."

Spring Salad

Submitted by: **Kathleen White**
"People are surprised when they taste this salad featuring an odd combination of ingredients, but it's a very good salad."

PARTY FOOD ▶

Prep Time: 10 minutes

Cook Time: 10 minutes

Average Rating: ★★★★★

What other cooks have done:

"I used red onions instead of green onions and dried cranberries instead of raisins. I heated the almonds in a pan over medium-low to medium heat with 1 to 2 tablespoons white sugar until the sugar melted. I let them cool, broke them apart, and then added them to the salad just before serving."

12	slices bacon	½	cup raisins
2	heads fresh broccoli, florets only	½	cup blanched slivered almonds
1	cup chopped celery	1	cup mayonnaise
½	cup chopped green onions	1	tablespoon white wine vinegar
1	cup seedless green grapes	¼	cup white sugar
1	cup seedless red grapes		

1. Place bacon in a large, deep skillet. Cook over medium-high heat until evenly brown. Drain. Crumble and set aside.
2. In a large salad bowl, toss together the bacon, broccoli, celery, green onions, green grapes, red grapes, raisins, and almonds.
3. Whisk together the mayonnaise, vinegar, and sugar. Pour dressing over salad and toss to coat. Refrigerate until ready to serve. **Yield:** 8 servings.

Per serving: 587 calories, 9g protein, 28g carbohydrate, 51g fat, 4g fiber, 44mg cholesterol, 500mg sodium

Cranberry Gelatin Salad

Submitted by: **Sharon Wolfe**
"Even people who don't like cranberry sauce like this tasty gelatin salad!"

HOLIDAY FARE ▶

Prep Time: 15 minutes

Cook Time: 10 minutes

Chill Time: 1 hour

Average Rating: ★★★★★

What other cooks have done:

"I mixed together 1 (8 ounce) package softened cream cheese, 1 cup sour cream, ¾ cup sugar, and ½ teaspoon vanilla extract. Once the salad had set, I spread this mixture on top. After taking this to dozens of gatherings, I now bring preprinted recipe cards with me for the onslaught of requests I get."

1	(16 ounce) can jellied cranberry sauce	2	cups boiling water
1	(16 ounce) can pitted dark sweet cherries, drained and chopped	1	(6 ounce) package cherry-flavored gelatin
1	(8 ounce) can crushed pineapple with juice	1	cup chopped pecans (optional)

1. In a medium saucepan over low heat, melt cranberry sauce.
2. Add cherries to the melted sauce. Stir in the pineapple with its juice. Remove mixture from heat.
3. In a medium bowl, pour the boiling water over the gelatin. Stir until all the gelatin has dissolved.
4. Add the gelatin mixture to the cranberry mixture and stir. Stir in pecans, if desired. Pour into a 9x13 inch pan and chill until set. **Yield:** 12 servings.

Per serving: 211 calories, 3g protein, 37g carbohydrate, 7g fat, 2g fiber, 0mg cholesterol, 58mg sodium

Roquefort Pear Salad

Submitted by: **Michelle Krzmarzick**

"This is the best salad I've ever eaten, and I make it all the time. It's tangy from the Roquefort cheese, fruity from the pears, and crunchy from the caramelized pecans. The mustard vinaigrette pulls it all together."

¼	cup white sugar
½	cup pecans
⅓	cup olive oil
3	tablespoons red wine vinegar
1½	teaspoons white sugar
1½	teaspoons prepared mustard
1	clove garlic, chopped
½	teaspoon salt
	Ground black pepper to taste

1	head leaf lettuce, torn into bite-size pieces
3	pears, peeled, cored, and chopped
5	ounces Roquefort cheese, crumbled
1	avocado, peeled, pitted, and diced
½	cup thinly sliced green onions

◄ COMPANY IS COMING

Prep Time: 15 minutes

Cook Time: 10 minutes

Average Rating: ★★★★

What other cooks have done:

"I've made this salad three times, and everyone wanted the recipe each time. I used spinach instead of leaf lettuce and added dried cherries."

1. In a skillet over medium heat, stir together ¼ cup sugar and pecans. Continue stirring gently until sugar has melted and pecans have caramelized. Carefully transfer nuts to wax paper. Allow to cool and break into pieces.

2. Blend oil, vinegar, 1½ teaspoons sugar, mustard, chopped garlic, salt, and pepper to taste.

3. In a large serving bowl, layer lettuce, pears, Roquefort cheese, avocado, and green onions. Pour dressing over salad. Sprinkle with pecans and serve. **Yield:** 6 servings.

Per serving: 429 calories, 8g protein, 33g carbohydrate, 32g fat, 6g fiber, 21mg cholesterol, 644mg sodium

Tropical Salad with Pineapple Vinaigrette

Submitted by: **Marianne**

"Bagged salad greens make this salad so simple."

FAMILY FAVORITE ▶

Prep Time: 20 minutes

Cook Time: 10 minutes

Average Rating: ★★★★★

What other cooks have done:

"I love salads, and this was so easy and delicious. I used precooked real bacon bits, canned pineapple chunks, and untoasted sweetened coconut to cut down on prep time."

6   slices bacon
¼   cup pineapple juice
3   tablespoons red wine vinegar
¼   cup olive oil
    Salt and ground black pepper to taste
1   (10 ounce) bag chopped romaine lettuce
1   cup diced fresh pineapple
½   cup chopped, toasted macadamia nuts
3   green onions, chopped
¼   cup flaked coconut, toasted

1. Place bacon in a large, deep skillet. Cook over medium-high heat until evenly brown. Drain, crumble, and set aside.
2. In a cruet or jar with a lid, combine pineapple juice, red wine vinegar, oil, and salt and pepper to taste. Cover and shake well.
3. In a large bowl, toss together the lettuce, pineapple, macadamia nuts, green onions, and bacon. Pour dressing over salad and toss to coat. Top with toasted coconut. **Yield:** 6 servings.

Per serving: 257 calories, 5g protein, 10g carbohydrate, 23g fat, 2g fiber, 8mg cholesterol, 258mg sodium

Spinach and Mushroom Salad

Submitted by: **Monique**

"This salad is one of my family's favorite ways to enjoy spinach."

COMPANY IS COMING ▶

Prep Time: 15 minutes

Cook Time: 20 minutes

Average Rating: ★★★★★

What other cooks have done:

"This salad is super delicious. I like to add in some diced chicken with the bacon."

2   eggs
4   slices bacon
2   teaspoons white sugar
2   tablespoons cider vinegar
2   tablespoons water
½   teaspoon salt
1   pound spinach
¼   pound fresh mushrooms, sliced

1. Place eggs in a saucepan and cover with cold water. Bring water to a boil. Cover, remove from heat, and let eggs stand in hot water for 10 to 12 minutes. Remove to cool. Peel and cut into wedges.
2. Meanwhile, place bacon in a large, deep skillet. Cook over medium-high heat until evenly brown. Drain, crumble, and set aside, reserving 2 tablespoons bacon drippings in skillet. Stir in sugar, vinegar, water, and salt. Keep warm.
3. Wash and remove stems from spinach; dry thoroughly and tear into pieces. Pour warm dressing over spinach and toss until coated.
4. Top salad with mushrooms, bacon, and egg. **Yield:** 4 servings.

Per serving: 234 calories, 10g protein, 8g carbohydrate, 19g fat, 3g fiber, 125mg cholesterol, 618mg sodium

Ramen Coleslaw

Submitted by: **Mary**

"This is nothing like the mayonnaise-based coleslaws that most people think of."

2	tablespoons vegetable oil	½	teaspoon salt
3	tablespoons white wine vinegar	½	teaspoon ground black pepper
2	tablespoons white sugar	2	tablespoons sesame seeds
1	(3 ounce) package chicken–flavored ramen noodles, crushed, seasoning packet reserved	¼	cup sliced almonds
		½	medium head cabbage, shredded
		5	green onions, chopped

1. Preheat oven to 350°F (175°C).

2. In a medium bowl, whisk together the oil, vinegar, sugar, ramen seasoning packet, salt, and pepper.

3. Place sesame seeds and almonds in a single layer on a baking sheet. Bake in the preheated oven for 10 minutes or until lightly brown.

4. In a salad bowl, combine cabbage, green onions, and crushed ramen noodles. Pour dressing over cabbage and toss to coat evenly. Top with toasted sesame seeds and almonds. **Yield:** 4 servings.

Per serving: 253 calories, 7g protein, 30g carbohydrate, 13g fat, 5g fiber, 0mg cholesterol, 543mg sodium

◄ OUT-OF-THE-ORDINARY

Prep Time: 15 minutes

Cook Time: 10 minutes

Average Rating: ★★★★★

What other cooks have done:

"I have made this recipe several times for my family and for gatherings; it's always a hit. To help keep the salad from getting soggy, I toast the ramen noodles along with the almonds and seeds. It's really nice on a buffet or for a potluck—but always wait until right before serving to add the noodles and nuts."

Chinese Napa Cabbage Salad

Submitted by: **Kay**

"This is an excellent way to use up that leftover cabbage from the garden."

¼	cup butter	1	large head napa cabbage, shredded
1	(3 ounce) package chicken–flavored ramen noodles, crushed, seasoning packet reserved	6	green onions, chopped
		¼	cup vegetable oil
		¼	cup rice wine vinegar
½	cup blanched slivered almonds	1	tablespoon soy sauce
½	cup sesame seeds, toasted	1	tablespoon sesame oil
		2	tablespoons white sugar

1. Melt butter in a large skillet over medium heat. Add crushed noodles, almonds, and sesame seeds. Sauté in melted butter until browned. Stir often to prevent burning. Add ramen seasoning packet and cool. Toss with cabbage and onions.

2. Whisk together the vegetable oil, rice wine vinegar, soy sauce, sesame oil, and sugar. Pour over salad. Toss and serve. **Yield:** 6 servings.

Per serving: 419 calories, 10g protein, 29g carbohydrate, 31g fat, 10g fiber, 21mg cholesterol, 616mg sodium

◄ AROUND-THE-WORLD CUISINE

Prep Time: 10 minutes

Cook Time: 15 minutes

Average Rating: ★★★★★

What other cooks have done:

"The dressing for this salad is first-rate—it's so light and flavorful. My husband doesn't like cabbage, so I use mixed salad greens. I also added sliced cooked chicken, shredded carrots, and mandarin oranges. If you don't have ramen noodles on hand, use chow mein noodles."

Artichoke Rice Salad

Submitted by: **Kathy Berliner**

"This recipe of my mother's has always been one of my favorites. Prepare it the night before and serve chilled."

MAKE-AHEAD ▶

Prep Time: 15 minutes

Cook Time: 20 minutes

Chill Time: overnight

Average Rating: ★★★★☆

What other cooks have done:

"I used 1 cup mayonnaise and a couple of jars of artichoke hearts, and this salad was terrific! Also, I didn't have any curry powder or parsley, but this salad still had tons of flavor."

4	cups chicken stock or broth		Salt and ground black
2	cups uncooked white rice		pepper to taste
3	(6 ounce) jars marinated	5	green onions, chopped
	artichoke hearts, chopped,	1	green bell pepper, chopped
	liquid reserved	¼	cup chopped parsley
2	cups mayonnaise	3	stalks celery, chopped
1	teaspoon curry powder		

1. Combine chicken stock and rice in a medium saucepan. Bring to a boil and reduce heat to low. Cook until tender, about 20 minutes.
2. Meanwhile, in a small bowl, combine artichoke liquid, mayonnaise, and curry powder. Season to taste with salt and pepper and set aside.
3. In a large bowl, combine artichoke hearts, green onions, green bell pepper, parsley, and celery. Mix in cooked rice and marinade mixture. Cover and chill overnight. Serve cold. **Yield:** 12 servings.

Per serving: 468 calories, 4g protein, 32g carbohydrate, 37g fat, 1g fiber, 22mg cholesterol, 709mg sodium

Three Bean Salad I *(pictured on page 3)*

Submitted by: **Cathy Castro**

"A delicious bean salad with extra kinds of beans and a zesty flavor!"

MAKE-AHEAD ▶

Prep Time: 10 minutes

Cook Time: 5 minutes

Chill Time: overnight

Average Rating: ★★★★★

What other cooks have done:

"I used slightly less oil and omitted the tarragon completely. This salad is delicious even when warm and freshly made."

1	(14.5 ounce) can cut green beans, drained	1	red onion, chopped
1	(14.5 ounce) can wax beans, drained	1	green bell pepper, chopped
		¾	cup red wine vinegar
1	(15 ounce) can red kidney beans, drained	¼	cup white sugar
		¾	cup vegetable oil
1	(15 ounce) can garbanzo beans, drained	¾	teaspoon powdered mustard
1	(15 ounce) can black beans, drained	½	teaspoon dried tarragon
		1½	teaspoons dried cilantro

1. In a large bowl, layer green beans, wax beans, kidney beans, garbanzo beans, black beans, onion, and bell pepper. Set aside.
2. In a small saucepan, mix the vinegar, sugar, oil, mustard, tarragon, and cilantro. Cook and stir over medium heat until sugar dissolves. Remove from heat and pour over bean mixture. Stir until all ingredients are coated. Cover and refrigerate overnight, stirring occasionally.
Yield: 10 servings.

Per serving: 378 calories, 8g protein, 48g carbohydrate, 18g fat, 8g fiber, 0mg cholesterol, 705mg sodium

Green Bean and Feta Salad

Submitted by: **Liz Herberth**

"A tasty salad using fresh green beans and feta cheese in a tangy dressing."

1½	pounds fresh green beans	¾	teaspoon salt
1	sweet onion, peeled and thinly sliced		Ground black pepper to taste
2	cloves garlic, chopped		Dash hot sauce
½	cup rice wine vinegar		Dash Worcestershire sauce
½	cup apple cider vinegar	4	ounces feta cheese, crumbled
⅓	cup canola oil		
1	tablespoon white sugar		

1. Bring a large pot of water to a boil. Add green beans and cook 4 minutes or until tender-crisp. Add onion and cook 1 more minute. Drain and rinse with cold water.

2. In a large bowl, whisk together garlic, rice wine vinegar, cider vinegar, oil, sugar, salt, pepper to taste, hot sauce, and Worcestershire sauce. Add bean mixture and cheese and stir until combined. Place in a nonreactive container and refrigerate overnight. **Yield:** 5 servings.

Per serving: 257 calories, 6g protein, 17g carbohydrate, 20g fat, 5g fiber, 20mg cholesterol, 617mg sodium

◄ **MAKE-AHEAD**

Prep Time: 15 minutes

Cook Time: 8 minutes

Chill Time: overnight

Average Rating: ★★★★☆

What other cooks have done:

"This is a great way to use garden beans. I cut the dressing in half, except for the sugar. This makes a large amount and is great for picnics. Kids even enjoyed this."

Barb's Broccoli-Cauliflower Salad

Submitted by: **Tom**

"This is a version of the classic broccoli salad with the addition of cauliflower. It can be prepared the day prior to serving and served chilled or at room temperature. Pecans can be used instead of sunflower seeds, if desired, and bacon lovers might want to add a few extra slices."

12	slices bacon	1	cup creamy salad dressing
1	head cauliflower, chopped	1½	tablespoons white wine vinegar
1	head fresh broccoli, diced	¼	cup white sugar
½	red onion, diced		
¾	cup sunflower seeds		

1. Place bacon in a large, deep skillet. Cook over medium-high heat until evenly brown. Drain, crumble, and set aside.

2. Combine bacon, cauliflower, broccoli, onion, and sunflower seeds.

3. Whisk together the salad dressing, vinegar, and sugar. Pour over salad and toss to coat. Refrigerate and serve chilled. **Yield:** 8 servings.

Per serving: 506 calories, 9g protein, 19g carbohydrate, 45g fat, 5g fiber, 38mg cholesterol, 529mg sodium

◄ **PARTY FOOD**

Prep Time: 10 minutes

Cook Time: 10 minutes

Chill Time: 30 minutes

Average Rating: ★★★★★

What other cooks have done:

"This was such a party-pleaser. I substituted toasted pecan pieces for the sunflower seeds and rice wine vinegar for the white wine vinegar. I used bottled coleslaw dressing for the creamy dressing. What a hit!"

Mediterranean Lentil Salad

Submitted by: **jen**

"This is a delicious lentil salad that keeps very well in the refrigerator."

AROUND-THE-WORLD CUISINE ▶

Prep Time: 15 minutes

Cook Time: 22 minutes

Average Rating: ★★★★

What other cooks have done:

"This was delicious! Instead of olive oil, I used fat-free Italian dressing and added a tablespoon of apple cider vinegar and two diced tomatoes. Yum!"

1	cup dried brown lentils	2	tablespoons lemon juice
1	cup diced carrots	½	cup diced celery
1	cup red onion, diced	¼	cup chopped parsley
2	cloves garlic, minced	1	teaspoon salt
1	bay leaf	¼	teaspoon ground black pepper
½	teaspoon dried thyme		
¼	cup olive oil		

1. In a saucepan, combine lentils, carrots, onion, garlic, bay leaf, and thyme. Add water to cover by 1 inch. Bring to a boil. Reduce heat and simmer, uncovered, for 15 to 20 minutes or until lentils are tender but not mushy. Drain mixture and remove bay leaf.
2. Combine olive oil, lemon juice, celery, parsley, salt, and pepper. Add to lentil mixture and toss to mix. Serve at room temperature. **Yield:** 8 servings.

Per serving: 148 calories, 6g protein, 17g carbohydrate, 7g fat, 6g fiber, 0mg cholesterol, 448mg sodium

Restaurant-Style Potato Salad

Submitted by: **Mary Ann Benzon**

"This is a traditional and easy-to-make potato salad."

RESTAURANT FARE ▶

Prep Time: 15 minutes

Cook Time: 17 minutes

Chill Time: 30 minutes

Average Rating: ★★★★

What other cooks have done:

"This is wonderful potato salad. The dressing is creamy and flavorful. For my family's personal preference, I used five hard-boiled eggs, mashing up the yolks into the mayonnaise mixture. I also left out the carrots."

2	pounds russet potatoes	1	tablespoon minced celery
1	cup mayonnaise	1	teaspoon minced pimiento
4	teaspoons sweet pickle relish	½	teaspoon shredded carrot
4	teaspoons white sugar	¼	teaspoon dried parsley
2	teaspoons chopped white onion	¼	teaspoon ground black pepper
2	teaspoons prepared mustard		Salt to taste
1	teaspoon white wine vinegar		

1. Bring a large pot of salted water to a boil. Add potatoes and cook until tender but still firm, about 15 minutes. Drain, cool, and chop.
2. In a large bowl, combine the potatoes, mayonnaise, sweet pickle relish, sugar, onion, mustard, vinegar, celery, pimentos, carrot, parsley, pepper, and salt to taste. Mix well. Chill and serve. **Yield:** 7 servings.

Per serving: 343 calories, 3g protein, 28g carbohydrate, 25g fat, 3g fiber, 19mg cholesterol, 229mg sodium

Fresh Tomato Salad *(pictured on page 263)*

Submitted by: **Karen Gray**

"This salad has fresh tomato, cucumber, onion, green pepper, and herbs."

5 tomatoes, coarsely chopped	2 tablespoons crushed garlic
1 onion, chopped	2 tablespoons white wine
1 cucumber, coarsely chopped	vinegar
1 green bell pepper, coarsely chopped	Salt and ground black pepper to taste
½ cup chopped basil	Feta cheese, crumbled (optional)
½ cup chopped parsley	

1. In a large bowl, combine the tomato, onion, cucumber, bell pepper, basil, parsley, garlic, and vinegar. Toss to coat and add salt and pepper to taste and feta cheese, if desired. Chill and serve. **Yield:** 7 servings.

Per serving: 42 calories, 2g protein, 9g carbohydrate, 1g fat, 2g fiber, 0mg cholesterol, 14mg sodium

◄ **FAMILY FAVORITE**

Prep Time: 15 minutes

Chill Time: 15 minutes

Average Rating: ★★★★☆

What other cooks have done:

"Delicious, healthy, and perfect for summer. I was able to go right outside and pick most of the ingredients from my garden. In our household, we enjoyed it even more by using sweet red bell peppers instead of green. Also, this tastes even better when mixed with crumbled feta or blue cheese."

Jambalaya Salad

Submitted by: **Louis**

"This is a New Orleans-style salad with shrimp, ham, bacon, rice, and Creole seasonings."

1⅓ cups water	½ cup sliced celery
⅔ cup uncooked long-grain white rice	¼ cup chopped onion
6 slices bacon	1 cup chopped fresh tomato
1 (6 ounce) jar tiny shrimp, drained	¾ cup Italian-style salad dressing
½ cup cubed ham	1 teaspoon dried thyme
½ cup chopped green bell pepper	¼ teaspoon chili powder
	1 clove garlic, minced
	¼ teaspoon salt

1. In a medium saucepan, bring water to a boil. Stir in the rice. Cover, reduce heat, and simmer 20 minutes.

2. Meanwhile, place bacon in a large, deep skillet. Cook over medium-high heat until evenly brown. Drain and crumble.

3. In a large bowl, mix together the cooked rice, crumbled bacon, shrimp, ham, bell pepper, celery, onion, and tomato.

4. Whisk together the salad dressing, thyme, chili powder, garlic, and salt. Pour over rice mixture and toss to coat. Serve warm or cover and chill until serving. **Yield:** 6 servings.

Per serving: 341 calories, 13g protein, 24g carbohydrate, 21g fat, 1g fiber, 61mg cholesterol, 668mg sodium

◄ **OUT-OF-THE-ORDINARY**

Prep Time: 15 minutes

Cook Time: 22 minutes

Average Rating: ★★★★★

What other cooks have done:

"I made this salad the night before I served it, and the flavor really intensified overnight. I also substituted frozen salad shrimp for the jar of shrimp. I doubled the recipe for a potluck at work, and there were only a few spoonfuls left. I will definitely make this again."

Spaghetti Salad I

Submitted by: **Kathy Young**

"Tangy pasta salad that's even better made the day before!"

MAKE-AHEAD ▶

Prep Time: 10 minutes

Cook Time: 15 minutes

Chill Time: 25 minutes

Average Rating: ★★★★★

What other cooks have done:

"This recipe has turned into one of the most requested dishes that I make. I use the larger elbow noodles (better for kids to handle). Great every time!"

1 (16 ounce) package spaghetti
1 (8 ounce) bottle zesty Italian-style salad dressing
1 tablespoon Italian seasoning
1 bunch green onions, chopped
1 cucumber, chopped
2 tomatoes, chopped
1 (2.25 ounce) can sliced black olives

1. Bring a large pot of lightly salted water to a boil. Add pasta and cook 8 to 10 minutes or until al dente. Drain and rinse with cold water.
2. Combine cooked pasta with Italian dressing, Italian seasoning, green onions, cucumber, tomatoes, and black olives. Toss to coat and refrigerate 25 minutes or overnight before serving. **Yield:** 8 servings.

Per serving: 339 calories, 9g protein, 49g carbohydrate, 12g fat, 3g fiber, 0mg cholesterol, 530mg sodium

30 minutes or less

Home on the Range Tuna Salad

Submitted by: **Teresa**

"A delicious, creamy tuna salad. Don't turn it down just because it has cottage cheese in it—try it!"

COVERED-DISH FAVORITE ▶

Prep Time: 10 minutes

Cook Time: 14 minutes

Average Rating: ★★★★★

What other cooks have done:

"Excellent! I eat this on wheat crackers, and it makes a perfect lunch. I did omit the green onions and added sweet pickle, but it was still great. I like it so much that I served it with tomato slices at a ladies' luncheon—it was a huge hit!"

2 eggs
1 (6 ounce) can tuna, drained
1 cup low-fat cottage cheese
¼ cup chopped celery
¼ cup chopped green onions
2 tablespoons chopped fresh parsley
1 teaspoon lemon pepper seasoning
¼ teaspoon celery salt
1 teaspoon lemon juice
¼ cup mayonnaise

1. Place eggs in a saucepan and cover completely with cold water. Bring water to a boil. Cover, remove from heat, and let eggs stand in hot water for 10 to 12 minutes. Remove from hot water and cool. Peel and chop.
2. In a large bowl, flake tuna. Add cottage cheese, eggs, celery, green onions, parsley, lemon pepper seasoning, celery salt, lemon juice, and mayonnaise; mix well. Chill until serving. **Yield:** 4 servings.

Per serving: 240 calories, 22g protein, 4g carbohydrate, 15g fat, 0g fiber, 131mg cholesterol, 577mg sodium

Fuss-Free Breads

288 Quick Breads

 *minutes or less*

Cinnamon-Sour Cream Biscuits

Submitted by: **Jennifer**

"I received a champion ribbon at the county fair for these biscuits. They're good warm or cool and are great for breakfast or anytime."

BLUE RIBBON WINNER ▶

Prep Time: 15 minutes

Cook Time: 12 minutes

Average Rating: ★★★★★

What other cooks have done:

"I just finished tasting one of these biscuits while it was still warm from the oven. They are yummy! They have a light, moist texture, which must be from the sour cream. Next time, I will increase the cinnamon as it was a little too subtle."

2	cups all-purpose flour		1	cup sour cream
2	tablespoons white sugar		2	tablespoons milk
½	teaspoon ground cinnamon		½	cup raisins
2	teaspoons baking powder		½	cup confectioners' sugar
¼	teaspoon baking soda		2	teaspoons milk
¼	teaspoon salt			Cinnamon (optional)
½	cup butter or margarine			White sugar (optional)

1. Preheat oven to 450°F (230°C).

2. In a large mixing bowl, combine flour, 2 tablespoons white sugar, cinnamon, baking powder, baking soda, and salt. Cut in butter. Make a well in center. Add sour cream, 2 tablespoons milk, and raisins, stirring just until combined. (Add a bit more milk, if needed.)

3. Turn dough out onto a floured surface and gently knead 8 to 10 times. Pat dough to ½ inch thickness. Cut with biscuit cutter, dipping cutter in flour between cuts. Place on a lightly greased baking sheet.

4. Bake in the preheated oven for 10 to 12 minutes. Cool slightly on wire racks.

5. Stir together confectioners' sugar and 2 teaspoons milk. Drizzle over biscuits. Sprinkle with additional cinnamon and white sugar, if desired. **Yield:** 1 dozen biscuits.

Per biscuit: 232 calories, 3g protein, 29g carbohydrate, 12g fat, 1g fiber, 9mg cholesterol, 257mg sodium

Biscuit Know-How

Warm, buttery biscuits are easy-to-make crowd-pleasers, but as fast and simple as they are to prepare, we have a few pointers to help you make your biscuits even better.

• Mix only until the ingredients just hold together. Overmixing the dough will develop the gluten in the flour and toughen the biscuits.

• Try making biscuit dough in your food processor. Combine dry ingredients in the processor bowl, add the fat, and pulse 6 or 7 times or until the mixture resembles coarse meal. Slowly add the liquid through the food chute, with the processor running, just until the dough forms a ball. The processor can easily overwork the dough, so watch it closely.

• Wrap leftover biscuits in foil, place in a plastic zip-top bag, and freeze up to 3 months. When you're ready to serve, thaw individual biscuits and heat, still wrapped in foil, in a 300°F (150°C) oven for several minutes or until heated.

• If you like biscuits with crusty sides, place them 1 inch apart on a shiny baking sheet. For soft sides, arrange them close together in a shallow baking dish or pan.

• If you accidentally leave your biscuits in the oven too long, gently scrape the flat burned undersides of your biscuits against a fine-toothed grater to remove most of the mistake. Do this over the sink because it's messy.

For more information, visit **Allrecipes.com**

Never-Fail Biscuits

Submitted by: **Madison**
"These biscuits are easy to make, and everyone enjoys them."

2	cups all-purpose flour	2	teaspoons white sugar
½	teaspoon salt	½	cup butter, chilled and
4	teaspoons baking powder		diced
½	teaspoon cream of tartar	¾	cup milk

1. Preheat oven to 450°F (230°C).
2. In a large bowl, combine flour, salt, baking powder, cream of tartar, and sugar. Cut in butter until mixture resembles coarse crumbs. Make a well in the center of the dry mixture and pour in milk. Stir until dough begins to pull together; turn out onto a lightly floured surface.
3. Roll dough out to ½ inch thickness. Cut dough into rounds using a 2½ inch biscuit cutter and place on an ungreased baking sheet.
4. Bake in the preheated oven for 10 minutes or until golden. **Yield:** 11 biscuits.

Per biscuit: 466 calories, 8g protein, 53g carbohydrate, 25g fat, 2g fiber, 66mg cholesterol, 797mg sodium

◄**FREEZER FRESH**

Prep Time: 14 minutes

Cook Time: 10 minutes

Average Rating: ★★★★★

What other cooks have done:
"These are wonderful, light biscuits. I used 1 cup buttermilk in place of the milk. I recommend using these for berry shortcakes or topped with peach slices and a dollop of whipped cream. This is a keeper!"

Cranberry Scones

Submitted by: **Cristina Gomez**
"A quick, basic scone recipe that's a great treat for Christmas morning."

2	cups all-purpose flour	1	cup fresh cranberries,
¼	cup packed brown sugar		roughly chopped
1	tablespoon baking powder	⅓	cup white sugar
¼	teaspoon ground nutmeg	1	orange, zested
¼	teaspoon salt	½	cup chopped walnuts
¼	cup butter, chilled and	¾	cup half-and-half
	cut into pieces	1	egg

1. Preheat oven to 375°F (190°C). Lightly grease baking sheets.
2. In a large bowl, stir together flour, brown sugar, baking powder, nutmeg, and salt. Cut in butter until mixture resembles coarse crumbs.
3. In a separate bowl, toss cranberries with white sugar; add to flour mixture. Stir in zest and nuts. Mix lightly.
4. In another bowl, beat together half-and-half and egg; slowly add to dry ingredients, mixing until dough forms. Knead dough 4 or 5 times, being careful not to overhandle. Divide dough in half. Turn out onto a lightly floured surface. Shape each half into a 6 inch circle. Cut each circle into 6 wedges. Place scones on the prepared baking sheets.
5. Bake in the preheated oven for 20 minutes or until golden brown.
Yield: 1 dozen scones.

Per scone: 212 calories, 4g protein, 29g carbohydrate, 10g fat, 1g fiber, 34mg cholesterol, 159mg sodium

◄**HOLIDAY FARE**

Prep Time: 20 minutes

Cook Time: 20 minutes

Average Rating: ★★★★☆

What other cooks have done:
"I used raisins instead of cranberries, and it turned out great. These are so easy to make. For more color, I brushed the top of each scone with egg wash so that they came out golden brown after baking."

Apple-Nut Muffins

Submitted by: **Laura**

"These are the best muffins ever. They're sweet, nutty, and full of apple flavor."

HOLIDAY FARE ▶

Prep Time: 12 minutes

Cook Time: 18 minutes

Average Rating: ★★★★☆

What other cooks have done:

"I added 1 teaspoon cinnamon to the batter. These are great heated for about 20 seconds in the microwave and served with some vanilla ice cream. Yummy!"

¾	cup butter	¾	teaspoon salt
1¾	cups white sugar, divided	1½	cups sour cream
3	eggs	1	(21 ounce) can apple pie
1½	teaspoons vanilla extract		filling
3½	cups all-purpose flour	1	cup chopped walnuts
1½	teaspoons baking powder	½	teaspoon ground cinnamon
1½	teaspoons baking soda		

1. Preheat oven to 350°F (175°C). Lightly grease muffin pans or line with paper liners.
2. In a large bowl, cream butter and 1½ cups sugar. Beat in eggs and vanilla. In a separate large bowl, combine flour, baking powder, baking soda, and salt. Stir into the creamed mixture alternately with sour cream. Fold in apple pie filling and walnuts. Spoon batter into prepared muffin cups. Combine remaining ¼ cup sugar and cinnamon; sprinkle over muffins.
3. Bake in the preheated oven for 16 to 18 minutes or until a toothpick inserted into center of a muffin comes out clean. **Yield:** 18 muffins.

Per muffin: 364 calories, 5g protein, 49g carbohydrate, 17g fat, 2g fiber, 64mg cholesterol, 336mg sodium

Maple Muffins

Submitted by: **Jan Bittner**

"Delicious, light muffins with real maple syrup."

HOLIDAY FARE ▶

Prep Time: 12 minutes

Cook Time: 20 minutes

Average Rating: ★★★★☆

What other cooks have done:

"Light, delicious muffin. I loved the maple syrup and added extra oats for more texture. Kids loved it for a snack!"

1½	cups all-purpose flour	¼	cup rolled oats
¼	cup white sugar	1	egg, lightly beaten
2	teaspoons baking powder	½	cup milk
½	teaspoon salt	½	cup real maple syrup
¼	cup shortening		

1. Preheat oven to 400°F (205°C). Grease muffin pan.
2. Sift together flour, sugar, baking powder, and salt. Cut in shortening until mixture resembles coarse crumbs. Stir in oats. Add egg, milk, and syrup. Stir just until dry ingredients are moistened. Fill muffin cups three-quarters full.
3. Bake in the preheated oven for 18 to 20 minutes. Cool briefly in pan before removing to a wire rack to cool completely. **Yield:** 1 dozen muffins.

Per muffin: 163 calories, 3g protein, 27g carbohydrate, 5g fat, 1g fiber, 19mg cholesterol, 190mg sodium

Doughnut Muffins

Submitted by: **Debbie**
"Muffins that taste like doughnuts, topped with a delicious cinnamon-sugar mixture."

⅓	cup shortening	½	teaspoon salt
1½	cups white sugar, divided	1¼	teaspoons ground
1	egg		cinnamon, divided
1½	cups all-purpose flour	½	cup milk
1½	teaspoons baking powder		

1. Preheat oven to 375°F (190°C). Grease muffin pan or line with paper liners.

2. In a large bowl, cream shortening and 1 cup sugar; beat in egg. In a separate bowl, stir together flour, baking powder, salt, and ¼ teaspoon cinnamon. Stir flour mixture into egg mixture alternately with milk. Spoon batter into prepared muffin cups.

3. Bake in the preheated oven for 20 minutes or until a toothpick inserted into center of a muffin comes out clean.

4. While muffins bake, combine remaining ½ cup sugar and remaining 1 teaspoon cinnamon. Remove muffins from pan and let cool for 5 minutes. While muffins are still warm, roll tops of muffins in cinnamon-sugar mixture. **Yield:** 1 dozen muffins.

Per muffin: 216 calories, 3g protein, 38g carbohydrate, 7g fat, 1g fiber, 19mg cholesterol, 139mg sodium

◄ KID-FRIENDLY

Prep Time: 10 minutes

Cook Time: 20 minutes

Average Rating: ★★★★★

What other cooks have done:

"I used ½ teaspoon Chinese five spice powder instead of cinnamon to make the topping. Dunk the muffins in melted butter before rolling them in the sugar mixture to help the topping stick."

Pecan Pie Muffins *(pictured on page 298)*

Submitted by: **T's mom**
"It's hard to believe there are only five ingredients in these wonderful little muffins! The brown sugar makes them taste like pecan pie."

1	cup packed light brown sugar	1	cup chopped pecans
½	cup all-purpose flour	⅔	cup butter, softened
		2	eggs, lightly beaten

1. Preheat oven to 350°F (175°C). Line miniature muffin pans or regular muffin pan with paper liners.

2. In a medium bowl, stir together brown sugar, flour, and pecans. In a separate bowl, beat butter and eggs together until smooth; stir mixture into dry ingredients just until combined. Spoon the batter into the prepared muffin cups. Cups should be about three-fourths full.

3. Bake in the preheated oven for 16 to 18 minutes for mini muffins or 22 minutes for regular muffins. Cool on wire racks. **Yield:** 30 mini muffins or 12 regular-size muffins.

Per regular-size muffin: 346 calories, 4g protein, 31g carbohydrate, 24g fat, 2g fiber, 84mg cholesterol, 162mg sodium

◄ 5 INGREDIENTS OR LESS

Prep Time: 10 minutes

Cook Time: 22 minutes

Average Rating: ★★★★★

What other cooks have done:

"I bought glass jars, mixed the flour and sugar and put in the bottom of each one, and topped that with the nuts. I put a ribbon on each jar with a 'finish the recipe' card calling for the butter and egg, and gave them to teachers for holiday goodies. Big hit!"

Pineapple Puffs

Submitted by: **Debbie**

"My grandma used to make these when I was a kid. They're very moist and very sweet. If you want to, you can also add some coconut."

FAMILY FAVORITE ▶

Prep Time: 10 minutes

Cook Time: 20 minutes

Average Rating: ★★★★☆

What other cooks have done:

"I added 1 teaspoon vanilla extract and ½ teaspoon ground ginger to help boost the pineapple flavor, and they were great! We like bigger muffins, so I will probably fill the cups a little fuller next time."

½	cup butter, softened	2	cups all-purpose flour
1	cup white sugar	½	teaspoon salt
1	egg	½	teaspoon baking soda
1	(8 ounce) can crushed	1	teaspoon baking powder
	pineapple, undrained	½	teaspoon ground cinnamon

1. Preheat oven to 350°F (175°C). Grease muffin pan or line with paper liners.

2. In a large bowl, cream butter and sugar until light and fluffy. Add egg; beat well. Stir in pineapple and its juice. In a separate bowl, mix together flour, salt, baking soda, baking powder, and cinnamon. Add to pineapple mixture; stir well. Pour batter into prepared muffin cups.

3. Bake in the preheated oven for 20 minutes or until a toothpick inserted into center of a muffin comes out clean. Cool for 10 minutes in pan; cool completely on wire racks. **Yield:** 1 dozen muffins.

Per muffin: 224 calories, 3g protein, 35g carbohydrate, 8g fat, 1g fiber, 38mg cholesterol, 276mg sodium

Orange Muffins

Submitted by: **Jenn Hall**

"Great breakfast muffin recipe."

KID-FRIENDLY ▶

Prep Time: 15 minutes

Cook Time: 25 minutes

Average Rating: ★★★★☆

What other cooks have done:

"I made these for a holiday tray, so I baked them in mini muffin pans. I added ¼ teaspoon nutmeg and stirred in ⅓ cup finely chopped dried cranberries. Everyone wanted more!"

2	cups all-purpose flour	1	tablespoon orange zest
½	cup white sugar	¾	cup orange juice
1	tablespoon baking powder	⅓	cup vegetable oil
½	teaspoon salt	1	egg

1. Preheat oven to 400°F (205°C). Grease bottoms only of muffin pan or line with paper liners.

2. In a medium bowl, combine flour, sugar, baking powder, salt, and orange zest; mix well. In a small bowl, combine orange juice, oil, and egg; blend well. Add to dry ingredients all at once; stir just until dry ingredients are moistened (batter will be lumpy). Fill prepared muffin cups two-thirds full.

3. Bake in the preheated oven for 20 to 25 minutes or until toothpick inserted into center of a muffin comes out clean. Cool 1 minute in pan before removing to a wire rack. Serve warm. **Yield:** 1 dozen muffins.

Per muffin: 176 calories, 3g protein, 26g carbohydrate, 7g fat, 1g fiber, 18mg cholesterol, 225mg sodium

Land of Nod Cinnamon Buns *(pictured on page 298)*

Submitted by: **Shannon**
"Easy overnight cinnamon buns that are gooey and rich."

1	(25 ounce) package frozen dinner roll dough	2	teaspoons ground cinnamon
1	cup packed brown sugar	½	cup raisins
¼	cup instant vanilla pudding mix	⅓	cup butter, melted

1. Lightly grease a 10 inch Bundt pan. Place frozen roll dough in pan and sprinkle with brown sugar, pudding mix, cinnamon, and raisins. Pour melted butter over rolls. Cover with a clean, damp cloth and then place in a cold oven for 8 hours.
2. Preheat oven to 350°F (175°C).
3. Bake rolls in the preheated oven for 25 minutes or until golden brown. Turn rolls out onto a serving plate and serve warm. **Yield:** 24 rolls.

Per serving: 430 calories, 16g protein, 79g carbohydrate, 7g fat, 4g fiber, 8mg cholesterol, 842mg sodium

◄ MAKE-AHEAD
Prep Time: 7 minutes
Stand Time: 8 hours
Cook Time: 25 minutes
Average Rating: ★★★★★
What other cooks have done:
"We made this on Christmas Eve and had it on Christmas morning. It is so easy, and everyone loved it!"

30 minutes or less

Great Garlic Knots *(pictured on page 297)*

Submitted by: **Sandy B**
"So simple and quick to make, these delicious knots of herb-seasoned bread will complete just about any meal. You can also eat these tasty knots as a snack between meals with your favorite spread slathered on top. Using fresh rosemary makes these knots especially fragrant."

1	(11 ounce) can refrigerated soft breadsticks	1	tablespoon chopped fresh rosemary
1	egg	1	teaspoon garlic powder
1	teaspoon water		

1. Preheat oven to 375°F (190°C).
2. Tie each breadstick into a knot; place knots on a baking sheet. Combine egg and water. Brush the knots with egg mixture and sprinkle with rosemary and garlic. Bake the knots according to the package directions. **Yield:** 1 dozen knots.

Per serving: 242 calories, 8g protein, 39g carbohydrate, 5g fat, 1g fiber, 53mg cholesterol, 596mg sodium

◄ 5 INGREDIENTS OR LESS
Prep Time: 15 minutes
Cook Time: 13 minutes
Average Rating: ★★★★★
What other cooks have done:
"Super simple! I used a garlic-butter spread that I got from our local deli, and I omitted the egg wash. My whole family gobbled these up."

Real Sopapillas

Submitted by: **Leaz**

"Sopapillas for any occasion. Serve hot with honey or your own homemade tostadas."

AROUND-THE WORLD-CUISINE ▶

Prep Time: 10 minutes

Stand Time: 20 minutes

Cook Time: 15 minutes

Average Rating: ★★★★★

What other cooks have done:

"I generously sprinkled these with cinnamon sugar after frying. They turned out great and disappeared immediately upon serving."

4	cups all-purpose flour	1½	cups warm water
2	teaspoons baking powder		(110°F/45°C)
1	teaspoon salt	4	cups vegetable oil
4	tablespoons shortening		

1. In a large bowl, stir together flour, baking powder, salt, and shortening. Stir in water; mix until dough is smooth. Cover and let stand for 20 minutes.

2. Roll out on a floured surface to ⅛ to ¼ inch thickness. Cut into 3 inch squares.

3. Heat oil to 375°F (190°C) in a deep fryer or heavy pan. Fry squares until golden brown on both sides. Drain on paper towels and serve hot. **Yield:** 2 dozen sopapillas.

Per serving: 160 calories, 2g protein, 16g carbohydrate, 10g fat, 1g fiber, 0mg cholesterol, 118mg sodium

30 minutes or less

Basic Crêpes

Submitted by: **Jen**

"Here is a simple but delicious crêpe batter that can be made in minutes. It's made from ingredients that everyone has on hand. Stuff with any fillings you like."

FROM THE PANTRY ▶

Prep Time: 10 minutes

Cook Time: 20 minutes

Average Rating: ★★★★★

What other cooks have done:

"If you're using a nonstick pan, shake it back and forth now and then while the crêpe cooks. When the crêpe begins to slip back and forth in the pan, it's ready to be flipped."

1	cup all-purpose flour	½	cup water
2	eggs	¼	teaspoon salt
½	cup milk	2	tablespoons butter, melted

1. In a large mixing bowl, whisk together flour and eggs. Gradually add in milk and water, stirring to combine. Add salt and butter; beat until smooth.

2. Heat a lightly oiled griddle or skillet over medium-high heat. Pour or scoop ¼ cup batter onto the griddle. Tilt the pan with a circular motion so that the batter coats the surface evenly.

3. Cook the crêpe for about 2 minutes or until the bottom is light brown. Loosen with a spatula; turn and cook the other side. Repeat for remaining batter. Serve hot. **Yield:** 4 servings.

Per serving: 217 calories, 7g protein, 26g carbohydrate, 9g fat, 1g fiber, 124mg cholesterol, 252mg sodium

Graham Griddle Cakes

Submitted by: **Kim**

"I've been making these for years. They are very tasty and have a great nutty flavor."

¾	cup all-purpose flour	½	cup chopped pecans
¾	cup graham cracker crumbs		(optional)
2	tablespoons brown sugar	1	cup milk
2	teaspoons baking powder	2	tablespoons butter, melted
¼	teaspoon salt	1	egg

1. In a large mixing bowl, combine flour, graham cracker crumbs, brown sugar, baking powder, salt, and pecans, if desired. In a separate bowl, stir together milk, butter, and egg. Add to the flour mixture and stir well.

2. Heat a lightly oiled griddle or skillet over medium-high heat. Pour or scoop ¼ cup batter onto the griddle. Brown on both sides. Repeat with remaining batter. Serve hot. **Yield:** 6 servings.

Per serving: 254 calories, 6g protein, 28g carbohydrate, 14g fat, 2g fiber, 49mg cholesterol, 395mg sodium

◄ KID-FRIENDLY

Prep Time: 10 minutes

Cook Time: 20 minutes

Average Rating: ★★★★☆

What other cooks have done:

"I substituted wheat germ for the graham crackers and chocolate chips for pecans. So good!"

Pumpkin Pancakes

Submitted by: **Ruth**

"These are good any season but taste best on cold winter mornings. You can use canned or cooked fresh pumpkin."

1½	cups milk	2	teaspoons baking powder
1	cup pumpkin puree	1	teaspoon baking soda
1	egg	1	teaspoon ground allspice
2	tablespoons vegetable oil	1	teaspoon ground cinnamon
2	tablespoons vinegar	½	teaspoon ground ginger
2	cups all-purpose flour	½	teaspoon salt
3	tablespoons packed brown		
	sugar		

1. In a large bowl, mix together milk, pumpkin, egg, oil, and vinegar. In a separate large bowl, combine the flour, brown sugar, baking powder, baking soda, allspice, cinnamon, ginger, and salt; stir into the pumpkin mixture until just combined.

2. Heat a lightly oiled griddle or skillet over medium-high heat. Pour or scoop ¼ cup batter onto the griddle. Brown on both sides. Repeat with remaining batter. Serve hot. **Yield:** 6 servings.

Per serving: 278 calories, 8g protein, 46g carbohydrate, 7g fat, 3g fiber, 40mg cholesterol, 613mg sodium

◄ HOLIDAY FARE

Prep Time: 20 minutes

Cook Time: 20 minutes

Average Rating: ★★★★☆

What other cooks have done:

"I had leftover pumpkin from Thanksgiving pies, and this was the perfect way to use it! I had some extra batter, to which I added ¾ cup flour, ½ cup sugar, and more chocolate chips to thicken the batter to cookie dough consistency. I dropped spoonfuls of dough onto a cookie sheet and baked at 350°F (175°C) for about 12 minutes. The cookies and the pancakes were both great!"

Applesauce French Toast

Submitted by: **Joan R**

"An unusual but delicious way to make French toast! Extra moist and extra chewy!"

2 eggs	2 tablespoons white sugar
¾ cup milk	¼ cup applesauce
1 teaspoon ground cinnamon	6 slices bread

1. In a large mixing bowl, combine the eggs, milk, cinnamon, sugar, and applesauce; mix well.
2. Heat a lightly oiled skillet or griddle over medium–high heat.
3. Soak bread in applesauce mixture, 1 slice at a time, until saturated with liquid.
4. Cook in hot skillet until lightly browned on both sides. Serve hot.
Yield: 6 servings.

Per serving: 132 calories, 5g protein, 21g carbohydrate, 3g fat, 1g fiber, 74mg cholesterol, 174mg sodium

French Toast Waffles

minutes or less

Submitted by: **Fred Fields**

"Tired of plain old waffles? Do you love French toast, but don't like the hassle of making it? Then try this recipe that combines the ease of waffles with the taste of French toast!"

1 cup pancake or waffle mix	½ cup cold milk
2 teaspoons white sugar	2 eggs
1 teaspoon ground cinnamon	1 teaspoon vanilla extract

1. Spray waffle iron with cooking spray. Preheat waffle iron.
2. In a large mixing bowl, combine waffle mix, sugar, and cinnamon. Stir in milk, eggs, and vanilla.
3. Pour ¼ cup batter onto hot waffle iron. Cook until golden brown. Repeat with remaining batter. Serve hot. **Yield:** 6 servings.

Per serving: 124 calories, 5g protein, 20g carbohydrate, 3g fat, 0g fiber, 72mg cholesterol, 354mg sodium

Great Garlic Knots, page 293

Pecan Pie Muffins, page 291

Land of Nod Cinnamon Buns, page 293

Butter Brickle Frozen Delight, page 328

Black Chocolate Cake, page 306

Apple Enchilada Dessert, page 321

Chocolate Layered Pie, page 317

Frozen Peanut Butter
Cheesecake, page 314

Peach Brûlée, page 325

Chewiest Brownies, page 339

Pig Picking Cake II, page 307

Desserts

Black Chocolate Cake *(pictured on page 300)*

Submitted by: **Jeanie Bean**

"This is a rich chocolate cake that uses cocoa powder and lots of sugar. It's my husband's all-time favorite."

(pictured on page 300)

2 cups all-purpose flour
2 cups white sugar
2 teaspoons baking soda
2 teaspoons baking powder
1 cup unsweetened cocoa powder
⅛ teaspoon salt
2 cups boiling water

⅔ cup shortening
2 eggs, beaten
2 teaspoons vanilla extract
1 (16 ounce) can chocolate frosting
1 (1.55 ounce) chocolate bar (optional)

1. Preheat oven to 375°F (190°C). Grease and flour a 9x13 inch pan.
2. Sift together the flour, sugar, baking soda, baking powder, cocoa, and salt in a large bowl. Set aside.
3. Combine boiling water and shortening, stirring until shortening melts. Stir shortening mixture into the flour mixture until blended. Beat in the eggs; stir in the vanilla. Pour batter into prepared pan.
4. Bake in the preheated oven for 30 minutes or until a toothpick inserted into center comes out clean. Frost cooled cake, if desired. Scrape a vegetable peeler down the edge of the chocolate bar to make chocolate curls, if desired; sprinkle over servings of cake.
Yield: 12 servings.

Per serving: 337 calories, 5g protein, 53g carbohydrate, 13g fat, 3g fiber, 35mg cholesterol, 297mg sodium

COMPANY IS COMING ▶

Prep Time: 15 minutes

Cook Time: 30 minutes

Average Rating: ★★★★★

What other cooks have done:

"Here's a trick I used: instead of water, heat 2 cups milk; after taking it off the heat, add 2 heaping teaspoons of instant coffee and use that mixture to dissolve the shortening. It really brings out the chocolate flavor."

Pralines, Coffee, and Cream Cake

Submitted by: **Mike Dmochowski**

"This is a great cake for parties and gatherings. I always get numerous requests for the recipe. It's so easy to make!"

1 (18.25 ounce) package white cake mix
3 eggs
1 cup coffee-flavored liqueur
½ cup vegetable oil
1 cup butter
1 cup packed brown sugar
1½ cups chopped pecans

1 (3.4 ounce) package instant vanilla pudding mix
1½ cups milk
1 (8 ounce) package cream cheese, softened
1 (12 ounce) container frozen whipped topping, thawed

1. Preheat oven to 350°F (175°C). Lightly grease and flour a 9x13 inch pan.
2. Combine cake mix, eggs, coffee liqueur, and oil in large bowl. Beat at medium speed with an electric mixer for about 2 minutes. Pour into prepared pan.

PARTY FOOD ▶

Prep Time: 15 minutes

Cook Time: 30 minutes

Average Rating: ★★★★★

What other cooks have done:

"I split the cake evenly with sewing thread, forming a top and bottom layer. I spread the frosting between the layers and, when I serve it, I put a small dollop of frosting on the side as well. This makes a lovely presentation."

3. Bake in the preheated oven for 25 minutes or until cake springs back when touched or a toothpick inserted into center comes out clean. Cool on a wire rack.

4. Meanwhile, combine butter and brown sugar in a medium saucepan. Heat, stirring constantly, over medium heat. Boil, stirring constantly, for 2 minutes. Add pecans and remove from heat. Stir mixture and immediately pour over cake. Cool cake in refrigerator.

5. Combine pudding mix, milk, cream cheese, and whipped topping; beat at medium speed with electric mixer until thickened. Spread over cake. **Yield:** 18 servings.

Per serving: 576 calories, 5g protein, 52g carbohydrate, 37g fat, 1g fiber, 79mg cholesterol, 440mg sodium

Pig Picking Cake II *(pictured on page 304)*

Submitted by: **Claudia Hamilton**

"From living down South and attending all the get-togethers for Pig Picking—barbecues where everyone 'picks' meat from the pig—I know that this cake is a sure winner with everyone, from southerners to northerners. This dessert brings us all together."

1 (18.25 ounce) package yellow cake mix	1 (3.4 ounce) package instant vanilla pudding mix
½ cup butter or margarine, softened	1½ cups chopped pecans, toasted and divided
4 eggs	½ cup flaked coconut, toasted and divided
1 (11 ounce) can mandarin oranges with juice	1 (8 ounce) container frozen whipped topping, thawed
1 (20 ounce) can crushed pineapple with juice	

1. Preheat oven to 350°F (175°C). Grease and flour 3 (9 inch) round pans.

2. In a large bowl, combine cake mix, butter, eggs, and mandarin oranges and juice. Beat with an electric mixer for 3 minutes. Pour batter into prepared pans.

3. Bake in the preheated oven for 19 minutes or until a toothpick inserted into center comes out clean. Cool on wire racks.

4. In a large bowl, combine pineapple and juice with pudding mix. Stir in 1 cup pecans and ¼ cup coconut. Fold in the whipped topping. Spread between cooled cake layers and on top of cake. Chill until ready to serve. Sprinkle with remaining pecans and coconut. **Yield:** 12 servings.

Per serving: 465 calories, 5g protein, 56g carbohydrate, 25g fat, 2g fiber, 72mg cholesterol, 512mg sodium

◀ FAMILY FAVORITE

Prep Time: 20 minutes

Cook Time: 19 minutes

Average Rating: ★★★★☆

What other cooks have done:

"This is a great cake. My family just loves it! It is especially good in the spring and summertime, as it is light and fruity. But one thing to remember—it really doesn't travel well, so it's best to make it where you're going to serve it."

Amaretto Divine *(pictured on page 4)*

Submitted by: **Janet Ayers**
"A luscious, special-occasion dessert."

COMPANY IS COMING ▶

Prep Time: 18 minutes

Cook Time: 15 minutes

Stand Time: 5 minutes

Average Rating: ★★★★★

What other cooks have done:

"I have made this several times with great results. I did have to bake the layers about 35 minutes, and the last time I made it, I just put 1 tablespoon of amaretto in the frosting, and it was not quite as strong. If you want to make a really impressive dessert that is fairly easy, I would recommend this one. It is absolutely beautiful when done."

1 (18.25 ounce) package yellow cake mix
2 cups nondairy amaretto-flavored creamer, divided
1¼ cups amaretto liqueur, divided
3 eggs
⅓ cup vegetable oil
1 (3.4 ounce) package instant vanilla pudding mix
2 cups heavy cream, whipped
6 (1.4 ounce) chocolate-covered toffee bars, chopped
  Chocolate syrup

1. Preheat oven to 350°F (175°C). Grease and flour 3 (8 inch) round pans.

2. Mix together the cake mix, 1 cup amaretto-flavored creamer, 1 cup amaretto liqueur, eggs, and oil until blended. Pour batter into prepared pans.

3. Bake in the preheated oven for 15 minutes, making certain the cake layers do not overbake. Allow to cool completely before frosting.

4. Combine pudding mix, remaining 1 cup amaretto-flavored creamer, and remaining ¼ cup amaretto liqueur. Set aside for 5 minutes. Fold whipped cream into amaretto mixture and beat at low speed with an electric mixer for 2 minutes or until thick. Stir in chopped chocolate-covered toffee bars, reserving some for garnish. Spread between layers and over cake. Drizzle cake with chocolate syrup and sprinkle with reserved toffee pieces. Refrigerate until ready to serve. **Yield:** 12 servings.

Per serving: 640 calories, 6g protein, 82g carbohydrate, 30g fat, 1g fiber, 92mg cholesterol, 510mg sodium

Red Velvet Cake II

Submitted by: **Rhonda**
"This cake is a bright spot on a holiday table."

1½	cups white sugar	2	teaspoons vanilla extract, divided
1	cup vegetable oil		
2	eggs	1	(8 ounce) package cream cheese, softened
2	ounces red food coloring		
1	teaspoon white vinegar	½	cup butter, softened
1	cup buttermilk	4	cups confectioners' sugar
1	teaspoon baking soda	½	cup chopped pecans
2½	cups self-rising flour		

1. Preheat oven to 350°F (175°C). Grease and flour 3 (8 inch) round pans.

2. In a large bowl, mix together white sugar, oil, and eggs. In a separate bowl, mix together food coloring, vinegar, and buttermilk. In a separate bowl, add baking soda to flour. Add flour mixture and buttermilk mixture alternately to the sugar mixture. Mix well. Stir in 1 teaspoon vanilla. Pour batter into prepared pans.

3. Bake in the preheated oven for 20 to 25 minutes or until a toothpick inserted into center comes out clean. Remove from oven and cool on wire racks.

4. Mix together cream cheese, butter, confectioners' sugar, and remaining 1 teaspoon vanilla. Stir in nuts. Spread frosting over cooled cake. **Yield:** 12 servings.

Per serving: 697 calories, 6g protein, 87g carbohydrate, 37g fat, 1g fiber, 77mg cholesterol, 602mg sodium

◄ FAMILY FAVORITE

Prep Time: 20 minutes

Cook Time: 25 minutes

Average Rating: ★★★★☆

What other cooks have done:

"This cake was a beautiful red color and unbelievably moist. I added an extra teaspoon of vanilla. I used store-bought vanilla icing, and it was fine."

Crowning Glory

Transforming a cake from plain and ordinary to stunning and irresistible is easier than you may think. The next time you've got a crowd to wow, try one of our quick and easy cake decorating ideas.

Fresh edible flowers, such as sweet violets, lavender, honeysuckle, rose petals, borage, bachelor's buttons, Johnny-jump-ups, and calendulas, make gorgeous and oh-so-easy cake decorations. For an added touch, dusting the flowers with superfine sugar gives a wonderful sparkly glow to your creation. Just be sure when using flowers as a decoration that they are clean, all the parts you are using are non-toxic, and that they are pesticide free.

Another great way to add color to a cake is to top it with fresh fruit. Pile fresh berries on top of a cake, sprinkle with confectioners' sugar, and garnish with fresh mint leaves. Kiwis, grapes, orange sections, and strawberries can be arranged on the top of a cake and glazed with a shiny syrup of melted apricot preserves or other fruit jam. Line the outside edge of a chocolate cake with strawberries for an elegant ring of color. Using caramel dipped, sugar-dusted, or candied fruit or rinds can also add a nice finishing touch to a beautiful cake. These are just a few of the many ways fruit can be used in decorating cakes.

Confectioners' sugar or cocoa powder lightly dusted over the tops of cakes makes a very nice finishing touch to any cake. Place parchment paper cut into fun designs, such as stars, polka dots, flowers, diamonds, vines, and waves, over the cake before dusting to make an attractive or whimsical statement.

For more information, visit **Allrecipes.com**

Grandma's Moist Cake

Submitted by: **Patricia Taylor**

"This very moist yellow cake recipe comes from my boyfriend's grandmother. We usually serve it with chocolate buttermilk icing."

1	cup butter, softened	1	cup milk
2	cups white sugar	1	tablespoon vanilla extract
4	eggs	2½	cups self-rising flour

1. Preheat oven to 350°F (175°C). Grease and flour 3 (8 inch) pans.
2. In a medium bowl, cream together butter and sugar with an electric mixer. Beat in the eggs, 1 at a time. In a small bowl, combine milk and vanilla and add alternately to the creamed mixture with the flour, ending with the flour. Do not overmix. Pour batter into the prepared pans.
3. Bake in the preheated oven for 15 to 20 minutes. Cake will pull away from the sides of the pans slightly when done. Allow cakes to cool in the pans for a few minutes before removing to wire racks to cool completely. Frost as desired. **Yield:** 12 servings.

Per serving: 395 calories, 6g protein, 54g carbohydrate, 18g fat, 1g fiber, 114mg cholesterol, 519mg sodium

David's Yellow Cake

Submitted by: **David S.**

"After trying different cake recipes that I thought were too dry, I decided to make up one of my own."

2	cups cake flour	1½	cups white sugar
2	teaspoons baking powder	8	egg yolks
½	teaspoon salt	1½	teaspoons vanilla extract
1	cup butter, softened	¾	cup milk

1. Preheat oven to 350°F (175°C). Grease and flour 2 (8 inch) round pans.
2. Sift together the flour, baking powder, and salt. Set aside.
3. In a large bowl, cream butter and sugar with an electric mixer until light and fluffy. Beat in the egg yolks, 1 at a time, and stir in vanilla. Beat in the flour mixture alternately with the milk, mixing just until blended. Pour batter into prepared pans.
4. Bake in the preheated oven for 25 to 30 minutes or until tops of layers spring back when lightly tapped. Cool 15 minutes in pans before removing to wire racks to cool completely. Frost as desired. **Yield:** 12 servings.

Per serving: 364 calories, 4g protein, 44g carbohydrate, 19g fat, 0g fiber, 184mg cholesterol, 308mg sodium

Cream-Filled Cupcakes

Submitted by: **Grace W.**

"Delicious and simple to make, these treats feature a creamy filling that's piped into chocolate cupcakes with a pastry bag. Frost with your favorite frosting."

3	cups all-purpose flour	1	cup vegetable oil
2	cups white sugar	2	teaspoons vanilla extract, divided
⅓	cup unsweetened cocoa powder	¼	cup butter, softened
2	teaspoons baking soda	¼	cup shortening
1	teaspoon salt	2	cups confectioners' sugar
2	eggs		Pinch salt
1	cup milk	3	tablespoons milk
1	cup water		

1. Preheat oven to 375°F (190°C). Line muffin pans with paper liners.
2. In a large bowl, mix together the flour, white sugar, cocoa, baking soda, and 1 teaspoon salt. Make a well in the center and pour in the eggs, 1 cup milk, water, oil, and 1 teaspoon vanilla. Mix well. Fill each muffin cup half-full of batter.
3. Bake in the preheated oven for 15 to 20 minutes or until a toothpick inserted into center of a muffin comes out clean. Cool.
4. Meanwhile, in a large bowl, beat butter and shortening with an electric mixer until smooth. Blend in confectioners' sugar and pinch of salt. Gradually beat in 3 tablespoons milk and remaining 1 teaspoon vanilla. Beat until light and fluffy. Fill a pastry bag with filling mixture. Push tip of pastry bag through bottom of a cupcake paper liner and fill cupcake. Repeat for each cupcake. Frost as desired. **Yield:** 3 dozen cupcakes.

Per cupcake: 196 calories, 2g protein, 27g carbohydrate, 9g fat, 1g fiber, 16mg cholesterol, 167mg sodium

◄ PARTY FOOD

Prep Time: 20 minutes

Cook Time: 20 minutes

Average Rating: ★★★★★

What other cooks have done:

"Instead of filling from the bottom, I filled the cupcakes from the top center before I topped them with store-bought chocolate frosting."

Amazing Corn Cake

Submitted by: **lois**

"This is a moist spice cake with a secret ingredient that no one will guess!"

KID-FRIENDLY ▶

Prep Time: 15 minutes

Cook Time: 30 minutes

Average Rating: ★★★★☆

What other cooks have done:

"My son and I prepared this cake and topped it with cream cheese frosting for a class project on corn recipes. The whole class loved it. The teacher had two slices, and the rest of it got spirited away to the teacher's lounge quicker than you can say A+!"

2¼	cups all-purpose flour	¾	cup white sugar
1	tablespoon baking powder	½	cup packed brown sugar
1	teaspoon baking soda	3	eggs
1	teaspoon ground cinnamon	1	cup vegetable oil
1	teaspoon salt	½	cup raisins
1	(14.75 ounce) can cream-style corn	½	cup chopped walnuts

1. Preheat oven to 375°F (190°C). Grease a 9x13 inch pan.
2. Stir together flour, baking powder, baking soda, cinnamon, and salt.
3. In a mixing bowl, combine corn, white sugar, and brown sugar. Beat in eggs and oil with an electric mixer until well blended. Mix in flour mixture. Stir in raisins and nuts. Pour batter into prepared pan.
4. Bake in the preheated oven for 30 minutes or until a toothpick inserted into center comes out clean. Cool. Frost as desired. **Yield:** 18 servings.

Per serving: 284 calories, 4g protein, 34g carbohydrate, 16g fat, 1g fiber, 35mg cholesterol, 360mg sodium

Aunt Anne's Coffee Cake

Submitted by: **Mary**

"This is the perfect cake for Sunday mornings spent reading the paper."

HOLIDAY FARE ▶

Prep Time: 15 minutes

Cook Time: 30 minutes

Average Rating: ★★★★☆

What other cooks have done:

"I like to think that I am a good cook, but I know I'm a lousy baker. Either this recipe is excellent, or I misjudged myself! I doubled the streusel topping and did not add it until the last few minutes of baking. Also, I thought the batter was a little dry, so I mixed in 2 to 3 tablespoons of apple juice. It was moist and flavorful."

¼	cup all-purpose flour	2	teaspoons baking powder
⅔	cup white sugar	½	teaspoon salt
1	teaspoon ground cinnamon	½	cup butter
¼	cup butter	1	egg
2	cups all-purpose flour		Milk
¾	cup white sugar	1½	teaspoons vanilla extract

1. Preheat oven to 350°F (175°C). Grease and flour a 9x13 inch pan.
2. In a medium bowl, combine ¼ cup flour, ⅔ cup sugar, and 1 teaspoon cinnamon. Cut in ¼ cup butter until mixture resembles coarse crumbs. Set streusel aside.
3. In a large bowl, combine 2 cups flour, ¾ cup sugar, baking powder, and salt. Cut in ½ cup butter until mixture resembles coarse crumbs. Crack an egg into a measuring cup and add milk to make 1 cup. Stir in vanilla. Pour into flour mixture and mix just until moistened. Spread into prepared pan. Sprinkle top with streusel.
4. Bake in the preheated oven for 25 to 30 minutes or until a toothpick inserted into center comes out clean. Cool. **Yield:** 15 servings.

Per serving: 230 calories, 3g protein, 34g carbohydrate, 10g fat, 1g fiber, 39mg cholesterol, 209mg sodium

Quick Cake

Submitted by: **Brenda Moore**

"A quick chocolate cake also known as Wacky Cake, this has no eggs or milk and is mixed in the same pan it's baked in."

1½	cups sifted pastry flour	¼	teaspoon salt
1	cup white sugar	1	cup water
¼	cup unsweetened cocoa powder	⅓	cup vegetable oil
1	teaspoon baking powder	¼	cup white vinegar
1	teaspoon baking soda	1	teaspoon vanilla extract

1. Preheat oven to 350°F (175°C).

2. Sift together the flour, sugar, cocoa, baking powder, baking soda, and salt into an ungreased 8x8 inch square pan. Make a well in the center and pour in the water, oil, vinegar, and vanilla. Mix until blended.

3. Bake in the preheated oven for 25 to 30 minutes or until a toothpick inserted into center comes out clean. Cool. **Yield:** 9 servings.

Per serving: 232 calories, 3g protein, 39g carbohydrate, 9g fat, 4g fiber, 0mg cholesterol, 246mg sodium

◄ **FAMILY FAVORITE**

Prep Time: 10 minutes

Cook Time: 30 minutes

Average Rating: ★★★★☆

What other cooks have done:

"Absolutely great cake and so simple to make! I served banana ice cream on the side, but it's delicious on it's own, too. Very moist."

Classic Tiramisu

Submitted by: **Carol**

"This classic Italian dessert made with ladyfingers and mascarpone cheese can be served in a trifle bowl or shaped in a springform pan."

6	egg yolks	⅓	cup coffee-flavored liqueur
1¼	cups white sugar	1	(1 ounce) square semisweet chocolate
1¼	cups mascarpone cheese		
1¾	cups heavy cream	1	teaspoon unsweetened cocoa powder
2	(12 ounce) packages ladyfingers		

1. Combine egg yolks and sugar in the top of a double boiler over boiling water. Reduce heat to low and cook for 10 minutes, stirring constantly. Remove from heat and whip until thick and lemon-colored.

2. Add mascarpone cheese to whipped yolks. Beat until combined. In a separate bowl, whip cream to stiff peaks. Gently fold whipped cream into yolk mixture and set aside.

3. Split ladyfingers in half; line the bottom and sides of a trifle bowl with half of split ladyfingers. Brush with half of coffee liqueur. Spoon half of yolk mixture over ladyfingers. Repeat layers. Chill overnight.

4. Scrape a vegetable peeler down the edge of the chocolate square to make chocolate curls. Dust tiramisu with cocoa powder and sprinkle with chocolate curls before serving. **Yield:** 12 servings.

Per serving: 575 calories, 10g protein, 60g carbohydrate, 32g fat, 1g fiber, 388mg cholesterol, 113mg sodium

◄ **PARTY FOOD**

Prep Time: 30 minutes

Cook Time: 15 minutes

Chill Time: overnight

Average Rating: ★★★★★

What other cooks have done:

"This recipe tastes terrific and makes a beautiful presentation in a springform pan. I added 2 teaspoons vanilla extract to the whipped cream and found that it enhanced the flavor of the mascarpone mixture. It's a good idea to brush the liqueur onto the ladyfingers using a pastry brush because you have more control, and the ladyfingers absorb just the right amount of liquid without getting soggy."

Frozen Peanut Butter Cheesecake *(pictured on page 302)*

Submitted by: **Angel Shephard**

"I'm not a cheesecake fan, unlike my husband, so this was my compromise."

HOLIDAY FARE ▶

Prep Time: 12 minutes

Cook Time: 12 minutes

Chill Time: 30 minutes

Freeze Time: 4 hours

Average Rating: ★★★★★

What other cooks have done:

"I reduced the rice cereal to about 1¾ cups and increased the chocolate chips (I used milk chocolate) to about 1¼ cups. I recommend taking it out of the freezer at least 15 minutes before serving."

⅓	cup butter	¾	cup peanut butter
1	(6 ounce) package semisweet chocolate chips	1	tablespoon lemon juice
2½	cups crispy rice cereal	1	teaspoon vanilla extract
1	(8 ounce) package cream cheese, softened	1	cup whipped cream
1	(14 ounce) can sweetened condensed milk	½	cup chocolate fudge sauce Chopped peanuts (optional)

1. In a heavy saucepan over low heat, melt the butter and chocolate chips. Remove from heat and gently stir in rice cereal until coated. Press, using the bottom of a glass if necessary, into the bottom and up sides of a 9 inch pie plate. Chill 30 minutes.
2. In a large bowl, beat cream cheese with an electric mixer until fluffy. Gradually beat in condensed milk and peanut butter until smooth. Stir in lemon juice and vanilla. Fold in whipped cream. Pour into prepared crust. Freeze for 4 hours or until firm. To serve, drizzle chocolate fudge sauce over slices of pie. Sprinkle with peanuts, if desired. Return any leftovers to the freezer. **Yield:** 8 servings.

Per serving: 645 calories, 14g protein, 59g carbohydrate, 43g fat, 3g fiber, 69mg cholesterol, 461mg sodium

Raspberry Mousse Cheesecake

Submitted by: **Dean Lawson**

"This is very rich and creamy. Probably the best cheesecake that I have ever eaten. This recipe tastes incredible with any flavor of jam."

CROWD-PLEASER ▶

Prep Time: 20 minutes

Cook Time: 25 minutes

Chill Time: 2 hours

Average Rating: ★★★★★

What other cooks have done:

"The topping for this cheesecake was way easy and tasted wonderful. I added a bit of red food coloring to it to give it more color, since I used cherry preserves. Delicious cheesecake!"

2	(8 ounce) packages cream cheese, softened	1	(9 inch) graham cracker pie crust
½	cup white sugar	1	cup raspberry jam
2	eggs	2	cups frozen whipped topping, thawed
½	teaspoon vanilla extract		

1. Preheat oven to 325°F (165°C).
2. In a large bowl, combine cream cheese, sugar, eggs, and vanilla. Beat with an electric mixer until light and fluffy. Pour into pie crust.
3. Bake in the preheated oven for 25 minutes. Cool completely.
4. Meanwhile, in a medium bowl, fold raspberry jam into whipped topping. Spread over top of cooled cheesecake and refrigerate for at least 2 hours. **Yield:** 12 servings.

Per serving: 372 calories, 5g protein, 42g carbohydrate, 21g fat, 0g fiber, 76mg cholesterol, 224mg sodium

No-Fuss Cinnamon Cheesecake

Submitted by: **Mellisa**

"When my friend Dee gave me this recipe, I was very skeptical. Who's ever heard of cheesecake made with crescent roll dough? This is so easy to make and very much in demand by my family. I make it all the time. Even my hard-to-impress mother-in-law asked for the recipe!"

2	(8 ounce) cans refrigerated crescent roll dough	1	tablespoon vanilla extract
2	(8 ounce) packages cream cheese, softened	½	cup butter, melted
1½	cups white sugar, divided	1	tablespoon ground cinnamon

1. Preheat the oven to 350°F (175°C).
2. Flatten one can of crescent roll dough and press into the bottom of a 9x13 inch pan. In a medium bowl, mix together cream cheese, 1 cup sugar, and vanilla until smooth. Spread cream cheese mixture over dough in pan. Unroll remaining crescent roll dough and place over cream cheese layer. Pour melted butter evenly over top of dough. Combine remaining ½ cup sugar and cinnamon and sprinkle over melted butter.
3. Bake in the preheated oven for 30 minutes or until top is lightly toasted. Cool and refrigerate until serving. **Yield:** 12 servings.

Per serving: 483 calories, 6g protein, 45g carbohydrate, 31g fat, 0g fiber, 62mg cholesterol, 556mg sodium

◄ OUT-OF-THE-ORDINARY

Prep Time: 15 minutes

Cook Time: 30 minutes

Average Rating: ★★★★★

What other cooks have done:

"This isn't like traditional cheesecake in taste or appearance, but it tastes great! If you skip the butter topping and just sprinkle the baked cake with confectioners' sugar, you have a cheese danish to serve for breakfast."

30 *minutes or less*

Cheesecake Cups

Submitted by: **Diana Doerner**

"Very easy recipe that kids can help make. Top with chocolate chips or cherry pie filling if you like."

16	vanilla wafer cookies	¾	cup white sugar
2	(8 ounce) packages cream cheese, softened	2	eggs
		1	teaspoon vanilla extract

1. Preheat oven to 350°F (175°C). Line muffin pans with paper liners.
2. Place one wafer cookie in the bottom of each muffin cup. In a medium bowl, beat cream cheese and sugar with an electric mixer. Beat in eggs and vanilla until smooth and pour over wafers in muffin cups.
3. Bake in the preheated oven for 15 minutes or until golden and set. **Yield:** 16 servings.

Per cheesecake cup: 172 calories, 3g protein, 15g carbohydrate, 12g fat, 0g fiber, 57mg cholesterol, 109mg sodium

◄ PARTY FOOD

Prep Time: 15 minutes

Cook Time: 15 minutes

Average Rating: ★★★★★

What other cooks have done:

"I made chocolate cheesecakes by adding 3 tablespoons unsweetened cocoa powder and an additional 2 tablespoons sugar to the cream cheese mixture. I used chocolate sandwich cookie tops as crusts and sprinkled them with chocolate chips."

Caramel Frosting I

Submitted by: **MaryKaye**

"I have had this recipe for over 30 years. Cream may be substituted for the milk for added richness."

5 INGREDIENTS OR LESS ▶

Prep Time: 10 minutes

Cook Time: 5 minutes

Average Rating: ★★★★★

What other cooks have done:

"A really great frosting! I used half-and-half, and it was excellent. I kept adding half-and-half until I reached a consistency I liked."

2	tablespoons butter	1	cup confectioners' sugar,
3	tablespoons milk		divided
½	cup packed brown sugar	½	teaspoon vanilla extract

1. Melt butter in a saucepan over medium heat; mix in milk and brown sugar. Boil vigorously for 1 minute.
2. Remove from heat and beat in ½ cup confectioners' sugar. Cool slightly and beat in vanilla and remaining ½ cup confectioners' sugar. Add more milk if frosting is too thick. Spread on cake immediately.
Yield: 12 servings.

Per serving: 93 calories, 0g protein, 19g carbohydrate, 2g fat, 0g fiber, 5mg cholesterol, 25mg sodium

Coconut-Pecan Frosting I

Submitted by: **Marsha**

"Traditional frosting and filling for German chocolate cake."

FAMILY FAVORITE ▶

Prep Time: 10 minutes

Cook Time: 10 minutes

Cool Time: 15 minutes

Average Rating: ★★★★★

What other cooks have done:

"I toasted my almonds and coconut to bring out the flavor. Everyone loved it. They said they never want canned icing again."

1	(14 ounce) can sweetened condensed milk	1⅓	cups flaked coconut
3	egg yolks	1	cup chopped pecans
½	cup butter	1	teaspoon vanilla extract

1. In a heavy 2 quart saucepan over medium heat, heat condensed milk, egg yolks, and butter for 10 minutes, stirring constantly, until bubbly. Remove from heat and stir in coconut, pecans, and vanilla. Cool for 15 minutes before spreading on cake. **Yield:** 12 servings.

Per serving: 296 calories, 5g protein, 23g carbohydrate, 22g fat, 1g fiber, 85mg cholesterol, 142mg sodium

White Chocolate Cream Pie

Submitted by: **Sara**
"Heaven and earth are united in this edible work of art."

5 (1 ounce) squares white chocolate, chopped	½ cup whipping cream, whipped
3 tablespoons heavy cream	1 (9 inch) pie crust, baked
1 (3 ounce) package cream cheese, softened	1 (1 ounce) square white chocolate, melted
⅔ cup confectioners' sugar	

1. Microwave 5 squares white chocolate and 3 tablespoons cream in a large bowl on high for 1½ to 2 minutes or until chocolate is almost melted, stirring after 1 minute. Stir until mixture is smooth.
2. Beat in softened cream cheese and confectioners' sugar. Gently fold in whipped cream until no streaks remain. Spoon into pie crust.
3. Microwave remaining square of white chocolate on high for 1½ to 2 minutes, stirring every 30 seconds, until melted and smooth. Drizzle melted white chocolate over pie. Chill overnight. **Yield:** 8 servings.

Per serving: 346 calories, 4g protein, 35g carbohydrate, 22g fat, 0g fiber, 29mg cholesterol, 184mg sodium

◄ MAKE-AHEAD

Prep Time: 30 minutes

Cook Time: 5 minutes

Chill Time: overnight

Average Rating: ★★★★☆

What other cooks have done:
"This takes hardly any time to make, other than letting it chill overnight. It is a perfect pie. I would recommend a chocolate cookie prebaked pie crust. Beautiful contrast in colors and flavors."

Chocolate Layered Pie *(pictured on page 301)*

Submitted by: **Jan H.**
"Chocolate pudding pie in a pecan-nut crust and topped with whipped topping tastes like heaven. Also known as a Voodoo Pie."

½ cup chopped pecans	1 cup confectioners' sugar
½ cup butter, melted	1 (5.9 ounce) package instant chocolate pudding mix
1 cup all-purpose flour	1⅓ cup milk
3 cups frozen whipped topping, thawed and divided	Additional chopped pecans
1 (8 ounce) package cream cheese, softened	Chocolate syrup

1. Preheat oven to 350°F (175°C).
2. Mix together ½ cup pecans, melted butter, and flour. Pat into the bottom and up the sides of a 9 inch pie plate.
3. Bake in the preheated oven for 18 minutes. Remove from oven; cool.
4. Meanwhile, in a mixing bowl, blend 1 cup whipped topping, cream cheese, and confectioners' sugar until creamy. Spread into cooled crust.
5. Whisk together pudding mix and milk. Spread over cheese layer. Spread remaining whipped topping on top. Chill 1½ hours. Top with additional pecans and chocolate syrup before serving. **Yield:** 8 servings.

Per serving: 542 calories, 6g protein, 55g carbohydrate, 35g fat, 2g fiber, 63mg cholesterol, 513mg sodium

◄ MAKE-AHEAD

Prep Time: 14 minutes

Cook Time: 18 minutes

Chill Time: 1 hour 30 minutes

Average Rating: ★★★★★

What other cooks have done:
"I added ¼ cup white sugar to the crust. I also added a teaspoon of vanilla to the cream cheese mixture. Finally, I topped the whipped cream with mini chocolate morsels. Super easy and scrumptious."

Sour Cream-Lemon Pie

Submitted by: **Michelle Davis**

"This pie is a favorite at our family gatherings. Top each slice with a dollop of whipped cream if you like. You can substitute ¼ cup cornstarch for the flour."

FAMILY FAVORITE ▶

Prep Time: 15 minutes

Cook Time: 20 minutes

Average Rating: ★★★★☆

What other cooks have done:

"I doubled the lemon zest and sour cream, increased the lemon juice to ⅔ cup, and decreased the milk to 1½ cups. Voilà! A truly flavorful lemon-sour cream pie for those of us who like things extra tart."

1	cup white sugar	1½	teaspoons lemon zest
½	cup all-purpose flour	¼	cup lemon juice
½	teaspoon salt	½	cup sour cream
2	cups milk	1	(9 inch) pie crust, baked
3	egg yolks		Whipped cream (optional)
¼	cup butter		

1. In a saucepan, combine sugar, flour, and salt. Gradually stir in milk. Cook, stirring constantly, over medium heat until thickened and bubbly. Reduce heat and cook, stirring constantly, 2 more minutes. Remove from heat.

2. Beat egg yolks slightly. Gradually stir 1 cup of milk mixture into yolks. Return yolk mixture to saucepan and bring to a gentle boil. Cook, stirring constantly, 2 more minutes. Remove from heat and stir in butter, lemon zest, and lemon juice. Fold in sour cream.

3. Pour filling into pie crust and cool. Top with whipped cream, if desired. **Yield:** 8 servings.

Per serving: 343 calories, 5g protein, 43g carbohydrate, 17g fat, 0g fiber, 106mg cholesterol, 347mg sodium

French Peach Pie

Submitted by: **Judy Richardson**

"This is an easy and impressive pie that's very good with fresh fruit."

MAKE-AHEAD ▶

Prep Time: 15 minutes

Cook Time: 5 minutes

Chill Time: 1 hour 10 minutes

Average Rating: ★★★★☆

What other cooks have done:

"I used a graham cracker crust and put sliced fresh strawberries on top of the crust before adding the pudding mixture. The strawberries were a great complement to the peaches!"

1	(16 ounce) can sliced peaches, liquid reserved	1	cup sour cream
1	(3.4 ounce) package instant vanilla pudding mix	¼	teaspoon almond extract
		1	(9 inch) pie crust, baked
1	cup milk	1	tablespoon cornstarch
		1	teaspoon lemon juice

1. Drain peaches, reserving ⅔ cup liquid. Stir together pudding mix, milk, sour cream, and almond extract for 2 minutes or until very smooth. Pour filling into pie crust. Chill for 10 minutes.

2. Arrange peach slices in a nice pattern over custard in pie shell.

3. In a small saucepan, mix together reserved peach liquid and cornstarch. Bring to a boil and cook for 2 minutes. Remove from heat and stir in lemon juice. Pour glaze over pie filling. Chill at least 1 hour. **Yield:** 8 servings.

Per serving: 268 calories, 4g protein, 32g carbohydrate, 15g fat, 1g fiber, 15mg cholesterol, 331mg sodium

Fruit Pizza with White Chocolate *(pictured on cover)*

Submitted by: **Lynisa**

"This recipe is very easy and delicious and loved by all in my town! It's a sugar cookie crust with a milky layer of white chocolate and cream cheese that's topped with your favorite fruit choices and a glaze. Use any fruit you like for the topping, and any fruit juice or juice from any canned fruits you like for the pineapple juice."

½ cup butter, softened
½ cup shortening
1½ cups white sugar
2 eggs
2¾ cups all-purpose flour
2 teaspoons cream of tartar
1 teaspoon baking soda
¼ teaspoon salt
1 (12 ounce) package white chocolate morsels
¼ cup heavy whipping cream

1 (8 ounce) package cream cheese, softened
1 pint strawberries, sliced
½ pint blueberries
½ pint blackberries
½ pint raspberries
½ cup white sugar
2 tablespoons cornstarch
1 cup pineapple juice
1 teaspoon lemon juice

◄ COMPANY IS COMING

Prep Time: 25 minutes

Cook Time: 17 minutes

Average Rating: ★★★★★

What other cooks have done:

"I used fresh pineapple, kiwi, strawberries, bananas, and fresh blueberries, and it turned out delicious. The white chocolate layer would be good as a fruit dip alone. I doubled the glaze and the white chocolate layer and made three pizzas for a school function, with three packages of sugar cookie dough as the crusts."

1. Preheat oven to 400°F (200°C). Lightly grease a large (13x15 inch) baking sheet.
2. Cream together butter, shortening, and 1½ cups sugar with an electric mixer. Beat in eggs. In a separate bowl, stir together flour, cream of tartar, baking soda, and salt. Beat flour mixture into butter mixture to form a stiff dough. Press dough into a ½ inch thick rectangle on prepared baking sheet.
3. Bake in the preheated oven for 14 minutes or until light brown. Let cool on a wire rack.
4. Meanwhile, in medium microwave-safe bowl, microwave white chocolate and whipping cream on high for 1 minute or until chips are melted and smooth after stirring. Beat in cream cheese with electric mixer until creamy. Spread on cookie crust.
5. Arrange fruit over filling. In a medium saucepan over medium heat, combine ½ cup sugar, cornstarch, pineapple juice, and lemon juice. Stir and cook until sugar dissolves and mixture thickens. Pour over fruit. Refrigerate until serving. Store leftovers in refrigerator.
Yield: 15 servings.

Per serving: 579 calories, 7g protein, 71g carbohydrate, 30g fat, 1g fiber, 68mg cholesterol, 314mg sodium

Blanca's Cherry-Cheese Tarts

Submitted by: **Blanca Castello**

"These miniature cheesecakes with graham cracker crusts and a rich cherry topping are absolutely the best. You can't have just one. It's a hit at every gathering!"

CROWD-PLEASER ▶

Prep Time: 15 minutes

Cook Time: 30 minutes

Chill Time: 30 minutes

Average Rating: ★★★★★

What other cooks have done:

"I made these for my niece's informal wedding reception, and they were a big hit! I topped them with cherry and blueberry pie fillings, and they were gobbled up. When making the crust, I melted the butter instead of cutting in cold butter—I felt it was easier, and they turned out just fine."

2	(8 ounce) packages cream cheese, softened
½	cup white sugar
2	eggs
1	teaspoon vanilla extract
1	teaspoon lemon juice
1⅛	cups graham cracker crumbs
2	tablespoons white sugar
	Pinch ground cinnamon
¼	cup butter
1	(21 ounce) can cherry pie filling

1. Preheat oven to 350°F (175°C). Line muffin pans with paper liners.
2. In a medium bowl, combine cream cheese and ½ cup sugar. Stir in eggs, vanilla, and lemon juice. Mix thoroughly.
3. Combine cracker crumbs, 2 tablespoons sugar, and cinnamon. Cut in butter until crust forms small crumbs. Put one spoonful of crust into each muffin cup and pat it down. Spoon a layer of cream cheese mixture over each crust.
4. Bake in the preheated oven for 30 minutes. Spoon cherry pie filling evenly over each tart. Let tarts chill for at least 30 minutes.
Yield: 26 servings.

Per tart: 143 calories, 2g protein, 15g carbohydrate, 9g fat, 0g fiber, 37mg cholesterol, 106mg sodium

Aussie Lime Pie

Submitted by: **Louise Griffin**

"A coconut-oatmeal cookie crust enhances the flavors of this easy lime pie."

⅔	cup rolled oats	1	teaspoon baking soda
⅔	cup flaked coconut	1	(14 ounce) can sweetened
⅔	cup all-purpose flour		condensed milk
½	cup white sugar	½	cup lime juice
½	cup butter, melted	4	egg yolks, beaten
2	tablespoons light corn syrup	2	teaspoons grated lemon zest

1. Preheat oven to 350°F (175°C). Lightly grease a 9 inch pie plate.
2. In a medium bowl, combine oats, coconut, flour, and sugar. In a separate bowl, combine melted butter, corn syrup, and baking soda until frothy. Add corn syrup mixture to oat mixture and stir until ingredients are well combined. Press mixture into bottom and up sides of pie plate.
3. In a medium mixing bowl, combine condensed milk, lime juice, egg yolks, and lemon zest. Beat at medium speed with an electric mixer for 1 minute. Pour mixture into pie crust.
4. Bake in the preheated oven for 20 minutes or until firm in center. Do not allow top to brown. Chill before serving. **Yield:** 8 servings.

Per serving: 449 calories, 8g protein, 60g carbohydrate, 21g fat, 1g fiber, 154mg cholesterol, 363mg sodium

◄ COVERED-DISH FAVORITE

Prep Time: 15 minutes

Cook Time: 20 minutes

Chill Time: 1 hour

Average Rating: ★★★★★

What other cooks have done:

"Turned out yummy! I thought the baking soda flavor came through too strongly, so I halved it the second time I made this pie, and the crust was perfect—sorta like eating a oatmeal cookie. Can't wait to experiment with other fillings, such as chocolate!"

Apple Enchilada Dessert *(pictured on page 300)*

Submitted by: **ReDonna**

"You could make this with peaches or cherries, too."

1	(21 ounce) can apple pie filling	½	cup white sugar
6	(8 inch) flour tortillas	½	cup packed brown sugar
1	teaspoon ground cinnamon	½	cup water
⅓	cup butter		Cinnamon (optional)
			Ice Cream (optional)

1. Preheat oven to 350°F (175°C). Lightly grease an 8x8 inch dish.
2. Spoon filling evenly onto tortillas and sprinkle with cinnamon. Roll up tortillas and place seam side down in prepared dish.
3. Bring butter, white sugar, brown sugar, and ½ cup water to a boil in a medium saucepan. Reduce heat and simmer, stirring constantly, for 3 minutes.
4. Pour sauce evenly over tortillas; sprinkle with extra cinnamon, if desired. Bake in the preheated oven for 20 minutes. Serve over ice cream and sprinkle with additional cinnamon, if desired. **Yield:** 6 servings.

Per enchilada: 483 calories, 5g protein, 88g carbohydrate, 14g fat, 3g fiber, 0mg cholesterol, 403mg sodium

◄ FAMILY FAVORITE

Prep Time: 7 minutes

Cook Time: 30 minutes

Average Rating: ★★★★★

What other cooks have done:

"This was very tasty, and I received many compliments for it. I added ½ cup pecans and additional cinnamon to spice up the apple pie filling. When the enchiladas were finished baking, I cut them in half, so they served 12. The portions were perfect—not too big and not too small. I highly recommend this!"

Banana-Chocolate Chip Dessert

Submitted by: **Michele O'Sullivan**

"Top with your favorite toppings; chocolate syrup and whipped cream are great!"

PARTY FOOD ▶

Prep Time: 20 minutes

Cook Time: 20 minutes

Average Rating: ★★★★★

What other cooks have done:

"This recipe is a real winner. It's a cross between a chocolate chip cookie and banana bread. I didn't have a jellyroll pan and wanted a thinner bar-type dessert, so I spread the batter on a baking sheet. I baked it for about 7 minutes less than the recipe calls for. Also, I stored the bars in between layers of parchment paper in an air-tight container to keep them from sticking together."

¾ cup butter, softened	1¾ cups all-purpose flour
⅔ cup white sugar	2 teaspoons baking powder
⅔ cup brown sugar	½ teaspoon salt
1 egg, lightly beaten	1 cup semisweet chocolate
1 teaspoon vanilla extract	chips
1 cup mashed bananas	

1. Preheat oven to 350°F (175°C). Grease and flour a 10x15 inch jellyroll pan.
2. In a large bowl, cream butter, white sugar, and brown sugar until fluffy. Beat in egg and vanilla. Fold in mashed bananas. In a separate bowl, mix flour, baking powder, and salt. Fold flour mixture into butter mixture. Stir in chocolate chips. Spread into prepared pan.
3. Bake in the preheated oven for 20 minutes or until set. Cool and cut into squares. **Yield:** 24 servings.

Per serving: 174 calories, 2g protein, 25g carbohydrate, 8g fat, 1g fiber, 24mg cholesterol, 134mg sodium

Banana Fritters

Submitted by: **Vicki G.**

"I was craving apple fritters but couldn't get to the doughnut shop. I didn't have apples, but I had some ripe bananas. That's when I came up with these. You won't be disappointed. They don't look pretty, but they taste delicious!"

KID-FRIENDLY ▶

Prep Time: 5 minutes

Cook Time: 8 minutes per batch

Average Rating: ★★★★☆

What other cooks have done:

"These were great! I tried substituting applesauce for the bananas, and my family could not get enough of them."

2 ripe bananas	1 teaspoon baking powder
2 tablespoons milk	½ teaspoon salt
2 eggs	¼ teaspoon ground cinnamon
1 tablespoon butter or margarine, melted	Pinch ground nutmeg
1 cup all-purpose flour	2 cups vegetable oil
3 tablespoons white sugar	1 cup confectioners' sugar

1. In a large bowl, mash bananas. Mix in milk, eggs, and butter until smooth. In a separate bowl, combine flour, white sugar, baking powder, salt, cinnamon, and nutmeg. Stir dry ingredients into banana mixture.
2. Heat oil to 375°F (190°C) in a deep fryer or heavy pan. Drop batter by spoonfuls into hot oil and cook, turning once, until browned, 2 to 8 minutes. Drain on paper towels and dust evenly with confectioners' sugar. **Yield:** 6 servings.

Per serving: 388 calories, 5g protein, 52g carbohydrate, 19g fat, 2g fiber, 71mg cholesterol, 280mg sodium

Sautéed Bananas

Submitted by: **Michelle**

"I got this recipe from a friend and changed it up a bit. It's very easy, and it looks fancy."

¾ cup heavy cream, divided
2 tablespoons butter, divided
3 tablespoons white sugar, divided
4 (1 ounce) squares bittersweet chocolate, chopped
4 bananas, peeled and halved lengthwise
⅓ cup dark rum

1. In a small saucepan over medium heat, combine ½ cup cream, 1 tablespoon butter, and 2 tablespoons sugar and bring to a boil. Remove from heat and stir in chopped chocolate until smooth. Set aside.

2. In a medium bowl, beat remaining ¼ cup cream with an electric mixer until stiff peaks form. Set aside.

3. In a large skillet over medium heat, melt remaining 1 tablespoon butter. Sprinkle remaining 1 tablespoon sugar evenly over surface of pan and cook until it begins to turn golden. Place bananas, cut sides down, in pan and pour rum over bananas. Continue to cook, basting with sauce, until bananas begin to soften.

4. To serve, place 2 warm banana halves on a plate. Spoon a little rum sauce over the top and drizzle with chocolate sauce. Top with whipped cream. **Yield:** 4 servings.

Per serving: 551 calories, 4g protein, 54g carbohydrate, 32g fat, 5g fiber, 78mg cholesterol, 78mg sodium

◄ COMPANY IS COMING

Prep Time: 15 minutes

Cook Time: 10 minutes

Average Rating: ★★★★★

What other cooks have done:

"I sautéed the bananas in brown sugar and cinnamon, shaved a little chocolate for a garnish on the whipped cream, and sprinkled some toasted slivered almonds on top. A definite hit."

Cherry Dessert

Submitted by: **Laurie**

"A cracker crust, a creamy middle layer, and cherry topping make this dessert a simple but wonderful treat."

1¼ cups graham cracker crumbs	½ cup white sugar
¾ cup butter or margarine, melted	Dash vanilla extract
	Dash almond extract
1 (8 ounce) package cream cheese, softened	1 cup whipping cream
	1 (12 ounce) can cherry pie filling

1. Preheat oven to 350°F (175°C). Grease a 9x9 inch baking dish.
2. In small bowl, combine graham cracker crumbs and melted butter. Stir well and press into bottom and up sides of prepared baking dish.
3. Bake in the preheated oven for 5 minutes. Cool.
4. Meanwhile, in large bowl, combine cream cheese, sugar, vanilla, and almond extract. Mix well. Beat whipping cream until stiff peaks form. Fold whipped cream into cream cheese mixture. Spread over cooled crust. Cover with pie filling. Chill until serving. **Yield:** 9 servings.

Per serving: 448 calories, 4g protein, 32g carbohydrate, 35g fat, 1g fiber, 64mg cholesterol, 336mg sodium

Lemon Lush

Submitted by: **Mrs. Kelly Z**

"A family friend shared this lemon and cream cheese dessert with me. It's a hit with my family, and I make it now for all our get-togethers."

1 cup butter, softened	2 (3.4 ounce) packages instant lemon pudding mix
2 cups all-purpose flour	3½ cups milk
2 (8 ounce) packages cream cheese, softened	1 (12 ounce) container frozen whipped topping, thawed
1 cup white sugar	

1. Preheat oven to 350°F (175°C).
2. In a medium bowl, cut butter into flour using a pastry cutter until dough forms a ball. Press into the bottom of a 9x13 inch baking dish.
3. Bake for 25 minutes in the preheated oven or until light golden. Remove from oven and cool completely.
4. In a medium bowl, beat cream cheese and sugar together until smooth. Spread evenly over the cooled crust. In a separate bowl, whisk together the lemon pudding mix and milk for 3 to 5 minutes. Spread over the cream cheese layer. Chill until set, at least 1 hour. Top with whipped topping and serve. **Yield:** 12 servings.

Per serving: 591 calories, 8g protein, 59g carbohydrate, 37g fat, 1g fiber, 88mg cholesterol, 521mg sodium

Peach Whirligigs

Submitted by: **Tally Flint**

"My mother-in-law makes this yummy dish every summer when peaches are in season. In autumn, replace the peaches with apples."

5	large fresh peaches, peeled, pitted, and sliced	2	tablespoons white sugar
2	cups water	2	tablespoons butter, melted
1¾	cups white sugar, divided	⅓	cup milk
2	tablespoons cornstarch	2	tablespoons butter, softened
1⅓	cups buttermilk baking mix	1	teaspoon ground cinnamon

1. Preheat oven to 425°F (220°C).
2. In large saucepan over medium heat, combine peaches, water, 1½ cups sugar, and cornstarch. Cook, stirring constantly, until mixture boils. Boil for 1 minute and reduce heat to low to keep warm.
3. In a large bowl, stir together baking mix, 2 tablespoons sugar, melted butter, and milk to form a soft dough. Turn out onto a floured surface and knead 8 to 10 times. Roll out into a 9 inch square.
4. Spread softened butter over dough. Combine remaining ¼ cup sugar with cinnamon; sprinkle over dough. Roll dough into a 9 inch log; cut into 6 (1½ inch) slices. Pour peach mixture into an 8x8 inch baking dish. Place dough slices, cut sides up, on top of peach mixture.
5. Bake in the preheated oven for 20 to 25 minutes or until puffed and golden. Serve warm. **Yield:** 6 servings.

Per serving: 456 calories, 2g protein, 88g carbohydrate, 11g fat, 1g fiber, 1mg cholesterol, 432mg sodium

◄ COVERED-DISH FAVORITE
Prep Time: 15 minutes
Cook Time: 30 minutes
Average Rating: ★★★★☆
What other cooks have done:
"This is a great recipe. I added a teaspoon of vanilla to the biscuit mix and used brown sugar and cinnamon instead of white sugar and cinnamon. I also added walnuts to the peach mixture when I poured it into the pan. Turned out great!"

10 minutes or less

Peach Brûlée *(pictured on page 303)*

Submitted by: **KeraKay**

"Quick and easy peach dessert. Serve with whipped cream or ice cream."

1	(15 ounce) can peach halves, drained	¼	teaspoon ground cinnamon
¼	cup packed brown sugar	¼	cup chopped pecans
			Whipped cream (optional)

1. Preheat broiler.
2. Arrange peach halves, cut sides up, in a shallow baking dish. In a small bowl, stir together the brown sugar, cinnamon, and chopped pecans. Sprinkle mixture over peaches.
3. Broil in the preheated oven 3 inches from heat for 2 to 3 minutes or until topping is browned. Serve with whipped cream, if desired.
Yield: 3 servings.

Per serving: 200 calories, 2g protein, 36g carbohydrate, 7g fat, 3g fiber, 0mg cholesterol, 13mg sodium

◄ 5 INGREDIENTS OR LESS
Prep Time: 5 minutes
Cook Time: 3 minutes
Average Rating: ★★★★☆
What other cooks have done:
"I used 4 fresh peaches instead of canned and added a tiny bit of nutmeg to the mixture. I baked at 450° for 10 to 15 minutes. Thanks for the recipe!"

Homemade Vanilla Pudding

Submitted by: **Rosemary**
"A delectable dessert. There is no substitute!"

2	cups milk	¼	teaspoon salt
½	cup white sugar	1	teaspoon vanilla extract
3	tablespoons cornstarch	1	tablespoon butter

1. In medium saucepan over medium heat, heat milk until bubbles form at edges. In a bowl, combine sugar, cornstarch, and salt. Pour into hot milk, a little at a time, stirring constantly to dissolve. Continue to cook and stir until mixture thickens enough to coat the back of a spoon. Do not boil. Remove from heat. Stir in vanilla and butter. Pour into serving dishes. Chill before serving. **Yield:** 5 servings.

Per serving: 167 calories, 3g protein, 29g carbohydrate, 4g fat, 0g fiber, 14mg cholesterol, 189mg sodium

KID-FRIENDLY ▶

Prep Time: 5 minutes

Cook Time: 20 minutes

Chill Time: 30 minutes

Average Rating: ★★★★☆

What other cooks have done:

"I put the sugar, cornstarch, and salt in my saucepan first and slowly added cold milk, stirring constantly. Then I cooked it until it thickened. No lumps!"

Chocolate Cream Pudding

Submitted by: **Mimi**
"Sugar, cornstarch, milk, and unsweetened chocolate are cooked, thickened with egg yolks, cooked some more, and then flavored with butter and vanilla."

1	cup white sugar	2	cups milk
2	tablespoons cornstarch	2	egg yolks
¼	teaspoon salt	2	tablespoons butter
2	(1 ounce) squares unsweetened chocolate, chopped	2	teaspoons vanilla extract

1. In a medium saucepan over medium heat, combine sugar, cornstarch, and salt. Stir in chocolate and milk. Cook, stirring constantly, until chocolate melts and mixture thickens. Remove from heat and stir in egg yolks. Return to heat and cook 2 more minutes. Remove from heat and stir in butter and vanilla. Chill at least 1 hour before serving. **Yield:** 6 servings.

Per serving: 286 calories, 5g protein, 43g carbohydrate, 12g fat, 2g fiber, 88mg cholesterol, 181mg sodium

CLASSIC COMFORT FOOD ▶

Prep Time: 10 minutes

Cook Time: 15 minutes

Chill Time: 1 hour

Average Rating: ★★★★☆

What other cooks have done:

"I served this cold at a dinner for 20 and got loads of compliments. Adding more chocolate made the flavor intense."

Grandma Grippin's Brown Pudding

Submitted by: **Karen Grippin Blankenship**
"The best baked pudding you have ever eaten!"

2	cups packed brown sugar	2	cups all-purpose flour
4	cups water	2	teaspoons baking powder
¼	cup butter	2	teaspoons ground
1	cup white sugar		cinnamon
½	cup butter, softened	½	cup milk

1. Preheat oven to 350°F (175°C). In a large saucepan, stir together brown sugar, water, and ¼ cup butter; bring mixture to a boil over medium heat.

2. Meanwhile, cream together white sugar and ½ cup softened butter with an electric mixer. In a separate bowl, combine flour, baking powder, and cinnamon. Blend flour mixture into butter mixture alternately with milk until smooth.

3. Pour boiling brown sugar mixture into a 9x13 inch baking dish and drop flour mixture by spoonfuls into the liquid mixture.

4. Bake in the preheated oven for 20 to 25 minutes or until set.

Yield: 10 servings.

Per serving: 460 calories, 3g protein, 83g carbohydrate, 14g fat, 1g fiber, 0mg cholesterol, 231mg sodium

◄ FAMILY FAVORITE

Prep Time: 15 minutes

Cook Time: 30 minutes

Average Rating: ★★★★★

What other cooks have done:
"This tastes less like pudding and more like drop biscuits in syrup. It was really delicious. My dough was really thick, so instead of dropping spoonfuls into the syrup, I rolled them into balls and flattened them out a little to resemble biscuits. They cooked up beautifully. I would make this again just for the biscuits!"

S'mores

Submitted by: **Star Truong**
"Quick, easy, and delicious indoor s'mores. They're messy but tasty."

5 INGREDIENTS OR LESS ▶

Prep Time: 10 minutes

Cook Time: 10 minutes

Average Rating: ★★★★☆

What other cooks have done:

"This is an incredibly easy and yummy dessert! I make my graham cracker crumbs in a food processor. Two packages in a box of graham crackers equals 3 cups of crumbs."

1	cup butter, melted	2	cups semisweet chocolate chips
⅓	cup white sugar	3	cups miniature marshmallows
3	cups graham cracker crumbs		

1. Preheat oven to 350°F (175°C). Butter a 9x13 inch baking dish.
2. In a medium bowl, combine butter, sugar, and graham cracker crumbs until well coated. Press half of crumb mixture into the bottom of prepared dish. Top with chocolate chips and marshmallows. Sprinkle remaining crumb mixture over the marshmallows and press down with a spatula.
3. Bake in the preheated oven for 10 minutes or until marshmallows are melted. Cool completely before cutting into squares. **Yield:** 24 servings.

Per square: 215 calories, 2g protein, 26g carbohydrate, 13g fat, 1g fiber, 21mg cholesterol, 151mg sodium

Butter Brickle Frozen Delight *(pictured on page 299)*

Submitted by: **Lorie**
"This dessert is a frozen winner! It can be stored in the freezer and served immediately when unexpected company arrives. It is a very rich dessert with layers of butter brickle, caramel sauce, whipped topping, and cream cheese."

MAKE-AHEAD ▶

Prep Time: 21 minutes

Cook Time: 18 minutes

Freeze Time: overnight

Average Rating: ★★★★★

What other cooks have done:

"Unreal! I made this for a dinner party, and everyone went crazy for it. No one complained about it being too sweet or rich—just cut it into smaller pieces if you're worried about that. Plus, you can't beat it for a make-ahead dessert!"

1¼	cups graham cracker crumbs	1	(8 ounce) package cream cheese, softened
⅓	cup butter, melted	1	(14 ounce) can sweetened condensed milk
¼	cup white sugar		
1	cup all-purpose flour	1	(12 ounce) container frozen whipped topping, thawed
¾	cup quick cooking oats		
¼	cup packed brown sugar	1	(12.25 ounce) jar caramel topping
½	cup butter, melted		
¾	cup chopped pecans		

1. Preheat oven to 350°F (175°C).
2. In a medium bowl, combine graham cracker crumbs, ⅓ cup melted butter, and white sugar until well mixed. Press into bottom of a 9 inch springform pan.
3. Bake in the preheated oven for 6 minutes or until set. Cool completely.
4. Increase oven temperature to 400°F (200°C).
5. In a large bowl, combine flour, oats, brown sugar, ½ cup melted butter, and pecans until well mixed. Lightly pat onto a baking sheet.

6. Bake in the preheated oven for 12 minutes or until light brown. Crumble while still hot. Cool completely.

7. In large mixing bowl, beat cream cheese until smooth. Beat in condensed milk until well blended. Fold in whipped topping.

8. Spread half of the cheese mixture over the crust in the springform pan. Sprinkle half of the oat crumbles over the cheese mixture. Spread half of the caramel sauce over oat crumbles. Repeat layers. Freeze until firm. Remove pan sides and serve dessert cold. **Yield:** 12 servings.

Per serving: 621 calories, 8g protein, 71g carbohydrate, 36g fat, 2g fiber, 66mg cholesterol, 386mg sodium

Four-Layer Delight

Submitted by: **Julie**

"This is great dessert for any time of year. You can easily change the flavor by substituting a different pudding in place of the butterscotch."

½	cup butter or margarine, softened	1	(8 ounce) container frozen whipped topping, thawed and divided
1¼	cups confectioners' sugar, divided	2	(3.4 ounce) packages instant butterscotch pudding mix
1	cup all-purpose flour	3	cups milk
1	cup chopped pecans	2	tablespoons chopped pecans
1	(8 ounce) package cream cheese, softened		

1. Preheat oven to 300°F (150°C). Coat a 9x13 inch baking dish with cooking spray.

2. In a bowl, cream together butter with ¼ cup confectioners' sugar. Mix in flour and 1 cup pecans. Press into prepared dish.

3. Bake in the preheated oven for 15 minutes or until very lightly browned. Cool completely.

4. Meanwhile, in a bowl, cream together cream cheese with remaining 1 cup confectioners' sugar. Fold in half of whipped topping. Spread over cooled crust.

5. Stir together pudding mix and milk and allow to set up slightly. Spread over cream cheese layer. Top with remaining whipped topping and sprinkle with 2 tablespoons nuts. Refrigerate until serving. **Yield:** 15 servings.

Per serving: 348 calories, 5g protein, 35g carbohydrate, 21g fat, 1g fiber, 20mg cholesterol, 337mg sodium

◄ HOLIDAY FARE

Prep Time: 20 minutes

Cook Time: 15 minutes

Average Rating: ★★★★★

What other cooks have done:

"I used chocolate pudding instead of butterscotch. To serve, I placed each portion in short, clear cups, and they were beautiful. Lots of praise when I brought out the dessert, and more after the first bite."

Pecan-Filled Cookies

Submitted by: **Laural Takashima**

"This wonderful, treasured family favorite is served at special occasions. Enjoy!"

HOLIDAY FARE ▶

Prep Time: 15 minutes

Cook Time: 11 minutes per batch

Average Rating: ★★★★★

What other cooks have done:

"This was a very good cookie that's not too sweet. These cookies do puff up, so the filling will just coat the top of the cookie instead of filling it if your indentions are not deep enough."

½	cup butter, softened	2	cups all-purpose flour
1¼	cups packed light brown sugar, divided	½	teaspoon baking soda
		¼	teaspoon salt
1	egg	½	cup chopped pecans
1	teaspoon vanilla extract	2	tablespoons sour cream

1. Preheat oven to 350°F (175°C). Grease baking sheets.
2. In a medium bowl, cream together butter and 1 cup brown sugar until smooth. Beat in egg and stir in vanilla. In a separate bowl, combine the flour, baking soda, and salt; stir into the sugar mixture. Roll the dough into 1 inch balls and place them 2 inches apart onto the prepared baking sheets. Make an indention in the center of each ball. Mix together pecans, sour cream, and remaining ¼ cup brown sugar; fill each indention with the mixture.
3. Bake in the preheated oven for 8 to 11 minutes or until light brown. Cool for a few minutes on baking sheets before removing to wire racks to cool completely. **Yield:** 2½ dozen.

Per cookie: 99 calories, 1g protein, 13g carbohydrate, 5g fat, 0g fiber, 16mg cholesterol, 77mg sodium

Pecan Sandies

Submitted by: **Mary Ann**

"Very good melt-in-your-mouth cookies. Makes a bunch."

HOLIDAY GIFT GIVING ▶

Prep Time: 15 minutes

Cook Time: 12 minutes per batch

Average Rating: ★★★★★

What other cooks have done:

"These don't spread much, so you can put a whole bunch on one cookie sheet. When rolled in white sugar, they are to die for!"

1	cup butter or margarine, softened	1	teaspoon vanilla extract
1	cup vegetable oil	4	cups all-purpose flour
1½	cups white sugar, divided	1	teaspoon baking soda
1	cup confectioners' sugar, sifted	1	teaspoon cream of tartar
		1	teaspoon salt
2	eggs	2	cups chopped pecans

1. Preheat oven to 375°F (190°C).
2. In a large bowl, cream together butter, oil, 1 cup white sugar, and confectioners' sugar until smooth. Beat in the eggs, 1 at a time. Stir in the vanilla. In a separate bowl, combine flour, baking soda, cream of tartar, and salt; stir into the creamed mixture. Mix in pecans. Roll dough into 1 inch balls and roll each ball in remaining ½ cup white sugar. Place balls 2 inches apart onto ungreased baking sheets.
3. Bake in the preheated oven for 10 to 12 minutes or until edges are golden. Remove to wire racks to cool. **Yield:** 8 dozen.

Per cookie: 92 calories, 1g protein, 9g carbohydrate, 6g fat, 0g fiber, 4mg cholesterol, 61mg sodium

Angel Crisps

Submitted by: **Paula**

"Here's a great recipe if you like sugar cookies. These are easy to make; they go fast in my house."

½	cup butter, softened	1	teaspoon vanilla extract
½	cup shortening	2	cups all-purpose flour
½	cup packed brown sugar	1	teaspoon cream of tartar
1	cup white sugar, divided	1	teaspoon baking soda
1	egg	½	teaspoon salt

1. Preheat oven to 425°F (220°C).

2. In a large bowl, cream together butter, shortening, brown sugar, and ½ cup white sugar until smooth. Beat in egg and stir in vanilla. In a separate bowl, combine flour, cream of tartar, baking soda, and salt; beat into the creamed mixture.

3. Roll dough into 1 inch balls. Dip the top half of the balls into water and then into remaining white sugar. Place balls, sugar side up, onto ungreased baking sheets. Flatten slightly.

4. Bake in the preheated oven for 8 to 10 minutes or until light brown. Cool on wire racks and store in an airtight container. **Yield:** 4 dozen.

Per cookie: 82 calories, 1g protein, 10g carbohydrate, 4g fat, 0g fiber, 10mg cholesterol, 72mg sodium

◄ **FAMILY FAVORITE**

Prep Time: 15 minutes

Cook Time: 10 minutes per batch

Average Rating: ★★★★★

What other cooks have done:

"These were definitely the best sugar cookies I've tried in a while. I added a little bit of amaretto to the batter."

Jam-Filled Butter Cookies

Submitted by: **Missi**

"This cookie recipe has been in my mother's family for more years than I've been alive. It's my favorite cookie—my comfort food!"

¾	cup butter, softened	1¾	cups all-purpose flour
½	cup white sugar	½	cup fruit preserves, any flavor
2	egg yolks		

1. Preheat oven to 375°F (190°C).

2. In a medium bowl, cream together the butter, white sugar, and egg yolks. Mix in flour a little bit at a time until a soft dough forms. Roll dough into 1 inch balls. If dough is too soft, refrigerate for 15 to 20 minutes. Place balls 2 inches apart onto ungreased baking sheets. Use your finger to make an indention in the center of each ball and fill each with ½ teaspoon of preserves.

3. Bake in the preheated oven for 8 to 10 minutes or until golden brown on the bottom. Remove to wire racks to cool. **Yield:** 3 dozen.

Per cookie: 82 calories, 1g protein, 11g carbohydrate, 4g fat, 0g fiber, 22mg cholesterol, 41mg sodium

◄ **5 INGREDIENTS OR LESS**

Prep Time: 20 minutes

Cook Time: 10 minutes per batch

Average Rating: ★★★★★

What other cooks have done:

"These cookies are buttery-sweet, and strawberry or blackberry preserves add a perfect finishing touch. They look lovely on a tray for tea-time or parties. I added a teaspoon of vanilla for an even sweeter-tasting cookie, and the results were delicious!"

Thick Cut-Outs

Submitted by: **Margo**

"A large batch of thick sugar cookies. These are the big, soft sugar cookies you have been looking for. Frost them while warm and sprinkle with colored sugar."

KID-FRIENDLY ▶

Prep Time: 17 minutes

Chill Time: 1 hour

Cook Time: 10 minutes per batch

Average Rating: ★★★★★

What other cooks have done:

"These cookies were delicious, and the dough was easy to work with! I used 1 teaspoon vanilla and ½ teaspoon almond extract in the dough. I used 6 teaspoons whipping cream for the 6 egg yolks."

2	cups butter, softened	7	cups all-purpose flour
2	cups plus 2 tablespoons white sugar	1	tablespoon baking powder
		½	teaspoon salt
4	eggs	4	cups confectioners' sugar
6	egg yolks	¼	cup vegetable oil
2½	teaspoons vanilla extract, divided	1	tablespoon hot water (or as needed)

1. In a large bowl, cream together butter and white sugar until smooth. Beat in eggs and yolks, 1 at a time, mixing after each addition. Add 1½ teaspoons vanilla. In a separate bowl, combine flour, baking powder, and salt; stir into sugar mixture. Cover dough; chill for at least 1 hour.
2. Preheat the oven to 375°F (190°C). Grease baking sheets.
3. On a floured surface, roll dough to ½ inch thickness. Cut into shapes using cookie cutters. Place 2 inches apart onto prepared baking sheets.
4. Bake in the preheated oven for 8 to 10 minutes. Cool cookies on baking sheets for 5 minutes; remove to wire racks to cool completely.
5. Mix together the confectioners' sugar, oil, and remaining 1 teaspoon vanilla until smooth. Gradually add enough hot water to achieve a spreadable consistency. Frost cookies. **Yield:** 6 dozen.

Per cookie: 148 calories, 2g protein, 21g carbohydrate, 6g fat, 0g fiber, 42mg cholesterol, 79mg sodium

Potato Chip Cookies II

Submitted by: **Barbara**

"This recipe adds pecans for extra flavor."

OUT-OF-THE-ORDINARY ▶

Prep Time: 15 minutes

Cook Time: 14 minutes per batch

Average Rating: ★★★★☆

What other cooks have done:

"A really good butter cookie with a slight crunch, this is like a crisped rice cereal candy bar. I thought it would be too salty or taste too much like potato chips, but you really don't taste the chips at all. Very easy to make."

1	cup butter, softened	1½	cups all-purpose flour
½	cup white sugar	⅔	cup crushed potato chips
1	egg yolk	1	cup chopped pecans
1	teaspoon vanilla extract		

1. Preheat oven to 350°F (175°C).
2. In a medium bowl, cream together butter and sugar until smooth. Stir in egg yolk and vanilla. Gradually stir in the flour until just blended. Mix in crushed potato chips and pecans. Drop by rounded spoonfuls onto ungreased baking sheets. Make a crisscross pattern on the top of each cookie using a fork dipped in water.
3. Bake in the preheated oven for 12 to 14 minutes or until edges are lightly browned. Cool on baking sheets. **Yield:** 2 dozen.

Per cookie: 161 calories, 2g protein, 12g carbohydrate, 12g fat, 1g fiber, 30mg cholesterol, 91mg sodium

Oatmeal-Banana-Raisin-Coconut Cookies

Submitted by: **MadameRambo**
"A new twist on an old favorite. Moist and yummy."

1¼	cups butter, softened	½	teaspoon salt
¾	cup firmly packed brown sugar	1	teaspoon ground cinnamon
½	cup white sugar	¼	teaspoon ground nutmeg
1	egg, lightly beaten	⅛	teaspoon ground cloves
1	teaspoon vanilla extract	3	cups rolled oats
1½	cups all-purpose flour	2	ripe bananas, sliced
1	teaspoon baking soda	1½	cups raisins
		1	cup flaked coconut

1. Preheat the oven to 375°F (190°C). Grease baking sheets.
2. In a large bowl, cream together the butter, brown sugar, and white sugar. Beat in the egg and vanilla. In a separate bowl, combine the flour, baking soda, salt, cinnamon, nutmeg, and cloves; stir into the creamed mixture until well blended. Stir in the oats, bananas, raisins, and coconut, 1 at a time, using a wooden spoon. Drop by rounded spoonfuls 2 inches apart onto prepared baking sheets.
3. Bake in the preheated oven for 11 to 13 minutes. Allow cookies to cool on baking sheets for 1 minute before removing to wire racks to cool completely. **Yield:** 4 dozen.

Per cookie: 124 calories, 2g protein, 17g carbohydrate, 6g fat, 1g fiber, 4mg cholesterol, 113mg sodium

◄ KID-FRIENDLY

Prep Time: 16 minutes

Cook Time: 13 minutes per batch

Average Rating: ★★★★★

What other cooks have done:

"I omitted the nutmeg and cloves. Also, I split the dough before adding the raisins and then added ½ cup raisins to one half and ½ cup chocolate chips to the other. Great recipe!"

Mississippi Tea Cakes

Submitted by: **Carol K.**
"This is my mother's recipe, which she got from her mother, and so on. My grandmother's advice is to enjoy these warm with a big glass of ice-cold milk!"

½	cup butter, softened	2	cups all-purpose flour
1	cup white sugar	1	teaspoon baking powder
1	egg	½	teaspoon baking soda
1	teaspoon vanilla extract	¼	cup buttermilk

1. Preheat oven to 350°F (175°C). Grease baking sheets.
2. In a medium bowl, cream together butter and sugar until smooth. Beat in egg and vanilla. In a separate bowl, combine flour, baking powder, and baking soda; beat into the creamed mixture alternately with the buttermilk. Drop by rounded spoonfuls onto prepared baking sheets.
3. Bake in the preheated oven for 8 to 10 minutes. Allow cookies to cool on baking sheets for 5 minutes before transferring to wire racks to cool completely. **Yield:** 3 dozen.

Per cookie: 73 calories, 1g protein, 11g carbohydrate, 3g fat, 0g fiber, 13mg cholesterol, 61mg sodium

◄ FROM THE PANTRY

Prep Time: 15 minutes

Cook Time: 10 minutes per batch

Average Rating: ★★★★★

What other cooks have done:

"I passed this recipe on to my sister to use for a dessert social, and the cookies turned out great! She had to bake a second batch for the guests, since we couldn't stop eating them fresh out of the oven. Try adding ¼ teaspoon of nutmeg for an extra kick of flavor."

White Chocolate-Chocolate Cookies

Submitted by: **Amy Woodruff**

"This is a reverse chocolate chip cookie—rich dark chocolate with white chocolate chips."

HOLIDAY GIFT GIVING ▶

Prep Time: 15 minutes

Cook Time: 10 minutes per batch

Average Rating: ★★★★★

What other cooks have done:

"Don't bake them for a second more than the recipe says; the cookies harden within a few minutes of cooling. These have the perfect texture and flavor—not too chewy but not too hard and with just the right amount of sweetness."

1	cup unsalted butter, softened	1¾	cups all-purpose flour
1	cup white sugar	2	teaspoons baking soda
¾	cup packed brown sugar	2	cups white chocolate chips
2	eggs		
1¼	cups unsweetened cocoa powder		

1. Preheat oven to 350°F (175°C). Grease baking sheets.
2. In a large bowl, cream together butter, white sugar, and brown sugar until light and fluffy. Add the eggs, 1 at a time, beating well after each addition. In a separate bowl, combine cocoa, flour, and baking soda; gradually stir into the creamed mixture. Fold in white chocolate chips. Drop by rounded spoonfuls onto prepared baking sheets.
3. Bake in the preheated oven for 8 to 10 minutes or until puffy but still soft. Allow cookies to cool on baking sheets for 5 minutes before removing to wire racks to cool completely. **Yield:** 3 dozen.

Per cookie: 171 calories, 2g protein, 22g carbohydrate, 9g fat, 1g fiber, 28mg cholesterol, 86mg sodium

Aunt Cora's World's Greatest Cookies

Submitted by: **Mary Hays**

"This is my Aunt Cora's recipe for the world's best chocolate chip-peanut butter cookies!"

CLASSIC COMFORT FOOD ▶

Prep Time: 15 minutes

Cook Time: 15 minutes per batch

Average Rating: ★★★★★

What other cooks have done:

"This is really a great cookie recipe! I added ¼ teaspoon salt and 1 teaspoon vanilla. They had a nice, delicate texture. Everyone loved them."

1	cup butter or margarine, softened	2	cups unbleached all-purpose flour
1	cup peanut butter	1	teaspoon baking soda
1	cup white sugar	2	cups semisweet chocolate chips
1	cup packed brown sugar		
2	eggs		

1. Preheat oven to 325°F (165°C).
2. In a large bowl, cream together butter, peanut butter, white sugar, and brown sugar until smooth. Beat in the eggs, 1 at a time, mixing well after each addition. In a separate bowl, combine flour and baking soda; stir into peanut butter mixture. Mix in chocolate chips. Drop by heaping spoonfuls onto ungreased baking sheets.
3. Bake in the preheated oven for 12 to 15 minutes or until lightly browned at the edges. Cool cookies on baking sheets for 1 minute before removing to wire racks to cool completely. **Yield:** 4 dozen.

Per cookie: 154 calories, 3g protein, 18g carbohydrate, 9g fat, 1g fiber, 9mg cholesterol, 100mg sodium

Macadamia Nut-Chocolate Chip Cookies

Submitted by: **Bev**

"Drop cookies with macadamia nuts and chocolate chips make delicious, crunchy treats for your family or gifts for your friends."

½	cup butter, softened	½	teaspoon baking soda
⅓	cup packed dark brown sugar	½	teaspoon salt
⅓	cup white sugar	1	cup macadamia nuts, chopped
1	egg	1¼	cups semisweet chocolate chips
1	teaspoon vanilla extract		
1⅛	cups sifted all-purpose flour		

1. Preheat oven to 375°F (190°C).
2. Cream butter, brown sugar, and white sugar together in a large bowl. Beat in the egg and vanilla until well blended. In a separate bowl, sift together flour, baking soda, and salt; gradually blend into the creamed mixture. Stir in chopped macadamia nuts and chocolate chips. Drop by rounded teaspoonfuls 2 inches apart onto baking sheets.
3. Bake in the preheated oven for 10 to 12 minutes or until the cookies are golden brown. Remove to wire racks to cool. **Yield:** 3 dozen.

Per cookie: 109 calories, 1g protein, 11g carbohydrate, 7g fat, 1g fiber, 13mg cholesterol, 79mg sodium

◄ HOLIDAY GIFT GIVING

Prep Time: 15 minutes

Cook Time: 12 minutes per batch

Average Rating: ★★★★★

What other cooks have done:

"I tried this recipe the other day, but I used white chocolate chips instead of semisweet chocolate. The cookie was awesome."

Pumpkin-Chocolate Chip Cookies I

Submitted by: **Beth**

"Try this unique combination of nuts, chocolate, spices, and pumpkin."

½	cup shortening	1	teaspoon salt
1½	cups white sugar	1	teaspoon ground nutmeg
1	egg	1	teaspoon ground cinnamon
1	cup canned pumpkin	½	cup chopped walnuts (optional)
1	teaspoon vanilla extract	1	cup semisweet chocolate chips
2½	cups all-purpose flour		
1	teaspoon baking powder		
1	teaspoon baking soda		

1. Preheat oven to 350°F (175°C). Grease baking sheets.
2. In a large bowl, cream together shortening and sugar until light and fluffy. Beat in egg. Stir in pumpkin and vanilla. In a separate bowl, combine flour, baking powder, baking soda, salt, nutmeg, and cinnamon; gradually stir into creamed mixture. Add walnuts, if desired, and chocolate chips. Drop dough by teaspoonfuls onto prepared baking sheets.
3. Bake in the preheated oven for 15 minutes or until light brown. Cool on wire racks. **Yield:** 4 dozen.

Per cookie: 96 calories, 1g protein, 14g carbohydrate, 4g fat, 1g fiber, 4mg cholesterol, 99mg sodium

◄ HOLIDAY FARE

Prep Time: 15 minutes

Cook Time: 15 minutes per batch

Average Rating: ★★★★★

What other cooks have done:

"I've made these cookies many times and like to experiment with the ingredients. Adding 1 teaspoon of pumpkin pie spice brings out the pumpkin flavor. A little extra cinnamon is another favorite addition of mine. I added applesauce in place of the shortening to lower the fat, and the cookies turned out soft and chewy."

Dishpan Cookies II

Submitted by: **Laura and Tammy**

"These cookies have a little of everything in them, except for a dishpan."

FAMILY FAVORITE ▶

Prep Time: 15 minutes

Cook Time: 10 minutes per batch

Average Rating: ★★★★★

What other cooks have done:

"Good and a little different from your average cookie. I used half chocolate chips and half butterscotch chips and really liked the flavor."

2	cups butter, softened	1	teaspoon salt
2	cups packed brown sugar	4	cups cornflakes cereal
2	cups white sugar	1½	cups rolled oats
4	eggs	2	cups flaked coconut
4	cups all-purpose flour	3	cups semisweet chocolate
2	teaspoons baking soda		chips
1	teaspoon baking powder		

1. Preheat oven to 350°F (175°C).

2. In a large bowl, cream together butter, brown sugar, and white sugar until smooth. Beat in eggs, 1 at a time, mixing well after each addition. In a separate bowl, sift together flour, baking soda, baking powder, and salt; stir into the creamed mixture until just blended. Mix in cornflakes cereal, rolled oats, coconut, and chocolate chips. Drop by heaping spoonfuls onto ungreased baking sheets.

3. Bake in the preheated oven for 8 to 10 minutes or until edges are lightly browned. Cool on wire racks. **Yield:** 6 dozen.

Per cookie: 174 calories, 2g protein, 25g carbohydrate, 8g fat, 1g fiber, 12mg cholesterol, 161mg sodium

Cranberry-Pumpkin Cookies

Submitted by: **Lucy Randall**

"Soft, cakelike cookies."

HOLIDAY FARE ▶

Prep Time: 20 minutes

Cook Time: 12 minutes per batch

Average Rating: ★★★★★

What other cooks have done:

"These were a huge hit! If you have a major sweet tooth, you may want to substitute sweetened dried cranberries for fresh. But most will appreciate the sweet-tart combo of the pumpkin and cranberries. My mother brought a batch of these to her workplace, and before lunchtime, I had a call asking if there were any more!"

½	cup butter, softened	1	teaspoon baking soda
1	cup white sugar	½	teaspoon salt
1	teaspoon vanilla extract	1	teaspoon ground cinnamon
1	egg	1	cup cranberries, halved
1	cup packed pumpkin puree	1	tablespoon orange zest
2¼	cups all-purpose flour	½	cup chopped walnuts
2	teaspoons baking powder		

1. Preheat oven to 375°F (190°C). Grease baking sheets.

2. In a large mixing bowl, cream butter and sugar until light and fluffy. Beat in vanilla, egg, and pumpkin. In a separate bowl, sift together the flour, baking powder, baking soda, salt, and cinnamon; stir into mixture until well blended. Stir in cranberries, orange zest, and walnuts. Drop by teaspoonfuls onto prepared baking sheets.

3. Bake in the preheated oven for 10 to 12 minutes. Cool on wire racks. **Yield:** 3 dozen.

Per cookie: 90 calories, 1g protein, 13g carbohydrate, 4g fat, 1g fiber, 13mg cholesterol, 139mg sodium

Cashew Cookies

Submitted by: **Amy Gjerdingen**

"Soft sour cream cookies with cashews and buttery frosting. These cookies immediately disappear after you make them. Try them—you'll fall in love!"

½	cup butter, softened	¾	teaspoon baking powder
1	cup brown sugar	¾	teaspoon baking soda
1	egg	¼	teaspoon salt
⅓	cup sour cream	1¾	cups chopped cashews
2	teaspoons vanilla extract, divided	½	cup butter
2	cups all-purpose flour	3	tablespoons heavy cream
		2	cups confectioners' sugar

1. Preheat oven to 350°F (175°C). Grease baking sheets.
2. In a large bowl, cream together ½ cup softened butter and brown sugar until light and fluffy. Add the egg, beating well. Stir in the sour cream and 1 teaspoon vanilla. In a separate bowl, combine the flour, baking powder, baking soda, and salt; gradually stir into the creamed mixture. Fold in cashew pieces. Drop by rounded spoonfuls onto prepared baking sheets.
3. Bake in the preheated oven for 12 to 15 minutes. Allow cookies to cool on baking sheets for 5 minutes before removing to wire racks to cool completely.
4. Meanwhile, melt ½ cup butter in a saucepan over medium heat. Cook until butter turns a light brown color, being careful not to burn it. Remove from heat and stir in the cream. Gradually beat in the confectioners' sugar and remaining 1 teaspoon vanilla until smooth. Spread onto cooled cookies. **Yield:** 3 dozen.

Per cookie: 161 calories, 2g protein, 18g carbohydrate, 9g fat, 0g fiber, 22mg cholesterol, 152mg sodium

◄ PARTY FOOD

Prep Time: 20 minutes

Cook Time: 15 minutes per batch

Average Rating: ★★★★★

What other cooks have done:

"Very good cookie. It has a delicious buttery taste. I chopped the cashews with my food processor, being careful not to chop them too much. These would make a good cookie for holiday baking, as I consider them to be a special treat."

Italian Cookies II

Submitted by: **Pam**

"This delicious, moist cookie is a favorite of ours. You'll love it."

AROUND-THE-WORLD CUISINE ▶

Prep Time: 20 minutes

Cook Time: 10 minutes per batch

Average Rating: ★★★★★

What other cooks have done:

"This is the perfect recipe to use up extra ricotta. The cookies are so moist and light. I ran out of vanilla before making the frosting, so I added about a teaspoon of lemon extract to cut the sweetness a little bit, and they came out great."

½	cup butter, softened	½	teaspoon baking soda
1	cup white sugar	¼	teaspoon salt
2	eggs	2	tablespoons butter, softened
1	teaspoon vanilla extract	2	cups confectioners' sugar
8	ounces ricotta cheese	¼	teaspoon vanilla extract
2	cups all-purpose flour	1½	tablespoons milk

1. Preheat oven to 350°F (175°C). Grease baking sheets.

2. In a medium bowl, cream together ½ cup butter and white sugar until smooth. Beat in the eggs, 1 at a time. Stir in 1 teaspoon vanilla and ricotta cheese. In a separate bowl, combine the flour, baking soda, and salt; gradually stir into the cheese mixture. Drop by rounded teaspoonfuls 2 inches apart onto prepared baking sheets.

3. Bake in the preheated oven for 8 to 10 minutes or until edges are golden. Allow cookies to cool on baking sheet for 5 minutes before removing to wire racks to cool completely.

4. Meanwhile, in a medium bowl, cream together 2 tablespoons butter and confectioners' sugar. Gradually beat in ¼ teaspoon vanilla and milk until a spreadable consistency is reached. Frost cooled cookies. **Yield:** 3 dozen.

Per cookie: 115 calories, 2g protein, 18g carbohydrate, 4g fat, 0g fiber, 22mg cholesterol, 78mg sodium

Zeppole

Submitted by: **Arvilla**

"Delicious fried cookies made with ricotta cheese. These are also known as Italian doughnuts."

FAMILY FAVORITE ▶

Prep Time: 15 minutes

Cook Time: 4 minutes per batch

Average Rating: ★★★★★

What other cooks have done:

"This is a great recipe for zeppole. I add at least a tablespoon of sugar to the mix to sweeten it up a little."

4	cups vegetable oil	2	eggs, lightly beaten
1	cup all-purpose flour	1	cup ricotta cheese
2	teaspoons baking powder	¼	teaspoon vanilla extract
	Pinch salt	½	cup confectioners' sugar
1½	teaspoons white sugar		

1. Heat oil in a deep fryer to 375°F (190°C).

2. In a medium saucepan, combine the flour, baking powder, salt, and white sugar. Stir in eggs, ricotta cheese, and vanilla. Mix gently over low heat until combined. Batter will be sticky.

3. Drop by tablespoonfuls into the hot oil, a few at a time. Fry until golden brown, about 3 to 4 minutes. Drain and dust with confectioners' sugar. Serve warm. **Yield:** 3 dozen.

Per cookie: 79 calories, 2g protein, 5g carbohydrate, 6g fat, 0g fiber, 14mg cholesterol, 38mg sodium

Zucchini Cookies

Submitted by: **Marian**

"These are moist, spicy cookies!"

½	cup butter or margarine, softened	1	teaspoon baking soda
1	cup white sugar	½	teaspoon salt
1	egg	1	teaspoon ground cinnamon
1	cup grated zucchini	½	teaspoon ground cloves
2	cups all-purpose flour	1	cup raisins

1. In a medium bowl, cream together butter and sugar until smooth. Beat in the egg; stir in zucchini. Combine flour, baking soda, salt, cinnamon, and cloves; stir into zucchini mixture. Mix in raisins. Cover dough and chill for at least 1 hour or overnight.
2. Preheat oven to 375°F (190°C). Grease baking sheets.
3. Drop dough by teaspoonfuls 2 inches apart onto prepared baking sheets.
4. Bake in the preheated oven for 8 to 10 minutes or until set. Allow cookies to cool slightly on baking sheets before removing to wire racks to cool completely. **Yield:** 3 dozen.

Per cookie: 81 calories, 1g protein, 13g carbohydrate, 3g fat, 0g fiber, 6mg cholesterol, 99mg sodium

◄ **FREEZER FRESH**

Prep Time: 15 minutes

Chill Time: 1 hour

Cook Time: 10 minutes per batch

Average Rating: ★★★★★

What other cooks have done:

"Be careful not to overbake. Take them out when they still look slightly doughy in the center. They also freeze very well. No one will know these have zucchini in them!"

Chewiest Brownies *(pictured on page 303)*

Submitted by: **Kristin Pan**

"These rich chocolate chewy brownies are not cakelike at all! Serve with ice cream and chocolate syrup, if desired."

1	cup unsweetened cocoa powder	¼	teaspoon salt
½	cup melted butter	1	cup all-purpose flour
2	cups white sugar	2	teaspoons vanilla extract
2	eggs	⅓	cup confectioners' sugar (optional)

1. Preheat oven to 300°F (150°C). Line an 8x8 inch square pan with greased parchment paper.
2. Combine the cocoa, melted butter, white sugar, eggs, salt, flour, and vanilla. Mix until well combined. Batter should be very thick and sticky. Spread mixture into prepared pan.
3. Bake in the preheated oven for 30 minutes. Cool completely before cutting into squares. Dust with confectioners' sugar, if desired. **Yield:** 2 dozen.

Per brownie: 139 calories, 2g protein, 24g carbohydrate, 5g fat, 1g fiber, 28mg cholesterol, 70mg sodium

◄ **CLASSIC COMFORT FOOD**

Prep Time: 10 minutes

Cook Time: 30 minutes

Average Rating: ★★★★★

What other cooks have done:

"These were really chewy. I changed the cocoa to ¾ cup, added 2 tablespoons of oil, and decreased the sugar to 1½ cups. Then I added chocolate chips and marshmallows for fun. They turned out moist, chewy, and very tasty."

Peanut Butter Fingers

Submitted by: **Mandy**

"These are soft and slightly chewy with a light peanut butter topping. My mom always made these when we were little."

KID-FRIENDLY ▶

Prep Time: 15 minutes

Cook Time: 25 minutes

Stand Time: 5 minutes

Average Rating: ★★★★★

What other cooks have done:

"I've been looking long and hard for this recipe and am so happy I found it. These were easy to make and tasted delicious! I like to substitute chocolate frosting for melted chocolate chips."

½	cup butter, softened	¼	teaspoon salt
½	cup white sugar	1	cup rolled oats
½	cup packed brown sugar	1	cup semisweet chocolate chips
1	egg		
⅓	cup peanut butter	½	cup confectioners' sugar
½	teaspoon vanilla extract	¼	cup peanut butter
1	cup all-purpose flour	3	tablespoons milk
½	teaspoon baking soda		

1. Preheat the oven to 325°F (165°C). Grease a 9x13 inch pan.
2. In a large bowl, cream together butter, white sugar, and brown sugar until smooth. Beat in egg, ⅓ cup peanut butter, and vanilla. In a separate bowl, combine flour, baking soda, and salt; stir into peanut butter mixture. Mix in rolled oats. Spread dough evenly into prepared pan.
3. Bake in the preheated oven for 20 to 25 minutes or until edges are firm. Remove from oven and sprinkle with chocolate chips. Let stand for 5 minutes. Spread melted chips to cover. Cool. In a small bowl, mix confectioners' sugar and ¼ cup peanut butter until smooth. Stir in milk, 1 tablespoon at a time, until drizzling consistency. Drizzle over dessert when cool. Cut into bars. **Yield:** 2 dozen.

Per bar: 184 calories, 3g protein, 23g carbohydrate, 10g fat, 1g fiber, 19mg cholesterol, 125mg sodium

Chocolate Scotcheroos

Submitted by: **Debbie**

"A very sweet bar cookie that can be made with crispy rice cereal."

FAMILY FAVORITE ▶

Prep Time: 15 minutes

Cook Time: 5 minutes

Chill Time: 30 minutes

Average Rating: ★★★★★

What other cooks have done:

"Very sweet and tasty. Probably my favorite use for butterscotch chips. I line the pan with a piece of buttered wax paper, press the cereal mixture into the pan, and use a pizza cutter to cut the bars when the mixture has cooled."

1	cup white sugar	1	cup semisweet chocolate chips
1	cup light corn syrup		
1	cup peanut butter	1	cup butterscotch chips
6	cups crispy rice cereal		

1. Butter a 9x13 inch pan.
2. In a saucepan over medium heat, combine sugar and corn syrup and bring to a rolling boil. Remove from heat and stir in peanut butter. Mix in rice cereal until evenly coated. Press mixture into prepared pan.
3. Melt chocolate and butterscotch chips in the microwave on high, stirring occasionally, until smooth and well blended. Spread over the top of the dessert. Chill for 30 minutes or until set. Cut into bars. **Yield:** 4 dozen.

Per bar: 118 calories, 2g protein, 18g carbohydrate, 5g fat, 1g fiber, 0mg cholesterol, 63mg sodium

Applesauce Bars

Submitted by: **Debbi Borsick**

"Moist and spicy bar cookies with frosting. An easy and quick afterschool snack. You can also sprinkle with confectioners' sugar instead of frosting."

¼	cup butter or margarine, softened	½	teaspoon salt
⅔	cup brown sugar	1	teaspoon pumpkin pie spice
1	egg	1½	cups confectioners' sugar
1	cup applesauce	3	tablespoons butter or margarine, melted
1	cup all-purpose flour	1	tablespoon milk
1	teaspoon baking soda	1	teaspoon vanilla extract

1. Preheat the oven to 350°F (175°C). Grease a 9x13 inch pan.
2. In a medium bowl, mix together butter, brown sugar, and egg until smooth. Stir in applesauce. In a separate bowl, combine flour, baking soda, salt, and pumpkin pie spice; stir into the applesauce mixture until well blended. Spread evenly into prepared pan.
3. Bake in the preheated oven for 25 minutes or until edges are golden. Cool in pan on a wire rack.
4. Meanwhile, in a medium bowl, mix together the confectioners' sugar and butter. Stir in milk and vanilla until smooth. Spread over cooled dessert and cut into bars. **Yield:** 20 servings.

Per bar: 135 calories, 1g protein, 24g carbohydrate, 4g fat, 0g fiber, 17mg cholesterol, 173mg sodium

◄ **HOLIDAY FARE**

Prep Time: 20 minutes

Cook Time: 25 minutes

Average Rating: ★★★★

What other cooks have done:

"This simple recipe is easy and delicious. I don't keep pumpkin pie spice on hand, so I substituted ½ teaspoon cinnamon, ¼ teaspoon nutmeg, and ¼ teaspoon cloves."

Ga Ga Clusters

Submitted by: **Saundra**

"Kids really love these peanut-chocolate candies."

1	(12 ounce) package semisweet chocolate chips	1	(16 ounce) package miniature marshmallows
1	(14 ounce) can sweetened condensed milk	2	cups dry-roasted peanuts

1. Lightly grease a 9x13 inch baking dish. In a medium saucepan over low heat, combine chocolate chips and milk; stir until chips are melted and mixture is smooth. Meanwhile, combine marshmallows and peanuts in a large bowl.
2. Pour melted chocolate mixture over marshmallows and nuts; mix together. Pour mixture into prepared dish. Cover and chill for 2 hours before cutting into bars. **Yield:** 1 dozen.

Per bar: 500 calories, 10g protein, 71g carbohydrate, 23g fat, 4g fiber, 11mg cholesterol, 260mg sodium

◄ **MAKE-AHEAD**

Prep Time: 5 minutes

Cook Time: 5 minutes

Chill Time: 2 hours

Average Rating: ★★★★★

What other cooks have done:

"These are just as good with milk chocolate chips. Instead of pouring into a dish, I dropped the batter by spoonfuls onto wax paper to set. Delicious!"

Chinese New Year Chocolate Candy

Submitted by: **Sam**
"An easy recipe to make!"

KID-FRIENDLY ▶

Prep Time: 5 minutes

Cook Time: 5 minutes

Chill Time: 30 minutes

Average Rating: ★★★★★

What other cooks have done:

"Since we really enjoy our chocolate and butterscotch in separate doses, I made mine with just the chocolate chips and added raisins, mini marshmallows, and toasted slivered almonds."

| 2 | cups semisweet chocolate chips | 2½ | cups dry-roasted peanuts |
| 2 | cups butterscotch chips | 4 | cups chow mein noodles |

1. Butter a 9x13 inch baking dish.
2. Melt chocolate and butterscotch chips in the top of a double boiler over simmering water. Remove from heat and stir in peanuts. Stir in noodles until well coated. Press into prepared dish. Chill for 30 minutes or until set; cut into squares. **Yield:** 2 dozen.

Per square: 276 calories, 5g protein, 26g carbohydrate, 18g fat, 2g fiber, 0mg cholesterol, 51mg sodium

Peanut Butter Cups

Submitted by: **Pam**
"These are a snap to make. They taste just like the ones from the store, if not better! They'll be gone in minutes."

HOLIDAY GIFT GIVING ▶

Prep Time: 10 minutes

Cook Time: 5 minutes

Chill Time: 30 minutes

Average Rating: ★★★★☆

What other cooks have done:

"I let each layer harden in the fridge before adding the next. I preferred the flavor of milk chocolate chips. Don't add too much peanut butter, or it will be like eating a huge spoonful of peanut butter."

| 1 | cup semisweet chocolate chips | 1 | tablespoon vegetable oil |
| ¼ | cup butter | ¼ | cup peanut butter |

1. Spray 12 mini muffin cups with cooking spray. In a microwave-safe bowl, microwave chocolate with butter and oil on high, stirring often, until melted, 1 to 2 minutes. Pour about a tablespoon of the chocolate mixture into each muffin cup.
2. Melt peanut butter in the microwave on high for 30 to 40 seconds. Spoon about 1 teaspoon of melted peanut butter over chocolate in each muffin cup. Top each cup with another tablespoon of chocolate.
3. Chill for 30 minutes or until set. **Yield:** 1 dozen.

Per cup: 143 calories, 2g protein, 10g carbohydrate, 12g fat, 1g fiber, 10mg cholesterol, 66mg sodium

Crispy Marshmallow Balls

Submitted by: **Fruger**

"These are yummy. I only make them around Christmas, so they are a real treat for the whole family. They are also easy to make."

4	cups crispy rice cereal	30	individually wrapped
1	(14 ounce) can sweetened		caramels, unwrapped
	condensed milk	1	(16 ounce) package large
1	cup butter or margarine		marshmallows

1. Pour rice cereal into a shallow dish or bowl.

2. In a double boiler, combine condensed milk, butter, and caramels. Cook, stirring constantly, over simmering water until melted and smooth.

3. Using tongs or 2 forks, dip marshmallows, 1 at a time, into caramel mixture and roll in rice cereal. Place on wax paper until set. **Yield:** 4 dozen.

Per candy: 123 calories, 1g protein, 19g carbohydrate, 5g fat, 0g fiber, 3mg cholesterol, 91mg sodium

◄ KID-FRIENDLY

Prep Time: 20 minutes

Cook Time: 10 minutes

Average Rating: ★★★★☆

What other cooks have done:

"This recipe was excellent! My family loved them! I used mini bamboo skewers, and it wasn't messy at all. I rolled half of them in toasted coconut. My hubby and his mom love coconut, and they really enjoyed this variation. Highly recommended recipe!"

Microwave Pralines

Submitted by: **Mary**

"Brown sugar, cream, salt, butter, pecans, and vanilla are microwaved and dropped onto wax paper to cool into bite-sized pralines."

1½	cups packed brown sugar	1½	cups pecan halves
⅔	cup heavy cream	1	teaspoon vanilla extract
⅛	teaspoon salt		
2	tablespoons butter or		
	margarine		

1. In a large microwave-safe bowl, combine sugar, cream, salt, butter, and pecans. Microwave on high 9 minutes, stirring once. Let stand for 1 minute. Stir in vanilla and continue to stir for 3 more minutes. Drop by teaspoonfuls onto buttered wax paper. (If mixture is too thin, allow to cool 30 seconds more and try again.) **Yield:** 3 dozen.

Per candy: 86 calories, 1g protein, 10g carbohydrate, 5g fat, 0g fiber, 6mg cholesterol, 20mg sodium

◄ HOLIDAY GIFT GIVING

Prep Time: 9 minutes

Cook Time: 9 minutes

Average Rating: ★★★★☆

What other cooks have done:

"I used half-and-half by mistake, and they turned out beautifully. I would coarsely chop the pecans next time so they are easier for the kids to eat, but overall, these are our new Christmas favorites!"

Metric Equivalents

The recipes that appear in this cookbook use the standard United States method for measuring liquid and dry or solid ingredients (teaspoons, tablespoons, and cups). The information on this chart is provided to help cooks outside the U.S. successfully use these recipes. All equivalents are approximate.

METRIC EQUIVALENTS FOR DIFFERENT TYPES OF INGREDIENTS

A standard cup measure of a dry or solid ingredient will vary in weight depending on the type of ingredient. A standard cup of liquid is the same volume for any type of liquid. Use the following chart when converting standard cup measures to grams (weight) or milliliters (volume).

Standard Cup	Fine Powder	Grain	Granular	Liquid Solids	Liquid
	(ex. flour)	(ex. rice)	(ex. sugar)	(ex. butter)	(ex. milk)
1	140 g	150 g	190 g	200 g	240 ml
¾	105 g	113 g	143 g	150 g	180 ml
⅔	93 g	100 g	125 g	133 g	160 ml
½	70 g	75 g	95 g	100 g	120 ml
⅓	47 g	50 g	63 g	67 g	80 ml
¼	35 g	38 g	48 g	50 g	60 ml
⅛	18 g	19 g	24 g	25 g	30 ml

USEFUL EQUIVALENTS FOR DRY INGREDIENTS BY WEIGHT

(To convert ounces to grams, multiply the number of ounces by 30.)

1 oz	=	¹⁄₁₆ lb	=	30 g
4 oz	=	¼ lb	=	120 g
8 oz	=	½ lb	=	240 g
12 oz	=	¾ lb	=	360 g
16 oz	=	1 lb	=	480 g

USEFUL EQUIVALENTS FOR LENGTH

(To convert inches to centimeters, multiply the number of inches by 2.5.)

1 in					=	2.5 cm			
6 in	=	½ ft			=	15 cm			
12 in	=	1 ft			=	30 cm			
36 in	=	3 ft	=	1 yd	=	90 cm			
40 in					=	100 cm	=	1 m	

USEFUL EQUIVALENTS FOR LIQUID INGREDIENTS BY VOLUME

¼ tsp						=	1 ml		
½ tsp						=	2 ml		
1 tsp						=	5 ml		
3 tsp	=	1 tbls			=	½ fl oz	=	15 ml	
		2 tbls	=	⅛ cup	=	1 fl oz	=	30 ml	
		4 tbls	=	¼ cup	=	2 fl oz	=	60 ml	
		5⅓ tbls	=	⅓ cup	=	3 fl oz	=	80 ml	
		8 tbls	=	½ cup	=	4 fl oz	=	120 ml	
		10⅔ tbls	=	⅔ cup	=	5 fl oz	=	160 ml	
		12 tbls	=	¾ cup	=	6 fl oz	=	180 ml	
		16 tbls	=	1 cup	=	8 fl oz	=	240 ml	
		1 pt	=	2 cups	=	16 fl oz	=	480 ml	
		1 qt	=	4 cups	=	32 fl oz	=	960 ml	
						33 fl oz	=	1000 ml	= 1 liter

USEFUL EQUIVALENTS FOR COOKING/OVEN TEMPERATURES

	Fahrenheit	Celsius	Gas Mark
Freeze Water	32° F	0° C	
Room Temperature	68° F	20° C	
Boil Water	212° F	100° C	
Bake	325° F	165° C	3
	350° F	175° C	4
	375° F	190° C	5
	400° F	200° C	6
	425° F	220° C	7
	450° F	230° C	8
Broil			Grill

Common Substitutions

Ingredient	Amount	Substitution
Allspice	1 teaspoon	• ½ teaspoon ground cinnamon, ¼ teaspoon ground ginger, and ¼ teaspoon ground cloves
Arrowroot starch	1 teaspoon	• 1 tablespoon flour OR 1 teaspoon cornstarch
Baking powder	1 teaspoon	• ¼ teaspoon baking soda plus ½ teaspoon cream of tartar OR ¼ teaspoon baking soda plus ½ cup buttermilk (decrease liquid in recipe by ½ cup)
Beer	1 cup	• 1 cup nonalcoholic beer OR 1 cup chicken broth
Brandy	¼ cup	• 1 teaspoon imitation brandy extract plus enough water to make ¼ cup
Breadcrumbs	1 cup	• 1 cup cracker crumbs OR 1 cup matzo meal OR 1 cup ground oats
Broth (beef or chicken)	1 cup	• 1 bouillon cube plus 1 cup boiling water OR 1 tablespoon soy sauce plus enough water to make 1 cup OR 1 cup vegetable broth
Brown sugar	1 cup, packed	• 1 cup white sugar plus ¼ cup molasses and decrease the liquid in recipe by ¼ cup OR 1 cup white sugar OR 1¼ cups confectioners' sugar
Butter (salted)	1 cup	• 1 cup margarine OR 1 cup shortening plus ½ teaspoon salt OR ⅞ cup vegetable oil plus ½ teaspoon salt OR ⅞ cup lard plus ½ teaspoon salt
Butter (unsalted)	1 cup	• 1 cup shortening OR ⅞ cup vegetable oil OR ⅞ cup lard
Buttermilk	1 cup	• 1 cup yogurt OR 1 tablespoon lemon juice or vinegar plus enough milk to make 1 cup
Cheddar cheese	1 cup, shredded	• 1 cup shredded Colby Cheddar OR 1 cup shredded Monterey Jack cheese
Chervil	1 tablespoon, fresh	• 1 tablespoon fresh parsley
Chicken base	1 tablespoon	• 1 cup canned or homemade chicken broth or stock. Reduce liquid in recipe by 1 cup.
Chocolate (semisweet)	1 ounce	• 1 (1 ounce) square of unsweetened chocolate plus 4 teaspoons sugar OR 1 ounce semisweet chocolate chips plus 1 teaspoon shortening
Chocolate (unsweetened)	1 ounce	• 3 tablespoons unsweetened cocoa plus 1 tablespoon shortening or vegetable oil
Cocoa	¼ cup	• 1 (1 ounce) square unsweetened chocolate
Corn syrup	1 cup	• 1¼ cup white sugar plus ⅓ cup water OR 1 cup honey OR 1 cup light treacle syrup
Cottage cheese	1 cup	• 1 cup farmers cheese OR 1 cup ricotta cheese
Cracker crumbs	1 cup	• 1 cup breadcrumbs OR 1 cup matzo meal OR 1 cup ground oats
Cream (half-and-half)	1 cup	• ⅞ cup milk plus 1 tablespoon butter
Cream (heavy)	1 cup	• 1 cup evaporated milk OR ¾ cup milk plus ⅓ cup butter

Ingredient	Amount	Substitution
Cream (light)	1 cup	•1 cup evaporated milk OR ¾ cup milk plus 3 tablespoons butter
Cream (whipped)	1 cup	•1 cup frozen whipped topping, thawed
Cream cheese	1 cup	•1 cup pureed cottage cheese OR 1 cup plain yogurt, strained overnight in cheesecloth
Cream of tartar	1 teaspoon	•2 teaspoons lemon juice or vinegar
Crème fraîche	1 cup	•Combine 1 cup heavy cream and 1 tablespoon plain yogurt. Let stand for 6 hours at room temperature.
Egg	1 whole (3 tablespoons)	•2½ tablespoons powdered egg substitute plus 2½ tablespoons water OR ¼ cup liquid egg substitute OR ¼ cup silken tofu pureed OR 3 tablespoons mayonnaise OR ½ banana mashed with ½ teaspoon baking powder OR 1 tablespoon powdered flax seed soaked in 3 tablespoons water
Evaporated milk	1 cup	•1 cup light cream
Farmers cheese	8 ounces	•8 ounces dry cottage cheese OR 8 ounces creamed cottage cheese, drained
Fats for baking	1 cup	•1 cup applesauce OR 1 cup fruit puree
Flour (bread)	1 cup	•1 cup all-purpose flour plus 1 teaspoon wheat gluten
Flour (cake)	1 cup	•1 cup all-purpose flour minus 2 tablespoons
Flour (self-rising)	1 cup	•⅞ cup all-purpose flour plus 1½ teaspoons baking powder and ½ teaspoon salt
Garlic	1 clove	•⅛ teaspoon garlic powder OR ½ teaspoon granulated garlic OR ½ teaspoon garlic salt (reduce salt in recipe)
Ginger (dry)	1 teaspoon, ground	•2 teaspoons chopped fresh ginger
Ginger (fresh)	1 teaspoon, minced	•½ teaspoon ground dried ginger
Green onion	½ cup, chopped	•½ cup chopped onion OR ½ cup chopped leek OR ½ cup chopped shallots
Hazelnuts	1 cup whole	•1 cup macadamia nuts OR 1 cup almonds
Herbs (fresh)	1 tablespoon, chopped	•1 teaspoon chopped dried herbs
Honey	1 cup	•1¼ cups white sugar plus ⅓ cup water OR 1 cup corn syrup OR 1 cup light treacle syrup
Hot sauce	1 teaspoon	•¾ teaspoon cayenne pepper plus 1 teaspoon vinegar
Ketchup	1 cup	•1 cup tomato sauce plus 1 teaspoon vinegar plus 1 tablespoon sugar
Lemon grass	2 fresh stalks	•1 tablespoon lemon zest
Lemon juice	1 teaspoon	•½ teaspoon vinegar OR 1 teaspoon white wine OR 1 teaspoon lime juice
Lemon zest	1 teaspoon, grated	•½ teaspoon lemon extract OR 2 tablespoons lemon juice
Lime juice	1 teaspoon	•1 teaspoon vinegar OR 1 teaspoon white wine OR 1 teaspoon lemon juice
Lime zest	1 teaspoon, grated	•1 teaspoon grated lemon zest
Macadamia nuts	1 cup	•1 cup almonds OR 1 cup hazelnuts
Mace	1 teaspoon	•1 teaspoon ground nutmeg
Margarine	1 cup	•1 cup shortening plus ½ teaspoon salt OR 1 cup butter OR ⅞ cup vegetable oil plus ½ teaspoon salt OR ⅞ cup lard plus ½ teaspoon salt
Mayonnaise	1 cup	•1 cup sour cream OR 1 cup plain yogurt

Ingredient	Amount	Substitution
Milk (whole)	1 cup	•1 cup soy milk OR 1 cup rice milk OR 1 cup water or juice OR ¼ cup dry milk powder plus 1 cup water OR ⅔ cup evaporated milk plus ⅓ cup water
Mint (fresh)	¼ cup, chopped	•1 tablespoon dried mint leaves
Mustard (prepared)	1 tablespoon	•Mix together 1 tablespoon dried mustard, 1 teaspoon water, 1 teaspoon vinegar, and 1 teaspoon sugar.
Onion	1 cup, chopped	•1 cup chopped green onions OR 1 cup chopped shallots OR 1 cup chopped leek OR ¼ cup dried minced onion
Orange zest	1 tablespoon, grated	•½ teaspoon orange extract OR 1 teaspoon lemon juice
Parmesan cheese	½ cup, grated	•½ cup grated Asiago cheese OR ½ cup grated Romano cheese
Parsley (fresh)	1 tablespoon, chopped	•1 tablespoon chopped fresh chervil OR 1 teaspoon dried parsley
Pepperoni	1 ounce	•1 ounce salami
Raisins	1 cup	•1 cup dried currants OR 1 cup dried cranberries OR 1 cup chopped pitted prunes
Rice (white)	1 cup, cooked	•1 cup cooked barley OR 1 cup cooked bulgur OR 1 cup cooked brown or wild rice
Ricotta	1 cup	•1 cup dry cottage cheese OR 1 cup silken tofu
Rum	1 tablespoon	•½ teaspoon rum extract, plus enough water to make 1 tablespoon
Saffron	¼ teaspoon	•¼ teaspoon turmeric
Semisweet chocolate chips	1 cup	•1 cup chocolate candies OR 1 cup peanut butter or other flavored chips OR 1 cup chopped nuts OR 1 cup chopped dried fruit
Shallots (fresh)	½ cup, chopped	•½ cup chopped onion OR ½ cup chopped leek OR ½ cup chopped green onions
Shortening	1 cup	•1 cup butter OR 1 cup margarine minus ½ teaspoon salt from recipe
Sour cream	1 cup	•1 cup plain yogurt OR 1 tablespoon lemon juice or vinegar plus enough cream to make 1 cup OR ¾ cup buttermilk mixed with ⅓ cup butter
Soy sauce	½ cup	•¼ cup Worcestershire sauce mixed with ¼ cup water
Stock (beef or chicken)	1 cup	•1 beef or chicken bouillon cube dissolved in 1 cup water
Sweetened condensed milk	1 (14 ounce) can	•¾ cup white sugar mixed with ½ cup water and 1⅛ cups dry powdered milk (Bring to a boil, and cook, stirring frequently, until thickened, about 20 minutes.)
Vegetable oil (for baking)	1 cup	•1 cup applesauce OR 1 cup fruit puree
Vegetable oil (for frying)	1 cup	•1 cup lard OR 1 cup vegetable shortening
Vinegar	1 teaspoon	•1 teaspoon lemon or lime juice OR 2 teaspoons white wine
White sugar	1 cup	•1 cup brown sugar OR 1¼ cups confectioners' sugar OR ¾ cup honey OR ¾ cup corn syrup
Wine	1 cup	•1 cup chicken or beef broth OR 1 cup fruit juice mixed with 2 teaspoons vinegar OR 1 cup water
Yeast (active dry)	1 (.25 ounce) package	•1 cake compressed yeast OR 2½ teaspoons active dry yeast OR 2½ teaspoons rapid rise yeast
Yogurt	1 cup	•1 cup sour cream OR 1 cup buttermilk OR 1 cup sour milk

Recommended Storage Guide

IN THE PANTRY

Baking powder and soda	1 year
Flour, all-purpose	10 to 15 months
Milk, evaporated and sweetened condensed	1 year
Mixes	
cake	1 year
pancake	6 months
Peanut butter	6 months
Salt and pepper	18 months
Shortening	8 months
Spices (discard if aroma fades)	
ground	6 months
whole	1 year
Sugar	18 months

IN THE REFRIGERATOR

Butter and margarine	1 month
Buttermilk	1 to 2 weeks
Eggs (fresh in shell)	3 to 5 weeks
Half-and-half	7 to 10 days
Meat	
casseroles, cooked	3 to 4 days
steaks, chops, roasts, uncooked	3 to 5 days
Milk, whole or fat-free	1 week
Poultry, uncooked	1 to 2 days
Sour cream	3 to 4 weeks
Whipping cream	10 days

IN THE FREEZER

Breads	
quick	2 to 3 months
yeast	3 to 6 months
Butter	6 months
Cakes	
cheesecakes and pound cakes	2 to 3 months
unfrosted	2 to 5 months
with cooked frosting	not recommended
with creamy-type frosting	3 months
Candy and fudge	6 months
Casseroles	1 to 2 months
Cheese	4 months
Cookies	
baked, unfrosted	8 to 12 months
dough	1 month
Eggs (not in shell)	
whites	1 year
yolks	8 months
Ice cream	1 to 3 months
Meat	
cooked	2 to 3 months
ground, uncooked	3 to 4 months
roasts, uncooked	9 months
steaks or chops, uncooked	4 to 6 months
Nuts	8 months
Pies	
pastry shell	2 to 3 months
fruit	1 to 2 months
pumpkin	2 to 4 months
custard, cream, meringue	not recommended
Poultry	
cooked	3 to 4 months
parts, uncooked	9 months
whole, uncooked	12 months
Soups and stews	2 to 3 months

Nutritional Analysis

Nutrition Analyses Based on Premier Databases

  Allrecipes.com is proud to provide ESHA Research's nutrient databases for recipe nutrition analysis. ESHA Research is the premier nutrition analysis provider for the world's nutrition and health industries, having provided nutrient information to health care providers and the world's top food manufacturing firms for more than 15 years. Its nutrient databases total more than 22,000 foods, track 165 nutrient factors, and combine nutrient data from over 1,200 scientific sources of information. For more information about ESHA Research, visit the website at **http://www.esha.com.**

Using Allrecipes.com Information with Care

  Allrecipes.com is committed to providing recipe-based nutritional information so that individuals may, by choice or under a doctor's advice, adhere to specific dietary requirements and make healthful recipe choices. The nutrition values that appear in this book and on **Allrecipes.com** nutrition pages are based on individual recipe ingredients. When a recipe calls for "salt to taste," we calculate sodium based on ¼ teaspoon or 1 gram of salt. While we have taken the utmost care in providing you with the most accurate nutritional values possible, please note that this information is not intended for medical nutrition therapy. If you are following a strict diet for medical or dietary reasons, it's important that you, first, consult your physician or registered dietitian before planning your meals based on recipes at **Allrecipes.com,** and, second, remain under appropriate medical supervision while using the nutrition information at **Allrecipes.com.**

Recipe Title Index

This index alphabetically lists every recipe by exact title.

General Recipe Index

This index lists every recipe by food category and/or major ingredient.

Favorite Recipes Journal

Jot down your family's and your favorite recipes for quick and handy reference.
Remember to include the dishes that drew rave reviews when company came for dinner.

Recipe	Source/Page	Remarks